THE LIFE

OF

JOSEPH ADDISON ALEXANDER, D.D.,

PROFESSOR IN THE THEOLOGICAL SEMINARY AT PRINCETON, NEW JERSEY.

BY

HENRY CARRINGTON ALEXANDER.

VOLUME II.

NEW YORK:
CHARLES SCRIBNER & COMPANY.
1870.

CONTENTS.

CHAPTER XVI.

Lines to John.—Good Advice.—Indoor Life.—News from Abroad.—Modern Oratory.—Impassioned Appeal.—Brilliant Preaching.—Archibald Alexander.—Teaching Children.—The Elder Brother.—His Method of Story Telling.—Old Bibles.—Henry James.—Knowledge of Passing Events.—Manner with Strangers.—Powers of Entertainment.—Concealing his Feelings.—As a Talker.—Afraid of Mannerism.—Extemporary Efforts.—The City with Foundations.—His Day Books.—No Display of Learning.—In Argument.—A Letter.—Tours about Home.—No previous Plan.—His Tastes in Travel.—Paintings.—Trip to Ticonderoga.—At Washington.—Visits Congress.—Ham and Eggs.—Avoids Publicity.—Ecclesiastical Courts.—Some People.—In his Study.—A Religious Instructor.—Amusing Letter.—Sharp Hit.......... Page 481

CHAPTER XVII.

Prelatists.—Good-natured Criticism.—Sharp Reviews.—Oxford Tracts.—Ritualists and the Chinese.—A Contrast.—Newmania.—Power of Sarcasm.—Many Articles.--List of Articles.—Reveal the Man.—Variety.--Overflow.—Rhythmic Peculiarity.—Abrupt Appeals.—True Poetry.--Genius Trammelled..........523

CHAPTER XVIII.

Papers for Children.--Ridge Recorder.--Chicken College.—Advertisements.—A Child of Nature.—Polygonal.—Judge Breckinridge.—Grateful Testimonies.—Early Recollections.—Wistar's Magazine.—A Favourite Scholar.—Interruptions.—Little Girls.—Children's Lives.—Rhyming Epistles.—Life of Wiss.—Don Patrick.—Wistar's Magazine.—Don Barbarossa.—The Lurid Leper.—House of Correction.—End of Children's Papers.—This was a Man..........542

CHAPTER XIX.

Laborious Studies.—Dr. Green.—As an Orientalist.—Felix Trembled.—A Friend of the Student.—Professor Phillips.—An Indiscretion.—Abundant Work.—Candour.—Amusing Sketch.—Park's Matriculation.—First Recitation.—Change of Feeling.—A First Impression.—Character of Class Instructions.—Facts from the Journal.—Memoirs of the Alexanders.—A Giant.—His Day Books.—Attachment of his Students.—He loved Confidence........ Page 566

CHAPTER XX.

A Great Teacher.—Letter to a Girl.—The Doctorate.—Isaiah begun.—Princeton of that Day.—Conversation of Brothers.—Dr. Alexander in New York.—Scheme of Lectures.—A Playful Letter.—Reading Books.—Preparing to Write.—Contempt for Conventions.—A Busy Biographer.—Introduction to Isaiah.—Hard Work.—Origin of Work on Isaiah.—Feats of Memory.—Grateful Employments.—Private Instructions.—Appearance of Work on Earlier Prophecies.—Correspondence........ 588

CHAPTER XXI.

Rapid Work.—Other Occupations.—Personal Characteristics.—Brilliancy in Pulpit.—Jewish Admirers.—Analytical Mind.—Steadfast Orthodoxy.—Constructive Powers.—Original Genius.—Not an Innovator.—Distaste for Metaphysics.—Biblical Mysticism.—Powers of Generalization.—Analysis and Synthesis.—Extract from Sermon.—Qualities as a Sermonizer.—Intellectual Symmetry.—Jeremy Taylor.—Dr. Chalmers.—Great Men Classified.—Appearance of Later Prophecies.—Rigid Translation.—Colloquies.—Engagement in Philadelphia........ 614

CHAPTER XXII.

His Popularity as a Preacher.—Preaching in New York.—Effects upon Cultivated Women.—A Lady's Estimate.—Effects upon Prominent Men.—His Printed Sermons.—His Piety.—He abhorred Notoriety.—Dr. Read.—Effects upon a Reporter.—An Anecdote.—Dr. McGill Hears him Preach.—Disdain of Art.—At the House of Dr. Harris.—Two Evenings with Dr. Alexander.—His Humour Inexhaustible.—The Second Evening.—Addisonian Inflection.—Unfinished Work........ 639

CHAPTER XXIII.

A Solace for Annoyances.—New Works Suggested.—Second Church, Philadelphia.—Chair of Church History.—A Change Contemplated.—A New Professor.—Personal Recollections.—Commentary on the Psalms.—Averse to Public Display.—Not Misanthropical.—Inauguration.—Dr. Miller's Decline.—Revival in Princeton.—Addresses during the Revival........ 659

CHAPTER XXIV.

Mother's Magazine.—Enjoying Himself.—Noting Coincidences.—Treatment of Books.—Marking Books.—University of Virginia.—Princeton Magazine.

—Primitive Church Offices.—Sickness of his Father.—Approaching his End —The Burial.—Deep Grief.—To a Fatherless Child.—Head of the House. —A Study Table........................ .... Page 674

CHAPTER XXV.

A Bookish Letter.—Sudden Call to Preach.—Local Novelty.—Scenes from his Window.—Among Men.—Death of his Mother.—Studying Church History. —Reading Danish.—In New Haven.—Interpretation.—How to Teach it.— Book of Travels.—Sails for Europe.—His Journals.—A Predicament.—Dr. Candlish.—His Sermon.—Its Effects.—Candlish Again.—A Scotch Guide.— Dr. Hamilton.—His Sermon.—Dr. Cumming.—In the Courts.—Shea and Talfourd.—A Concert.—Mr. Binney.—Hears Melvill.—His Sermon.—Over to France.—M. Cocquerel.—M. Pressensé.—On the Rhine.—A Latin Conversation.—Two Priests.—Holland.—Mr. Chalmers.—Returns Home...691

CHAPTER XXVI.

Death of Relatives.—Daily Studies.—Too Exegetical.—Dr. Cattell.—Shaving-Book.—Meeting of the Brothers.—Daily Records.—Comical Adventure.— The Gift of a Cutter.—Dr. Schaff.—Dr. Smith's Visit.—Another Interview. —Final Conclusions.—Church History.—A Foreign Student's Estimate.— Relations with his Colleagues.—Not Unfeeling.—Dr. Hodge.—The Elder Brother...................... 730

CHAPTER XXVII.

A New Book.—Pallavicino.—Visit to Richmond.—House of Dr. Moore.—Domestic Incidents.—Remembering the Children.—Clifton.—From Staunton to Lexington.—Dr. Dabney.—New Monmouth.—Dr. Ramsey.—Impression of Dr. Wilson.—Visits to his Relations.—Polite Conversation.—Self-forgetfulness.—Preaching in Staunton.—Social Traits.—Col. Baldwin.....750

CHAPTER XXVIII.

Daily Readings.—Dr. Waldegrave.—Repertory Essays.—Fertility of Invention.—Plan for Isaiah.—Preaching for his Brother.—Death of Dr. Rice.— Mode of Working.—A Literary Curiosity.—Frequent Changes.—An Important Proposition.—Letter to Mr. Scribner.—His Commentaries.— Knowledge of Many Authors.—No Parade of Learning.—Publication of Acts.—At Home.—Family Worship.—As a Talker.—Recreation.—Sarcasm. —His Study.—Visitors.—Humming Tunes.—An Incident.—Little Kindnesses..769

CHAPTER XXIX.

Dr. Dabney.—Writing in New York.—A Graphic Letter.—Professor Hepburn.—Fond of Experiments.—Proposed Journey.—Extract from Journal.—Deep in his Work.—Biblical History.—Commentary on Acts.—Affairs in New York.—Method of Teaching History.—Letter to Dr. Schaff.—Summer Work.—A Memorable Interview.—Brilliant Conversation.—For Whom he Wrote.—Arrival of Dr. James Alexander.—Journal.—Professor Cameron.—Fruits of his Ministry........ .... Page 797

CHAPTER XXX.

Visit to Richmond.—Mrs. McClung.—Letter to Dr. Hall.—A High Compliment.—Writing in New York.—An Adjourned Meeting.—A Musical Festival.—Many Studies.—Erasmus.—A Latin Classic........................819

CHAPTER XXXI.

Decline of Health.—Versatility.—Conversation in the Cars.—Knowledge of the Reviews.—His Piety.—Rare Humour.—Life of Hall.—A Readable Letter.—Wit and Humour.—A Portrait.—A Happy Home.—An Instance of his Kindness.—His affectionate Softness.—Manner of Giving.—Sincerity and Affection.—Visiting the Sick.—At his own Fireside.—A Joyful Tribute.830

CHAPTER XXXII.

A Humorous Letter.—A Long Journey.—Love of Change.—A Military Parade.—A Crimean Soldier.—Review at Quebec.—Self-Identification.—All Right.—Travelling Incognito.—The Unknown.—Thrice Transplanted.—As a Linguist.—List of Languages.—Summary of Languages.—Dialects.—Few Equals.—List of Articles.—In the Repertory......................849

CHAPTER XXXIII.

A Heart-Searching Prayer.—The Departing Saint.—A New Sorrow.—His Brother's Death.—An Affecting Sermon.—Letter to Dr. Hall.—Change in his Looks.—Seminary Changes.—Last Message to the Students.—Impressions of Dr. Hodge.—Visible Decline.—Anxiety of Friends.—Last of his Diary.—His last Readings.—Jottings in the Margin.—Growing Worse.—A Slight Improvement.—A Note from Dr. Jones.—A last Letter.—Bishop of Carlisle.—Grateful for Little Kindnesses.—Last Books Read.—Still Weaker.—Asleep in Jesus.—Longed for Rest.—He Died Silent.—Appearance after Death.—Undeveloped Power.—The Burial.—Tribute of Dr. Burrowes.—Dr. Humphrey's Address.—Characteristics.—Use of German Critics.—His last Article.—Epitaph of Edwards....................868

INDEX..905

CHAPTER XVI.

A FULL and steady light upon the period on which we now enter is denied us. Often when Mr. Alexander was engaged in writing for the press, or absorbed in some other occupation, and sometimes merely from a temporary lack of interest in his journal, he made scarcely an entry for a series of years that can shed much light on his daily habits. We have now arrived at such a period; the diary for 1841 and 1842 consisting of little but rough notes of sermons and lectures, and containing no account of his studies. Fortunately there are other quarters to which we may look for information and not altogether without success. The great difficulty will be to avoid a certain appearance of sameness in the treatment of periods which resemble one another like the successive ages of prosperity. Such annals, agreeably to the saying of Montesquieu, are generally tiresome. The effort in this case will be to interweave as much as possible of the personal element with these tranquil records, and to give as many glimpses as possible of the subject of these memoirs; who was still young, being little over thirty, and in the ardour of a disposition that was noted for its masculine energy and its boyish elasticity.

In January, Mr. James Alexander was sounded, through a letter from Mr. Maxwell, about the vacant chair of Church History in the Union Theological Seminary, Virginia. He could have given no encouragement to this invitation. The number of calls which he received was never known even to his own family during his lifetime. His diaries, however, show that nearly every one of them gave him much anxiety, and occasioned many secret communings with God. He was satisfied after experiment, that the climate of lower Virginia was not suited to his health. There were other reasons, and very obvious ones, why he should cling to Princeton with great tenacity, and why the charms of a great city often seemed tame to him in the comparison.

The younger brother still amused himself with his boys. The following verses were written in honour of the birthday of one of them:

AD JOANNEM.

"It seems but yesterday, my friend,
Since I a little sonnet penned,
On being told
That you, whom I so long had known,
But still regarded as my own,
Were twelve years old.

"But in the space of three short years
How changed my little friend appears
In form and mien!
For he, who then had only passed
A dozen birth-days, has at last
Beheld fifteen.

"And in these days, so fleet and few,
How many follies rise to view,
Like shadows dim:
Sins for which nothing can atone
But a Redeemer's blood alone;
Oh, trust in Him!

"Let the time past for sleep suffice:
Cease, cease to dream! awake, arise!
Up, up, dear John!
The night of life is well nigh past;
Eternal daylight, sure and fast,
Comes stealing on."

The following letter accompanied the lines:

"AUGUST 2, 1840.

"MY DEAR JOHN:

"I trust that you have not forgotten, in the devotions of this day, that it completes your fifteenth year. I hope that the year upon which you now are entering will, by the grace of God, be better than the fifteen which have preceded it. This is a very favourable time to form good resolutions and correct bad habits. Resolve that in your sixteenth year you will endeavor to obtain a more complete command over your temper than you ever had before. Resolve to be more punctual and diligent in study. If you have begun to be remiss in your religious duties—I mean in prayer and in the reading of the Scriptures—now retrace your steps. If you have begun, like many others of your age, to feel ashamed of what is good, and to dislike all thought on serious subjects, now is the time to crush such feelings while they are yet weak. If you have begun to feel a secret longing after objects which you have been accustomed heretofore to look upon as sinful and unworthy of a man, now is a good time to repress all such desires, and resolve that you will act to the last upon the principles in which you have been educated. Let your character be formed before your studies are completed; let it be formed upon true Christian principles; and then, I trust in God that you will be able to vanquish the temptations of the world hereafter. If I may venture to express another wish, it is that before your sixteenth year is completed, you may be disposed to make a profession of religion; which is nothing more than agreeing to act in accordance to the truths which you profess to believe. If you can join sincerely in the prayers of the church, and really desire what you ask for in those prayers, I see no reason why you should not openly avow yourself a follower of Christ. Is it because it would debar you from pleasures which you wish to enjoy? You can do without them; you will be happier without them; and a young man who enters into life with a religious character has this advantage: that he escapes a thousand solicitations and temptations, to which otherwise he would be exposed. Besides, he is always more respected; let the irreligious say what they will. But I fear that this subject may be disagreeable. If so, you will excuse my introducing it; and believe that I have done so from a sincere regard to your present and eternal happiness. I heartily congratulate you on your birthday, and remain, with the kindest wishes, your affectionate friend,

"JOS. ADDISON ALEXANDER."

On the 28th of September, Dr. Murray dismissed the students with a very able address. The next day the Rev. James W. Alexander was appointed by the Alumni of the

Seminary to pronounce a discourse on Transcendentalism, in Philadelphia, during the session of the next General Assembly. This was probably the beginning of the famous article in the Repertory* which was attacked by Professor C. S. Henry and defended so ably by Dr. Hodge. The article in question was the joint production of Professors Alexander and Dod; the former contributing the part about the German Idealists, and the latter the part about Cousin. The incidents of the time were few. Now and then a lecture could be heard in Princeton from some scholarlike visitor who came from a distance. The address before the literary society of the College this year was from the Rev. Dr. John Johns, then of Baltimore, and now the venerable Bishop of Virginia. It was an elegant and finished discourse on "The Pleasure of Acquiring Truth as an Incentive to the Pursuit of it." Commencement passed off very well. One of Mr. Alexander's brothers was a graduate. Dr. Green read a noble historical paper on Dr. Witherspoon's administration of the College. It was received with extraordinary favour. The shower in the evening in no wise marred the delightful quality of the atmosphere. It was the first Commencement Dinner since the foundation of the College at which there was no wine.

The traces of the in-door life at the Breckinridge House are slight but not uninteresting.

The first winter storm was on the 13th of November; and as dark a one as anybody could recollect. The wind howled; and the ground was soon covered many inches deep with snow. Little cared the tough student for all this. Like De Quincey, he could mock at the rage of the elements as he sat before his comfortable faggots and urged on his mighty tasks. Yet we may take it for granted that his large heart was sometimes moved as he thought of the poor and houseless.† What troubled him many degrees more than ice or snow or tempest, was the increasing difficulty of modifying the phases of his

* See Princeton Rev. 1839. Jan. p. 37: also Princeton Essays, Edinb. p. 498.

† His diaries of other dates seem to justify this inference.

study apparatus. Change them about as he would, the table and the chairs, though in bran-new combinations, *would* be like the same objects under former arrangements. He was always pursuing yet never overtaking the phantom of a perfectly satisfactory adjustment of his furniture. This was a *bonum* not to be attained in a state of so much infelicity and disappointment as the present; and he felt it keenly. At a clerical meeting held this month at Dr. Maclean's, Dr. Miller, Dr. Carnahan, and Professor James Alexander chatted about the times and opinions of Jefferson, and kindred topics.

The year 1841 opened with stirring news from the East. Beirât, Tyre, Sidon, and Acre taken by the Allies; the isle and city of Chusan by the English; Napoleon's body brought back to France; the abdication of several sovereigns in Europe. No one had a more open ear for such intelligence than Mr. Alexander. He was also a most careful reader of missionary intelligence. One of his books is largely filled with a digest of the missionary journals, illustrated by his own neat maps and diagrams. He was very critical in his tastes in this respect.

On the 10th of January, Dr. Archibald Alexander preached at night to the young men, and with power: "My son, if sinners entice thee, consent thou not." It was one of his happiest efforts, simple and affecting. He scourged the prevailing vices of the place with a whip of scorpions. On the 12th, Dr. Parker, formerly of China, was in Princeton, and addressed the Seminary students. He was accompanied by a Chinese scholar. It is not improbable that Mr. Alexander availed himself of this opportunity to air his Chinese vocabulary, which was not yet large.

From the diary of the elder brother, I copy the following record:

"February 14. Addison preached a very impressive discourse in the evening in the church, from 'This is a faithful saying.'"

I make still another for Feb. 18:

"Thursday. Thawing. This day I had the unspeakable satisfaction of having at dinner in my house my dear honoured parents and all their children; all, through Divine mercy, in the enjoyment of health. Blessed be God who hath preserved us! and may the blessing of our fathers' God rest in saving influences on the beloved heads of all concerned, and on all who have descended or shall yet descend from them!"

During the month, Professor James Alexander was unanimously chosen President of Lafayette College, but declined the honour. He was afterwards approached by the Rev. Shepherd Kollock with solicitations from Norfolk, which were met in the same way. His diaries are still full of beautiful Latin prayers, conceived much in the manner of Augustin's in the early chapters of his Confessions. One day this month, Mr. Addison Alexander preached at night on the text "Behold the Lamb of God!" one of his best sermons; though much depended on the delivery. His picturesque and imaginative efforts were always more or less warm and impressive. He could not help thus blending fancy and feeling. It was impossible for him to commit the fault so severely censured by his brother, of mistaking the language of imagination for that of passion.

His own theoretical views on this subject are probably indicated by the marks which he scribbled in the first volume of Dr. Stevens's book* on the great mistake of the Methodists, a short time before his own death. He *double-scores* this:

"It is the great mistake of modern oratory, especially in the pulpit, that it confounds oratory with poetry; but it was never the mistake of this greatest of preachers."

Nor was it the mistake of Mr. Alexander. He also marks this:

"It is doubtful whether he ever made a congregation laugh."

* The History of the Religious Movement of the eighteenth century, called Methodism, &c., by Abel Stevens, LL. D., New York, 1859.

It is certain Mr. Alexander never did. With all his brilliancy of wit and fancy, he never carried this strange fire into the sanctuary. He looked to heaven for the divine flame, and his lips were in a manner touched with a coal from off God's altar. He, as well as Whitefield, whom he so little resembled in most other things, was full of reverence while in the temple of Jehovah, and, as in the case of the English preacher, the people often saw the light upon his brow like that irradiating the face of Moses, though "he wist not that his face shone." "They felt, nevertheless," as Dr. Stevens says in a passage which Mr. Alexander has marked with his approval, and which may stand as his own description, "that though he had come down to them from the mount of transfiguration, and was shining with its glory, yet he had gone up to it from among themselves."

The sermon of all others which most palpitated with plaintive and contrite emotion was the one on the broken heart. A gentleman of New York who heard it in Duane street, once said to me that he considered it the greatest sermon he ever heard; and that the preacher seemed carried up on the occasion in question to heights of impassioned appeal he had never known him to reach before.

One of his latest pupils, a descendant of President Davies, declares :

"I have heard many orators, sacred and profane. For me Dr. Addison Alexander was prince of them all."

To the vehemence of Luther without his violence, he loves to remember that he added some of the touching tenderness of Melanchthon ; to the solemnity of Jonathan Edwards without his terrors, the simplicity and directness of Samuel Davies. With the dialectics of an uninspired Paul, this pupil thought that he mingled much of the reverent love of John the Divine.

"And over all he threw the radiance of his own peculiar genius." "Concerning many," he continues, "of his discourses I could literally adopt the language of Peter Bayne: 'For our part we confess that our admiration is intense. They appear to us to have the true poetic glow; that fusing, uniting fire burns over them, whose gleam compels you to drop your measuring line or gauging apparatus and utter the word genius. To accompany the preacher in his high flight, seems to us like sailing with that archangel whom Richter in his dreams saw bearing the immortal through the endless choirs and galaxies of immensity; only that here we do not tremble and cry out at the overpowering spectacle of God's infinitude, for the softening light of the cross falls continually around us.'

"But sometimes that wonderful intellect would gather up and disclose the awful. In such moods he seemed to realize Andrew Marvel's appalling thought:

"'But at my back I always hear
Time's winged chariots hurrying near;
And yonder all before me lie
Deserts of vast eternity!'

"He seemed to see the people before him, as the dramatic historian of the French Revolution saw its actors when he cried out: 'Light mortals, how yet walk your light life-minuet over the bottomless abysses, divided from you by a film?' At such times, it was agony to hear him; the agony of intense, awful interest in human life and eternal destiny. He seemed impassioned; transfigured. A new baptism fell upon him; a rapture of burning eloquence poured from him. His utterance became swift, almost or quite beyond example: his voice, tremulous with strong emotion, deepened into sonorous rotundity. The whole man was affected, swayed by the mighty impulse. Then, as his glance, usually veiled by the drooping lid, blazed out,

'Swift as the lightning in the collied night,
That in a gleam unfolds both earth and heaven,'

one almost shrank from the intense white light gleaming from that ordinarily calm blue eye."

But the gleam, he says, was not always that of the lightning. Not unfrequently would be seen and felt the soft glow of a more tender emotion, the

"Light intellectual and full of love."

The writer of this sketch then proceeds as follows about the sermon on the sacrifices of God:

"Never, to my latest moment, shall I forget one rendering of his sermon on 'The Broken Heart' (Ps. li.: 17). The germs of it are in the published form, but *only* the germs. Having wrought up the audience to a state of quickened sensibility and vivid sympathy, he described the altar with the mysterious veil behind it; the approaching penitent, bearing, visible, a bleeding heart, thrilling and throbbing with its own divine sorrow; and as it is laid on the smoking altar, a hand from within the veil receives the bleeding oblation, while a joy, calm but deep as infinity, fills the penitent's soul; and the preacher cries out in an ecstasy of emotion, 'The sacrifices of God are a broken spirit; a broken and contrite heart, O God, thou wilt not despise!' Then the silence, painful in its intensity, yields to a long-drawn, tremulous sigh from the entire congregation. The rapt preacher stands with eyes swimming in softened light, and brow bathed with splendours not of earth. That is the scene I love to recall—that the posture in which to remember the reserved and misjudged scholar of Princeton." "With eye upturned and suffused, but beaming mild radiance, as from starry depths, and a light like that which painters throw around the cross which he preached so exclusively, I hear him evermore proclaiming those precious, comforting words, 'The sacrifices of God are a broken spirit; a broken and a contrite heart, O God, thou wilt not despise.'"

The 17th of April was the 69th birthday of Dr. Archibald Alexander; in reference to which event his oldest son records: "Blessed be God for continuing to us his valuable life so long!" Although Dr. Alexander was now on the borders of seventy, he was in pretty vigorous health, with an increasing tendency to flesh. Mrs. Lundy Duncan has given a true as well as lively and affectionate picture of him, in a foot-note to one of the pages in an intelligent volume suggested by her visit to the United States. She says he bore a wonderful resemblance in his looks and ways to Wilberforce, as well as in his character. He took no exercise; and spent hours every day in solitary meditation on the truths and problems of philosophy and revealed religion. The portrait of him by his gifted son cannot be retouched with advantage; but there are little facts about him with which many would like to be acquainted. This is not the proper place for most of them.

A survivor of this period cannot refrain, however, from saying here that his recollection is most vivid and pleasing of the days when he used to sit in the old man's lap and recite to him long strings of Latin words, or hear from him by the light of his study lamp the beautiful and melting Bible stories which he was so fond of telling children. He dwelt most on the accounts which are furnished in the first and second books of Samuel. This circumstance has almost caused the writer in later years to prefer the accounts of little Samuel and the boy David even to the inimitable pathos of the Book of Genesis and that (with the single exception of the life of Christ) most sweet and heart-stirring of all human narratives, the story of Joseph. Of the incidents belonging to the Jewish monarchy in the days of the Prophets and the Kings, he derived his deepest and most awakening impressions from this source. He would here record also his sense of the inestimable value of other instructions which it was his privilege to receive from his venerable teacher at a somewhat later day; as for example, in Latin grammar, arithmetic, geometry, and physics; and his pleasure when the sash-door of the study communicating with the gate to the Seminary would open, and the venerable man would return to hear his lesson. Before proceeding to the task, his gray-haired preceptor would commonly address to him some kind word or other in a cheery tone of voice; he would sometimes also pare an apple and scrape it with an ivory paper-folder, and in all such cases would insist upon his little pupil's taking the lion's share of the spoil. It is true, there were moments when that speaking countenance inspired awe and even dread; sometimes, but very rarely, his reproofs were severe and painful to the feelings of the listener; but the obedient child had nothing to fear, but, on the contrary, everything to look forward to; and the teacher's leaning was ever to the side of leniency, rather than of harshness or rigour. Indeed, his gentleness, patience, tact, happy wisdom, and loving-kindness, knew no ordinary bounds.

The same disposition, as we have seen, appeared in all his intercourse with grown men. His reproofs were commonly conveyed in silent glances of the eye; when he uttered them, however, in words, they were at times scathing. I have heard it said that a fanatical religionist of the type formerly, and perhaps still, prevailing in some parts of the country, once called upon him and interrogated him as to his evidences of personal piety. Provoked at his significant silence, the man is said to have exclaimed, "Have you *no religion*, Dr. Alexander?" "None to speak of," was the quiet reply.

I resume the thread of narrative, if it may be called such. On the 3d of May, and in spite of his earnest and recorded protestations, Dr. James Alexander, then holding the Latin and Rhetoric chair in the College, was unanimously invited to return to his former charge in Trenton; but without the result desired. Mr. Alexander was informed of these negotiations in a letter from his brother, who was at the time in Trenton. The natural scenery of the month of May was wonderfully enchanting; and the lively breath of this bright charming spring must have exhilarated Mr. Alexander to the utmost. His elder brother, writing under the same roof, says:

> "I have found no temple so inspiring as the open vault of heaven and the green earth. Everything around me breathes of Divine benignity. The sparrow has laid her young in a rose-tree just beside my door-sill; another has built in the vine by the wood-house. The blue-birds seem to be tenanting the house I prepared for them over the arbour, and I am looking for the return of the wrens to the lodge above the swing. The indigo-bird and some unknown pied bird appear among my young elms. The cat-bird sings almost all day in the large cherry-tree by our ice-house and in the orchard just beyond. Bob-o'Lincoln indulges in his capricios morning, noon, and night. But no song so affects me as the plaintive note of the robin, heard at a distance in the evening. It tells of solitude and care. It is such a strain as, were I a bird, I could not choose but sing myself."

Flowers and blossoms were out in profusion. The common air was an elixir vitæ. The 29th was hot, and portended summer. Late in the month, Mr. Addison Alexander went to Albany; returning June 7th, having passed through New-York, Philadelphia, and Washington. The journals and letters embodying the results of these trips are seldom more than barren statements of his entering and leaving such and such places, and doing such and such every-day things.

The two scholars had both a rare knack with the pen. One night in June, the elder brother wrote two Sunday-school stories after tea. It is hard to say which was the fastest reader and writer, or which could tell the most interesting stories, and write the best children's books. Their modes of entertaining were widely unlike, and were altogether unique.

With the younger brother's methods the reader has by this time become tolerably acquainted. The older brother's plan was to take a boy into his lap or on his knee, and tell him the story of Troy, or of Romulus, or of wandering Ulysses; and he agreed with "Addison" in believing that bright children no less than men felt the power and charm of the stories of the few mighty poets. He knew well how to beguile an evening in this way with outline views—oral or pictorial, as the case might be—of Laocoon, the Trojan horse, Achilles dragging Hector, the brothers Sleep and Death, the web of Penelope, the Hall of the Suitors, and the like. Or if something of a lighter kind was desired, he would change the muscles of his face, sing (in his round sonorous voice), whistle, imitate different kinds of birds, and engage in sportive dialogues with fantastical personages who were the creatures of his fancy and of the moment, sometimes throwing in something pleasant from Mother Goose or the fables of Æsop and La Fontaine.

I find that Dr. James Alexander lectured in Trenton before the Mechanics' Institute on the 29th of June. His efforts to please and edify the working classes, under the style of "Charles Quill," were not unrewarded, and he was prouder of their good opinion than of the compliments received from the fastidious and learned. He was once presented by a Mechanics' Association with a handsome gold-headed cane, as a token of their good opinion.

On the 9th of August, the subject of this narrative returned from New-York; having received the hospitality of Netherwood, the beautiful residence of James Lenox, Esq. It were impossible for a man of Mr. Alexander's tastes not to be particularly interested in Mr. Lenox's noble collection of English Bibles. He sought every chance, whether in Europe or the United States, of increasing his knowledge of the editions, versions, and manuscripts of the inspired volume. He regarded Coverdale as he would have done one of the great diamonds. The old renderings of Wickliffe and Tyndale had for him an unfading interest; and he stops many a time in his exposition of a passage to laugh inwardly at the queer and almost comic turn they so often give to a familiar sentence.

Mr. Lenox writes that his impressions of him socially, beyond the short and hurried intercourse of business meetings at Princeton, were confined to Mr. Alexander's visits at his house many years ago when he resided in the country. Of these he can say that they afforded him

"An apprehension of his character differing from that usually entertained by those who saw him under other circumstances; vivacity and humour were a source of constant enjoyment."

This is the unanimous testimony of those who knew him well.

The following penetrating and suggestive view of his character is from the pen of Henry James, Esq. of Cambridge, Mass., formerly of Princeton, and could have been written only by one who, like Mr. James, was on social and personal grounds an intimate acquaintance and favourite companion of "the solitary:"

"I was familiar, of course," says Mr. James, "with the prestige of his immense erudition, his brilliant wit, his incisive judgment; but I confess my imagination was always far more acutely piqued by the mystery of his inner life. He habitually lived in the utmost personal remoteness from the world; and yet his sympathy with all mundane interests, and his judgment of all mundane problems, were as keen and sagacious and enlightened as if he dwelt in the very centre of the popular life and movement. He had, by nature, or temperament, all that the ascetic vainly strives to acquire by culture; so that a certain childlike charm of innocence was seen to underlie his mature intellectual activity, and soften, to the eyes of those who knew him, his otherwise commanding lineaments. I never knew any one in whose native honesty I so confided as I did in his. I have known many persons, of course, in whose cultivated integrity I should feel a perfect faith; but he seemed to me to have been born honest, and to be incapable, not only of actively telling, but even of passively acting, a lie. It was a constant problem to me, therefore, how this man, so unlike the mass even of cultivated men, so singularly gifted by nature as he was, so free from all *personal* frailties, so independent of all *personal* ties, contrived to live in the chaste sanctuary of his own thought, and what was the habitual tenour of his bosom experience toward God and man. It was delightful to see him with children. He revelled in their society, as if he had here found at last the dimensions of true manhood, and they rejoiced in his; for while he gave them a heart as young and unperverted as their own, he lifted them by the most playful and engaging wiles of wisdom to a level, for the moment, with his own ripe understanding.

"This, in fact, was the ground of my lively interest in Mr. Alexander, and the ever-growing argument of my admiration, how he managed to combine, as he did, in his personal character so much innocence with so much knowledge, so much modesty with so much culture, so unfeigned a personal humility with so indisputable a conventional eminence over other men."

The writings of Mr. James himself have long been before the public, and have attracted no little attention from scholars and theologians; and therefore in praising the talents and disposition of his old friend, he will not be suspected of any bias toward a narrow and sectarian "orthodoxy." It is one instance out of many of the admiration and love felt for the Princeton Professor by those whose opinions on a number of important subjects differed *toto cœlo* from his own. There was in him a centre of attraction, as well as of repulsion, altogether aside from any mere power of intellect or agreement in doctrine or sentiment.

A return to the chain of incidents will now bring us once more into the atmosphere of the schools of learning. The accounts from abroad were disastrous. Princeton was startled on the 12th of August by the afflicting tidings of the death of the Rev. John Breckinridge. "This," writes Professor James Alexander, "is solemn news to me." They had been warm friends, and occupants of the same dwelling. The whole town mourned for him, and the College Professor never ceased to speak of him with a kind of tender and melancholy affection. His picture was soon hanging by the side of Dr. Miller's, over the Professor's mantelpiece. Dr. Breckinridge was a man of great sweetness and strength of character. His administrative talents were of a high order, and his moral courage, which never shrank from religious conversation in any company, awakened much admiration in his friend. His memory is precious.

The college was in a somewhat disorderly state. The President's veto of the Bank Bill came just upon the back of excitements produced by the final award of college honours, and was followed by disturbances among certain of the students. These events perhaps had little effect on the solitary life of Mr. Alexander, but they were all pondered by him, and must have entered to some degree into the tissue of his thinking. He was not a mere student. His library was but the innermost of concentric circles. Who was there better informed than he of the bustling scenes in the vicinity of the College? Who more thoroughly acquainted with the contents of the current reviews and newspapers? Yet he was in no sense either a busybody or a politician. His thoughts radiated from his comfortable chamber to the ends of the earth. His sympathies embraced the continental world of letters and the lands of the heathen.

Perhaps the best idea of the quiet Oriental professor, as he appeared when he laid aside his mask and his armour, is to be had from pictures drawn by his intimates. The Rev. John

Hall, D.D., of Trenton, a friend who was afterward and always much cherished by Mr. Alexander, writes that he has no special recollections of him previous to his own removal from Philadelphia to Trenton, which occurred in 1841. He had met him before on his own occasional visits to Princeton, when he always staid at Dr. Alexander's.

> "Like other persons," he says, "who fell in with him under such circumstances, I never found him the distant, unapproachable character, such as he was imagined by strangers who judged of him by his reputation as one absorbed in study, and as having almost a misanthropical aversion to 'society.' My impressions of him, as in those days, are of a genial, affectionate, talkative, humorous companion; one whose tastes and habits confined him very much to books, but whose manner, countenance, and talk showed him to be alive to (and wonderfully acquainted with) the world and everything going on in it, even to trifling matters, which most persons supposed never came to his notice, or would be disdained if they had. It has often caused expressions of astonishment how he could know so much of a world in which he mingled so little, of subjects which lay so far out of his track, of people of all sorts of whom it was supposed he knew and cared nothing."

The recollections of this gentleman of his friend's manners when unexpectedly confronted with strange but congenial "company" will strike some readers with surprise; but they agree with what is said by another of his most valued and intimate associates, as well as by one of his most esteemed pupils. It was not always the case, indeed, that Mr. Alexander felt sufficiently at his ease to throw off all appearance of constraint in this happy way. Often when strangers were introduced into the circle of which before their entrance he had been the lively centre, he became bashfully silent, or from some cause or other failed to mingle freely or joyously in the social intercourse. But if at the moment of embarrassment he was not singled out as an object of prominent notice, he was apt to be contented, and to make the best of the situation. There can be no doubt whatever that even when he was absolutely speechless on such occasions, his eyes and ears and mind drank in everything that was going on, and often (as his diaries attest) with unalloyed, and sometimes very keen, enjoyment.

The same writer proceeds to say:

"He sometimes staid with me in Philadelphia when he went to preach there, and was always, not only a most welcome, but most agreeable guest. If there was other company, he was as unembarrassed and pleasant as any; never showing a disposition to shrink from the circle, and uniformly taking his part as if he enjoyed it. There, as well as afterwards in Trenton, he would sit with me after the family had retired; and his chat was so lively and inexhaustible that I had usually to tell him of the lateness of the hour to get him to his room."

The same kind friend bears witness to his almost unequalled powers of entertainment, and the varied and never-failing resources of his conversation. This was what struck everybody who knew him very well. He was never at a loss for a subject or an exciting opportunity. He seemed to have whole libraries and encyclopædias, not to mention histories, grammars, dictionaries, poems, works of travel, works of biography, works of romance, quarterly magazines, reviews, newspapers, religious journals, religious and literary diaries; in short a vast amount of what was in books, what was in paper covers, what was in print, what was in manuscript, at his fingers' ends. He was acquainted, too, with what one most wishes to know about men, whether of the past or of the present; their characters, their acts, their probable motives, their personal traits and appearance, the causes of their success or failure, and a thousand additional particulars, many of which no one else would think of. No one was better informed about political or ecclesiastical measures. He knew much of the unwritten history of the church. The geography and scenery of the world were as familiar to him, apparently, as those of New Jersey. His summer jaunts in America, his journeyings in Europe, the details of what had happened or was happening, in Princeton, Philadelphia, New York, and the domestic incidents in his father's and brother's families, were themes on which he loved to descant when he was exactly in the mood for it. In very truth, he seemed to know almost everything, and to excel other people in talking about what they knew as well as he did. Yet he never overburdened his discourse, either with egotism or pedantry. He never harangued or soliloquized. His fireside intercourse was governed throughout by good sense, unaffected courtesy, genuine kindliness and a rare absence of self-obtrusion. His knowledge was implied rather than asserted.

Says Dr. Hall:

> "Like his father, he knew everybody—all our ministers, the Princeton men of College and Seminary, and from his acquaintance with what they were doing (and the same may be said of a much larger extent of individuals in all churches and in literary and common life), one would have supposed he had a large intercourse with society. Anecdotes, traits of character, observation of *minutiæ*, knowledge of all kinds of books, familiarity with current literature, observation of human nature, discernment of foibles and virtues, contempt of pretenders, appreciation of the humblest goodness or modest ability, come to my mind as characterizing his talk."

He did not like to make an exhibition of his feelings, and never did so, except when really constrained by some ungovernable impulse. There was a fount of tenderness in him which sometimes broke out in the pulpit in a gush of impetuous emotion. More commonly it disclosed its existence only in his acts, and the occasional tones of his voice. He did things, little things often, which no one unless an arrant hypocrite, would ever have dreamed of doing but from the suggestion of a gentle and loving heart. His honesty was beyond the breath of suspicion. It was his honesty, united to his stern sense of what was right and what was seemly, and the electric suddenness and brightness of his rare sarcasm, that made him feared by those who had been once blinded by it, as well as those who heard the report of it, and were not aware of his more attractive and genial qualities.

His wit and humour were brought out constantly at the house of this friend. There was never lack of provocation or rejoinder. An evening spent with Mr. Alexander at Mr. Hall's would have been in this respect like an evening spent with Lamb or Jerrold. But the announcement of a visitor too often broke the charm. If his brother James chanced to be present, Mr. Alexander's spirits knew no bounds. The walls would sometimes ring with the laughter of the children, as well as with the uncontrollable merriment of those who were older and wiser. Thomas Hood or Sheridan could hardly have been more extravagantly facetious than he was sometimes. But even then he kept his own countenance, and never in the slightest degree transgressed the limits of decorum. His boisterous mirth was all for the little ones. In his encounters with grown-up men and women, his talk was always full of good nature, sparkle, dry retort, whimsical fun, but was never undignified, and seldom unmixed with grave discourse or dialogue on serious subjects. He had a way of passing abruptly from one extreme and one topic to another, in a manner almost peculiar to himself. He allowed himself to drift enjoyably on the current. There was always a tie of connection in his own mind between his thoughts, but he did not stop to tell others what it was. He let himself alone, and thus made himself one of the most charming of companions. He talked most about little things and every-day matters; but he never went far without throwing out some lively hint or broad generalization about books or men, or some shrewd poignant comment upon life or manners; almost invariably, too, there were graphic touches of description, and now and then finished pictures; and then there were withal those innumerable flashes of fine intellectual mirthfulness and friendly feeling. He bore no close resemblance to any of the celebrated literary talkers. His conversation was more unexaggerated and (if I may say so) more unconscious of itself. He never seemed to be thinking of himself except when he fancied that he was an object of curiosity to others, and then the thought chilled his faculties of speech and his sense of genial comfort. When he was "making himself entertaining," he was interested in his subject, or his hearer, or his surroundings, and lost to everything else.

To his fascination in private, his friend bears cheerful testimony. His exact words on this point need not be withheld:

"You know how much hilarity there was in his private hours, when in good spirits; how jocosely he saw and spoke without undignifying himself, as so many men of wit do. Of his seasons of depression I know nothing, though I have heard his brother James speak of such. He could use satire, and be severe, but he was conscientiously just and considerate. He had a great indifference to 'showing off.' Was it pride or modesty? How ridiculous everything like forwardness seemed to him! He could not tolerate affectation, vanity, assumption. Even the commonplace ways of doing one's best to be seen, he perhaps too much disdained."

This almost morbid aversion from everything that looked like display of self, had its effect upon his manner of preaching. Yet his feelings would often get the better of him, and make him eloquent in spite of every half-voluntary effort on his part to be calm and unimpressive. Sometimes his soul seemed on fire, and he then set everything before him in a blaze. His hearers would observe a deathly stillness; would weep, shudder, tremble; would almost shout aloud. This was not often but sometimes the case, when Mr. Alexander was yet in the flush of his powers, and in the prime of his florid health and exuberant animal spirits.

"It was a fault of his doings in the pulpit that he seemed to be afraid of the least approach to mannerism. There was a sort of carelessness in his reading and preaching which sometimes gave the appearance of hurry or negligence. He would not try to give *effect* to a hymn or chapter by his mode of reading, and usually tumbled into his sermon as if it was to be despatched as soon as possible. But he soon showed that he felt his subject, and though he got no nearer to artificial oratory or elocution, there came an earnestness and often an awful solemnity in his tones which literally *thrilled* his audience. His voice was delightful, and to me more melting in pathetic parts than any I ever heard, excepting perhaps Jenny Lind's. Some of his long sentences, rolling on to a grand climax, occur to me, which have made me put my handkerchief to my mouth lest I should *scream*. It of course happens with his printed sermons, as with all others that were delivered with feeling and melody, that their effect can be realized only by those who are so familiar with his manner of delivery that they can hear him while they read."

Dr. Hall thinks that his performances without the book were nearly or quite equal to his more laboured efforts, when he spoke with every assistance from the manuscript.

"I can imagine him untrammelled by manuscript, and left to the working of his feelings, before a sympathetic audience, where he should lose all diffidence, transcending in power what he would write. He had such a control of language, such an unhesitating command of the very words, such capacity to make plain, that had he been a pastor, I think his great strength and usefulness would have been in off-hand preaching. He had no excuse for making a sermon from study, as his mind was already so furnished with the materials."

This is no vain speculation. No one who knew Mr. Alexander in private as Dr. Hall did, could doubt that his genius would be excited by contact with some great occasion, and that he might under such circumstances surpass all his previous exhibitions of power and eloquence. But in the opinion expressed above, he differs from many, and I think from Mr. Alexander himself. The judgment of a public speaker is not perhaps to be trusted in a question touching the excellence of his own oratory, or touching even the comparative proficiency he may have attained in a particular mode of address. There are other valuable judgments on this point which go to corroborate that of Dr. Hall. It may be that any defects in brilliancy of imagination, copiousness of fancy, or vehemence of passion, which some think they have noticed in Mr. Alexander's extemporary efforts as compared with those in which he used the manuscript, may be owing purely to his constitutional reluctance to display himself, his feelings, and his fancies before the world. In the study he could overcome the repugnance. In the pulpit, possibly, he found it more difficult to do so.

On the other hand, his memory was so surprising that he retained a sermon in his head after reading it over once; this he admitted to his brother James; and it is not improbable that he sometimes preached *memoriter* when it was supposed that he was creating his discourse *de novo.*

I happen to recollect an instance of this kind. One Sun day night, the preacher, who had been expected to officiate in the First Church in Princeton, was absent, or for some reason unable to speak, and Mr. (then Dr.) Addison Alexander was applied to to take his place. Seeing at once how the matter stood, he swiftly ascended the steps of the pulpit, and after the preliminary services, in which he seemed to be altogether at his ease, poured out one of the most enrapturing and overwhelming discourses to which I ever had the privilege of listening. It was spoken of by some as an extempore effort, but was the famous sermon on the " City with Foundations," which is printed in his works. He fairly ravished me with his enchanting imaginative pictures, and his wild bursts of music and pathos. He went through it as a summer wind goes through the trees before the outbreak of a thunderstorm. His voice was plaintive, but too low for the greatest popular impression. His tones, however, were diversified, and to him perfectly natural; though his intonation was singularly peculiar, and by the rules of rhetorical elocution, faulty. But it was the best manner for *him,* and with its wailing cadence and rising inflection was extensively copied by his students, much to their own detriment and somewhat to the astonishment and amusement of their audiences. But there was no time to see or think of faults. The speaker was in breathless haste, and was going at 'railroad speed.' Sometimes he would glide in nobly and gracefully to the end of a paragraph or period, very much as a locomotive glides in through a fair prospect to the swinging bell which indicates the next stop. Now and then he would suddenly lift his right hand with a sort of upward wave, and then drop it again. This was almost his only ges ture. To change the figure used just now, the sermon was a widening and foaming torrent, and closed in a perfect cataract of glorious imagery and high religious feeling.

Of all Mr. Alexander's sermons this one is the most imaginative, in the popular sense of that term, that is, the most ornate and highly wrought, the most full of rare and captivating fancy. It is also, in the strictest sense of the term, a noble work of imagination. It is, from beginning to end, a mass of gorgeous imagery, describing the kindred yet opposite illusions of the saint and the worldling. The peroration is descriptive of the rupture (fearful in the one case, and transcendent in the other) of these life-long deceptions. The Christian who had sought the glimmering city in the sky, with faint heart but steadfast purpose, finds that all beneath that city is shadow, and that this alone is substance. He awakes from his dream to pass an eternity in transport. The wicked man awakes from his dream also; he had thought the world was every thing, and had made light of the celestial vision as a puerile vanity. He awakes to shame and everlasting contempt.

It is as sustained a description as any thing in Bunyan; but is not at all quaint, not primitive, not antique, homely or crude. It is perfectly modern; and very rich in its elaborate colouring, as well as superb in its minute finish. The difference between the two in these respects is analogous to the difference between Perugino and Paul de la Roche. It was one of the earlier and more florid efforts for which, in after life, he had a supreme contempt. Macaulay thus despised the essay on Milton, and pronounced its noble ornaments gaudy.

Mr. Alexander's vocabulary was not more immense than his selections from it were eminently choice. The writer, upon the store of whose recollections I have just been drawing, after speaking of the fluency and charm of his speech whether in the private circle or in the pulpit, is naturally led to speak of his written style:

"His command of language must strike every reader of his commentaries, &c. So simple, too; so familiar, easy, colloquial often. It reads *fast*, as it was written. His English is more Saxon than his brother's, and its clearness and immediate intelligibleness suit better those who do not, or cannot, study as they read."

The same gentleman was struck, like all others, with his friend's "diversity of knowledge, reading, tastes, &c." He thinks he was told by one of Mr. Alexander's brothers that he had read all Coke on Littleton. In literature

"He knew no limits. Did he not begin a sort of Biographia Literaria of himself? It seems to me either he told me so, or that I heard something of the kind was found among his papers."

His impression is that Mr. Alexander once told him he kept a record of all the books he read.

Dr. Hall is substantially right here. Mr. Alexander once said he meant to write a literary autobiography, but he never carried it out. He, however, kept a sort of biographico-literary diary; which is for the most part a mere record of his daily employments, and innumerable projects and schemes of study. In this journal he commonly put down the names and description of the books he read, and sometimes entered in it also his judgment upon their contents. Sometimes, though very rarely, he makes his entry in the form of a critical notice or fragment of a review-article. His favourite way of indicating when he began and when he finished a volume, was by marking the dates in the book itself. The presence of a date on any page showed that he had read up to that point. His day-books abound in frequent traces of his exegetical labours, and are sprinkled over with Hebrew, Arabic, and Syriac characters. They are also enriched with quotations and original fragments in various of the modern languages. Sometimes he fills a page with minute accounts of what is doing in Princeton or elsewhere. Occasionally he indulges in a delineation of character. When he travelled, his best journals commonly took the form of letters to his friends at home. These foreign letters are minute and exact enough on all points to satisfy the most rigorous demands of his correspondents. They would sometimes be tedious were they not so full of change, so gracefully voluble, so witty, learned, sensible, and graphic, so affectionate, so characteristically expressive of the writer's shifting moods and whims, so charged with laughing abandon and animal spirits, so free from the usual contagion of the guide-books, so artfully simple and natural in style, and so smoothly and legibly written with the pen, in his round, fair manner.

His freedom from all pedantic effort to show his learning has been noticed by every body who ever knew him. With all his information, he kept it as much as possible in the background, though using it freely when occasion really called for it. Whether at home or abroad, whether in his letters or his conversation, he showed himself the gentleman and scholar as distinguished from the vain and noisy pretenders to these titles.

On this point, Dr. Hall says:

"I need not add how far he was from displaying or talking about his knowledge, his reading, &c.; how well he escaped the airs of a learned man; how young and fresh he was to the last."

With all his lively traits, too, his profound respect for all the decencies and proprieties of religion was known and read of all men.

"Those who best knew his cheerful moods know also how serious and reverent he was in every thing sacred. No associations seemed to tempt him to transgress the 'that is required' and 'that is forbidden' in the Third Commandment. Yet who was further from sanctimoniousness, or cared less for mere forms and appearances?"

Dr. Charles Hodge has done justice to the scope and brilliancy of his colleague's intellect, and with his own foreign training and his life-long companionship with men of mark and learning, Dr. Hodge will not be accused of forming his opinion of Mr. Alexander rashly, or upon insufficient data. He might, indeed, be suspected of some partiality toward one whom he had admired from a child; but the reader must be struck with his evident fairness of statement, and the tone of deliberate moderation which distinguishes the paragraphs in which he refers to Mr. Alexander's intellectual ascendancy over his fellows:

"This ascendancy was due partly to his extraordinary talents. He seemed to have the power to acquire and to do, in the best manner and with the greatest ease, whatever he chose to attempt. He was a great linguist. He learned Arabic and Hebrew when yet a boy, without any instructor. He became familiar with almost all the modern languages of Europe, apparently without effort. But this in him was not a peculiar and solitary gift. He acquired all things apparently with the same ease. In most cases it was not the language itself, so much as its literature, which occupied and interested him. And yet the science of language and comparative philology were with him favourite subjects of study.

"His mind was analytical and comprehensive. He could unravel the most complicated mass of details and discover the principle by which they were reduced to order. This power he displayed to great advantage in the treatment of the Old Testament History, which he so taught as to make that economy appear as an organic whole, each part assuming its proper relation to every other part, and all culminating in the fuller revelation of the new economy.

"Few men had the ability to argue with greater clearness and force, as is evinced in the introductions to several of his commentaries and in his Biblical essays.

"His style was distinguished not only for perspicuity, but for singular felicity and propriety of language. It was a great pleasure to listen to him, with the attention directed to that particular point. No man could say more in few words. His memory was not only encyclopædic but, remarkably tenacious. Some of his feats of recollection are well known to his friends, which seem almost incredible. More than once he has come into my study, and taken a sheet of paper and written down in alphabetical order the first, middle-names, and the surnames of thirty or forty students, after having heard them called over the day before promiscuously in the process of matriculation. The fertility of his imagination was strikingly exhibited in many of his sermons, and in the poetic effusions in which he sometimes indulged. Taking him all in all, he was certainly the most gifted man with whom I have ever been personally acquainted."

Dr. Hodge speaks of his "Introductions" as showing in a high degree the power of argument. Some of his expositions and critical articles are equally remarkable in this respect. His novel presentation of the argument for the canon of Scripture, in his work on New Testament Literature, will here occur to the reader. His refutation of the papal claim from the Saviour's words to St. Peter; his progressive proof of the sacred writer's purpose in the first Gospel, and in the second, and in the Acts; his discussion of the point whether the brothers of our Lord were the sons of Mary; his repeated discomfiture of German grammarians and lexicographers on their own ground, in the Isaiah; and his proof of the strictly paradoxical character of many of our Lord's sayings, are other instances that occur to me. The most sustained and lengthened of his arguments pure and simple, however, is his work on the Primitive Offices; which is in form as logical and polemical as Chillingworth's.

In the following letter, he chides his correspondent humorously for multiplying his labours with a view to ensnare his Princeton friend into compliance:

"PRINCETON, March 29, 1842.

"MY DEAR SIR:

"The Sunday work I could do for you without inconvenience; but I do not choose to come down and return on that day, and I have an engagement on Monday morning, besides writing enough to keep me busy until late at night on Saturday. I know your sympathy with my official burden is extremely weak, and it may be for that reason that my own with yours is not the strongest possible, especially in reference to those embarrassments which spring from an extraordinary multiplication of public duties. I take for granted that the services of which you speak on Monday and Friday are voluntary appointments of your own (providential emergencies being, of course, subject to no rule), and venture to suggest that if you are not able to fulfil them, they ought not to have been made. All this, in substance, I remember to have heard from you on similar occasions, and have merely given it a new direction. But seriously, I do believe that by preaching at my usual place in this vicinity, on Sunday afternoon, and attending to my duties on Saturday and Monday, I am likely to do more good than by leaving all these in order to do what I can do just as well in the vacation of three months and more, during which it is impossible to suppose that you will not need help as much as you do now. Mr. Yeomans was here yesterday, but only on his way to New York. Very sincerely yours,

"J. A. ALEXANDER."

The astonishment with which the fact is accepted that Mr. Alexander knew much of the world, and had the rare gift of reading the human heart, notwithstanding his recluse habits, would be greatly lessened were it generally known how much he travelled, and what a keen observer he was of all he saw on these journeys. He delighted to leave home somewhat mysteriously, and to return without previous announcement. He loved to go off without a plan either for place or time, to remain *incognito*, and to be absent as long as the trip continued to be pleasant. Now and then he had a companion in these tours, but commonly preferred to be alone. Even during the sessions of the Seminary, he was sure to seize every occasion of preaching in Trenton, or Philadelphia, or New-York, or elsewhere, and would, under these circumstances, spend the whole of Saturday in roaming about the town or city he visited, or in speculating upon the probable characters of the people he saw passing to and fro on the streets and at the hotels. He had a strange passion for riding in public vehicles, attending large public gatherings, seeing startling sights and shifting crowds of people; but he especially liked the bustle and perpetual variety of the large city hotels. He seemed to feel perfectly comfortable, when he could thus survey the world in miniature and at the same time be pretty confident that nobody recognized him, or, if any one did, that no one would venture to disturb him. But he took the highest satisfaction in those little jaunts which were almost unpremeditated, and which were not complicated with any ministerial "appointments." He loved to take his passage on the Camden and Amboy steamboats, and to snuff the salt breeze from the sea. He has given in the Princeton Magazine an amusing account of one of these trips to Camden, in which he exhibits a perfect acquaintance with the route, and with the minutiæ of what is done on these boats and on the connecting railway. He was just as familiar with the Bay of New-York, and the noble spectacle of shipping at the wharves and in the roadstead, and with the noise, confusion, rush, and daily incidents of the Hoboken and Jersey City ferries. Sometimes he "enlarged his brief," and struck out for new regions. He would get upon a train of cars and dash into the interior of New-York, or Pennsylvania; or he would visit the lakes, or the mountains, or the great rivers. He once took it into his head that he would visit all the notable cities of the United States and Canada, and did visit nearly all of them during successive summers. The general scheme of travel, embracing many separate and independent journeys, was often arranged beforehand, with lucid comprehension and refined accuracy; but the method of travel on each particular journey was left to be decided by the current of events. It was most usual with him to have no chart or *programme.* Nothing could exceed the utterly planless character of some of his excursions. It diverted his mind to be passive and let chance determine the question whither he should go, where he should lodge, and what he should have for his breakfast, his dinner, or his supper. He often let the waiters choose for him. He often started to go to one point, and afterwards changed his mind and went to another and perhaps the very opposite. This was not from any want of voluntary firmness. It was done deliberately, and was the way in which he saw fit to recreate his jaded feelings and faculties of mind, which, however capable of severe tension and long endurance, of course sometimes needed unbending, and now and then craved absolute repose. It was the expression, too, of a fresh and original mind which sought out new or adventurous paths. It was his own way of enjoying himself to his heart's content in the intervals of labour. Once, when he was in Europe, and in quest of a certain town towards which he had been making all speed, he was apprized of the fact that he had reached it; and on the instant, and for no reason in the world but pure caprice, determined to go somewhere else, and refused to stop at the place indicated.

When he visited New-York, he commonly staid at a public house. This was more convenient, and enabled him the better to fulfil the ends for which he had left home. He went from one hotel to another, until he had seen them all. He would take one meal at one *café* or *table d'hôte* and another at another. He had the greatest talent for enjoying himself in strange places, and in looking eagerly at little but unnoticed things. His European journals show how much of his enjoyment abroad was derived from other scenes besides those which travellers usually make most of; scenes on shipboard, on the highway, in the intercourse of foreign society, and especially scenes presenting anything that was droll or characteristic. He went to parts of old towns which are not approached by voyagers. He read all the old signs, and especially those in strange characters. Foreign signs and street-cries were among his hobbies. He loved anything that was racy and of the soil. He at first preferred Amsterdam to Paris. He never tired of comparing what he saw abroad with what he had seen which was most like it at home; and of noticing resemblances between certain persons in England or Scotland or on the continent and certain persons in the United States; and between the incidents of his earlier and of his later European journeys, which were divided by an interval of exactly twenty years. His memory for these incidents, and for the names, faces, dates and circumstances to which they were related, was admirable almost to the point of perfection. Large portions of his foreign diary are taken up with descriptions of the children he saw in the streets. Some of these excited more admiration in his mind than Nôtre Dame. He had a comical way of calling all children "babes," and all young men "youths." He had a classic taste in music, and an untutored but sound Gothic taste in architecture; but he was a modern in his taste for painting, and confesses, with a sort of whimsical compunction, that he prefers Delaroche to Raphael. What struck him most at the Louvre, was that the great room was a quarter of a mile long. He liked the Dutch painters as a class better than the Italian or even the French. The homeliness and visible truth of the pictures which crowd the walls of Amsterdam, Leyden, and Antwerp, took hold of him with power. He had no scruples about disclosing what were the emphatic judgments of his mind on all such points. It is very characteristic of him that the paintings which he most fancied in Paris and in Holland, as well as in Great Britain, were portraits of children, the children of celebrated kings. At the *Trippenhuis* in Amsterdam, which could boast many of the choicest pieces of Rubens, Rembrandt, Teniers, Gerard Dow, Vandyck and others, and which contained the famous Boar Hunt of Paul Potter, the thing that riveted and fascinated him was the full-length portrait by Vandyck of the two children of Charles the First. He did not affect an emotion which he did not feel, when confronted with the old masters. The repetition of sacred subjects soon became tedious to him, and the idolatrous worship of "Saints" and "Holy Families" was something that he could not understand or imitate. He said he would not give the pictures of the children of Charles the First by Vandyck, and of Edward the Fourth, by Paul Delaroche, for all the Madonnas and Holy Families of the greatest masters.

He loved to seize upon the salient traits of a new people or spoken language, at a glance of his eye or ear. If he discovered that he had made mistakes, he was careful to take them back. His journal of one day is in little things sometimes in flat contradiction of the journal of the preceding. The complexion, size, features, manners, accent, habits, of a population afforded him endless sources of amusement. Types and sub-types of national and individual character were always observed and discriminated by him. He had constructed an unwritten science on this whole subject.

But it is of his more ordinary jaunts and journeys, his remarkable "travels about home," that I had proposed speaking. He sometimes travelled in company with one or more of his young scholars. It was a rare thing for him not to have a boy under the ferule. One of these went with him on his second voyage to Europe, but this was after the relation between them of preceptor and pupil had long since ceased. I remember a visit with him to Fairmount Water-works at Philadelphia, and his "taking an ice cream" there. Afterwards we walked along the "verdurous wall" of the Schuylkill till we came to the massive portals of Laurel Hill cemetery. The grassy margin of the river, shining in the sun, and the picturesque acclivity and profuse shade of the heights capped with obelisks were greatly admired by him. An accident prevented our admittance. On the way, he talked in his most sportive and fascinating manner. The day was enchanting, and his keen pleasure in everything he saw, unbounded. The length of a coal-train on the Reading Railway, as it crossed the long bridge near Fairmount, aroused his wonder.

When in Philadelphia, and merely on the wing, he commonly put up at Jones's, then the principal hotel in the city, and one of Mr. Alexander's favourite stopping places. Very often, notwithstanding all efforts to the contrary, his friends would find him out and invite him to their houses, or urge him to occupy their pulpits. All this he would take very good-naturedly, but would complain a little bitterly to his travelling companion of the "breach of his incognito."

"For months beforehand," writes one of his nephews, "my kind instructor had been talking of a trip with me to Ticonderoga; which place he had previously visited alone himself. A trip was accordingly taken, not to Ticonderoga, but to Washington. This trip to Ticonderoga became a proverb in our subsequent intercourse, and was used to denote any journey in which we jointly participated. He always spoke of such a journey, as 'our projected trip to Ticonderoga.'"

That journey to Washington is one of the most memorable events of the writer's life. It was during the palmy days of the American Senate, when Winthrop was speaker of the House, and Webster, Calhoun, Preston, Benton, McDowell, and others equally or scarcely less famous, were the lions of the legislative chambers. The whole tour was marvellous and exciting to a raw lad without any knowledge whatever of the great world; but the scenes and occurrences at the capital blotted out the vivid memory of any thing else. As the two rode by the various public buildings, he pointed them out and explained their uses, and described what was done, or what was to be seen within their walls. As they passed the Patent Office, his manner, which had been very gracious, suddenly changed. Without the least warning, he seized his fellow-traveller (who was alone with him in the hack), and forcibly directed his face towards the new object of interest, telling him as he did so, in quick, sharp, peremptory tones, to look out of the window and see what was to be seen; and that it was not worth while to leave one's home unless one was disposed to look about one and use one's eyes. There was all the menace and fire of legitimate authority in his tone, as he said this, but he did not seem to be angry. It has sometimes struck me as possible, that he wished to lodge a favourite lesson in the mind of his pupil, and could think of no way of doing it at once so easy and effectual as this summary process. The ebullition was as transient as it was extraordinary. He was presently in a high glow, and played the part of a Mentor with as much kindliness as knowledge and discretion. Mr. Alexander held in contempt every thing like laziness, revery, stupidity, and idiotic listlessness. All approaches to these baneful-states he cordially reprobated. The travellers repaired every morning to the Capitol, and he took great pains in showing his young *élève* the many attractions of the edifice and the grounds. He was perfectly content to stay there all day, strolling under the green trees, watching the movements of the children, examining the pictures and statuary, surveying the fine prospect of the Potomac and the verdant fields adjacent which is commanded by the higher parts of the building, and above all attending the debates of Congress. When gently reminded, about two o'clock, of the importance of sustaining nature with food, he would say, "I can do without my dinner," but would pleasantly yield to the urgency of an appeal which if suggested by the cravings of appetite, was certainly fortified by considerations of reason. He listened to the interesting speeches. Colonel Benton one day spoke for hours while they were there. But what interested him most was

22*

scrutinizing the personal features and bearing of members, gazing upon the animating *tout ensemble*, studying the manners of men and the varieties of human character, witnessing the calling of the roll, and of the yeas and nays, and what he has styled "the pretty play of passing between tellers," watching the easy grace and adroitness of the pages, and the free employment by members of newspapers and government "stationery," and familiarizing himself (if such a term applies to who needed little further instruction) to the rules and usages of parliamentary decorum, the order and form of the various motions, and the operation of such devices as the previous question, the motion to adjourn, and the series of other dilatory feints. His eyes wandered from a wearisome declaimer to the prominent members who retained their seats, to the gad-abouts and whisperers, to the sycophants, to the vain or handsome men, to those who noiselessly glided to and fro in the passages, or moved or stood in groups in the open spaces, at the door, and in the lobby. He appeared to see through it all, and could and did unravel the mesh from beginning to end. He invited the attention of his young charge to the fact that the really great men did not put themselves in the foreground, never vociferated or bawled, were not always on the floor, and seldom uttered a word except on important questions. One day, in the left hand gallery, the strangers looked down upon the tall, gaunt figure of John C. Calhoun, of South Carolina, who was silently pacing the area near the reporters' desks, with his head bowed forward, and his iron-gray hair brushed high over his forehead and falling in long, straggling locks about his ears. He did not open his mouth to speak during the whole time they were there. Mr. Alexander also directed the notice of his pupil to the vacant seat of the Senator from Massachusetts, and told him to pay attention to the man who should sit in it. Soon after a dark-browed man, of a swarthy complexion, with deep sunken eyes and a certain look of hidden power, entered the door and occupied this very seat. He was dressed in a blue coat with brass buttons, and was the impersonation of Senatorial gravity. Mr. Webster spoke three words while the Princeton visitors were in the chamber, and these were from his seat. They were the words, "Let it pass."

Another point of great attraction at Washington was the huge arm-chair of Dixon H. Lewis, which was at least twice as large as any other. While the tourists were looking at it, the unwieldy member took his seat and filled it amply. Mr. Alexander seemed a little annoyed, but not at all provoked, that his own ability to occupy one of the ordinary arm-chairs should excite the surprise and comment of his fellow-traveller.

Some of Mr. Alexander's impressions of what he saw at different times at Washington, may be gathered from the Princeton Magazine, in which he has embodied them in articles of a serious nature, as well as in several truly laughable *squibs* or *jeux d'esprit.* One of these articles is signed "Nos," and intituled, "Ham and Eggs. A Plea for Silent Legislation." The effort of the satirist is to show, that the union of speaking with law-making is as purely conventional as that of ham and eggs; of which a friend once remarked, "Why should those two things always go together? The only effect is to spoil them both." The writer refuses to endorse that opinion in its literal application, but adopts it as a general principle of broad range and with a striking bearing on the method of Congressional debates. It will be seen that he has anticipated Carlyle in his clever *mot* about "wind and tongue." After a page of strenuous reasoning and telling sarcasm, he thus concludes the paper:

"The practice of oral discussion had its origin when books were rare, and the accomplishment of reading saved a felon from the gallows. Why should it still be kept up, as a part of legislation, or an indispensable preliminary to it, in a day when hackney-coachmen read upon their boxes, and a beggar will not beg till he has seen the morning paper? We might as well have link-boys with our gas-light, or hot bricks with our furnaces. Does a man take his night-cap and dressing-gown along with him, when he goes by railroad from New-York to Philadelphia for an hour's business, as he did when he went by the old line of stages, and spent a night or two at way-side taverns? It is shameful that . . . . our legislation should be just where it was in the days of Wittenagemote, when the Saxon nobles franked public documents with the sign of the cross, and scored appropriation bills upon the walls with chalk or charcoal. Let us have no more of this exploded and explosive nonsense. Let the Constitution be amended so as to forbid all talking, except so far as may be absolutely necessary, for the purpose of passing bills and resolutions, and making formal motions for the conduct of the public business. To suppress all clamour about voting blindly, in the dark, and what not, let no legislative act be passed until ten days after it is introduced, and in the meantime let the press groan with arguments, appeals, and explanations upon both sides. More will read them than will now listen to the endless twaddle of our conscript fathers and brethren. No man will then be at the mercy of reporters, but will speak for himself to all who read him. And many a man who cannot speak, at least in the Temple of the Winds, can write intelligibly on an interesting subject. Such is our device for the cure of this inveterate disease of the tongue, or rather of the lungs; for we believe, after all, the chief ingredient of our legislative eloquence is wind.

"To avert the criticisms of physicians, druggists, and apothecaries, we make haste to add, that this form of phthisis is entirely *sui generis*, arising from excessive strength of lungs, and ending in consumption of the public money, time and patience."

To appreciate all this as it deserves, the reader ought to have taken a trip with this honest critic to the legislative chambers, and to have before him, as he peruses these trenchant paragraphs, the look of mischievous fun that often played over the writer's face when, in his soft voice and unhesitating rapid tones, he uttered such "ower true" pleasantries as this is, *vivâ voce*.

Mr. Alexander abhorred notoriety. This led him, as some thought, to hide his light too much under a bushel. On this head, one of his best and most discerning friends writes:

"He avoided publicity in forms where he would have appeared to the greatest advantage." *

The same friend thinks he must have refused a large number

* The Rev. J. Hall, D.D., in a letter to the biographer.

of invitations to give literary lectures, orations, sermons on prominent occasions. I have evidence that he refused a pressing invitation from Prof. Henry to lecture before the Smithsonian Institution. He would never consent to a nomination for the General Assembly, or to be moderator of Synod or Presbytery. He was fond of attending the debates of the ecclesiastical courts, but seldom spoke, and then in few words. Now and then he would seem to forget himself, and enter pretty fully into the merits of a question. His speeches, however, were invariably short and conversational, and commonly made to facilitate the progress of business.

Dr. Hall is satisfied that the chief reason for his customary silence was the consciousness that whatever he should say would be sure to draw unusual attention to the speaker. Another reason unquestionably was a contempt for the American habit of mere declamation. It is certain that he took a more active part in the debates of the church judicatories which were held in Princeton, than in any others; and probably not only because they were more convenient to his study, and because he wished to set a right example before the young men, but also because in Princeton he was better known to the people at large than elsewhere, and his movements on such occasions would therefore not be likely to attract so much curious notice as in a strange town or village.

"But you know how accurately and fully he could *report* a debate when it was over, and reproduce the peculiarities of the speakers."

Nothing about him was more wonderful than his astonishing acquaintance with the forms of parliamentary procedure. It was not merely great, it was well-nigh perfect. It was that of the most accomplished expert; and I am persuaded that no speaker or clerk of the House of Representatives; no hanger-on of years' standing at Washington or Westminster could rattle off the exact expressions, in the right place, and in the proper order, with more rapid *nonchalance* than he could. His children's books are filled with real or imaginary diaries of such proceedings, and nothing he ever wrote is more amusing than some of the burlesque debates he has recorded in Wistar's Magazine. The satire in these inimitable performances is sometimes so broad that any child can see it; but sometimes, again, it is terse and delicate, like that which has embalmed the pithy sayings of La Rochefoucauld.

In this connection I am reminded to say that perhaps the most vehement sarcasm Mr. Alexander ever wrote, is contained in a contribution of two pages to the same magazine, which is entitled "Some People." * It is at times as "tart as the Quarterly" under Gifford. Occasionally it seems to have almost the savagery of John Lockhart, in his roughest style; but a benign purpose shines through every one of its caustic sentences.

The reader will not find his attention flag in the attempt to read the short extracts which follow:

"Some People imagine that the only way in which they can be disagreeable is by ill nature or severity. They never dream that they may be too gracious, or that most men can bear any thing in manner with more patience than that bland assumption of superiority, which shows itself in patronizing condescension."

"Some People cherish the delusion, that in order to enjoy the pleasures of taste, they must be inventors, or at least performers. They forget that the great majority must always be the passive recipients of such impressions. Under this delusion many waste their lives in making themselves mediocre draughtsmen or musicians, and still more deny themselves such pastimes altogether, when both classes might derive untold pleasure from thankfully enjoying what is done by others, without ambitiously attempting it themselves. If the same mistake, which thus exists about the fine arts, were equally operative in literature, what would the result be? If no man dared to read a poem without writing one, the world would either have too many writers to be read, or too few readers to let writers live.

"Some People think it is a conclusive argument against a given course of conduct, that if all men followed it, society could not exist. In the shallow ethics of the world, no formula is more approved than

*Princeton Magazine, p. 280.

'What if every body did so?' The same logic would demonstrate that, because if all were doctors there would be no patients, men must all be patients and none doctors; or because if all preached there would be no hearers, therefore none must preach and all must hear without a preacher. The most valuable functions are precisely those which would be worthless if they could be universal." . . . .

The rhythm of the last trenchant saying was no doubt unconscious, but is very characteristic of the writer.

"SOME PEOPLE, if they condescend to read these paragraphs, may feel disposed to poach upon my manor and write others, whether in mere continuation, or by way of parody or refutation. All such are hereby notified that they may spare themselves the labour and exposure which they meditate, as the feelings which prompt to such a course had better be kept secret than exposed to public view; and as to the continuation of these thoughts, it is commonly conceded that the person who begins to say any thing is for the most part the best qualified to finish it."

The fiercest part is omitted in these selections, though it is all a masterpiece of cutting sense and brevity. It is true Juvenalian satire; a lashing of the follies of the age, or rather of the race, and from a wholesome motive.

Among the testimonials of this period is that of Dr. Rice of Mobile, who was then a student of the Theological Seminary, and who soon began to frequent his study again, after long years during which they had seldom met. The Professor was engaged at this time upon his great work on Isaiah, which, in addition to his labours in the Seminary, left him very little liberty for chat with his friends. He recollects that he said to him on one occasion, that his study was always open to him. If he should come in and find him busy, he would take no notice of him, unless he had some special matter of inquiry; but it would not interrupt or disturb him for him to stay there and read or examine books. If he was at leisure for a "crack," he would sit down and talk to his pupil as he believes no other man ever could talk. He was certainly the most agreeable companion, he says, that he has ever known.

"His apprehensions were so quick; his knowledge was so extensive and accurate; his learning so varied and profound; his imagination was so high; his fancy so bright, lively, playful (albeit it was occasionally a little grotesque, though it was always refined); his wit so sparkling, though it was sometimes terrible as the forked lightning; his humor so large, sweet, racy and genial, that his society at this time afforded a strange pleasure not unmingled with awe."

The evidence as to his social capacities and sympathies when engaged in talk with people he knew well, is clear and striking:

"In intercourse with his friends and intimates, he was unpretending, modest, and without affectation. He never seemed conscious of any superiority. He certainly never manifested such a state of mind."

In reference to Mr. Alexander's religious state at this time, Dr. Rice says that when he entered the Seminary and became acquainted with him again, he found that he was a rapidly advancing Christian. He does not think he has ever met with one who grew in grace more consistently and constantly. So transparent a character could not fail to reveal himself to those with whom he was associated as intimately as this Professor was with his pupils. Every teacher is known by his class; by some of them; by those who from more favourable opportunities of seeing him than others, or from superior natural qualifications, are most competent to judge. A public instructor, especially a religious instructor, is like "a city set on a hill, which cannot be hid." The testimony on this point, as regards Mr. Alexander, if respect be had to the sterling credit and high competency of the witnesses of his course at this period, is exceedingly important and gratifying.

Alluding to the extraordinary clearness, distinctness, straightforwardness, and compactness of his instructions in the class-room, the same pupil testifies as follows:

"These instructions were characterized by great directness; he went straight to the point by the best and shortest way; by intensity or force; and by extraordinary elegance and felicity of diction.

"Add to this his vast, brilliant, powerful imagination, and you have the characteristics of his preaching."

When listening to him in the pulpit, he was always thinking of some mighty cataract:

"He always brought Niagara Falls to my mind. I had the same sense of power, and sublime, magnificent beauty. In the lecture-room he was like a powerful locomotive in motion upon a straight and level railroad track."

The following letter to an old correspondent which begins as an effusion of one of the transcendentalists,* who were then much in vogue in Princeton, and afterwards falls into the quaint, old Covenanter manner, and winds up in the style of the Ritualists.

"DEC. 23, 1842.

"MY DEAR SIR:

"Since I last wrote I have become a transcendentalist, and look with loathing on the vulgar, sensuous, one-sided pragmatism of your phraseology. The doings of which you speak are natural developments of that unworthy realism, in which your stand-point, I lament to see, remains unmoved by all the strenuous attacks of O. A. B., C. S. H., and other faithful followers of Cant and Cozen. If I can leave the regions of pure reason long enough to speak of such material concerns, I will do you to wit: that on Sabbath first (whilk is Yule), I was to have given a screed of doctrine against all such superstitious rags of Popery in our chapel; but a letter from that painful minister, Mr. W. moving me to give him my countenance at his visitation on that day, hath led me to transfer my witness-bearing from Yule itself to the first day of the incoming year, the individual day whilk you have named in your epistle; so that I may not homologate or condescend to your gracious invite without resiling from this new and special ordering of the affair, which would be both indecorous and kittlesome to them concerned; for which cause I make bold to crave the liberty of naming [☞] the first Sunday after Epiphany, profanely called the eighth of January, when it will give me pleasure to unite with you in

* I use this term as he did, not technically or of the followers specifically of Aristotle or of Kant, in Europe, but of the upstarts and tyros in the United States who were going crazy over the Germans.

the inimitable services of our excellent Liturgy, aided by the swelling tones of the organ, and the affecting sight of a reading-desk arranged on the Apostolic model. N. B. Please to allow your verger or sacristan to adjust the fald-stool (reverently) to my inferior altitude, or my introit will be less impressive than I could desire. If this day does not suit you, name any later one; or if you insist upon it as 'vital,' I can make a new arrangement here, and preach for you on the Feast of Circumcision, as you request. Please to preserve this letter, as it may be necessary to publish the correspondence. At any rate, it must appear sooner or later, as I write always in the manner of Walpole, with a view to posthumous celebrity."

CHAPTER XVII.

The Biblical Repertory and Princeton Review was now in the full tide of prosperity. From the moment that Mr. Alexander put his broad shoulder to the wheel, and gave his whole strength to the work, the Review had received an impetus that greatly raised it in the public estimation, and carried it forward to a point of eminence in the regards of wits and scholars that it had never before attained, and had not at first aimed to reach This was several years before he became the nominal editor Some of his own articles, in particular raised a stir among the quid-nuncs like that produced by a squall upon a smooth sea. Hitherto he might sometimes be mistaken for his brother Jacob; but now his speech and his manner alike bewrayed him: the hands were incontestably the hands of Esau. On this point, Professor Hart says:

"I knew nothing further of Addison until after his return from Europe, when he signalized himself by a series of brilliant articles in the Princeton Review, which attracted very general attention. The first two or three especially, in which he gave free rein to his power of sarcasm, were much read and quoted in College. The articles which I remember most distinctly as having created a sensation at the time of their appearance, were the following: a Review of the Rev. Calvin Colton's Reasons for Leaving the Presbyterian and Entering the Episcopal Church; a Review of the Discussion between Dr. Boardman and Bishop Doane, in regard to the Apostolical Succession; * a Review of Bishop Onderdonk's Pamphlet, 'Episcopacy Tested by Scripture.'"

This last named article is not upon Dr. Addison Alexander's list of his own pieces, or upon other lists of them within my reach; nor is it in his style. The manner is grave, sedate, and courtly, and well becoming that high-toned polemic, Dr. Miller.

But another article in reply to the Bishop's rejoinder, in the October number of the same year, is by a very different pen, and in a very different style. It was in a style calculated to excite the fear, that the Assyrian had suddenly found his way to the very centre of the camps of the extreme High Churchmen; or (to borrow another figure from the enemies of Israel), in a style suited to provoke the exclamation, "The Philistines are upon thee, Samson." It is entitled "New Theory of Episcopacy," and opens in these dulcet but ringing tones:

"It is no safe thing to meddle with our ancient friends, the Prelatists, since their last discovery. As might have been expected from its magnitude and value, they have grown exceedingly tetchy with respect to the treatment of their great arcanum by the uninitiated. They seem to imagine, like the alchemists of old, that the whole world is waiting in suspense for the results of their experiments; holding its breath till the universal menstruum or elixir is discovered. No one is allowed either to feel or feign indifference. And even when the mystery is divulged, what can we do? If we let it alone, we are enrolled as converts; if we handle it at all, it is always too roughly. High church episcopacy is indeed, botanically speaking, a most tender herb, liable not only to be crushed by the broad foot of vulgar non-conformity, but also to be blasted by the merest breath of argument. It cannot bear the east wind of discussion, but must have an atmosphere created for it, like a rare plant in a hot-house, to be looked at but not touched. To this discreet arrangement we have no objection, but are heartily content to stand at any distance not entirely out of sight, craving no other privilege than that of furnishing a brief description, now and then, for the gratification of 'the uninformed.'"

This menace was terribly fulfilled in the course of this article, and a series of later articles on the same general subjects, by this new Democritus, or Lucian, whose repartees were enthymemes, and whose scathing refutations were in the form of jests. In explanation of his last phrase, he goes on to say:

"We are ashamed to acknowledge our belief that some even of those

* Dr. Hart adds, that great mirth was provoked by an article of Mr. Alexander on his old friend Dr. Cox's book on Regeneration. But with this Mr. Alexander had nothing to do. The article was by another hand.

who read the Repertory, far from knowing all about THE TRACT, before we introduced it to their notice, had never yet discovered its existence. 'Not to know me argues thyself unknown,' would be a keen retort, and we are far from justifying our poor friends from the charge of guilty ignorance, the rather as it has not been for the want of zealous efforts on the part of zealous 'churchmen' to apprize the world that they and their superiors are *in esse*. But as the Eastern proverb says, 'The hen may lay a thousand eggs and the owl never know it, however loud the hen may cackle.'"

He then proceeds to show, as essential to a just appreciation of the subject, that this particular theory of high Prelacy is a new one, and that this new theory is put forward as a binding doctrine of the word of God, which no man can deny and be guiltless.

No one in reading these strictures can fail to see that his aim in these witty and exasperating articles was not to wound the feelings of individuals, but to pierce with ridicule a system which he believed to be absurd and pernicious, and yet so encased in self-esteem as to be in one sense invulnerable to the shafts of mere dialectics. Not that he undervalued the weapons of a strictly argumentative warfare, even in this controversy. In his later essays on Church-order, which were finally gathered into the volume entitled, "New Testament Offices," he has fully vindicated the claims of syllogistic reasoning, and has demonstrated, in the most rigorous method, that the high-church system is a system that, logically considered, is "twice dead, plucked up by the roots."

It is evident from the whole drift, as well as particular statements of this article, that its author was not fighting against the ecclesiastical polity advocated by Hooker, but against the American caricature of the system invented at Oxford. He speaks in one place of "The fathers of the English Church, (those noble souls whom we as well as prelatists delight to honour)," and plainly intimates that they were of another mind upon these subjects. He holds that the adherents of the "Tract" party ought to blush that they are successors of Thomas Cranmer and John Jewell. Of the "Discourse" of Bishop Griswold himself, "the parent of the doctrine," which is attacked in the Repertory, the reviewer writes:

"There is nothing in it to impair the feelings of personal respect for his character which we believe to be generally entertained. Our opinion of his argument is known already; but we feel ourselves bound, as well in justice as in Christian charity, to say that, in maintaining his opinion, he is simple, modest, earnest, and we doubt not, most sincere."

And Bishop Onderdonk himself is dealt with in a spirit of sarcastic irony, but not of deliberate malice.

Of him the reviewer says:

* * * "The operation which it was our duty to perform upon this precious offspring of his intellect and fancy, was indeed a painful one, and we were not at all displeased to see the tender father much distressed, and even angry. The first gush of feeling, about six months ago, while it indicated sensitiveness of the highest order, no doubt gave relief by giving vent to deep emotions. *Hinc illæ lacrymæ!* The wound inflicted on the Tract was not yet healed; but we are now rejoiced to learn that it is convalescent."

The article reviewing the reply of Bishop Onderdonk, was followed in 1836 by the exquisite showing up of Calvin Colton, and in 1841 by the annihilating review of Bishop Doane. The former is perhaps the best known of the series. Both articles will be found in the published volumes of the Repertory. The article on Bishop Doane's Rejoinder to Dr. Boardman was in part the work of other pens; though its raciest paragraphs were, with a single remarkable exception, undoubtedly the work of Professor Addison Alexander. The article in which he brought out into such conspicuous notice the name and features of Mr. Calvin Colton, is wholly his own, and his portrait of the amiable "American in England," is informed by a humour as fine and as enjoyable as any thing in the *Mémoirs* of Beaumarchais. It would have been relished, as those were, by Voltaire, by Marie Antoinette, and by 'old Goethe;' if only these lovers of wit had lived in our days, and been acquainted with the men and manners of the two countries, and with the shallow pretensions of certain transatlantic authors to shine as great lights in the ecclesiastical firmament. But the article, though containing personal attacks, breathes no spirit of personal malice. It is a frank and cutting, but parliamentary and just, and even kind, exposure of the most arrogant and foolish claims.*

He gives his readers the benefit of one of Mr. Colton's pleasant anecdotes, prefacing it with the remark:

"Those who are familiar with his writings, are aware that, excepting wit, he has all the gifts of an accomplished jester."

He then adds:

"We like this tale, and wish to make a 'practical improvement' of it. Mr. Colton considers it a capital joke that a cobbler should presume to 'stir a parson up.' And so it is; but is it not a better joke that Mr. Calvin Colton, of all men in the world, should undertake to settle, in half a dozen flimsy chapters, what never could be settled to mutual satisfaction by a Cartwright or a Hooker, an Usher or a Baxter?"

The only extract I shall take from the article on the Oxford Tracts and their fond admirer in New Jersey, is an encomium of the style of the English writers, especially John Henry Newman:

"If there is one improvement more conspicuous than any other, in the taste and practice of contemporary writers, especially in England, it is the exchange of pompous rhythm and pedantic phraseology for homely plainness and pure native idiom. That this exchange is perfectly compatible with beauty of the highest kind, has been proved by the example of some noted English writers, and by none more clearly

* Dr. Beach Jones writes that he knows of nothing in our language which for sharp and delicate raillery, sustained irony, and sportive wit and humour, equals this article, and that he has found others, much better versed in literature than himself, whose opinions coincide with his own. Dr. Moore, Dr. Cuyler, Dr. Halsey, and many others have expressed themselves in much the same way.

than by several of the Oxford theologians. To our taste, Newman, as a writer, stands preëminent; as being more musical and elegant than Pusey, and at the same time less mawkish and more masculine than Keble. But in all three, and especially in Newman, what attracts us is the restoration of the old English freedom as to the length of sentences and variety of structure, but without those harsh inversions, and sesquipedalian vocables by which many of the best early writers are disfigured. In a word, the grand improvement is the happy combination of a free and flowing with a chaste and simple style; whereas of old, the flowing writer was almost in every case an incorrect one, and the simple writer was an awkward and a constrained one."

The style of the ambitious American prelate is then contrasted unfavourably with that of the Oxonian. The article is mainly argumentative, but dreadfully biting.

The last of this series of slashing essays in the Princeton Repertory is the one in the volume for the next year (1842), on "High Church Episcopalianism." In it occurs the following ludicrous parallel between the Ritualist party in the church and the Chinese nation.

"We have heard the question asked, how such pretensions should be treated; and we answer, just as the Europeans and Americans treat the claims of the Chinese to be regarded as the only civilized nation upon earth. High-churchmen are in this respect the Chinese of Christendom. The points of resemblance are too glaring to be missed: the same awful reverence for trifles; the same enlightened scorn of weightier matters; the same self-worship; the same polite, compassionate contempt of others; the same serene determination to sweep every thing before them; and the same success in doing it. High-church and the Celestial Empire fill corresponding blanks in civil and church history. Both are highly respectable and highly useful. We have no more doubt that one exists for some important end than that the other does. But what the final cause, in either case, may be, we should not like to determine. We are very unwilling to believe that a whole people exists only to be laughed at. And yet how is it that the greatest nation upon earth, in point of numbers, is the only one which history exhibits in an aspect purely ridiculous? Other people have their oddities, but these have nothing else. It is not merely their costume and physiognomy. Their most solemn acts of government, of legislation, of negotiation, and of war, are comic, and in many cases farcical. It is impossible to read of them without a smile. There is something so intrinsically droll about them that the gravest writers are compelled to be amusing. The characteristic feature of the Chinese manners is a sort of grave buffoonery, the more diverting, as the Chinaman is always solemnly unconscious of his own absurdity. In every national and individual act, they seem to say, We are the people, and wisdom shall die with us. It is not to be wondered at that such a nation should include a Board of Ceremonies in its constitution. To them life itself is but a series of ceremonies. Every thing is ceremony. Man is a ceremonial puppet, made to go through certain evolutions and manœuvres, to assume certain postures, and to utter certain words at the bidding of the Hang Quo, or master of ceremonies, or under the bamboo of a red-button Mandarin. It is just the same with Sinicism in religious matters. If you wish to place religionists of any sect beyond the reach of ridicule or reason, you must begin by making them as unreasonable and ridiculous as possible; and then they are forever proof against both wit and wisdom. As soon as any one has learned to look upon the paring of his nails and the adjustment of his eyebrows as a vital matter, he is perfectly impregnable. You cannot reach him. Reasoning, of course, is thrown away upon him. Ridicule he looks upon as sinful, because nothing is too small for him to reverence. And after this perversion of the intellect has gone to certain lengths, the smaller a thing is the greater it becomes in his esteem. Matters of life and death are little in comparison with matters of arrangement and grimace. Tell him that what he eats is wholesome or unwholesome, and he hears you not. But tell him which way he must look, and in what posture he must eat, and he is all attention. Tell him that what he is about to drink is poison, and his only answer is a vacant stare. But tell him that the cup is in the wrong hand, or the wrong edge next his mouth, and he is thankful. When a man has reached this point, he might as well shave his head, and thenceforth be inaccessible to all approaches except such as may be made through the Ho Ping, or ceremonial code, and the decrees of the Lee Poo, or ceremonial council. One effect of such a system is to make those who live under it supremely self-complacent. What do the Chinese care for foreign trade? They have every thing they want at home. What is geography to them? They are content to know that China is the centre of the universe. They allow the savage English and Americans to leave the howling wilderness and clamour at Canton for tea; but when the English become smugglers they determine to destroy them. This contempt of other nations seems unconquerable, even by hard blows and bloodshed. Through the smoke of battle they are still seen as grotesque and self-important as before. Every junk that puts out from the coast is to destroy the British fleet; and when it fails they are as confident as ever that the next will be successful. And when all has failed, they purchase their own safety with some millions of bad dollars, and then publish in the Government Gazette that, 'though the English demons made a bold attack, the imperial commander, with his rumbling thunder, considerably damped the ardour of the fierce barbarians.' We think we have seen battles gained at home in the same manner; and we fear that even bishops might be found who, as to both these articles of spurious silver and rumbling thunder, might successfully compete with all the Mandarins of the Celestial Empire. We commend this illustration to our friends who are annoyed by the absurd pretensions of their High-church neighbours. When we hear the latter prate of an 'unauthorized ministry,' 'uncovenanted mercy,' and the 'danger of dissent,' let imagination conjure up before the hearers some familiar form from the Chinese Museum, and we venture to assure them they will find it much more difficult to keep their countenances than to keep their temper."

The great severity and keenness of these telling articles against the then inconsiderable party of the Ritualists (or Puseyites, as they were called in that day) excited the surprise of some who knew the reviewer's intrinsic gentleness of heart, and the beaming delight he took in children. These perhaps too much disregarded the other and sterner side of his character. For the rest, it must be admitted that his attack upon the victims of *Newmania*, as he facetiously termed it, was, after all, a counter attack, and an attack that was not made without great provocation. It was made, furthermore, with a wholesome design, and from an outraged sense of Catholic tolerance.

"It was this essential charity of his nature," writes one* who knew him intimately, and differed from him widely, "this almost feminine repugnance to ostentation in religious things, that explained what I have heard attributed to him as a blemish, namely his scorn-

* Henry James, Esq., of Cambridge.

ful and sarcastic treatment of the High-church pretension. The principle of an authority over the conscience of men had grown so obsolete in our religious practice, that it might by this time have been pronounced fairly dead and buried, were it not that certain ministers of the Episcopal Church, in seeking how to distinguish themselves from the ordinary gospel ministry, had wit enough to make a gain out of the fact by daintily manipulating the small ecclesiastical or reactionary temper which yet survives in many a belated bosom amongst us, and converting the church for their sake into a peaceful sunny *aquarium*, as it were, which shall have no link of connection with the great outlying sea of human interests, and where every fossil fish of pure ecclesiastical lineage may undergo a cheap coxcombical rehabilitation, and frolic and flounder and spout water, as if it were still vitalized by the living springs of God's providence, and not by the factitious fountains of men's sectarian impudence and cupidity. Dr. Addison Alexander's humane and righteous instincts were outraged, *not* beyond measure by this insincere and faithless behaviour on the part of high-church episcopacy, and he accordingly did ample justice to its pretensions, whenever he was called upon to speak of it."

This is the way the thing strikes a man who, protesting as he does against the ordinary ecclesiastical distinctions, may be regarded as an outsider and an unprejudiced witness.

The subject is thus handled by Professor John S. Hart, in a letter to the editor of this volume:

"Addison's power of sarcasm was unequalled; and when he began writing for the Princeton Review, * he seems to have thought there were certain ecclesiastical and theological assumptions which needed to be met with wit rather than argument, and whose authors deserved punishment rather than refutation. He castigated them accordingly with merciless severity."

* Dr. Hart writes: "Perhaps I ought to add in this connection that the change of the name of the Review from the 'Repertory' to the 'Princeton Review,' was made by Addison's suggestion, at the time that he began his connection with the editorship. So at least I understood from himself. He had a great fancy for local names; quoting the Edinburgh Review as an instance; and his ambition at that time seemed to be to make the Princeton Review equally world renowned; and his first articles, named above, had many of the characteristics which marked the 'swashing blows' administered by Jeffrey and Sydney Smith, in the earlier volumes of the Edinburgh.'"

It was to be observed, however, that after a few years from the date of Mr. Alexander's first appearance as editor of the Review, he rarely indulged in this vein.

"If the fact of his abstaining was due," as Dr. Hart already supposed it to be, "to a growing conviction that a different line of controversy was better suited to the proprieties of theological discussion, the fact does great credit to his conscientiousness. There are few temptations harder to resist than the temptation to use sarcasm and ridicule, when one has manifestly been gifted with these powerful weapons."*

The subsequent efforts of the witty iconoclast in this new image-controversy, were made up almost entirely of pure disputation; and were as grave and courteous in manner as they were ruthless in logic and polite in diction. In the reply to Bishop Southgate, in 1844, he again goes out of his way to eulogize such men as "Bishop Meade, of Virginia," and the fathers of the English church. The criterion by which he discriminated, was the acknowledgment of the other as "sister churches."

But these essays in the Episcopal controversy were but a part of what he was printing in the Biblical Repertory. Every number teemed with the fruits of his studies, and cogitations, and variable feelings. Most of these articles were written without a thought beyond the passing moment; much that is in them is, of course, ephemeral; but some portions of each are worth preservation, either for their learning, their intellectual brilliancy, their wit, their humour, their kindliness, their logic, their eloquence, or their style. All of them are remarkable for their abundant, even overflowing knowledge, and their plain, intrepid, scholarlike, and harmonious English. The dic-

* "The shafts which Addison hurled were not only keenly pointed, but hurled with a force which it was next to impossible to resist. Few opponents, in or out of the church, could have stood up against the terrible weapon which seemed ever lying within reach of his fingers and yet which, during the last twenty years of his life, he forbore entirely to employ."—J. S. H. So that he did not, as Dr. Johnson said of Junius, mistake the venom of the dart for the vigour of the bow.

tion might not always suit a purist or a *petit maître*, but even in the most eager and discursive passages it has a fine idiomatic flavour about it, and the "noble negligence" so much commended, and so happily illustrated, by Dryden. By the end of 1842 he had written fifty articles for the Review; * some long, some short; some elaborate, and some very cursory; profound and superficial; grave and gay; critical, exegetical, conversational, historical, philological, biographical, oratorial. To describe them by exhaustive epithets would be impossible. Several of them will be referred to in other connections. I shall now merely give from the author's private list the titles of the pieces from 1833 to 1843—the catalogue for ten years. He continued to write for the Review as long as he lived:

* Strong traces of his fondness for the remains of classic literature, for old and colloquial forms of English, and for familiar as well as recondite but happy parallels to something in the text, are to be found even in his Isaiah: nude and slavishly critical as his discussion has been regarded by many. Take, for instance, the following passages in his first volume: What he says about the Stabat Mater and Cowper's Ode to Friendship, p. 109. The mechanical interpretation of a "thousand splendid passages of classical and modern poetry," p. 273. Homer's description of Thebes, 526. Horace's of Troy, p. 573. A quotation from Claudian. Cicero's "Evasit," &c., p. 627. Cicero and Cæsar. *Clypea*, p. 390. A Quotation (by Lowth) from Lucretius, p. 496. A Latin verse from *Sedulius*, p. 65. Ovid, p. 336. Lucan. Horace, p. 558. Virgil, p. 562. Demosthenes, and Æschylus's Prometheus, p. 95. Chittim, Cyprus, Josephus, *Citium*, Cicero, p. 406. Macpherson's Ossian, p. 435. Burns (so Barnes) weeping over Isaiah, xxv: 8, p. 435. The descriptions in the Koran and in Quintus Curtius, of the *Mirage*, p. 582. Various allusions of Herodotus, Strabo, Diodorus, &c. *passim*. Poetry and Botany, p. 576. Mixed metaphors in Oriental style, pp. 453 and 485. A beautiful extract (by Barnes) from Mungo Park's journal, p. 496. Hamlet against Gesenius, on ghosts, pp. 571-572. Milton's Flood, p. 265. The Compression and breviloquence of Isaiah xxii: 13, p. 394. Rephaim: "Gigantic Shades," p. 276. Image of Downfall of British Empire. Accessory Ideas that would be Natural, p. 347. Ditto of Desolation of Mississippi Valley, p. 350. Illustration by the Duke of Wellington, p. 369. The Mediæval *maires du palais*, p. 395. The "Lamia" of the Ancients and the Vulgate, p. 569. Boswell's "Curds," p. 132. "Filling Another's Shoes." "Colloquial English," p. 399. "Just as We Might Say," &c., p. 387. "What of the Night?" "What o'clock?" p. 382.

		PAGE.
Murdock's Mosheim	1833	47
Life of Farel	"	145
Theories of Education	"	165
Bush on the Millennium	"	204
Cyril Lucaris	"	212
German New Light.	1834	366
Rowland Hill	"	372
Guericke's Church History	"	407
Roger Williams	"	449
Art of Writing	"	491
Bush on the Psalms	1835	73
Stewart's Sketches	"	134
Barnes on the Gospels	"	149
Stuart's Greek Grammar	"	233
Presbyterian Policy	"	272
Bush's Hebrew Grammar	"	341
Civilization of India	"	401
New Theory of Episcopacy	"	573
Rosenmüller	1836	1
Hengstenberg, Ewald, Freytag, &c.	"	58
Calvin Colton	"	390
Robinson's Gesenius	1837	88
Gleanings from German Periodicals	"	198
Isaiah vii: 8	"	558
Early letters of Melanchthon	1838	1
Part of Article on Henry's Christian Antiquities	"	153
Nordheimer, Vol. I.	"	196
Hengstenberg on the Pentateuch	"	542
Inaugural Address (Scripture Guide)	1839	201
Part of article on Bush on Genesis.	"	271
Kenrick's Theology	1840	283
Plea for Bishops	1841	1
New Works on Isaiah.	"	159
Nordheimer, Vol. II.	"	250
Part of Article on Bishop Doane	"	450
Robinson's Palestine	"	583
High-Churchism	1842	129
Works on Genesis	"	199
Whately's Kingdom of Christ	"	584

The articles here named, and those that followed them from the pen of Dr. Addison Alexander, not only reveal the scholar and the gifted writer, but show us *the man* in his personal characteristics, tastes, prejudices, and partialities. They were written with as much freedom, and disregard of precedents and critics, as if they had been dashed off for the newspapers. I venture, just here, to take an extract from a notice of his death in the Sunday-school Times for Feb. 4, 1860:

"Dr. Alexander's essays and reviews in the 'Biblical Repertory,' the theological quarterly published at Princeton, have been numerous, and have been marked with profound ability. They have by no means been limited to philological or exegetical subjects, but have embraced almost every variety of topics suited to such a magazine. Some of his earlier reviews were characterized by a keen, trenchant wit. All of them have been marked with a vigour and richness of imagination more to be expected in a poet and a man of elegant letters, than in the mere bookworm he was reputed to be."

After touching casually upon another topic, the writer proceeds in pretty much the same strain:

"Dr. Alexander was a signal proof, if any were needed, that the study of languages, even when pushed to their most abstruse points, does not necessarily make one dry and dull. The United States probably never produced a scholar of more secluded and solitary habits, one who came nearer to the character of the mere bookworm that we read of in some European countries. Yet his writings and his pulpit discourses were as simple and perspicuous as if he had been a mere English scholar. His sentences are as limpid in their flow, and glide as gently and smoothly into the reader's understanding, as those of the Joseph Addison after whom he was named. This wonderful simplicity, both of his thoughts and his language, combined often with a fervid eloquence, and always with profound and comprehensive views, made his pulpit performances exceedingly attractive."

It is the judgment of some thorough Biblical scholars, that Dr. Addison Alexander's contributions to the Review set forth his splendid literary abilities in a much stronger light than any of his other writings. It is very certain he wrote in the quarterlies and magazines with a bold, free hand which was somewhat fettered when engaged upon the commentaries. He wrote in the same free way in his newspaper squibs, children's books, and some of his letters, and in his European journals The greater part of what he did, however, in this reckless, slap-dash style, was not intended for preservation and, though on merely literary grounds it is often exquisite, is for other but equally weighty reasons kept back from the eye of curious readers. The essays in the Repertory, on the whole, give one the best notion of the variety of his gifts and accomplishments as a writer of English. They give the best notion, too, of his masculine tastes, his general knowledge, his progressive moderation, his sterling good sense, his genial humour and true politeness, his fine wit, his facetious irony, his power (never used without provocation) of withering sarcasm, and the marvellous cunning of his diction. Viewed as an unbroken collection, these pieces certainly possess extraordinary merit; and all the more so that some of them were floated off as the veriest waifs. One who wishes to know what he could do in the way of elaborate orations, should read his printed sermons. When writing these discourses (as he says himself of the immortal English dramatist), he now and then "let his imagination fairly boil." For passion, music, movement, contour, and sustained climax, and rare rhetorical command of the united forces of logic and eloquence, we shall look in vain over his writings for any thing comparable with these discourses. But the essays in the periodicals, and more especially the Repertory, are interesting as being mostly unstudied, and wholly uninfluenced by the thought of an audience. They are the spontaneous overflow of a brimming vessel. The first thing that strikes one is the evident strength of the mind and hand that made them. Notice is then attracted to the diversity of their subjects and plans, the capricious changefulness of their author's whim and genius, the graceful sweep and curve of the sentences, the all but fluid volubility of the diction, the sonorous rhythm, occasionally, of the bolder passages, but in ordinary the homely but racy idioms of the fireside. These essays show the man of taste, the man of feeling, the man of the world, quite as much as they do the theologian, the slashing critic, and the professional censor. I am not now speaking of the evidences they disclose of his scholarship; which are certainly not greater than are afforded by his exegetical writings; nor even of the indications they furnish of the generous interest he took in contemporary literature, even in its lighter forms, and in current politics and passing affairs; nor of his love of Scripture and discriminating knowledge of human motives and character; but of the capacity they evince as a writer who, had he so chosen, might have been remembered among the classics of his native tongue. We find the same richness of matter, the same wisdom and propriety of thought, the same modest independence of authority, the same freshness of view and novelty in the mode of treatment, the same suggestiveness and originality, in all his writings. The same fondness for old sayings, proverbs, apothegms, paradoxes, traditions, touches of nature and obsolete forms of speech, reappear constantly. The same happy interchange of large and small words, of long and short sentences, of technical and familiar terms and phrases, will be admired in all that he has left, whether in print or manuscript. The rhythmical structure which always marks his impassioned writing is, of course, to be met with everywhere in his sermons and addresses; but may also be detected even in his commentaries, and especially in his paraphrases.* It is often discernible even in his most condensed summaries and recapitulations. It does not occur so often in the critiques and essays. These have much more freedom as to manner. The Review of the Scripture Guide (his inaugural address) is, as we might have expected, full of this wild melody. The closing syllables of the peroration come

* Notice, for instance, his comments on Mark x: 40, xii: 17, 27, parts of the preliminary analysis to chapter xiii, and comments on xiii: 14; also his own remarks upon "measured prose," under ix: 48. See also on Matt. xvi: 26; last words on Isaiah liii: 12, and Sermons, vol. I, p. 187, *et passim.*

rolling in like the sea-waves at flood. There are passages in his discourses which affect me somewhat as does the golden diapason of the hexameters in Homer, or the strange, irregular music of the choruses in Sophocles. Yet, like De Quincey, he seldom or never degenerates into blank-verse prose. These measured periods (which are everywhere mingled with simple and unmeasured phrases) could not have been formed with deliberation, for the manuscript in such cases always betrays unusual excitement. Yet the rhythmic peculiarity of such sentences could not have always escaped his notice, for, in a few instances, scraps of this kind of writing are divided off into metrical feet, as if for purposes of scanning, or else of mere critical scrutiny. He has grossly caricatured this manner in some of his burlesques for children. My conjecture is, that he did not aim at it at all, but was conscious of the tendency, and when he wrote fast and under strong influence, often gave way to it, and afterwards made it a subject of reflection, if not animadversion. The most singular thing about the whole matter is, that in these passages the sense is never once sacrificed to the sound. The nice precision and curious felicity in the use of words, and couplets of words, is never more apparent than in these musically rounded sentences and clauses.

There is something of this kind in the English Bible, especially in Revelation. In the sermons, this trait is more conspicuous in the imaginative and emotional parts which directly precede the short, abrupt, and often startling appeals to the conscience. Take the following passage as an illustration :

"If, my hearers, it be true, as I believe, and as you believe, and as God's Word assures us, that in reference even to the case of those who shall assuredly be saved, or as assuredly be lost, 'it doth not yet appear what they shall be;' if it be true that even those who are already saved, not merely in God's purpose, but in fact, beyond the reach of all disturbing and retarding causes, even they who are rejoicing at this moment in God's presence as the spirits of just men made perfect, if even they are unable to enclose in their conceptions that illimitable ocean into which they have been plunged but for a moment; if it be true that even those who are disembodied spirits and now drinking of the cup of divine wrath, can, in the anguish of their torment, form no definite idea of the volume and duration of that stream of fire which forever and forever fills their cup to overflowing; if both these souls, however different in their actual condition and their prospects for eternity, are forced alike to cry out in a triumphant burst of grateful joy, and a convulsion of blaspheming horror, 'it doth not yet appear what we shall be!' oh, with what multiplied intensity of emphasis may those whose future state is still unsettled, who are still upon the isthmus between hell and heaven, wavering, vacillating, hanging in terrible suspense between the two, unable or unwilling to decide their fate, and waiting, it would almost seem, until some heaving of the ocean of eternity should sweep them from the earth, they know not, think not, care not whither, oh! with what emphasis might such exclaim, as they hang over the dizzy verge of two unchanging, everlasting states, 'it doth not yet appear what we shall be.'"

Dr. Alexander had all the qualities of the rhapsodist as well as the chronicler. He could play the part of an improvisatore as well as that of a raconteur or annalist. His powers were of an order and degree that fitted him as well for the domain of poetry as for that of history and eloquence. An eminent physician once remarked to me, "Dr. Addison Alexander was a born poet."

On this head, an old and intimate friend* of the subject of this memoir finely observes:

"His character included all the elements of the loftiest enthusiasm, and, as the phrases are not exactly co-extensive, all the chief elements of the true poet: originality of thought, vivid and cultivated feeling, an active imagination, a love of the beautiful and sublime in nature and art, a sense of the perfect, and vast power of exact and pointed expression. Not that genius which fitfully soars and shines, and then plunges into darkness and filth; but that which is consecrated by Christian inspiration, and derives its strongest impulses from communion with Jesus and eternal realities, the great thing wanting—as a prince of critics, Dr. Andrew P. Peabody, so forcibly remarks—in so much of our American poetry. 'If he had not been occupied with the de-

* Rev. Paul Eugene Stevenson, Paterson, N. J.

lights, the poetry, if you please, of profound philosophical and theological thinking, he might have made his mark as a poet.'

"Since it is said that poetry has never been defined, and hence the whole field is clear, I shall venture to think my definition not far from right when I say that true poetry consists of striking thoughts, including feeling and imagination, so expressed as to make a high order of rhetoric, the form of the whole being modified and rendered musical by more or less of recurrent measure. This excludes commonplace and prosaic measured lines, which claim a name as if there were magic in mere measure; and, on the other hand, it leaves to rhetoric its own splendid domain, with unlimited liberty of discernment, judgment, reasoning, feeling, imagination, rhythm, and power of expression; unless a higher muse, whose work is the crown of accumulative series, is called in to shape and beautify the whole, and fill it with the music of 'harmonious numbers.'

"Judged by this standard, Dr. Alexander had the powers, not only of a fine prose writer, but of a poet, even to the possession of a soul, an ear, and a skilful hand for music, we are reminded, by the short poems which, during intervals of relaxation from severer thinking, so readily flowed from his pen. One thing I think is certain: if he had given scope and use to those powers, he would have avoided some of the intellectual and æsthetic blunders of many eminent sons of genius, e. g., the cloudy verbosities of Byron, not now to refer to black, polluting immoralities, and the tame, prosaic phrases of Tennyson. He would be sure to place himself in that school of poets who, like Thomas Campbell, in the Pleasures of Hope, and Henry Taylor, in Philip Van Artevelde, have gone upon the principle, that while a poet may deal in rare words as well as rare thoughts, and avail himself of every allowable poetic license, fog helps neither poetry nor prose, and hence, for one thing, the way to be a de-lightful writer is to be a day-lightful writer."*

Many have lamented that he did not unbend himself more, and give more scope to his fertile literary genius, when he was writing for the press.

"I have always thought," remarks Professor Halsey, himself an accomplished writer and an experienced critic, "that had he given his life simply to literature instead of theological science, his wonderful

* Mr. Stevenson here follows in the footsteps of Archbishop Whately. See his Preface to Bacon's Essays.

mastery of diction, with his brilliant imagination, would easily have won a rank equal to any that has been achieved in American authorship. Several hymns composed by him, and some fugitive pieces in the Princeton Magazine, as well as his articles in the Princeton Review, reveal an ability in this direction, which makes us regret that he had not taken in hand some grand theme which might have made him the Macaulay or Prescott of Church History; or perhaps but deepens our feeling of loss, when we think he was called away ere his wonderful genius had yet essayed its chief endeavour." *

* Every reader of the smallest child's-book from the hand of Dr. Addison Alexander has noticed his fondness for memoirs and historical relations; and has felt the influence of that elastic freshness of spirits and liveliness of parts which could throw a kind of romantic or sentimental interest over the most trifling and often absurd incidents. The same qualities reappear in his graver essays. He loved to review a volume of travels, and to dissect the character of the author. Historical and literary themes pleased him quite as well as philological.

CHAPTER XVIII.

It was most natural that one of Mr. Alexander's undoubted social tendencies, rarely manifested though they seemed to be, should sometimes thirst for the pleasures of society. This he evidently did, but seldom when at home with the members of his father's or his brother's household, and among his own fragrant bookshelves. Here he found abundant scope for his affectionate feelings and exuberant playfulness, not only in intercourse with the family, but in the company of the little folks; among whom in course of time he numbered his special favourites by the score, if not by the hundred.

"He was not," says Dr. Hodge, "very much inclined to society.* He never visited (at least in Princeton), except in going to see one or two of his friends at their studies. The relaxation and diversion of mind which others found in social intercourse, he found in amusing himself with children. He always had one or more in the constant habit of going to see him. For these he would write amusing tales, with great care and skill in penmanship, and of diverse forms. Nothing more characteristic of the man could be found than a collection of his writings for his juvenile companions, teeming with humour, with originality, and good feeling."

The number of these *brochures*, little and big, which are still extant, is exceedingly great; and many others have perished or have been lost. The boys or girls whom he thus delighted to fascinate and please, were commonly his pupils; and he would sit *tête-à-tête* with one or more of them for hours, sometimes interrupting, and sometimes carrying on, his other work while

* This remark must, of course, be taken with the proper and intended modification.

they were occupying his settee or cane-bottomed chairs. His chief, and commonly his first, business was to write their lives.

"I have," says Dr. McGill, "in primer form, folded and stitched and paged, with the leaves uncut, an amusing biography of a child in my own family which he composed from her conversation about the place and playmates she left in coming from Allegheny to Princeton."

I suppose that I have heard of thirty or forty of these whimsical literary efforts. At least half a dozen of such biographical pamphlets by him have been in my hands. They are usually very small square volumes, covered with blue, pink, green, or brown paper, and written upon unruled sheets. In some cases they were slim duodecimos bound in leather. He was always careful to write them in a neat hand, to number the pages, and to prefix a title page and append an index. Not a few of them are printed with a pen. Every thing is complete, from the record of copyright to the "Finis" and table of typographical errata. He seemed to have an unappeasable rage for this kind of composition. No event was too small to be noticed, and some of these accounts now possess a real value for the facts which they have preserved as in amber. It is needless to add that these narratives were almost always contrived so as to awaken the sense of the ludicrous. The ironical gravity of some of them is equal to some of the best passages in Pickwick.

He would sometimes write down a journal of his travels with one or more of his little scholars.* He loved to make

* One of the most formal of these records is now lying before me, and is entitled, "Journal of the Exploring Expedition, 1842." I give a few words from the elaborate preface :

"The Board then proceeded to appoint the officers of the Expedition; when James L. Beffo was unanimously chosen Geographer, Hydrographer, and Historiographer; and Col. ———, late of the New-York and Erie Railroad, was at the same time appointed Civil Engineer. The expedition was ordered to set out immediately, and on its return to lay its journal before the Board. Both these orders were complied with, and the Board was pleased to direct that the journal should be published in its present form. The utmost care has been these minute diaries, and it was truly wonderful how much he remembered. He could take down the confused jargon of con versation in a railroad car with more than the exactness of a stenographic reporter. On these occasions he was known as James L. Beffo, and his little friends received various assumed names.

But about this time, or to be more exact, a few years earlier, he conceived the idea of writing and editing a burlesque newspaper; somewhat in the style of several of his youthful publications, but for lads and lassies, and all in fun. It was to be really printed with the pen, but issued from an imaginary printing press. This was the origin of the "Ridge Recorder;" tattered fragments of which are now lying on my table. These are parts of two numbers which were issued at "Breckin-Ridge" respectively on Dec. 28, 1838, and Jan. 16, 1839. They are ludicrous imitations of some of the New Jersey country newspapers; and are wholly filled with the trivial incidents of household ménage.*

The news articles are in a style as pompous as a Spanish bulletin. The following may serve as a specimen:

employed to secure the highest degree of typographical correctness, and no expense or labour has been spared in the illustration of the work, by means of the most splendid engravings. With these advantages, the Journal is committed to the public without any hesitation or misgiving as to its reception."

As a specimen of his abilities as a verbatim reporter, I might copy his transcript of the talk of some lawyers on the train, who were returning from the trial of Monroe Edwards. The principal persons engaged in it were the Hon. Thomas F. Marshall, of Kentucky, who had been defending Edwards, Col. Stone, and Judge Kent. The Journal is illustrated with diagrams, bills of fare, and street signs.

* In the left-hand corner it bore upon its face the following startling announcement in exquisite fine print: "Published as often as convenient, at the corner of the Piazza and the Gravel Walk. Terms—nothing per annum. Advertisements—$.00 per line. Communications may be addressed to the editor, postage unpaid, No. 11 Heath st." The advertising columns are admirably filled, and the proposals of the supposititious tradesmen, &c., are designed to interest very little children.

"On Monday, November 19, the reigning Duke and Dutchess de la Ridge arrived and took up their abode in the ducal palace. Their heir, the Marquis of Carrington, came with them. Prince George of Cabello had previously arrived, under the care of his gouvernante. Signore Addisono Alessandro had preceded them about a week. The crown prince of Essemby, during the absence of the Duke and Dutchess, had resided with his illustrious grandparents, where he still continued on account of the arrival of his Electoral Highness the Lord Proprietor."

"Thursday, Dec. 5. A stove* was erected in the grand Entrance Hall, and the pipe carried through the southwest chamber, where accommodations have been fitted up for the Crown Prince. His Highness partook of a collation this evening in the grand *salle-à-manger*."

There also appears the following:

"The curiosity of the good people of the Ridge has been much excited by certain mysterious visits of two distinguished foreigners, Don Ricardo d'Istocktoni and the Chevalier Giovanni Potterini. It is conjectured that they are engaged in secret negotiations with the Minister of Foreign Affairs. A few days will probably disclose the secret. The Chevalier and Don Ricardo travel incogniti, without attendants, and unarmed."

In a very grandiloquent editorial he heralds the advent of a new poet, and gives seventy-three short verses as a sample of his great production. The following is headed "Chicken College:

"The annual course will commence on the first of January as follows:

On Feeding, by Professor Cray.†
On Scratching, by Speckled Hen.
On Roosting, by Broken Leg, jr.
On Laying, by Black Hen.
On Cackling, by Red Rover.
On Crowing, by C. Chanticleer.
On the Diseases of Hens and Chickens, by P. W. Pip.
On Pulline Jurisprudence, by W. Wagtail.

* Which went by the name of its inventor, Kisterbock.
† Peter Cray, a man-servant at the Breckinridge House.

A limited number of students may obtain accommodation in the Hen Roost, by applying to Professor Chanticleer, Dean of the Faculty."

There is also subjoined the following little piece of laughing satire:

"At a meeting of the Anti-milking Society, held in the Cow-house, on the seventh of December, Mr. Applegate's cow was called to the trough, and *Our Cow*, Esq., appointed Secretary. On motion, it was resolved that the practice of milking cows is cruel, unjust, and oppressive; and that we will resist it to the utmost. It was resolved that a Committee of Vigilance be appointed to aid fugitive cows in their escape from oppression. The proceedings of the meeting were ordered to be published in the Ridge Recorder."

Among the advertisements, I notice this:

"ROAN HORSE respectfully informs the inhabitants of the Ridge that he has opened an office in the stable, where he will promptly answer all calls for his professional services as a beast of burden. Reference: Sir Peter Cray, Master of the Horse." tf w2 xyz.

There are, in addition, prices current, an account of a dreadful massacre, and a résumé of foreign news. The familiar words, Terms, Wanted, and For Rent, are to be seen on the first page. There are agricultural, literary, and political departments; a list of letters remaining in the Post Office at Breckinridge; a Shipping List; and articles on the Weather, Election Frauds, Fashionable Arrivals, and Select Schools. There is, too, an account of a "grand concert," and the following card appears under the title:

"RAN AWAY—From the subscriber, on Christmas Eve, a fine Carp Rhine Cat, with blue eyes and yellow hair. Any person restoring the said animal will receive nothing at all. OLD BLACK."

Under the head of Political, I find the following:

"The important change mentioned in our last as probable, has taken place. The Loudon Administration is at an end. The Dinah Administration has succeeded it. This may be regarded as a signal triumph of the African over the Anglo-Saxon party. The late Premier resigned the seals of office in the evening of the eleventh; the new Premier assumed them in the afternoon of the twelfth. We are not yet informed what policy will be adopted by the new administration."

Under the head of "GREAT WATER," I notice this ludicrous imitation:

"Last night a destructive water broke out in the Kisterbock, and raged for ten minutes without intermission. It was at length subdued by the preternatural exertions of the Kisterbock Water Company, whose hose was considerably wetted."

The following gives us a peep at "the Great Unknown" himself:

"The subscribers continue to relate their adventures to admiring audiences in the Northeast Upper Room. Price of admission, one burnt almond. Apply to either of the undersigned.

"PETER ARUN.
"OLD BLACK."

Much of the letterpress of the "Recorder" resembles the finest copperplate. I have observed but one erasure in either of the numbers now in my possession.

There are readers who may think that Mr. Alexander demeaned himself in thus letting himself down to the level almost of infancy. Not so think many wise and prudent judges of human nature, and friends of the abrupt and solitary scholar. Nor did he ever think so himself. He was himself a child of nature as well as of art. *Aquila non captat muscas*, was no motto of his. He evidently thought with Dr. Johnson, that "The true strong and sound mind is the mind that can embrace equally great things and small." He could sympathize with Dr. Clarke, who reluctantly stopped his leap-frog with the boys on seeing Beau Nash approaching, saying, as he did so "Here comes a fool." Many seem strangely to forget that it was in this rare power of running nearly the whole gamut of things possible to the mental faculties that a large part of Mr. Alexander's superiority consisted. Others might write amusing children's books, but not such as he, or such books as he wrote. Variety and symmetrical proportion were the objects respectively of the centrifugal and centripetal tendencies which made up so large a part of his intellectual character. Of course such assertions are liable to qualification as to the degree of their truth. What I aim at is to express the nature rather than the measure of the excellence. The man who could thus tickle the ears and warm the hearts of little children, could (had he so pleased) have charmed senates, and did captivate and control some of the most intellectual assemblies in America, and expose to mocking ridicule some of the most illustrious scholars of Germany. He put the learned infidels of the old world, and the sciolists of the new, to the torture of his refined but inexorable criticism, and has applied the knout of his galling sarcasm to the back of conceited folly everywhere. The changes in his intellect were as great as those in his feelings. On this and kindred points, A. A. Rice, M.D., of Kentucky, writes thus:

"Dr. Addison Alexander was one of the most 'polygonal' men I ever knew; nor do I believe that there was any one, outside of his own immediate family who had the opportunity of looking at him upon every side of his character. For me, he was as a colossal statue placed upon an elevated pedestal, which I could only look up to and wonder at. The only time, during the fourteen years that I lived in Princeton, that I came in direct contact personally with him, was when I was about nine years old, and he was then a man grown, and was, I think, a tutor in the college. It was then, as it continued to be during his life, a characteristic of his, to find a relaxation from mental activity in the society of children, rather than of grown persons, and for their amusement he would pour forth wit and humour with a profusion amply sufficient to establish the fact that he was one of the wittiest men of the day. I well remember into what convulsions of laughter he used to throw me by his narrations concerning 'Old Blaque' and 'Peter Arrhen.' I give you his own spelling of these names,* which

* He spelt these names in all manner of ways.

I doubt not are familiar sounds to you, as well as to many others, now men and women, who in their childhood were fortunate enough to attract his attention. Nor were these witty and humorous deliverances confined to spoken narratives. His pen was as prolific as his tongue, and I am sure that quite a volume of his facetiæ could even now be found, if they were sought for in the proper quarters. There was one story that he told me which made a very vivid impression on my mind, haunted my waking thoughts, and was reproduced in my dreams for many years afterwards; which I found was a wonderful travesty of Moore's Epicurean, when I saw that book after I was grown."

Many of the boys who owed their first or strongest impulse to Mr. Alexander, have since obtained merited distinction. Among these I may perhaps reckon Judge Samuel M. Breckinridge, of St. Louis, a son of the Rev. Dr. John Breckinridge, a grandson of the late venerable Dr. Samuel Miller, and a blood relation of one branch of the Alexander family, though not connected in this way with the subject of this memoir. He writes that the time he spent in Princeton after the death of his mother, under the roof and special care of Dr. James W. Alexander, who stood to him *in loco parentis*, was about a year, reaching from the autumn of 1838 to the autumn of 1839, when he was from ten to eleven years of age. During the most of that time, he was the room-mate of the protean linguist; and though Prof. James Alexander, whose duties were in the college, had taken charge of his studies, many of his recitations were made to Mr. Addison Alexander, who was his "very intimate and much loved friend." Judge Breckinridge goes on as follows:

"During that time he found recreation, and I infinite pleasure, in a little paper, edited (and with a pen printed) by him; very irregular in size and contents and times of issue, but full of fun in prose and verse, in editorial and (what purported to be) communicated matter, and rich in advertisements of all sorts, &c. It is a source of constant regret to me that in the breaking up of my father's remaining establishment at Princeton, when in 1839-40 he went to New Orleans as pastor, and in the sale of his effects after his death in 1841-2, while I was absent, and at any rate too young to appreciate fully the value of these papers, and many others of a like nature and also written by Dr. Addison Alexander, this collection of what was even then very precious to me was lost or destroyed, and the most careful search and inquiry has given me no trace of them.* That year was one of the most profitable to me I ever spent; made so by Dr. James Alexander's teaching and his brother Addison's, and the benefits I could not fail, though so young, to derive from them."

With the end of this year Mr. Breckinridge left Princeton, and did not return till the autumn of 1842, when he entered the college as a Sophomore. He concludes in the following language:

"I remember, of course, many incidents and facts, and there are endless personal recollections; but they are rather of that kind which make an impression ineffaceable on one's mind and memory, and yet can only in a very unsatisfactory way be communicated to another. Certainly Dr. Addison Alexander was one of the most rarely gifted men of his time; with marvellous capacity for acquiring knowledge and imparting it: and to me he manifested the wonderful wealth of his nature, in showing that his great labours, rare acquirements, and devotion to his profession and the duties of his place, left him still able to unbend, and, with fit opportunity, to enjoy with all the simplicity of a child the sports of children, and at the same time to make them useful and instructive. I never loved one out of my own immediate family more; very few so much."

The grateful testimonies of this kind would make up quite a little library. Few of them can be given here. They all present the same outlines and the same warm and pleasing colouring. There are numbers of men and women now living who look back with delight to the days when *fronde super viridi*, or upon "The Rocks,"† or on "The Mound," or in "The Tan Path," or under the green willows of "Piccadilly," or within the ceiled walls of one of Mr. Alexander's divers studies, they

* These included, unquestionably from the description, specimens of the Ridge Recorder.

† A group of picturesque fragments within the Breckinridge inclosure, resembling the summits of precipitous crosses.

were regaled with stories and amusing dialogues, and initiated into the absurd and tantalizing mysteries of the "Jarvach," or the "Cappadocian"; and who can remember his toils, as an infant biographer, newspaper editor, and magazinist.

> "I knew Anselmo. He was sage and pious;
> Learning and genius had their shares of him;
> But he was changeful as a wayward child,
> And pleased again by toys which childhood please;
> As book of fables graced with print of wood,
>
> * * * * * * * *
>
> Or the rare melody of some old ditty,
> That first was sung to please a Persian cradle." *

And I hold it no detriment to "the scholar 'breathing libraries,'" to exhibit all sides of his character; and even to lay stress

> "On that best portion of a good man's life,
> His *little*, nameless, unremembered acts
> Of kindness and of love."

A favourite pupil, and friend of years' unbroken intimacy, writes, that the only reason for his saying any thing is that he profited perhaps more than any other by Mr. Alexander's great love for children, and for teaching children. His earliest recollections of him are of

"Being taken to see him in his rooms in the 'Tombs,' † when in my petticoats, and afterwards of being sent with messages to 'Noah's Ark,' in Canal street."

He can now scarcely distinguish between his personal recollections of these visits, and the accounts his instructor used to give him of them in later years.

"It was when I was a school-boy, about ten or eleven years old, that

* Slightly altered from the original.
† His rooms under the Seminary Chapel.

he took a fancy to attach me to him more permanently. Going on some errand to his study in his father's house, he entertained me in a long conversation, and engaged me to come again with the promise of writing something for me. That was the beginning of a constant and close association, in which he gradually took possession of the whole of my leisure time, detaching me from my school playmates almost entirely. At first, the chief attraction was the magazines and letters which he wrote for me, which are now in my possession.

He made him tell him the principal events of his life which he could recollect, which he incorporated in little books entitled "Life of Wiss."

"Then commenced the "Wistar's Magazine," beginning with an advanced volume and number; of which he would give me usually a number a fortnight, interspersed with long letters in rhyme, one of which, covering a folio sheet, was wrapped in an immense package. After letting me open this, he withheld it for several days (to my intense disappointment), and at last yielded it to my entreaties. This magazine continued for two or three years, running through two series; showing a fertility of invention and command of language equal, I think, to any of his productions, and certainly among the most curious of his literary remains."

All this naturally awakened as strong a love as a boy ever felt for a man not his own father. The pupil was under no constraint in the presence of the master, and felt no fear of him. If the teacher was preoccupied or out of patience with him, he had only to wait "and all would come right." In this way the strange, or as some fancied, the unsocial scholar, obtained the most perfect mastery over the boy's affections and mind. And to this the pupil thinks he owes the impetus which this teacher gave to his studies.

"While visiting him in this way, he began to teach me. The first lessons I recollect from him, entirely apart from my school tasks, were in the Latin verb."

He made him recite this in the four conjugations, active and passive, through, and without a mistake. Any slip, although immediately corrected, required him to commence again from the beginning, till he had thus gone through the whole successfully. Then, in the same way, he took the active and passive of each conjugation together, then of two conjugations together, then of three, and finally of four. The disgust the pupil felt after getting almost through and then losing all by a single slip may be imagined. It was some weeks before he finally accomplished the feat, and the delight when it was safely done he shall never forget. At the same time, he was making him write translations from Latin books and thus

"Gradually implanting a love for this language and desire for acquisition to which I owe most of what I know."

He believes he was not twelve years old when his friend proposed, much to his joy, to take him entirely from other schools and prepare him for college. From this time for two years he was with him almost constantly, "morning, noon, and night," studying in his room, and going back in the evening very frequently to read with him. His method of teaching was greatly varied, constantly exciting fresh interest by proposing something new. He gave short lessons in the grammar, which were to be memorized with absolute accuracy. The translations exacted were pretty long. He made his pupil write a good deal, translating back into Latin something he had before read; besides writing exercises from some school-book. He learned by heart a considerable amount of Latin verse. While under this tuition, he also began the study of Greek, going through two books of the Anabasis, and making constant use of the pen in his lessons.

At the same time, and under the charm of profound secrecy, he gave him some lessons in Hebrew. He learned to read the text with ease, and mastered the regular verb as completely as he had done the Latin verb, and besides reading and writing French in the ordinary way, the teacher would insist for a week at a time on holding no communication with his scholar except in that language, making him "Frenchify" English words, when he could not command French ones; so that notwithstanding "the indescribable jargon," the learner gained some knowledge of words and forms.

"All this time he was inspiring me with a love for history and literature. He read to me, making me take notes. He caused me to write copious condensations of historical books. He talked much about historical characters and writers, and in this way insensibly gave me a knowledge of the outlines and relations of history such as no boy would be likely to get by his own reading. He would read poetry to me, too, with immense enthusiasm. I shall never forget the night of my first introduction to Shakespeare, by his reading to me the murder scene in Macbeth, nor my first knowledge of Sir Walter Scott, (except the punishment a previous teacher gave me in the Tales of a Grandfather,) in his reading the tournament scene in Ivanhoe. So with Milton. Few things have left a stronger impression on me than the classic simplicity of his taste in literature, by which I was kept from inferior authors during the period when I would have been most injured by them."

All this did not seem to interrupt the teacher's own work, for when most intently engaged in writing, he would frequently break off and talk for awhile about other things, and often then about the subject that was engaging him.

"Quite often I took advantage of his exuberant good humour to get off my lessons; for if on trial I found he was inclined for 'a free,' as he used to call it, I could sometimes induce him to continue it the whole time which was to have been occupied in preparing my lessons."

Another interruption which this pupil used to welcome, came from his love of "flitting." He not only removed from house to house, but from room to room; turning his bed-room into his study, and *vice versâ*; changing the book-cases in his rooms so as to give them a new aspect.

"Several times on going to his study in the morning, I would find him so engaged, and would help him take his books down and put them up differently; and when all was done, he would feel quite refreshed, and say that it was 'the next best thing to moving.'"

Once during these years he took this pupil with him on a trip to New-York, Boston, Albany, Washington, etc.

"His spirits always rose when travelling. He was fond of riding in omnibuses, going the whole length of the route, and then taking another in a different direction; always picking up something to tell, in the queer characters and scenes he met, and sometimes exciting the wonder of the people by talking to me in Persian verse, and making me answer with some verses he had taught me by ear. The record of one of these journeys was written in Wistar's Magazine. He more than once wrote for my amusement minute accounts of other journeys which he made. One winter, he read me the journal of his first voyage to Europe, and seemed much to enjoy the desire it awakened to see the same scenes. I little thought, then, that I was destined to make the voyage in his company. Any reminiscences of that voyage would be superfluous, as he kept a most copious journal daily, not a word of which he would allow me to see, either then or afterwards, as I have never yet obtained a sight of it."

This gentleman's visits to Mr. Alexander were kept up with no decrease of familiarity or kindness on the part of the latter during his college course. On the contrary,

"He often read with me, and advised me; and during the year after my graduation, and during my seminary course, I saw him frequently."

Mr. Alexander's liking for children was by no means restricted to boys. No one was more sensible than he to the attractions of blooming girlhood, and his study was often rendered charming by the rosy faces and laughing eyes of the daughters of his friends and colleagues. A lady who has a vivid recollection of him, testifies to this fact. She says:

"A prominent characteristic was his great liking for little girls. In his brother's family, where he resided at the time referred to, the children were all boys. But he always found in some of the families in the neighbourhood a *pet*, who was urged to come often to his study, and who never failed to meet with a warm welcome when the tap of the little visitor brought Dr. Alexander to the door. On such occasions, he would entertain his guest by telling marvellous stories, or by writing her name for her in ever so many different languages, or by singing or repeating some lines in an Oriental tongue, and then translating the strange sounds to her. Or sometimes she would try her skill in writing for him on a slip of paper. Such a fragment, with perhaps nothing upon it but the writer's name in childish characters, would be carefully put away, and months afterwards be produced from the depths of his pocket-book to show that he had kept it, and perhaps to tease the little penman on account of the bad writing, which was her best not long before.

"Writing a book for his especial favourite, was a great pleasure promised sometimes. The writer well remembers a tiny volume, regularly bound, but its pages *written* by Dr. Alexander, not printed, her 'Life,' which he got up to please her. It was inscribed upon the back 'The Life of ——— ———.'

"Perhaps for want of material in the history of a life of eight years or thereabouts, the little book contained a number of digressions from the subject and some blank pages. But there it was, a *real book*, and with great delight she used to display it to her young companions."

He never ceased to take a deep interest in those of whom he was ever fond. He kept up a pretty active correspondence with some of the half-grown young ladies who had enjoyed the privilege of his company and instructions. Sometimes his letters were in rhyme, but commonly in a vein of grave or facetious prose. These were often made the vehicle of advice and counsel, as well as of mental stimulus. I give below parts of one of his rhyming epistles to a little girl. After adverting to her expected departure to a neighbouring city, he kindly refers to her life which he had promised to write:

"This has led me to fear that you may not be here when the work is complete. So I send you this sheet, that you may not suspect any wilful neglect or intentional failure. I deeply bewail your departure, and would keep you here if I could. But as this cannot be, and as I may not see you again very soon, is it too great a boon that I venture to ask, or too irksome a task I impose, in beseeching that as soon as she was at home in the city, she would, just out of pity, take a pen and ink, without stopping to think, and at once, my dear Nan, fill a sheet, as you can, I am sure without trouble; and should it be double, why so much the better; for how can a letter from you be too long? I know it is wrong and dishonest to flatter, and this is a matter in which I may seem to approach that extreme, yet I feel bound to say that I would, any day, very cheerfully pay double postage to see a long letter from thee, which would please me as much as if written in Dutch, and be answered at once. But I write like a dunce, to suppose you will care, when you get settled there, for your poor country friends; and to make some amends for so foolish a thought as that you could be bought with the bribe of a letter, I have something better to offer, instead of what you have read. It is this, that if you will consent to do what I now request, I will do my best, by hook or by crook, to finish the book, and will bring it down when I come to town. And if you will employ a man or a boy, a girl or a woman, at some painting room in the city, to do a good likeness of you, and then send it to me, it shall certainly be without any expense to *your side of the fence.*

"But I almost forgot to inform you of what might have puzzled you sadly, and made you feel badly, if left unexplained, as it would have remained if some little thing had not happened to bring the affair to my mind; and lest it should find its way out again, before this poor pen can have time to go through what I wish it to do, I think myself bound, without going around any longer, to tell what I might just as well have told you before; but you know there is more satisfaction in knowing what one has been going to tell, but did not, than in just hearing what you never had thought of, or wished to know aught of; and therefore I may take upon me to say, that this little delay in expressing my views, will not only amuse, but afford you delight. Yet I own that the sight of my sheet, almost done, has already begun to make me repent of my evil intent and malicious desire to raise still higher your high curiosity. Yes, the monstrosity of such a course strikes me now with great force. So I give up my plan, and proceed, my dear Nan, to inform you, without any winding about, that the paper enclosed is a letter composed more than three weeks ago; but the mail is so slow that I wish I had kept it. Please now to accept it, as not yet too late, although much out of date; and now, my young friend, as I draw near the end of my letter, I feel, I must own, a good deal of regret and concern at your speedy return to the State of your birth, which is certainly worth more than Jersey, since you were born there, and I too; yet I should have preferred very much to have heard that you meant to remain. But regrets are now vain, and I wish you, at parting, a prosperous starting, and easy transition, a pleasant position, a happy abode, and a bountiful load

"Of enjoyments below, and of gifts from above,
In the beautiful City of Brotherly Love;
(And thus I reveal to you for the first time,
That what you are reading is written in rhyme)
And with a regard which I feel for but few,
I bid you, dear Nannie, a final
Adieu."

There is another, sent to a cousin in Virginia, which beginning with the usual common-place doggerel, closes in a strain of pathetic sincerity. I give the concluding part:

"Give my love to all in Livingston Hall, from the dear grandsire, beside his fire, to the youngest boy who is at his toy; and believe that I, before I die, will certainly try to darken once more that friendly door, and again behold that happy fold with its lambs at play. Until that day, * * * do not forget a far distant friend, who can only send his love by mail; and do not fail, when the lights grow dim, to pray for him who prays for you, and your household too, that it long may thrive with its elders alive, its brothers five, its sisters seven, and one in heaven. And oh, that He, before whom she rejoices now, would teach us how, by any pain, by any cost, we may regain what we have lost! It may be done, she may be won, there is a way, but only one. If we believe and love the Lord, we shall receive the same reward. Though now we grieve, and now are sad, we shall be glad, as she is glad! That we all may meet, in the golden street of the heavenly city, our long-lost Kitty, no more to part—thus from the heart will ever pray

"Your cousin A."

Of all the children's books the most unique and brilliant are the Wistar's magazines. Three of these little waifs are are now hidden under my outstretched hand. Two of them are stitched in dark red wrappers, and one in dark green. On the back of one of them are strange characters that look like Æthiopic. The Life of Wiss, which is also lying near me, is less than half the size of these, and is in bright blue. The hand is large, bold, regular, and characteristic. This biography is kept up for a while in the Magazine. The little periodical contains a store of choice writing. "Yes and No," is an account of two boys James and John, one of whom could not say yes, and the other could not say no. It is in a high degree ingenious, and is wholesome in its practical tendency.

But the most remarkable thing in these little books is a verbal *galimafrée* entitled, "Don Patrick: A Romance of Terra del Fuego." A single extract will give a sample of the whole:

"On the summit of the Amazon, above the green fields which are watered by the Hecla and its tributary streams, there stood in ancient times a fortified sirocco! From its frowning entablature the martial canzonet, as he paced to and fro with his easel on his shoulder, could behold the verdant glaciers of Owhyhee, and occasionally catch the dying echo of some distant *mal di testa*, as it died away among the capsules of the lofty prairies. Here the youthful Masorites were wont to angle for the aloe and the centipede, the choicest dainties of a Gentian's table; while above them, in the logarithms of St. Chlorine, an extenuated monkey of the order of Sangamon, wearing his rosary of snow-white azure, chanted the solemn and sublime replevin of the Vandal Church. In this romantic spot, before the days of Salamanca, or perhaps while she was reigning, lived an aged Virtuoso, who could trace his cosmogony to Upas the Valerian, through many generations of illustrious Flamingoes."

In January, 1842, Wistar's Magazine was enlarged to the size of a goodly duodecimo of one hundred and thirty-four pages, bound in soft dressed leather almost as fine as calf. It appeared after this in double columns, needing five or six more issues, irregularly numbered, to complete the second volume. The numerous title-pages are in different styles of printing: some in large letters, and some in small; some in black letters, and some in pale; some in Roman capitals, and some in German text, or else in different kinds of ornamental characters. There is similar variety in the literal or material execution of the whole volume. Some of it is printed with a pen, and some merely written. Some of it is in very large type, and some of it in type so small as almost to suggest the use of a microscope. The number of erasures and interlineations is exceedingly small. There is equal diversity in the substantial contents of these very curious pages. The work is intended either to ridicule, or, as sometimes seems to be the case, merely to parody, the current magazine literature of the day. The first table of contents reads thus:

> "To the Public. The Ghost, a Poem. Letter from the Man. Letter from Old Black. Geographical Essay. The Two Shirts (Poetry). John P. Baratier. Royal Names. Correspondence between Arun and Bald. The Bray Legislative Proceedings. Literary and Philosophical Intelligence. To our Readers and Correspondents."

With very few exceptions it is purely ironical; in some cases sharply satirical. It is, however, not devoid of salutary instruction.

The piece on Baratier, for instance, is a serious article, and ends with words which the editor could hardly make use of without thinking of himself.

> "He was what is called a prodigy; but such persons, even when they live long, seldom do as much for the world as those who begin early and improve more steadily for many years."

There are two letters from Old Black; both of which are written in sentences scarcely one of which contains more than three words, and these the shortest and plainest that the vulgar colloquial English affords. The duelling correspondence between Arun and Bald is carried to great length through successive numbers. "The Ghost" is continued almost to the end of the volume. Hardly a number is destitute of a record of "Legislative Proceedings," e. g. of the "House of Boys," "House of Grannies," "Convention of Characters," "House of Correction." The Geographical Essay is read before the "Little Boy" Lyceum. Various personages figure in character, either occasionally, or all through the book, as for example: James L. Beffo (the editor), Gaspard de la Foix (the proprietor), Sophonisba Saltmarsh Pepperwell, Dr. Bald, Mrs. Bald, Old Black, Peter Arun, The Man, Mr. Flag Ship, Don Barbarossa, Oliver Oaf, Mr. Ossifrage, Captain Cumberland, and M. W. Mott. Some of these merely flit across the stage, but others are more constant in their periodical appearance. The characters of Dr. and Mrs. Bald, of Black, Arun, and Captain Cumberland are the most distinctly drawn. There are here and there graphic strokes which remind one of some of the old writers. The verisimilitude is kept up throughout. The most extravagant characters are never, unless intentionally, confounded, and in the "Convention of Characters" who have figured in Wistar's Magazine, each speaks *propriâ voce*, and sustains his part admirably in the confused and grotesque dialogue. The "humour" of Don Barbarossa is to utter sonorous periods in which there is the most scrupulous choice of words and epithets, and often a delightful rhythm, but never a grain of sense. "The Man" pours out a mass of ingenious and plausible contradictions. After awhile "The Man" disappears, and Barbarossa absorbs his character into his own. His favourite formula is that he rises "to express his silent contempt." Mr. Flag Ship speaks in a fervid and sophomorical strain, and with continual repetition of such phrases as "the sun was peering like a mettled courser," "pillowed on the lap of ocean," "through a canopy of gorgeous clouds tinged with molten gold." Black is an ignorant, malapert, quick-witted, and provoking old servant-maid. Arun is the waggish but harmless Mephistophiles who ironically presides over the uncouth convention, comprehends the situation at a glance, laughs at it inwardly, and coolly enjoys his own wit and the perplexity and blunders of his associates.

Here is a specimen of the style of Don Barbarossa, in which he appears to have snatched a grace from "The Man:"

"A friend has directed my attention to a series of sedentary articles, contained in a mephitic publication called Wistar's Magazine, and purporting to give a syllabub or syncope of my late lamented father's autobiography. I read the successive theorems with wonder and disgust. The suppuration, the political economy, the shameless volubility of this synonymous hydrographer, surpass belief. My parochial duties as a military man prevent my writing now in the requisite malignity. I therefore content myself with asserting the barefaced veracity of this audacious eulogist, and promising, as soon as my hypocrisy admits of it, to furnish an abundant and curtailed corroboration of his vapid memorandi." *

* There is possibly a shade of the same influence observable in the following heroics from the same pen:

THE LURID LEPER.

BY DON BARBAROSSA.

In that spasmodic region where mankind
Are deeply synchronous and vaguely blind,
Where elemental anodynes prevail,
And Stygian carols ventilate the sail;
Where man is analyzed, and nature's voice
Bids esoteric fallacies rejoice—
In that far distant soporific land
There dwelt an adipose, erotic band.
Their crimson viaducts, their bland petards,
Their synalœpha and æolic guards,
Their imbecility, their chevaliers,
Annulled and scarified them many years.
At length a leper of laconic form
Appeared, sophisticated on a storm;
His eye mellifluous, his nose malign:
His lurid colour vilified the Rhine;
While in his air a sudorific sneer
Of calligraphic anguish did appear.
On either side of his Savannah ran
A tall, narcotic, evanescent man;
While all around a cloud of granite spread,
White as a coal, and as a lily red.
From this a salamander floated in
And stood where once a terebinth had been;
Paused for a moment, shook his amber mane,
Then rushed at once upon the leper. Vain
Were all his efforts to propel the pang.
His bones were crumbled by the murderous fang.
He shrieked, he sympathized, he vainly tried
To draw an inference, with ghostly pride;
And thus without a groan, the lurid leper died.
Above his grave a ghostly catacomb
Rises, like Chimborazo over Rome.

The article entitled "Proceedings in the House of Correction" is too good to be lost:

"The Speaker took the chair at one o'clock. Several honourable and learned criminals presented petitions, which were referred to the appropriate committees. The Committee on Ways and Means reported a new mode of picking locks. The Committee on Foreign Relations reported a bill for the relief of Dutch cousins, which was read twice and committed. The House resolved itself into Committee of the Whole Hog on the bill to rob the exchequer, which was read by sections and amended. The House resumed, and Mr. Footpad rose to a question of privilege, viz.: Has every member of the House the privilege of robbing and cheating all the rest? Mr. Lightfinger moved to amend by adding the words, *if he can*, which was agreed to. The motion was then carried without a count. The Speaker having resigned the chair, the House proceeded to elect a Speaker, when Fox Wolf, Esq., was chosen, and having been conducted to the chair by Messrs. Footpad and Lightfinger, spoke as follows: 'Gentlemen of the House of Correction, my heart swells with unwonted emotion as I take this venerable chair. I hope you will believe me when I say that I shall do my utmost to deserve your favour.' The Committee on the Judiciary was instructed to report a bill to abolish all imprisonment. The debtors present resolved to repudiate their debts. On a motion made by Mr. Vagrant Rogue, the Speaker decided that it was not in order to pick a member's pocket within the bar. The following bills were read a third time and passed: A Bill for the Suppression of Courts, Justices, and Constables. A Bill for the Encouragement of Highway Robbery. A Bill to make Gunpowder and Cold Steel a Legal Tender. A Bill to Incorporate the Worshipful Society of Knaves. The members were then called on for petitions. Mr. Gag presented a petition for a dollar. Mr.

Thither the pilgrim, in his fell canoe,
Eludes the gnomon and the wild haloo,
And as he vilifies his deep career,
In which a panoply of lights appear,
Dethrones the universe, dissects the stars,
Pursues Pygmalion in his lambent cars,
Assails the carabine, ascends the Alps,
And builds a wigwam of a thousand scalps.
More of thy history I may not tell,
But bid thee, Lurid Leper, now farewell.

Starling petitioned for his freedom. [A message from the Hangman by his private secretary, John Ketch, jr., Esq.] Mr. Cunning brought in a bill for robbing Peter to pay Paul, which was laid upon the table. Mr. Goosygoosy Gander offered the following resolutions: Resolved that we are free and independent. Resolved that we will assert our rights at any cost or hazard. Resolved that the Speaker be requested to prepare a discourse proving that prisoners are free, and that he deliver the same to Buncombe at his earliest convenience. A message was received from the gaoler [with the prisoners' dinners] which was laid upon the table, and then taken up, until it passed (into the stomach), after which the House adjourned." *

I here close the account of these children's-papers. When the multitude of these amusing trifles is taken into the account, and when it is considered that these things were thrown off spontaneously, to relieve his own mind, and to delight those even to notice whom is thought to be beneath the dignity of some men who aspire to the name of greatness; above all

* The subjoined card, entitled "Error Corrected," needs no comment:

"*To the Editor of Wistar's Magazine:*

"SIR, In your report of proceedings in the House of Boys (p. 14), I find these words: 'Mr. Baby moved the previous question, and Mr. Stout the floor. In order to define my position, I beg leave to state the question as it stood when I made my motion. On the introduction of a bill, a motion had been made to reject it, and another motion to lay the motion on the table, and a third to lay the second on the table, and a fourth to postpone the second indefinitely; whereupon a point of order was made, and the Speaker decided that the fourth was in order. From this decision an appeal was taken, and a motion made to lay the appeal upon the table, and another motion to postpone this, in order to take up a motion to refer the whole subject to a committee, which last motion was withdrawn in order to make way for a motion to postpone indefinitely, which was followed by a motion to lay the motion for indefinite postponement on the table, which latter motion was amended so as to include the other motions, and this amended complex motion was decided to be out of order, from which decision an appeal was taken, and a motion made to lay this appeal upon the table, upon which motion I had the honor to move the previous question. In the hope that I have made this simple case of parliamentary order as perspicuous to you and to your readers as it is to me, I beg leave to subscribe myself

"Your humble servant,

"BOANERGES BABY."

when it is remembered what were the magnitude and excellence of the works he was at the time producing, and the toils he was engaged in on the very days during which he was thus disporting himself; one is tempted to say, though in a sense somewhat different from that of the Roman writer,

> "O mortalem beatum cui certo scio ludum nunquam defuisse. Hunccine hominem tantis delectatum esse nugis!"

And I confess when I think of it, I again and again revert to the exquisite tact of the great dramatist in putting these words, descriptive of Brutus, into the mouth of Antony:

> "His life was gentle; and the elements
> So mixed in him, that Nature might stand up
> And say to all the world this was a man."

CHAPTER XIX.

As the year 1843 opened, it found Mr. Alexander, as was his wont, occupied with Scripture exposition. The journal affords a few entries which may be of interest as showing the direction he was giving to his studies, and in general the way in which he was employing his time.

"January 16. In a fit of ennui I took up the Philoctetes to-day; was delighted with it, and spent the whole afternoon and a good part of the evening at it; till, with the aid of Edwards's absurd but useful version, I got through it. The three main characters are beautifully drawn. The sufferings of Philoctetes are so described as to make me feel them. I know nothing in dramatic poetry finer than Neoptolemus, his reluctance to deceive, his repentance, and his noble reparation. Ulysses is less prominent, but finely contrasted with the other two. The reader is made to sympathize with the physical condition of Philoctetes, the intellectual power of Ulysses, and the moral qualities of Neoptolemus, head, heart, and body. The whole is exquisitely natural."

On February 9th, I find him reading Exodus xv; in De Wette, the half of Joshua in Hebrew and DeWette, with Maurer's notes. Having satisfied himself as to the form which he should give to his "treatise on Church government," he this day began to write the book, and before bed-time had completed nineteen pages. He records, that it is his purpose to give the hours of daylight, and as many before daylight as he finds necessary, on Tuesdays, Thursdays, and Saturdays, to the writing of his book aforesaid. On the intermediate days he wished to write lectures, viz: Mondays on Isaiah, Wednesdays on Nahum, Fridays on Introduction.

"After dark in the evening I read history, biography, topography, the news, &c. I have been reading more of Jefferson's letters; beautiful style, but dangerous and full of notions."

The book on Church government, mentioned above, afterwards took the form of essays, and was published in the Princeton Review, and then, with additions, in a volume entitled "Primitive Church Offices," and after his death with still further additions from the Princeton Review, under the title, "Exegetical Essays."

During the summer, he was attending to his usual Seminary duties, and preaching every Sunday afternoon in a school-house at Queenston, a suburb of Princeton; occasions which will long be remembered by those who were privileged to attend those rich expository exercises. He also wrote a compendious Hebrew grammar for the use of his classes. During the year, he was also giving instructions to C. W. Hodge, then, as subsequently, one of his favourite pupils and most valued friends, and now his successor in the chair of New Testament Literature and Biblical Greek.

The following extract from the diary will give some idea of his method of preparing and writing his sermons:

"Oct. 1. Read Mark ii. 1–12, and the parallel passages in Matthew and Luke, as explained by Calvin, Kunoel, Bloomfield, and De Wette. Also Winer's explanation of 'breaking up the roof' in his Realwortbuch. I intended to preach on this passage at Queenston; but as they did not send for me, I spent an hour or more in expounding 1 Peter, v. 1–5, extempore and audibly, as a preparation for the sermon which I think of preaching on that text before the Presbytery this week. Having gone through it once, I began again and finished it a second time. As my mind was now full of the subject, I began after tea to write, and finished about half of what I meant to prepare, before I went to bed at eleven."

He had again taken up his Commentary on Isaiah. The following extract will sufficiently indicate his method of preparation:

"Nov. 2. Wrote four pages of my sermon before breakfast, and read Blunt on Genesis ix. and Nehemiah xi. in De Wette. Read Jarchi, Kimchi, Aben-Ezra, the Michlal Jophi,* Luther, Calvin, Grotius, Junius, Cocceius, the Dutch Annotations, Pool's Synopsis, Vitringa, Clericus, Gill, J. H. Michaelis, J. D. Michaelis, Lowth, Rosenmüller, Augusti, Gesenius, Maurer, Hitzig, Hendewerk, Barnes, Henderson, De Wette, Ewald, and Umbreit, on Isaiah x. 33, 34. Wrote the first draft of a commentary on these verses. At night wrote out my notes on the same."

The reminiscences of his colleague, the Rev. Dr. William Henry Green, of Princeton, are exceedingly valuable just here, as few others had such a near view of his habits as a learned man; and of all his friends few were so well qualified to speak judiciously of his attainments. The two professors were warmly attached to each other, and as their departments often crossed, there was a good deal of correspondence between them relating to points of Biblical scholarship, and the boundaries of their respective chairs.

Dr. Green says the first time he ever saw Dr. Addison Alexander was in the pulpit at Trenton, shortly before he came himself as a student to the Seminary. He had no suspicion who the strange minister was when the service began, but he had not proceeded far in his discourse before he felt sure that he was "listening to the prince of American preachers." His text was, "Awake, thou that sleepest, and arise from the dead, and Christ shall give thee light," one of the most striking and masterly of his discourses. Dr. Green's admiration of him as a speaker was always mingled with wonder:

"Dr. Alexander's discourses, even those which were most simple and least elaborate, such as his talks at conference and other religious meetings in the Seminary and elsewhere, always bore marks of his transcendent genius, which eschewed the commonplace paths trodden by ordinary men, and hewed out a fresh passage for itself. Though he dealt with old-fashioned truths, they were always presented in a new light, or approached by unexpected ways, or exhibited in novel

* Of Abenmalech.

forms. I knew no greater intellectual treat than to hear him pouring out his massive thoughts in that vigorous English of his, which set forth his conceptions as sharply and clearly as if they were pictured on canvas, while he carried you up some mighty climax, or exposed the follies and inconsistencies of unbelief, or turned his withering sarcasm upon open opposers or false-hearted friends of true religion, or unfolded some of the grand themes of God's Word."

His rapid and impetuous but distinct utterance, and his accurate emphasis, together with his earnest manner and quick movements, which seemed extorted from him by strong feeling, and were impressive if not always graceful, brought his audience into lively sympathy with him and with his subject; so that

"His preaching delighted while it instructed and impressed his hearers. The crowds which flocked to hear him while he occupied Dr. Boardman's pulpit, during the absence of the latter in Europe, showed how his ministry was appreciated."

Dr. Green's familiarity with the Hebrew and Arabic adds weight to his testimony as to Dr. Alexander's consummate scholarship as an Orientalist. As a teacher of Hebrew, he regarded him as a great one for the advanced minds. For the others he was also a good teacher, but often terrified and sometimes discomfited them.

"I knew him," he writes, "as a teacher only in the capacity of an instructor in Hebrew. His lectures were prepared after my course of study was completed. It was to facilitate their preparation and afford him the leisure for giving a course on O. T. history, thus relieving the venerable Dr. Miller to whose department this had previously belonged, that I was made Dr. A.'s assistant."

His rapidity, his thorough mastery of his subject, and his wonderful fertility of invention were the sources of his great excellence, and of some defects, as a teacher.

"His own mind moved so fast, and study was to him such a delight and constant occupation, that he perhaps had scarcely consideration enough for dull and laggard pupils, though manifesting a great interest in those who were really making satisfactory progress, and preserving a lively memory of those ever after who were the best students in each class which came under his instructions. His amazing versatility led him to be constantly devising new methods of communicating his knowledge, or presenting his subjects, which however suggestive to those who were able to follow him, proved perplexing to those who were in the early stages of study."

When a fault occurred, he was sometimes unsparing in his strictures.

"When deserved, he could administer rebukes which would be felt. The neglect into which Hebrew was apt to fall in the second year, was very trying, or certainly not very stimulating, to a professor. His patience used to be severely tested by our class, I remember; until one day, after numbers had been called upon to recite, with the constant answer, 'not prepared,' he announced for the next lesson four verses, perhaps a third or a fourth the usual quantity, and added, 'I wish I had some gauge by which to measure the capacity of the class.' I need not add that the class did better afterwards. Subsequently it fell to his lot to hear the speaking of one of the classes. I have heard him say that he disrelished this task; for criticise as gently as he could, the students who had undergone the process were sure to be coming to his room the next day to ask if he did not think they had mistaken their calling in seeking the ministry."

This reminds me of something that happened in the presence of several living witnesses. A number of gentlemen, members of the Board, were once dining at Dr. Addison Alexander's, and among them the late Dr. Gurley; when the conversation fell on the foolish sermons that are sometimes preached. Dr. Gurley then asked Dr. Alexander whether he recollected what I am about to relate: A student took for his text in the oratory, "As Paul reasoned of righteousness, temperance, and judgment to come, Felix trembled." He went on to say, that we know Paul's opinions on these points; and thereupon he gave what he said he supposed to be the burden of Paul's discourse before Felix. When the young man had finished, Dr. Alexander remarked, approaching the subject in his circuitous way, that it was hard to say in a given case how much we had preserved to us of an Apostolic sermon. Sometimes only the subject was recorded. At other times, it seemed, an epitome was given. There were cases in which we had the introduction and conclusion, and other cases in which we had the main discussion. This, he said, was a case where the main topics were merely suggested. We knew nothing of the exordium or peroration, and could only guess at the argument. He did not think it possible in such a case to supply the omission. He did not believe that *any* body could preach the sermon which Paul delivered before Felix. But of one thing he felt sure, and that was, that the young brother had not preached Paul's sermon in the oratory that night; for if Paul, on the occasion referred to, had preached the sermon they had just heard, *Felix never would have trembled.* As he told this story, the speaker looked round furtively at Dr. Alexander and awaited his reply. The professor looked a little disconcerted, and admitted that he had a faint recollection of hearing and criticising a sermon on that text, though he "thought that in this case the stone had gathered some moss in rolling."

It is remarkable that most or all of these tart sayings of his, and every one of his scorching or annihilating review articles, belong to this earlier period. In after years his feelings greatly softened towards human infirmity.

Professor Green himself always experienced the most generous kindness from him as an instructor. He was always warmly received and made to feel that he was welcome, when he sought an explanation of difficulties, or wished further information, or desired counsel. Books were freely lent him, and time lavished upon him in the way of special instructions in Arabic, etc., and he was encouraged to push his studies under his general direction further than they were carried in the regular course. Like courtesies were extended to any of his pupils who were disposed to avail themselves of them, though he could also be curt to impertinent intrusion.

"You probably remember," he says, "the obtrusive questioner whom he put down by the reply, 'I prefer the dogmatic method of instruction.' You also remember the generosity with which his house in Steadman street was thrown open to the occupancy of students until every room was filled."

There was no end to his little benefactions. The world never knew of them, and he too much scorned its good opinion. His sharp retorts were sudden, and often innocuous, explosions. His kindness shone on unregarded, like the common light of day. We pay more attention to flashes of lightning than to the steady beams of the sun. He would go as far as any man to serve a friend, and he warmed towards people he saw in his travels, with the impulsiveness of a boy.

Another pupil, himself now a professor * writes:

"I was a pupil of Dr. Addison Alexander for one year only, and that the first year of the course at the Seminary. It was fashionable then to be afraid of him. ——— used to say that he went into his recitation room thinking of the sign-board on a railroad, 'Look out for the locomotive! † Once when he asked me at the close of a recitation to come to his study at a certain hour, the members of my own little coterie bade me an affectionate farewell. When I returned safe, they pretended to be very much astonished, and to be incredulous that the *awe-full* professor only wanted me to study Arabic. But I had been taught to admire Dr. Alexander before he went to Princeton, so that I had only to learn to love him, and this I did easily and quickly as any Freshman will a great professor who is courteous to him and inspires him with the hope of doing something in this world."

The subjoined account by his esteemed friend, the late Rev. Dr. Joseph H. Jones, of Philadelphia, is very true and graphic. The picture of the seemingly abstracted student who yet saw and remembered everything, slowly moving about the streets *incognito*, with his hands behind his back, is nature itself:

* The Rev. Professor Charles Phillips, of Chapel Hill, N. C.

† Which so much amused the English tourist, Captain Hammond.

"He was often in our city, where he was greatly admired as a preacher, but was rarely the guest of any private family. He had many invitations from those who would have deemed it a privilege to entertain him, but he usually went to the hotel. I do not recollect that he ever consented to stay at my house in Philadelphia except when be came to occupy my pulpit. On such occasions his reserve was laid aside. He was very communicative and social, full of anecdote and sprightly remarks about persons, books, and passing events. Nobody could be more entertaining. He had an instinctive dislike of crowds, of the artificial customs and many of the requisitions of fashionable society. In a large and promiscuous assembly he was generally taciturn, and seemed to be alone. Magna civitas, magna solitudo. I never met him at a public dinner, nor at a large evening party. To see him walking by himself in our streets, with hands clasped behind his back, he appeared to be musing in a sort of reverie, as if unconscious of any thing around him. While in this state of apparent abstraction, he was a very close observer of every thing. His recollection of persons and events was as remarkable almost as that which Xenophon ascribes to Cyrus. He never forgot any one that he ever knew, and often surprised graduates of the Seminary who had been absent many years by addressing them by name. He was so much disposed to 'keep to himself' when in Philadelphia, remain incognito, and look out from his retreat upon men and things, that none of his friends ever heard or saw half as much of him as we desired."

After one of these visits, in a letter to Dr. Hall, he refers to his love of preaching, and to an indiscretion into which it had led him:

"PRINCETON, *July* 13, 1843.

"MY DEAR SIR:

"One of my few weaknesses is an incapacity to say no, especially when asked to preach, and for this I am sometimes sufficiently punished. E. g. I foolishly consented to preach a third time in Philadelphia last Sunday for Mr. Willis Lord, who was suffering from influenza. After preaching twice for Mr. Jones, I had the pleasure of a walk from Third street, below Lombard, to Broad, above Chestnut, and back again in a perspiration, being solaced at the close of the walk home by the gentleman who escorted me, with an assurance that if it had been any day but the Sabbath, he would have brought a carriage. The next time I shall choose to preach there on a week-day. That night I lost my rest, and on Monday was quite uncomfortable, but executed my purpose of going viâ Amboy to New-York, which I reached in a highly influenzial state. I am now quite hoarse, with a cough, sore throat. and general feeling of dislocation. This may pass off soon, or it may not. I shall make it a reason, however, for declining your flattering invitation, and thus destroy the hopes which my first sentence no doubt excited. Let me add, for your further consolation, that Dr. Alexander is still in Virginia; that Dr. Miller does not sleep from home when he can help it; that Dr. Hodge preaches for Boardman; that Dr. Carnahan and Dr. Maclean have engagements in College; that Dr. J. W. Alexander preaches in the white Church here, while Dr. Rice (I think) administers the communion in the coloured one; and that Dr. Dod has to examine on mathematics on Monday morning, July the 24th. Thus you see that neither the working bee nor the 'drone' can give you any help on the day you mention.

"P. S. I find that Dr. Hodge is to preach for Boardman on the 16th inst. In answer to a message, he says he does not know now whether he could go to Trenton on the 23d."

It will be seen from the sketch which I give below, by the Rev. Dr. B. T. Lacy, of Missouri, that Mr. Alexander was now at, but not at all past, his intellectual climacteric. The account is from one who saw him several times under circumstances well fitted to call out his latent but strong social traits, but who knew him still better as an instructor and preacher:

"During the years from 1843 to 1846, the duration of my stay at the Seminary, Dr. Addison Alexander was in vigorous health, and in the very maturity of his productive powers. He had passed the years of his laborious studies, during which he had made such magnificent attainments in scholarship, and laid up such ample stores of profound and varied erudition; and now he was prepared to give to the world the valuable and splendid results of so much research. He was in the midst of his work on Isaiah, and had completed the first volume. His time was entirely occupied, and he allowed nothing to interfere with his allotted tasks."

While his secluded habits were regretted by many of his friends, and were the occasion of disappointment during his life time to those who, from congeniality of tastes and similarity of studies and pursuits, would have coveted his friendship, yet they can now see how well it was that his valuable time was left undisturbed; for in the mystery of God's purpose but a few years more were given him in which to work for his generation and posterity.

His singular impartiality and honesty as an interpreter and a polemic, have impressed themselves on the minds of a whole school of exegetes and preachers which he may be said to have founded. His ardent pupils and readers have sometimes fretted at his intellectual moderation. On this point the pupil from whom I last took extracts, writes forcibly. He says that:

In all his instructions, *truth* was the one subject of investigation and the great object to be attained. Perfect candour and unswerving honesty marked all his methods and all his conclusions. He never once suspected him of a partial presentation of the evidence designed to sustain a system or a theory. His ability and clearness in the presentation of the proofs which sustain and establish the system of doctrine and polity of the Old School Presbyterian Church, in connection with the entire fairness and frankness with which all objections and claims of opposing systems were stated, produced the happiest and most satisfactory results on the opinions and convictions of his classes. He can distinctly recall, in some instances, a sense of disappointment at the apparent deficiency of proof which would be adduced for dogmas loudly maintained by the confident assertions of authors, and held by the writer in common with others. But when the whole subject was fully examined, and the evidence on every side collected and compared, he would receive the conclusion with a clearer conviction of its truth, and rest in the doctrine with a stronger, because more intelligent faith. In no one instance did the teacher's searching and honest analysis shake his pupil's confidence, or disturb his belief in regard to any one of the distinctive doctrines of our Church. This result has been of incalculable advantage to him in fixing his individual opinions, and influencing the whole course of his ministry. He also learned from his teacher more respect for the opinions and systems of others. While his instructions strengthened his scholar's faith, they also tended to enlarge his charity.

In the style of his composition and in his extempore remarks, the same writer says:

"He greatly excelled any man I have ever known. He appeared to possess complete mastery over language. Not one element of excellence seemed wanting. Concise, almost laconic, without any meagreness of expression, simple and clear to transparency, without the sacrifice of beauty and felicity. He was without an affectation or a mannerism, and with a perfect adaptation of the expression to the subject and the occasion. All the varied excellencies of style which appear in his reviews, his commentaries, and his sermons, were equally apparent in his class instructions, and in the brief but comprehensive and beautiful prayers with which he opened the exercises."

The impression of Mr. Alexander which prevailed among most of the new students was not altogether agreeable. It took time and a little wisdom to know him as he was. The popular view was that he was a Colossus of intellect, a mighty scholar, a trenchant wit, a prince among teachers, preachers, and reviewers; but one whom it was dangerous to speak to except in the most guarded words. To this day, there is a ludicrous exaggeration in many minds of traits in the professor which were the product of a strong will and an elastic and impulsive temperament.

The life-like and amusing sketch which follows is from the pen of the Rev. James Park, of Nashville, Tennessee; who went through the usual curriculum at Princeton Seminary at this time, beginning with the session of 1843. Mr. Park's statements are of such a peculiar nature as almost to defy abridgment:

"I went to Princeton," he says, "in August, 1843, and was there two or three weeks before the session opened. It was my first trip from home. Dr. A. Alexander and Dr. Miller were the only persons thereof whom I had ever heard any thing particularly. The students who had been there before, seemed specially pleased to 'post' me in regard to the professors, and were particularly communicative in reference to Dr. Addison, giving me some terrible descriptions of scenes that had occurred in his class-room. When the term opened, the students came in with remarkable punctuality, and the 'old ones' seemed very kind and attentive to the 'new ones,' and took special pains to put us on our guard as to 'Dr. Addy.' When the bell rang for us to assemble in the oratory, I entered with the crowd, but with fear and trembling. I was to have my first sight of 'Dr. Addy.' I had called on Dr. A. Alexander and Dr. Miller, and had been treated so kindly, and was made to feel so easy by those good old fathers that I had no fear of them. Dr. Hodge I had seen several times, but had not been introduced to him. Dr. Addison I had not seen at all. He came in with his father, walking immediately behind him, with a port-folio under his arm. Dr. A. (sr.) read a portion of Scripture and prayed, after which Dr. Addison opened his port-folio, handed his father a strip of paper, opened a record book and laid it on the desk, also an inkstand and pens."

The young Tennesseean watched every movement he made with something like the feelings of a martyr. Dr. Archibald Alexander announced the first business in order, the matriculation of new students, and requested them to ascend the rostrum when their names were called.

"When the first name was called, and the student advanced, Dr. Addison rose from his chair, and when the student went up on the platform and presented his credentials, Dr. Addison, with a quick, energetic gesture, told him to 'take a seat on that chair.' I wondered what they were going to do with the poor fellow; whether it was possible they were going to *examine* him right then and there; or what will they do? Dr. Addison looked at the papers handed him by the student, announced the contents, which seemed satisfactory, read the obligation to be signed by the students, and then pointing to a line on the record book, said, 'Write your name there, sir!' I am sure no one ever looked upon a man with more awe than I did upon him. When my name was called, I went up, presented my diploma, which was duly announced, and was told to sit down and write. I should like to see that specimen of chirography now! I am not at all sure my name was spelled rightly. I know it was not traced in my usual style. When I returned to my seat it was with a feeling of thankfulness that that much of it was over, and I was still alive. And then, as I sat there and gazed upon that expanse of shining white forehead, those ruddy cheeks, those flashing eyes, that mouth so expressive of firmness and decision, that whole form so indicative of energy and strength, mental, moral, and physical, I wondered whether Luther on his way to the Diet of Worms was half such a man; and then whether such a fool as

I felt myself to be could ever meet him in a class-room without provoking his fury and incurring inevitable disgrace."

At length the matriculations terminated, the time for the different classes to meet their respective professors was announced, and the students were dismissed.

They were soon called upon to put their mettle to the proof. The account of the first recitation to Dr. Addison Alexander is a little startling:

"Our first contact with Dr. Addison was on Hebrew Grammar. He had a roll of the class alphabetically arranged, and called upon the students in that order, always looking steadily at him who rose in reply to the name called; but that roll we never saw any more after the last name on it was called once. He knew every man and called him by his right name after he had once responded to it, and the roll was no longer used.

There were two of the name of Park in the same class, and they were distinguished by their first initials, as Mr. O., and Mr. J. It was only at the third recitation, that the professor reached their names on the roll.

"Every member of the class had manifested some trepidation when he was first called up. My first appearance on the floor is memorable. I had begun to get homesick, not a strange circumstance considering this was my first separation from my family and friends; and my youthfulness favoured it too, for I was next to the youngest student in the Seminary. I rose *promptly*, *very*, at the call of my name, with quickened breath and bounding pulse. Dr. A.'s spectacles were wonderfully bright, yet not so bright as the eyes looking through them. He asked a question; I answered; he smiled; several students tittered. A second question, followed by the answer; Dr. A. smiled more perceptibly; all the class snickered, and I broke out in a sweat. A third question was answered; several students guffawed. *Rap*, *rap*, *rap*, on the desk, and with an indignant voice Dr. A. called out, 'Order in the class! I see nothing to laugh at.' And then to me, 'That will do, sir,' and called the next. I sat down in a state of terrible excitement, perplexed, confused, and ashamed, supposing I had exposed myself to the contempt and ridicule of the class, and resolved to start home the next day. When the class was dismissed, I was pushing my way to the door, anxious to escape from the gaze of the students, for some of them were still disposed to laugh at me; but as I approached the door, Dr. A. called to me, beckoning with his finger, 'Mr. J. P.! Mr. J. P.! I was afraid not to go to him, and yet only expected to hear him say, 'Young man, you had better go home, you are too much of a ninny for this place,' or something else that would be as bad."

Instead of this, he asked him about two other young men in Tennessee, who he had heard were coming to Princeton (sons of Drs. Edgar and Lapsley, of Nashville).

"While this was going on, the class passed out, and then he said, 'Mr. P., I will remain in the class-room a few minutes each day after the recitation to answer any inquiries the students may have to make concerning difficult points they may meet with, and I hope you will feel perfectly free to ask me any questions relating to your studies at such times. And at any other time that I am not engaged in class, I would be glad to have you call at my study, whenever you want any explanations or assistance.' It was all done with such simplicity, and with a countenance and voice so full of kindness, that I choked with emotion, stammered my thanks, and when he had passed out, hurrying to my room I locked the door and sat down and wept like a child."

From that moment all his feelings towards him changed, and while he still revered the dreaded Professor of Hebrew beyond any man he ever saw, he loved him with a deep and abiding affection.

Mr. Park's own language is essential to the effect of what follows:

"When my emotion subsided, and I had washed my face and brushed my hair, a rap on the door led me to open it. ——— * came in, his countenance bright with good humour, to explain the conduct of the class during my recitation. He said every one saw my excitement when I was called up; my first answer was given in full voice, tremulous from agitation; the second, in a tone loud enough to have been

* A classmate; himself a distinguished clergyman in one of the great cities of the Southwest.

distinctly heard at a distance of forty yards; and the third, as if Dr. A. was in a mill in full clatter, and I on the outside thirty or forty feet from the door."

The mark made upon him by the considerate manner and generous offer of Dr. A. to him after *that first recitation* is ineffaceable.

"His kindness and sympathy overpowered me, and over afterwards I felt indignant at the bare suggestion of his being unfeeling or uncongenial. As long as I remained at the Seminary nothing ever occurred to cause me to change my opinion. His heart was as great as his head. No man ever won my affections so completely; and it was an instantaneous transformation. The terrible dread and dreadful terror of him up to that time was never afterwards experienced by me. Still I had lost none of my profound reverence for him, nor did my desire to appear well before him abate one whit; but I had a new motive."

There were men in every class who seem to have taken the measure of their teacher, and who still entertain for him the most reverent admiration. The class of 1843 appears to have been full of such men. He was to each one of these gentlemen *magnus Apollo*, and seems to have strongly impressed upon them the stamp of his shaping influence. A clergyman of St. Louis,* who was then one of his students, writes:

"The impression he made upon me when I first saw him, which was at Princeton in 1843, and in the presence of the other members of the faculty of the Seminary, was one of awe mingled with intense curiosity to hear him and to know more of him."

This impression was not so much owing to what he had heard of him, as it was derived from his striking appearance and attitude.

"His youth, in comparison with his father and the venerable Dr. Miller, as well as with Dr. Hodge; his stout, full figure, more imposing when sitting than when upon his feet; his perfectly erect and motion-

* The Rev. Beverley Tucker Lacy.

less position; his resemblance in contour of face and head to the first Napoleon; his proud, solemn, and solitary expression of countenance: and more than all, his most remarkably developed forehead, so capacious and so perfect in its outline, a mighty dome of thought, almost as impressive as the head of Webster, and far more beautiful; all combined to awaken a profounder interest than had been excited in me by the appearance of any other man.

"This impression once made was never lost; it was continually renewed in many hundred interviews. Indeed, it produced something of a habit of gazing steadfastly at him when we supposed it would not attract his attention, and it caused me to give closer attention to to all he uttered in conversation, in the class-room, or in the pulpit. I remember distinctly an idea which often occurred to me while under his instructions at Princeton; that he possessed more wisdom than belonged to other men, and that he occupied a place in the temple of knowledge somewhat similar to that of the ancient priesthood who delivered their responses to the enlightened but heathen nations of the world."

Hence his instructions became to this pupil somewhat oracular, and he felt the necessity of attending to every word. He says that he has never been led to expect so much from any man as from him, and that he was never or seldom disappointed.

The same writer testifies that his class instructions were marked by wonderful clearness, conciseness, and comprehensiveness.

"The manner," he says, "was apparently stern and rather abrupt, and the utterance unusually rapid, but distinct. His explanations were not only satisfactory, but exhaustive; not only clear, but transparent, and but seldom repeated. At times he manifested a degree of impatience which I think was unreasonable, and which always betrayed itself in a severity of reproof, and a keenness of sarcasm overwhelming in their effects."

The writer bears witness that whenever he became satisfied that he had been guilty of injustice, or had violated the proprieties of the occasion, he generously and candidly made all reparation. As a teacher, he thinks he was at this time too much feared, and that there was too great a distance observed between him and his pupils, "especially those of dull and blundering minds." This was not the result of any intention or preference on his part, but owing to the peculiarities of temperament to a great extent not within his control.

It is my own opinion that even "dull and blundering minds" received great profit from Mr. Alexander, where they were not also lazy, conceited, or excessively timid. My recollections, however, date back to a period much later. I know that the laborious teacher aimed at a benefit that should be general, and would have considered that he had failed in his work unless he had supposed he had raised the average level of scholarship and capacity in every class.

The journal, meagre as it is, affords a few particulars. On November the 7th, I find him reading Blunt on the 14th chapter of Genesis, and the 2d chapter of Esther in De Wette. Before breakfast he prepared his notes for recitation. He then walked and meditated on, "Say among the heathen the Lord reigneth." He examined the class that day on Genesis i. 4–6, and analyzed verses 7–10 for them. Later in the day he perused Calvin on the eleventh chapter of Isaiah, with new delight and admiration. "Such sense! such piety! such style!" are his exclamations over this great author. At night he read Grotius, Junius and Cocceius on the same, as well as the debates in Congress, and Bridges on the 119th Psalm. One day can hardly be distinguished from another. This one was the image of hundreds, so far as extant records are concerned. There was perpetual variety in the midst of general resemblance. If we could have entered his study about this time, or possibly somewhat later, we should have found his floor, and a structure of temporary shelves which he had erected, extending entirely across the room, covered with the learned treatises of all nations having any bearing upon the work in hand. Dictionaries and cyclopædias; the Versions; the Rabbins; vellum folios; quarto and octavo grammars; Vitringa, Calvin, the Fathers, the classics, the Germans, the latest English authors, the infidels and the Christians, were tossed pell-mell about the rounds of his chairs, and under the huge legs of his table. There he sat entrenched among his forces, and girdled, like a leaguered camp, by strong redoubts and escarpments. His dark, soft brown hair was thinning somewhat on the top of the head, and was becoming slightly gray. Rosy health painted his cheek, and added to the comely roundness of his person and the sparkle of unusual pleasure in his eye. He wore gold spectacles, and was in every sense a Saxon rather than a Gaul. His voice could be heard through his closed door, as in chirruping mood he sang his Arabic and Persian songs, blew tunes upon his ivory paper-folder, or murmured strange words in tones which might have deceived an inexperienced bee-hunter. Then he would pause, whirl the leaves of a lexicon, murmur again, whistle, soliloquize, cross and recross the floor, resume his seat, and so *da capo*. Sometimes perhaps, when bending over Jarchi or J. D. Michaelis, a funny thought would strike him, and he would laugh aloud, quickly uttering the syllables, "ha, ha, ha."

I am able to present at this point the testimony of the Rev. Dr. A. A. Hodge, of Allegheny City, and Professor of Theology in the Western Theological Seminary. After speaking of the mighty changes, some of them terrible or sad ones, wrought by the late civil conflict, he observes:

"But the *past*; the men, the friends, the beloved teachers, associates, lessons, and associations; are all safe. Their deathless memories, sweet and large, form an abiding home and a peaceful contentful rest. And there, in the centre of the innermost circle, the Alexanders, father and sons, render the scene sacred and precious. I never go to Princeton without visiting their graves, and I never think of them without having my poor staggering faith in God and in regenerated humanity strengthened. Let us uncover our heads and thank God for them!"

His reminiscences will be found interesting. As a little boy he was admitted to unusual intimacy with Professor Addison Alexander, and saw much especially of his humorous side. He wrestled with him on the floor, teased him for his stories and "sat amazed while he sang English, French, German, Italian, Turkish, Latin, Greek, Hebrew, and Arabic songs or chants."

Then he went to school and college, and the intercourse was suspended. When he entered the Seminary in 1844, he met him as a stranger, in his infrequent visits to his study, sitting nervously on the edge of his chair, ready to go as soon as the promptly despatched business was over. "In the class-room he amazed as well as instructed us, as with inexhaustible fulness, and an almost baffling rapidity, he poured forth streams of light."

He then compares himself and his fellow-students to "half-fledged birds" striving "eagerly with outstretched necks and ineffectual wings" to follow the glowing portent in its track through the heavens.

"The prominent impression I received from him was that I was beholding a giant putting forth his great strength; but behind it all possessing an unfathomable reservoir of reserved force. The work done was great in itself, but appeared dwarfed by the contrast inevitably suggested of possibilities lying just below the surface, of absolutely indefinite extent. When contemplating him, I often thought of the great Ark, pregnant with all animate creation, carrying a world of possibilities, but on a new sea; apparently not steered on the shortest courses to the harbours frequented by ordinary practical merchant-men."

He was almost equally struck by the professor's evident piety, and with the remarkable quality of his prayers.

"Then there was the habitual and all-prevalent tenderness and devoutness of his spirit. Whenever he prayed, while his sentences ran on condensed and rapid, each a complete confession, supplication, or doxology in itself, through all breathed the tender, yearning, trustful spirit of a child. While holding himself morbidly aloof from the intercourse of men, it was evident that his heart was in tender sympathy with all human joys and sorrows, and that it nestled close to the heart of Christ."

During the next two years, Dr. Addison Alexander was closely engaged upon his commentary, and his journal becomes itself. a mass of mere interpretation. It was his habit, when at work upon a new volume, especially in the preliminary stages, to jot down in his day-book every new thought or suggestion as it occurred to him. Many of these are fresher than the statements in the printed book, but they are not in every case his matured opinions, and as casting no reflected ray upon his life at this time, need not be inserted here. Sometimes the entries of an exegetical kind are made in a hand so small as almost to require glasses to read them. The Hebrew text is beautiful. The penmanship throughout is free and bold, and often very elegant. Back-hand prevails, but the old-fashioned quill-pen-hand of "the fathers," inclining gracefully to the right, is nearly as common. He wrote much in the legal, and now and then in the commercial style. In the midst of these grave comments occur multiplied repetitions of his own full name, and the names of acquaintances; notes to imaginary friends or diplomatic characters, signed by Launcelot Andrews or James L. Beffo, and the curt correspondence of suppositious duellists.

Every motive of friendship and affection constrained the brothers to be much together. I find Dr. James Alexander enumerating among a series of reasons why he ought to be contented with his situation in Princeton, of which he sometimes tired, that he was among friends of eminent learning and wisdom; and he mentions besides the names of those now living, his father, Dr. Miller, and his brother Addison.

It gives me pleasure to introduce here the impressions of one who knew the Seminary teacher well, and could appreciate him, and who was long his neighbour and visitor, and latterly one of his closest friends and comforters.*

The writer says his acquaintance with Dr. Addison Alexander began in February, 1844, when he himself entered the

* The Rev. D. Abraham Gosman, of Lawrenceville, N. J, one of the American translators of Lange.

Seminary, and continued with a growing intimacy until his lamented death. Through all this period he found him a valued instructor, counsellor, and friend. It was then quite a prevalent opinion in the Seminary that it required some courage to enter his study, and that the venture could only be made upon some urgent consideration, but the result of his first interview convinced him that the opinion was groundless, and this conviction grew stronger and stronger the more perfectly he came to know him, during his subsequent student life, and in all his intercourse with him afterwards.

> "The frankness and cordiality with which he received me, gave me confidence, and upon stating my wishes and plans, I met with that ready sympathy and kindness which were never intermitted, and which have laid me under obligations I can never repay."

No one could be in his presence any length of time without being impressed with his extraordinary powers and attainments, and with his

> "Entire freedom from pride and ostentation, and from any apparent consciousness even that he was 'from his shoulders and upward' above the ordinary rank of men. This was perhaps the most distinct and universal impression which he made."

The eagerness with which nearly all the more intelligent and deserving of his old pupils have come to the rescue of Mr. Alexander's character for humility, amiable feeling, conscientious efforts towards the improvement of his classes, depth and liveliness of sensibility, and the earnest and tender piety, not only seems to establish the existence of these and kindred traits in their preceptor, but also furnishes strong evidence that he made his classes love as well as fear him. Some of his pupils talk now as if they would have fought for him. No mere proud scholar, and certainly no misanthropist, could have so powerfully moved so many hearts. The man who excited such feelings must have been himself a person of large and noble affections.

The testimony offered in this volume ought to be sufficient

to silence the calumny that Mr. Alexander was habitually morose or cold-hearted. Never was an impression more ill-founded. It was just as far from the truth that he was not a man of singular practical wisdom. Hear an affectionate pupil on these heads, and one who for many reasons and in many ways enjoyed his intimacy.

"So far from being distant and cold, no one came to him with confidence who did not meet with confidence. He had no time for mere idlers, but to help those who were in earnest was his delight. His time was at their command, and yielded not reluctantly and grudgingly, but with evident pleasure. His sympathies were quick and tender. He entered easily and fully into our perplexities and trials, and although living a comparatively secluded life, his advice upon all practical questions was always clear and judicious. Results uniformly attested its wisdom. Recalling now the various occasions upon which I went to him for counsel upon matters varying from those of a day to those which were to decide my life-course, I cannot bring up an instance in which his advice was not correct, as time and events have shown. In cases as to which my own judgment differed from his, I have had reason to regret not listening to his counsel."

CHAPTER XX.

The reader has been made acquainted with Mr. Alexander's disposition to hunt novelty in nearly every field of pursuit. But in affairs of importance it would be an error to suppose that he surrendered himself to every capricious suggestion. In little things, he undoubtedly pursued the phantom of ever-multiplying and ever-shifting variety, for its own sake, and as a refreshment both to mind and body. But in these as well as in greater matters, he was actuated after all not so much by love of change as by hatred of sameness; and as regards the main business of his life, he was impelled in these perpetual turnings and transformations chiefly by the absence of any mere pride of opinion, by the exuberance and restless productiveness of his genius, by a sincere and ardent love of truth, and an honest disdain of consistency where consistency is but a name for wilful perversity, and above all, by the continual discovery of new and often really better methods of study or instruction, and the advances he was daily making in knowledge and the ability to use it to the best advantage.

On this subject a friend of this and later periods writes with great justice:

"You are familiar with his peculiarities as an instructor. His mind seemed to tire of any thing like routine or monotony. His love of variety appears even here; and while it was restrained within the bounds which the routine teaching required, it led him to change his methods frequently. Plans which were laid down at the beginning of the session, were soon interrupted or thrown aside for what seemed to him to promise better results. It was not caprice, but his earnest desire to carry his class through the fields open before him, yet without retarding their progress towards the end, which led to these changes. Results showed how wisely they were made. He never probably took the same course with any two classes. And yet no real student, I think, ever failed to feel how clearly the end had been kept in view, how successfully and steadily it had been pursued, and what large and varied knowledge had been gained through the very changes which at the time may have seemed arbitrary, and only to be regretted.

"There are few men who could easily or safely adopt the same course, but with him it was a grand success. He not only thoroughly understood what he attempted to teach, but understood how he could best teach it. He kindled the minds of the students into ardour and enthusiasm; never suffered them to weary; turned them aside into pleasant openings which skirted their pathway, while they were still perhaps unconsciously pressing towards the end, and that more rapidly than if they had been plodding in one weary round. It may safely be said that as there have been few teachers who were so admired by their students, so there have been few who have conferred as great and lasting benefits."

It is more than doubtful whether under any one of these methods alone, or any single method whatever, no matter how comprehensive or felicitous, he could have awakened the same interest or imparted the same amount of knowledge. It is very certain that his own spirits would have flagged under a system of monotonous routine; the wings of his daring intellect would have melted like wax in such an atmosphere. He could not, in such a state of things, any longer cleave the cloud or mount towards the sun. He must be disporting himself in an element of delight, or else he lay panting on the earth incapable of putting forth any proper exertion, or at least unable to brace his faculties for any valuable and sustained effort.

Here is a letter to a little girl, which contains some pretty compliments:

"PRINCETON, February 28, 1844.

"DEAR ———:

"Last Thursday we celebrated the birthday of Washington, and to-day I propose to celebrate the birthday of ———. Do you know who is just completing her eleventh year? A friend of mine whom I have not seen for more than two months. When I saw her last she was very plump and rosy, but I do not know how the city air may have agreed with her. A year ago this very day her throat was sore and her jaws tied up; but she soon got over that. If you know who she is, and should meet her in the street, tell her that I wish her many, many happy birthdays. And now, as for yourself, my little friend, I wish to thank you for your very kind and interesting letter. The account of what you saw on Christmas-day was very entertaining. But you neither told me how you were, nor said a single word about your new home, or your new friends, or your studies, or a hundred other things of which I wish to hear. I want to know, for instance, who is ——— ———'s successor as your bosom friend, and how you are coming on in Latin and Hebrew? Do you know the meaning of חַזָּת הָאַרְנֶבֶת? This is not my Hebrew pen, and I am very much afraid that I have written it illegibly. If so, I can try it again in my next. I wish I had some Princeton news to tell you; but you get it all, no doubt, from your other correspondents. The Rev. Dr. Seabury preached in Trinity Church last Sunday. Old Mrs. Millet was buried the same day. The roof of the Seminary was on fire this morning, but was soon extinguished. Professor Henry has determined not to follow 'you all' to Philadelphia. The house next to this will be vacant in April. Do come back and take it! Jemmy has told me twice to send his love to you, and beg you to write again. Have you read the Letters to a Very Young Lady?* My glass, which you refused to take, has been at Capt. Crabb's for several months. I am sorry you always think me joking when I want to have your likeness taken. You ought at least to be daguerreotyped, for my satisfaction, and at my expense. If you do not choose to have it done for me, I will have it done for myself when I come to see you. There must be three copies: one for you, one for ———, and one for me; but I am to have the prettiest and the one most like you. In the mean time you must choose in what position they shall take you, where you will put your hand, and whether you will have a flower in it, or a roll of music. Do you ever sing now? If you do, here is a little song for you to practise on:

> "Sakee beyari badeh keh amud zemani gul
> Ta beshkeneemi taubeh deegher der miyani gul
> Hafiz wesali gul telabi hemchu bulbulan
> Ian koon fedai khaki rehi baghebani gul." †

* By Dr. James Alexander.

† This was his favourite Persian song, and is about a rose.

"You can see how pleased I was to get your letter by the speed with which I answer it; for I hardly think you expected an answer in six months. But in earnest, ——, I was very much delighted, and almost the only reason for not writing sooner was that I did not wish to plague you and give you the trouble of answering my letter as soon as you received it. Now take notice, little woman, you are not to answer this until you are at leisure and would rather write than not; and if that time never comes, although I shall be sorry not to hear from you, I shall neither be offended nor suppose that you have forgotten me, which I do not mean to believe until I have it from you in black and white. I am glad you like the marker; it was made by my sister. I am sitting up at night to write this letter, or everybody here would be sending love to you. I hope you will always be as much beloved as you are now, and deserve it as well.

"Sincerely yours."

The next letter to Dr. Hall is in the usual vein of badinage. The allusion to the Doctorate is an ironical expression of his known opinion of it. Another allusion is explained by the fact that he had a peculiar horror of men who put on sanctimonious airs and talked about their hearts. He was like the statesman who said, that whenever he heard a man talk much about his honour, he at once set him down for a rascal. The best irony in the letter is in the first sentence of the postscript:

"PRINCETON, September 17, 1844.

"DEAR AND HONOURED SIR:

"Your anxiety to keep your eye upon me when I come to preach at Trenton is altogether natural, considering your precarious situation there, and the excellent train into which matters have been brought. Just at present, however, I am on another scent. You say nothing about politics. You are requested to write an article on the march of mind, or the holiness of virtue, as you please. I was called Doctor * by every body in my late visit to New York. Oh, my good sir, what can this portend? If I know my own heart, I shall not allow our relations to be much affected.

Yours truly,

J. A. ALEXANDER."

"As it requires a good deal of peculiar talent to distinguish the

* He received the degree from Rutgers College.

delicate vein of humour running through my first paragraph, I add in a translation, that I expect to preach three times at Elizabethtown next Sunday, and twice in Princeton the Sunday after that. But for this, the plan which you propose would be highly agreeable. You will rejoice to hear that I am convalescent; but you see my hand trembles, and my pen too, though of steel."

The latter part of April was beautiful. The pastures and grain-fields smiled with verdure; the woods were in tender leaf, and the orchards were bending under odoriferous blossoms. The aspect of May was equally lovely. The country had scarcely ever looked so green. A lap of gracefully-sloping meadow and tilled land, now in rich colour, might be seen to advantage from the Steadman-street corner of the front Library lot. On the 27th, Mr. Alexander and one of his brothers returned from a jaunt which had carried them through New York, Philadelphia, Baltimore, Washington, York, Columbia, and Harrisburg. The General Assembly was in session. The final examination was going on at college. A great Whig convention at Trenton was spoken of. Webster, it was thought, would speak.

The older brother writes to Dr. Hall:* "Addison is just completing a bargain with Wiley & Putnam for the publication of his 'Commentary on Isaiah.' He will print it in a very leisurely manner, as it is not fully written out. It will be chiefly for clerical readers, etc. and will make a large octavo volume. He has laboured very much at it, and has gone over almost every part with his pupils."

I do not know that the brothers consulted much together over questions presented in the study of Isaiah. Professor James Alexander never heartily gave in to some of the views propounded in his brother's volumes. They did, however, talk much together about difficult and curious points suggested in the critical reading of Matthew. The elder brother gave the younger many striking views of passages in the New Testament, and himself wrote a large part of a popular Commentary

* Fam. Let. I. p. 395.

on the first Gospel, of which his brother Addison spoke in terms of strong eulogy.

On the 9th of June, the two brothers accidentally preached from the same text, Isaiah, 57: *ult.* the one at the college, and the other at Queenston. As I look back upon it through the sunshine of boyish remembrance, this strikes me as about the golden age of Princeton. The senior professors at the Seminary were not only alive but hale and vigorous, and their influence upon the Church was at its height. Professor Addison Alexander was in the full glow of perfect health, and splendid attainment and reputation. At the college, Professor Henry experimented and lectured, as none else could. Professor Dod inspired his mathematical class with admiration and zeal, and the dead languages and Belles Lettres became a delightful entertainment in the hands of such a man as Professor James W. Alexander. There were many charming families in the place; literary men abounded, in and out of the faculties; the preaching to be heard in any of the pulpits was of the highest order, and the general educational tendencies of its schools were unequalled. The Princeton of that day was truly Athenian. Not that I would pretend that the standard of scholarship was so high as it ought to be, or has since become; but there was, so to speak, a vital oxygen in the air, to breathe which almost gave a man a smattering of knowledge and taste, and to live in which was itself a tolerable education. There is something too subtle about these academic and collegiate influences for the litmus of exact analysis. What I speak of is found in its perfection at Oxford and Cambridge, and, in various degrees, at Yale and Harvard, and the University of Virginia. Each of these and similar places, is now at least a little hoary, and gives its own distinctive impress, without regard to the extent of the course, or the diligence of the pupil. But, besides having this air of antiquity and this liberal aroma, Princeton was graced at that time by the presence of quite a constellation of intellectual and famous men.

In July, Professor James Alexander proceeded to New

York, and pronounced an address before the Societies of the University. The day was very warm, and the house crowded. He was sought after by certain persons from Boston, who wished him to be called to the Bowdoin-street Church; but he could not favour the project.

The following thoughts were struck out in talk between the brothers James and Addison, some time in August. There was entire concurrence between them, but Dr. Addison Alexander's peculiar stamp is upon several of the expressions:

"Almost all extemporaneous preachers have this fault: they talk about the *way* in which they are preaching. Thus: 'After a few *preliminary remarks*, I shall proceed to,' etc.; or, 'What I shall lay down will take the form of general principles.' 'I come with hesitation,' etc. 'I shall be more brief on this point.' 'You will observe that in this discussion I do so and so.' Avoid all such observations. More generally still, avoid all that brings the speaker's personality before the hearer. A better model than our honoured father, in this, there could not be."

I give below the opinion of one who is now a rector in the Episcopal Church, * and whose writings have long been extensively known:

"Seeing Dr. Addison Alexander," he says, "almost daily, for several years, receiving from him some of the most powerful impressions my mind has ever received; honoured by his unsolicited approbation of my literary efforts; indebted to him for literary labours; this profound critic and scholar, this powerful and trenchant reviewer, this remarkable and, in my experience, unrivalled preacher, was personally as little known to me as if we had inhabited different planets. The students generally felt equal admiration of his power and respect for his reserve. His life of recluse study was to all of us a problem; with most, the instincts of scholarship solved it, without the elements of romance and mystery. It was nevertheless very surprising that, in our age, and in America, a man possessing the practical force of Luther, and the genial scholarship of Erasmus, should have lived in an atmosphere like that which, to our Protestant imagination, surrounded St. Dominic, or Loyola; and in one of the great thoroughfares

* The Rev. W. W. Lord, of Vicksburg, Miss.

of America, and one of the great universities of the world, should seem to invest himself with the solitude of the Thebaid, or the seclusion of a monastery."

On the 2d of October, the Rev. James W. Alexander removed, with his family, to New York, to take charge of the Duane-street Church, whose call he had accepted. He was installed the next day, and remained in this situation until 1849, when he returned to Princeton, to occupy the chair of Church History and Government, which had been left vacant by the retirement of Dr. Miller. This removal to New York was, in some respects, a trial to Mr. Alexander, though it added inducements to his frequent desire for travel. The settlement of another brother in the same city soon and greatly increased its domestic attractions. The first house occupied by the new pastor was No. 83 White street; and there the great scholar from the country would "gather *the babes*," as he facetiously called them, and, putting them before him on a sofa, would describe all the odd characters of the neighbourhood, and tell them new tales about Old Black and Peter Arun. He had great sympathy with his toiling brother in his new and heavy cares; and sometimes exhorted him to take summary measures with the troup of idlers, busybodies, and charlatans who devoured his time, and cut him off from the smallest chance of rest or leisure.

The elder brother writes, about this time, to Dr. Hall, at Trenton: "Visitors knock and ring 'frae morn till e'en.' Addison says, I should practice self-denial—*at the door*." * These little witty *mots* were too common and incessant to be taken down; otherwise a creditable volume might have been made of his speeches of this kind. But, as has often been remarked, he never crossed the limits of propriety, and did not fail, even in these little things, to "magnify his office."

The Isaiah was by this time fairly in the hands of the publisher. It appears from a letter to Dr. Hall, of October the 30th, that Dr. James Alexander sometimes sought *nepenthe* from his

* Fam. Letters, Vol. II., p. 30.

anxieties in the rooms of Mr. Wiley, and in the fresh books and pamphlets from the continent. He writes: "As Addison is printing [Isaiah] with Wiley & Putnam, I have the entrée there, and enjoy a grand gloat on the arrival of each steamer." He always had the knack of making friends with "the trade," and picked up many a new word or happy thought as he roamed among the shelves, or lingered at the counter to bandy foreign epithets with some bibliophile, or whiskered and moustached polyglot from Germany. He was much addicted to Anglo-Saxon, and comparative grammar, and loved to burnish up his wits with such accomplished bookmen as Mr. Garrigue and Mr. Westermann. He spoke French and German well, and Latin creditably, and could hold his own in a short conversation with an Italian or a Spaniard. He also knew something of the Dutch, and latterly of the Danish, Swedish, and Norwegian. He often visited the synagogue, and sometimes had a brush with one of the Jewish doctors. One of his sextons, a faithful simple-hearted fellow, by the name of Peter Tarlsen, belonged to the land of the Skalds and the Edda, and from him he derived much instruction.

The following scheme of lectures and private reading was observed by Mr. Alexander, during the greater part of the year 1845, and shows the nature of his occupation at that period:

"February 22, 1845. Plan for the next session, if I live:

Introductory lecture on the studies preliminary and auxiliary to Interpretation.

Study of Hebrew grammar, with occasional lectures on Biblical philosophy, criticism, and archæology.

Analytical lectures on the books of the Old Testament, in their order, with specimens as Hebrew lessons.

Messianic Prophecies, with the first class.

Acts of the Apostles, with the second class."

There can be no doubt that this plan was adhered to with great tenacity, and that Mr. Alexander was now devoting all his best energies to the critical interpretation of the Bible.

His Isaiah (that is, his first part) was approaching completion.

The next letter is in the playful vein again. He sends a student to preach at Trenton.

"Friday, March 14, 1845, 2 o'clock, P. M.

"MY DEAR SIR:

"As misfortunes never come alone, our invalidity has been synchronous (see the dictionary). I have been under medical treatment for some days—principal symptoms nausea and a very severe headache. Furthermore, I have put off two exercises till next Monday, and have just begun an article for the Repertory which ought to have been written at the beginning of this week, and must be done to-morrow night. Again, it is next Sunday that my father is to preach in the chapel: besides that, he declines going away from home at this season. You say nothing about *a third* person; but, in the plenitude of my benevolence, and with a great sacrifice of feeling, I have engaged Mr. James E. Moore, of Belvidere, N. J. of our first-class, to preach for you. It is very likely you will not thank me for this officious overstepping of my commission; but one must run the risk of such censures and mistakes, in the sacred cause of friendship. Mr. Moore has friends in Trenton with whom he will stay; but I have intimated the probability of your paying his expenses. If he should not please the fastidious taste of your metropolitan audience, it will be a salutary mortification of your ambitious views. James has just spent two days with us.

"And now, my dear sir, how shall I express my condolence with your sufferings, and the pleasure which it would have given me to aid you in your labour of love; a privilege to which I still look forward, in the course of the present season, with feelings which defy description, and, in the meantime, have the pleasure and satisfaction of subscribing myself Yours very truly,

J. A. ALEXANDER."

"P. S.—As my late indisposition has affected my mind, it may be prudent not to let this letter go beyond the Session and Board of Trustees.

I have only had your letter half an hour. You need not send for Mr. M."

His youngest brother, H. M. Alexander, Esq. of New York, communicates the following important reminiscences:

"He is connected with my earliest recollections. My chief delight was in hearing his stories; which he poured out with prodigious prodigality. He instituted a *bund* which he called the Cappadocian Society; a mysterious and awe-inspiring institution to me, the meetings being held in a darkened room, and what was not said and done being far more impressive than that which was. He mixed songs composed by himself with stories which never ended, and always broke off at the most interesting parts. Two of these songs, which always introduced two ghosts, or mysterious characters, I can sing the tunes of now.* He was always cheerful; and, as a child, my recollections of him are not connected with a single unpleasant association. When I began to study Latin and Greek he became my instructor, and was such, from time to time, until I entered college. I do not think I learned much of the regular studies I pursued with him (which was no doubt my own fault), but I learned a mass of other things which sometimes seem to me to be all that I know now. I studied in his library; and he would talk to me for hours, on subjects which interested him, precisely as if I was his equal in age and knowledge. He would never read aloud to me, but would pour out the contents of volumes digested and made plain, some of which I remember now. I never saw any one who might be said to devour a book as he did. He appeared to take up a page as soon as he looked at it, just as a sponge takes up a spot of water from a slate. I recollect once expressing a doubt whether he had actually read something, he turned the leaves so rapidly: whereupon he handed me the book, and recited, almost verbatim, every sentence on a page or two.† He took a wonderful delight in the men and history of the time of the Georges, and would talk incessantly about them. I became, in this way, acquainted with that period as I am with no other. There was no need to read on any subject. He would read a book, and then pour it out in a condensed form, retaining all that was interesting, and supplementing it with everything he knew upon the subject from other sources. I am surprised when I look back, at the way in which he used to consult me upon the matters he wrote for publication. Often he would alter what he had written, upon my making an objection, even when the objection was merely the thoughtless remark of a boy

* I remember the tunes spoken of, but do not associate them with the ghosts.

† The same brother says he has seen him read a long paragraph (say a large part of a page) more carefully, but only once, and then repeat it word for word.

of fourteen. When he was writing his Commentary on Isaiah, he caused to be made two standing desks reaching from one end to the other of his large study. These were two stories high. On the lower story he placed the folios and quartos, and on the upper the octavos. I should estimate that these stands held about fifty volumes, all of them open. He would first pass down the line where the commentaries were, then go to the lexicons, then to other books; and when he was through, he would hurry to the table at which he wrote, write rapidly for a few minutes, and then return again to the books: and this he would repeat again and again, for ten or twelve hours together. While this was in progress, nothing seemed to be an interruption. He would answer every question asked, or would stop and give some amusing description of what he had seen or heard on a trip to New York or Philadelphia, and then go on with his work. He was much troubled with toothache, and the hot weather affected him a good deal, and I have often heard him say that the best relief from both these annoyances was some difficult passage to explain. I used to go often with him when he travelled; when he seemed to gather more amusement from the people he saw, and what he heard them say, in a day, and would make the thing more interesting in detailing it, than most men would in a year. His powers of sarcasm were dreadful. His reproofs were usually given in this way; and I am sure the particular thing reproved was never repeated, without the recollection of the reproof. His admiration and love for his mother were unequalled. Her ability and manners he constantly spoke of in the most affectionate and exalted terms. I have seen him, numbers of times, leave his writing to go to her and read the verse he was commenting upon, and ask what she supposed it meant; and I once heard him say, her common sense, in certain matters of this kind, was worth more than all the commentaries in the world.

"He seemed to have a morbid appetite for reading what to every body else was the merest drudgery. I do not recollect the books now, but I remember well how I wondered to see him reading them, and to hear him burst into laughter at something. When I asked him what it was, he would reply, 'Nothing; you would not think it funny.'

"He was also fond of law, and of courts, and causes—of whatever kind they might be. I have known him spend day after day in our courts, listening to cases (civil, not criminal cases,) which every body else who could, would shun. He often came to my office, where my partners would be amused at his asking for the printed cases, in any suits going on, which he would devour for hours at a time. These cases consist of the pleadings, such testimony as is important to be laid before the higher court, the charge of the judge, and the points of law relied upon by the lawyers on either side.

"He was very fond of attending trials in which Mr. O'Conor was engaged, and said he was a man of genius. He said it was delightful to be thoroughly convinced by the argument of the counsel who first spoke, and then to be convinced of precisely the opposite. He said juries should have several days before being called on to render their verdict.

"He had a sovereign contempt for the usual ways of doing things by societies and associations, where there was no direct object in view. I recollect a humorous article he wrote about conventions, in which he gave pretended reports of the rag-pickers' convention, etc. I think this was a great mistake; for there is nothing which so aids people engaged in the same thing as to learn how others do it. You, no doubt, know how terribly severe he used to be on the use of big words where common, small ones would answer—such as commence for begin, converse for talk; *et id omne genus.* I intended to mention the satisfaction he took in listening to preaching, however stupid to me, provided it was not pretentious. He was often thrown in the way of hearing an old minister who had to leave the ministry because no one could stand his long, tedious sermons. I have frequently laughed at the attention he paid this old gentleman, and the pleasure he expressed on coming home.

"I doubt whether he ever thought whether anything was wholesome, or unwholesome, or whether it was imprudent to sit in a draught, or drink ice-water when heated. He constantly said that he rejoiced that he did not know enough about anatomy to be alarmed when he was ill, or be in pain lest it should prove a vital organ. Perhaps a little more attention to these things might have lengthened his life."

The account given in this communication of Mr. Alexander's mode of study when preparing his great Commentary, is confirmed by other evidence. His seclusion was more uninterrupted than ever, and his rapid movements in his room, from window to window and backwards and forwards over the floor, which were in plain view of the street, excited much attention and remark. What could it mean? Was the professor taking exercise? or was it only one of his freaks of fancy—one of his comical vagaries in the way of diversion? But there was no concealment of his purposes. Dr. Gosman writes:

"When I first entered his study, he was busy with his great exegetical labours upon Isaiah; and every available spot seemed to be occupied with the works of the great authors, ancient and modern, upon that book. His thorough conscientiousness led him to verify every reference he made. I cannot vouch for the truth of the story prevalent among us students at the time, that some brother minister, looking around upon the massive folios lying open for reference, girdling the whole room, began to deplore the great misfortune which the learned professor had suffered, in having so many valuable books wetted and damaged, but can easily believe it true." *

The Cappadocian Society changed greatly in its character in after years, being reduced to a mere club of children who sat round Dr. Alexander's green-morocco table, and talked nonsense with him and for him. Its sessions seemed to afford him much refreshment, and his little scholars not a little merriment. He was one of the busiest of biographers. He made it a point to write the life of each member, and loved to make odd puns on each name. The boys and girls he seated upon his settee, contenting himself with a hard-backed chair. He used to tell me a boy could not study in an easy-chair, or in a lounging position; that it was useless to try; that it was well if the chair was a little rough and uncomfortable, for it then acted as a spur to industry. He seemed to be in earnest when he said this, though he may have been in fun. Some of his best stories were matured and told at these meetings. He spent much time in playfully satirizing the little follies and weaknesses of his pupils; but only for the purpose of correcting these bad habits in them, and in such a manner as to cause the blooming creatures to love him all the more.

At one time he had a favourite seat under two large willows, on the east side of his father's house, which he called Piccadilly; and he would take his little playfellows with him there,

* This account is literally true.

and sometimes read, and sometimes puzzle them with dark sayings, and tell them stories, and make fun for them in various ways. He had a door cut in the wall communicating with this spot. A Baltimore oriole had its nest in one of these trees, and he and the bird picked up quite an acquaintance, and he became really fond of it. Either the same or another oriole frequented the spot for several successive summers. Another of his resorts had been "the mound" at the Breckinridge House. The spacious yard there had enabled him to take more exercise than he was wont to do elsewhere. There were children, too, on every side of him. His brother's return to Princeton subsequently threw him once more among the former scenes, but the faces that had then beamed on him were gone,

> "And the names he loved to hear
> Had been carved, for many a year,
> On the tomb."

There are no journals of this year. In their absence, the following letter from Mr. Alexander to his eldest brother may give an insight into his thoughts, now that he was just on the eve of publishing.

"PRINCETON, February 10th, 1846.

"MY DEAR BROTHER:

"In my Introduction to Isaiah, with which I am now busied, I wish to correct the use of Lowth's theory of Hebrew poetry, by showing that the peculiarities which he insists upon exist, to some extent, in the animated prose of all languages. You can help me in this by getting down the names of a few writers, ancient and modern, in whom you think there is the nearest approach to the Hebrew manner. A welcome addition (if you could make it without search or labour), would be that of a few *examples* of parallelism and strophical arrangement in prose. Of the last, I have as yet no examples, except those furnished by the French preachers, when they end a number of successive paragraphs with a text, as a kind of burden or refrain. * *

Yours,

J. A. ALEXANDER."

About the middle of the month, Mr. Alexander was refreshed by a visit from his brother James, who had run down from New York. These meetings of the brothers, after absence, were marked by all the warmth of a friendship that was not susceptible of decrease or change, and all the unaffected carelessness of an intercourse that was restrained by none of the conventional formalities and restrictions. When the New York pastor was able to slip away from his visiting list, and his study in White Street, to the pleasures, not found elsewhere, of a night under his father's roof, his spirits rose, his merry face beamed, and his sonorous voice rang from cellar to tile. Every one at his father's experienced something of the same glow. The old people were in a glee, and the two brothers who had been separated often, became as hilarious as if they had drunk wine; though they had taken nothing but water.

The following pleasant letter to his brother shows that he was just about to print his Isaiah. It seems the celebrated "Introduction" to this volume was not the offspring of painless idleness:

"February 24th, 1846.

"My Dear Brother:

"I have bound myself to bring out a volume of Isaiah in a few weeks, and am still over head and ears in my "Introduction," which has cost me an amount of labor out of all proportion to its length and value. I can keep myself at work only by giving up every thing else. As to leanness (metaphorical of course), I am a skeleton to you, who always can do more the more you have to do, and do it better.

I am on the point of printing my "Introduction," with running titles in the lateral margin, after the old fashion still retained by Bancroft and Prescott. This is intended partly to save room, and avoid the common American method of enumerated sections; partly to gratify a typographical penchant of my own. If you think it unadvisable for any reason, I should be thankful for a hint to that effect.

Yours truly,

J. A. A."

The volume on the earlier prophecies of Isaiah was now ready for the public; having gone from the author's hands into those of the printer. It was awaited with much anxiety, especially by the city pastor.

On the 24th of March, Dr. James Alexander tells Dr. Hall that "Addison's first volume [Isaiah] is all 'in hands' and daily expected." * And on the 8th of April he writes, "I this day corrected the title-page of Addison's book." Very soon after this, the portly book was given to the public. It was issued from the press of Wiley & Putnam. Its appearance had been delayed by various causes, and especially by its author's growing sense of the difficulty of the undertaking, and of his own incapacity to do it justice, together with a natural reluctance to confess how little after all had been accomplished. † The idea and plan of this work struck his mind about the year 1835, and he at once set about the collection of his materials. During the next few years, it was wholly, and some parts of it repeatedly, reduced to writing. About the year 1842, he found the difficulties of the undertaking so great that he laid the work aside, determining to publish first upon the minor prophets; and did actually prepare a commentary upon Obadiah, and gathered materials for the remainder of the task. In 1843, he again took up the Isaiah, and worked upon it steadily until it was completed. From this statement, meagre as it is, the reader can form a pretty correct notion of the nature and extent of his studies, during the years in which this work was in progress. "Often," says his brother Samuel, "have I seen him with from ten to twenty volumes open before him, which he consulted, one after another, in order to discover the views of different writers on the particular passage under consideration; and so remarkable was his memory, that when he began to write, he had no occasion to refer to these authors, but would, seriatim, give their opinions and answer them *currente calamo.*"

Speaking of his memory, the same brother assures me that Mr. Alexander could announce the Christian name and middle letter of every one of the old graduates of the Seminary, if only the surname were given him.

I have known him to do something perhaps as surprising as even that. He has submitted jocularly to my examination,

* Fam. Letters, Vol. II. p. 49. † See his Preface p. vii.

and told me without hesitation where he was, and what he was doing, on any day of any year I chose to name. This was when I was a boy, and one of his private pupils. He spoke on the instant; except in a few cases, when he would say, "Let me see!" and would make a pause, but never a very long one. My impression is, that he restricted the examination to certain particular years (including his first journey in Europe); but am not quite sure that there was any restriction at all. I have no recollection that he ever made a mistake. He would also consent to be catechized about the kings and queens of ancient or modern Europe, having previously familiarized himself with certain lists or tables of his own construction. He would usually (perhaps invariably) have it in his power to tell the name of the king or sovereign, together with the exact dates of his birth and death, or, perhaps, of his coronation and chief exploits. This used to fill me with wonder; but it was not more strange than other feats of his of the same kind. He would examine his class in the Seminary on the minutest details of Greek and Hebrew scholarship, with a rapidity and cleanness of finish that put one in mind of the machinery in a pin-or-needle factory. No one was ever known to trip him But the grandest triumph of his memory was the ease and perfection with which it grasped all the extant comments on Isaiah. I have heard him say, repeatedly, and in the most natural and modest way, that he had a remarkable faculty for "remembering *trains of thought.*" Little did I know, at the time, that it was a part of his meaning that he could sweep thirty or forty volumes with his eye, and then reproduce the gist of them, without need of further reference, and without danger of confusion or mistake. While on his sick bed he told a friend that he had the whole book of Matthew constantly spread out before his mind. He has told me he often carried a sermon in this way, and that he has recovered the whole train of ideas without omitting a sentence, though without care or wish to reproduce the very words. He was a prodigy of exactness in his recollection of dates: though he showed his wisdom by undervaluing the gift in others. He used to say that the essential thing was relative not absolute chronology; and that history might be written intelligibly in a descriptive way, without a particular date being given. He, however, greatly vexed the souls of the feeble-minded in the Seminary, with the innumerable "periodologies" of the German historiographers.

Another instance of his power of memory occurs to me as I write. It was his invariable exactness in hitting the right word, in his lectures, and especially in his prayers, and in his more elaborate stories. His lectures were, of course, carefully thought out, and no doubt many of the important sentences were in his mind when he went into the class-room; but his prayers in the family circle were offered twice in the day, and were indefinitely varied as to the language, which must have been, in large part, the prompting of the occasion. Yet any one of them might have been stereotyped at once. This consummate knowledge and choice of the English vocables implied a faculty of recollection of the most tenacious grasp and the utmost readiness.

One of his students writes:

"The minute accuracy of his memory, extending to the smallest diversity of punctuation or accent in different editions, contrasted in a remarkable manner with his grand comprehensive views, and his bold, sweeping, but philosophic generalizations. His statement threw a broad, strong light over the whole subject; and then every obscure or doubtful point was placed in the focus of a powerful lens, which revealed every line, and detected every flaw, even the slightest or the finest. Not unfrequently he held the book unopened, and would conduct the entire examination with his eyes closed. When, in the rapid mode of his questioning, he would pass from student to student, and to the different parts of the lesson, it was truly astonishing how he would prompt and correct, from memory, the hesitation and blunders of those who were intently looking upon the page, and on the alert to keep pace with him. This prompt and rapid method possessed the advantage of securing the attention, and exciting to constant activity the faculties of some, while it served to confuse and embarrass the minds of the slower and more diffident."

When I was a boy, he used to say to me unexpectedly in the midst of other conversation, "Now I am going to talk without thinking!" and would proceed incontinently to pour out the most harmonious periods that contained not one syllable of sense. I was overwhelmed with torrents of strange words and incongruous images. He would then suddenly break out laughing, as if to himself; having probably begun to think again. He seemed to have the power of suspending his reason and giving a free rein to his fancy and memory. These *tours de force* which I witnessed in my childhood, have convinced me that he could produce such pieces as the "Fandango of Osiris" almost automatically.

Mr. Alexander committed to memory, with ease, entire books of the Hebrew and English Bibles, and if he had set himself to the task, I do not doubt in the least that he could have committed the whole of either. This verbal mastery of the original Scriptures has been thought wonderful in the case of eminent learned Jews. Several ancients and moderns have got the poems of Homer by heart. A Roman priest,* it is said, could begin at a designated line of one of the Italian poets and recite a hundred lines, backwards or forwards according to the caprice of his listener. There is a gentleman connected with one of the Chinese missions, who can do something of this sort with several of the Latin classics. Dugald Stewart somewhere tells the story of a French marquis, who made a hand-book of France from recollection, describing every chateau in the kingdom. There is a little uncertainty hanging over the fact in some of these and the like cases. There are some things, however, of this nature which are incontestable. When Macaulay was caught tripping in a line of the "Paradise Lost," Prescott says, he came back a few days after with a book in his hand and the light of triumph in his eye: "I do not think," quoth the historian, "that you will catch me tripping in the *Paradise* again;" and Prescott says, they did not.† The Cardinal Mezzofanti

* See Life of Mezzofanti. † See Life of Prescott, by Ticknor.

had an all but miraculous remembrance of entire dictionaries and grammars.*

* Professor John S. Hart has kindly permitted me to see the advance sheets of his work[1] entitled "The Schoolroom," from which I select the following extract. The anecdote about Mr. Alexander I had heard before, and Dr. Hodge vouches substantially for it, in his reminiscences of his departed colleague:

"A distinction is to be made between memory as a power of the mind and the remembrance of particular facts. One or two examples will illustrate this difference. The late Dr. Addison Alexander, of the Theological Seminary at Princeton, had memory as an intellectual power to a degree almost marvellous. The following instance may be cited. On one occasion, a large class of forty or fifty were to be matriculated in the Seminary, in the presence of the Faculty. The ceremony of matriculation was very simple. The professors and the new students being all assembled, in a large hall, each student in turn presented himself before the professors, had his credentials examined by them, and if the same proved satisfactory, entered his name in full, and his residence, in the register. When the matriculation was complete, and the students had retired, there was some bantering among the professors as to which of them should take the register home and prepare from it an alphabetical roll—a work always considered rather tedious and irksome. After a little hesitation, Dr. Alexander said, "There is no need of taking the register home; I will make the roll for you;" and, taking a sheet of paper, at once, from memory, without referring to the register, and merely from having heard the names as they were recorded, proceeded to make out the roll, giving the names in full, and giving them in their alphabetical order. This was a prodigious feat of pure memory; for in order to make the alphabetical arrangement in his mind, before committing it to paper, he must have had the entire mass of names present in his mind by a single act of the will. Some of the wonderful games of chess performed by Paul Morphy are dependent in part upon a similar power of memory, by which the player is enabled to keep present in his mind, without seeing the board, a long series of complicated evolutions, past as well as prospective and possible. The same is true of every great military strategist.

"In all these cases, there is an act of pure memory; a direct and positive power of summoning into the mind its past experiences, such as can only take place where, either by natural gift or by special training, the memory as a faculty of the mind is in a high state of vigour. But there are other cases, in which a man is enabled to recall a great number of particular facts by a

[1] "The Schoolroom; or, Chapters on the Philosophy of Education." By John S. Hart, LL.D., Principal of New Jersey State Normal School. Eldredge & Brother, 17 & 19 South Sixth Street, Philadelphia, Pa. pp. 59, 60.

I have not the data to go upon in the case of Mr. Alexander, which would authorize me to say he could do any of the particular things just described, that have been so much lauded in others; nor would I venture to say he was equal to any one of the great prodigies of memory of whom we read accredited accounts; but it is within bounds to allege, that his mind was one of this rare and surprising class. It must be considered, how little time he had for efforts of this character; and how opposed he was to every kind of pedantry and vain show. He committed nothing to memory for the mere sake of the feat; but he had committed to momory the inflections, and syntax, and multitudes of the words and phrases, of certainly twenty-four languages without counting English. He had his past life always lying before him in a bird's-eye view, which included each separate day for months and years together. He could recite whole catalogues of names, without omitting an initial; he could repeat the express words of a lengthened conversation, days after it had taken place, and even the disconnected and broken sentences he had heard in a night-journey in the cars; he could read a heavy volume in a strange tongue, and then sit down and give a digest of every chapter, and almost every paragraph; and he could write voluminously for hours, and then repeat blindfold what he had written. "He would," says Dr. Jones, of Bridgton "at the opening of a new session, call the roll of a class comprehending, it may be, forty or fifty new students, and from that day onward, each name and face was known to him." A gentleman who has favoured me with many reminiscences offers the following apology for his own seeming extravagance:

"To one not knowing Dr. Alexander as I did, my estimate of him may seem extravagant, and I should suspect myself of bias, did I not remember that far better judges than myself rate him quite as high as

---

species of artifice or trick, which does not imply any special mental power, and the study of which does not tend, in any marked degree, to develop such power."

I have done; and that it was precisely the ripest scholars, and the choicest minds among his students, who carried away from the Seminary, and who have since retained, the strongest impression of his truly extraordinary powers; and who will ever regard him as unrivalled in his generation, in the original strength and compass of his mind, and in the variety, value, and thoroughness of his acquirements."

The following letter is to his brother James, and was intended to accompany, or rather succeed, a presentation copy of the new work:

"PRINCETON, May 11th, 1846.

"MY DEAR BROTHER:

"I judge from the complaisance of your remarks, that H. did not forget to present you with a copy of Isaiah 'from the author.' Will you urge him to send me on two copies by the first private hand, and, if possible, this week. I wish to make a sacrifice of one or two copies to foreign missions, and at the same time discharge an old debt by acknowledging several presents of books from former pupils now 'in the field.' My only creditors in this way are, Joseph Owen, John E. Freeman, and Walter M. Lowrie—the last on a very small scale; the first to the amount of several valuable works; and the second by several valuable remittances, including a very curious copy of the Koran, which I think you have inspected. I overlook the smallness of Lowrie's claim, in consideration of his superior ability to profit by the book, and make it useful.

"Yours,

"J. A. A."

He kept up his old interest in little girls, and taught them as well as boys. One of his favourite topics with them was French; another was history, especially as related to geography and chronology, and to the study of human character and motives. He made his lessons easy and delightful, and mingled them with free conversation and stories. There are many who recur to these hours spent with the terrible professor, with a sense of grateful obligation.

A lady of Virginia who enjoyed his instructions for a time, though at a later period, and who has been fortunate in her intellectual guides, has told me that when teaching her history and chronology he never made use of a text-book, and displayed that thorough acquaintance with the whole subject which his reputation for learning might, indeed, have led her to expect, but which, notwithstanding, could not fail to strike one with astonishment and admiration. She goes on to say:

"He gave these lessons during the few hours of leisure left from other engagements and studies; and yet never was he at a loss, among the longest lists of kings and emperors, either for a name or a date. By this *living* treatment of the subject, where the teacher acted as a substitute for the silent book—and more than a substitute (for he was a speaking compendium of many books), even the dry bones of chronology assumed shapely and attractive forms; so that his pupil made easy and pleasurable progress.

"What tended still further to relieve the monotony of recitation, was the occasional outburst of that wonderful flow of humour which so distinguished him. This was the natural rebound and relief of that severe intellectual tension demanded by a studious and thoughtful life. The effect was necessarily heightened by the striking contrast such pleasantries presented to his well-known attainments and profound learning."

The work on the earlier Prophecies of Isaiah was published early in May. If not the noblest product of his genius, it is certainly the most imposing monument to his industry. It is not and was not designed to be a popular commentary, but an original and exhaustive exhibition of the bare sense of the prophet, and a confutation of the sciolists who have marred that sense or obscured it.

It does not come within the scope of these personal memoirs to attempt any elaborate critique upon the Isaiah. It is everywhere conceded to be one of the most important contributions, if not the one most important contribution, to the study of the Hebrew prophets and especially of the son of Amoz, that has been made since the days of Vitringa. This is certainly the opinion of some in Scotland, France, and America; and there are many who place this work far above all others on this subject, not excepting that of Calvin. Dr. Alexander's work is confessedly superior to the Geneva Reformer's on the score of verbal exegesis and the visible display of ancient and modern learning, while it is deemed at least equal to it on the score of logical coherence. *La Réformation*, the organ and vehicle of some of the finest continental scholarship, noticed its first appearance in terms of exalted encomium, and testified that its author had shown himself master of the entire German literature of his subject.* Dr. Eadie, his eminent British editor, in a most able introduction to the volume (in which every previous and sound writer on Isaiah receives what was fitting in the way of measured praise), places Dr. Addison Alexander, of Princeton, above them all, not even excepting Vitringa and Calvin: though Dr. Eadie is exceedingly cautious and discriminating in his statements. In Germany, and among the Jews, Alexander on Isaiah is admired wherever known. Dr. Schaff tells me it is the fate of all modern commentaries to be little known in Germany unless exhibited in a German dress.

His correspondence, never copious, may now furnish us a few hints. The subjoined letter to Dr. Hall is on the usual topic of "ministerial supplies." He closes with a serio-comic reference to his Isaiah, about which his friend was already fully informed:

* "M. de Lengerke, professeur à Königsberg, auteur d'un commentaire sur Daniel, a publié, en deux volumes, une traduction des Psaumes avec un commentaire. C'est ici le lieu de mentionner aussi une explication des trente-neuf premiers chapitres d'Esaïe par Alexander, professeur de théologie à Princeton, aux Etats-Unis. Ce fruit de l'érudition américaine nous a paru remarquable, entre autres par la connaissance complète de la littérature allemande sur Esaïe, dont l'auteur fait preuve, soit dans le commentaire même, soit dans l'introduction où il cite et apprécie tous ses prédécesseurs. Otto de Gerlach a donne le second volume de ses notes sur l'Ancien Testament, qui comprennent maintenant tous les livres historiques. Winer a commencé une nouvelle édition de son dictionnaire biblique.

"Nous avons enfin à annoncer les premières livraisons d'une dogmatique catholique de J. Kuhn, qui aura quatre volumes. La troisième partie de l'Esquisse d'un système de philosophie de J.-H. Fichte est une théologie spéculative et appartient à la philosophie de la religion."—*La Réformation*, 1847.

"PRINCETON, April 17, 1846.

"MY DEAR SIR:

"The consummation which you so devoutly wish for, in your own case, has been virtually realized in mine: that is to say, my call to the ministry, at least in the foreign field, has expired, or been suspended until after the third Thursday of May instant. But in consideration of your torpor, both intestinal and cerebral, I think I may venture to resume my functions as a bishop *in partibus infidelium pro hâc vice* (how hard it is to stop writing Latin when we begin); I will therefore undertake to fill your pulpit on the day proposed, provided you allow me the right to send a substitute, should I find myself hard pushed, or even morally unable to attend in person. To this indispensable condition I shall understand you to assent, unless I hear from you again; at the same time, I may add, for your encouragement, that my present intention is to come myself, and that if I send a substitute, it shall be the oldest I can get; for I know, with sorrow, your unamiable prejudice against the young and rising generation, and your culpable backwardness in giving them an opportunity to try their gifts. If anything should happen to remove the necessity of my assistance (such as the arrival of a Free-Church minister, a seaman's chaplain, or the like), I shall be very far from counting it a slight, to be relieved from my engagement until better times. It will, no doubt, give you pleasure to learn that I have made up my mind to prepare a work upon Isaiah, for which I have been long engaged in gathering materials. I hope to go to press within a month; any aid in the way of subscriptions or donations will be thankfully received; any minister obtaining ten subscribers will be entitled to a copy at half-price—all communications post-paid.

"Very truly yours,

"J. A. ALEXANDER, D.D. F.A. PS. FGS. M. C."

CHAPTER XXI.

THE month of June was filled with the exciting intelligence of the great battles in Mexico that had been fought in May under Taylor. Mr. Alexander devoured all the despatches, and knew the geographical and strategical bearings of every one of the military positions. The elder brother's diaries are filled with excerpts from the daily papers containing the despatches.

The commentator now threw himself with all his heart and soul into the work of preparing a second volume of his Isaiah for the press. He was now writing on the later Prophecies. For this purpose he characteristically sought the town. He went there for the sights and the noise. He had also another reason which is thus referred to by his brother, in a letter of July 22: "Addison is in my place in New York, but for no reason but that he may have more perfect seclusion in order to complete his work. He has finished to the end of the 57th chapter, since the first volume was published. He is almost overwhelmed by it, and I do not wonder that he escapes all engagements when he can." * It was a Herculean task, but the author had great powers and an indomitable desire. Sometimes his purpose flagged; but he went on, and at length wrote his last page. There were moments of wavering, when this man upon the mountain-top needed to have his hands upheld by others, but, in the final issue, the victory over all difficulties was achieved, and the Amalek of German infidelity was overcome. It was an era in the history of American interpretation. The heaviest part of his toil had been gone over already in Princeton.

* Fam. Let. Vol. II. p. 55.

The commentary was flowing rapidly from his pen. He was indeed writing under great difficulties. Though by the almanac the summer was now over, the weather was yet nearly, or quite, as oppressive as in July. There was, however, a perceptible sea-breeze towards evening; gushes of delicious coolness floating inland from the Battery at fitful intervals, and reaching as far as Chambers street, where the absorbed student had been sitting hour by hour, denuded often of his upper vestment, regardless of the stifling heat, through a number of weary days, or drinking in the whiffs of gracious oxygen, and crowding all his enormous energies into the one task of putting the last ink on his Isaiah. Fortunately the nights were comfortable while he had been writing at this rate of speed. Lope de Vega, Balzac, or G. P. R. James could hardly fill a page in shorter time. His hand moved incessantly over the paper, and the wet sheets (as had happened in the case of Scott and Wilson) often dropped like sibylline leaves at his feet, and covered a large space on the floor. The greater part of the work had been done in the noisy solitude of a hotel far 'down-town.' The volume was made from title-page to index during this one vacation. Now his brother is able to announce to Mr. Hall, "Addison has finished his second volume, including a large introduction."

I give below an interesting letter to his mother:

"83 White St., New York, July 27, 1846.

"My Dear Mother:

"I have just got through the second Sunday very comfortably; having preached again twice, and dined again at Mr. Field's, in Chambers street. There was a sudden and violent shower in the afternoon, just at the hour of service, which, as Peter Taarlsen says, 'made us tinner.' I suppose he meant the audience, for I grieve to say, that no such effect was produced upon the preacher. The time passes here like a dream. I write all day; greatly aided by the noise and letting nobody into the room, even when they get into the house. Except from this account a visit from John Hall, who came into the study just as if he had stepped out an hour before. I must also except a visit from our Hanoverian friend who dined with you last winter. He is still more 'uncouraged,' or rather, he is starving. Going out in the evening is delightful, and refreshes me completely. I see nothing disagreeable here, even at this season, but the stench; and that I do not see but merely smell. I have not suffered in the least from heat. I know all the children in the neighbourhood by sight, but am not 'personally acquainted,' as old Mr. —— says, when he introduces me to the elders and deacons. I should like to have my old summer coat brought on for me to wear in the house, as the Roman toga which James lent me, trips up my heels when I go up and down stairs. I have finished chapter fifty-nine, and have but seven more to do. With the leave of Providence, I mean to see the end of it before I leave New York. In the meantime, honoured madam, I rémain as ever,

"Your loving Son,

"J. A. ALEXANDER."

Once more his success was received with expressions of praise and satisfaction from all quarters of the camp of Israel.

These were days of enormous intellectual production; and notwithstanding his labours on Isaiah, he did not neglect his class duties, or his sermons, or his new foreign languages, or his excursions among the bookshelves. He still loved to open the "Green Book" (but in Arabic), Aben Ezra, and the Targum of Onkelos, or of Jonathan; the histories of Mariana and Thiers; and the great Latin and Greek authors. He stamped his image and superscription upon his classes in the old imperial way.

The estimate which follows is from the hand of one* whose general cultivation, and whose competency as a translator from the German, were perceived and recognized by Mr. Alexander. The relations between them were those merely which subsist between teacher and pupil. It will be noticed, however, that the writer testifies with great cordiality to his preceptor's companionable qualities.

"He will always be to me an object of admiration. With his celi-

* The late Rev. Edward L. Yeomans, D.D. of Orange, N. J. the translator from Kurtz & Schaff.

bate, solitary ways, he was so communicative and social; with his independence and severity of manner, he was so genial; with his abhorrence of uniformity—a kind of perpetual mental discontent, and what his students often felt as indecision in his views, or non-committal; he was still so uniform, reliable, and true; and he could keep the routine of the class-room so brimful and dripping with the current of information and thought, as fresh in substance as it was monotonous in manner and flow; that he will, I suspect, always be the most sharply marked character of all the famous ones of his time, in the memory of Princeton students; and he will fall behind none in their affection.

"He was a strange combination of the solitary and the genial, even in the lecture-room. Often his manner, in entering the room, delivering his lecture, and going out, was automatic; and would not suggest the presence of an audience. He seemed to see no one. His call to prayer, as soon as he reached the desk, waited for no one. He lectured looking on a book and turning the leaves without reading; with rapid, monotonous utterance, regardless of hurrying pens and aching fingers and half-caught sentences below. And he stopped so short at the end of the chapter or the hour, and so unceremoniously left, that we sometimes did not know he was done till we raised our heads from our greedy notes, and saw him already out of the door."

This picture is as true as it is graphic.

The impression made upon this intelligent hearer, and fastidious critic, by his preaching, and which is conveyed to the reader in the paragraph now about to be given, one should say was derived principally from his efforts in the seminary chapel; which were commonly different in almost every respect from those which so often enchanted intellectual audiences in the great towns. Sometimes Dr. Addison Alexander spoke exactly in the way here described. At other times there was less, indeed scarcely any, animation or visible unction. But there were times when the whole force of his genius and fiery emotion broke upon his selectest auditories like a whirlwind, and drove them before him like chaff upon a threshing floor. His grandest exhibitions of this character were in Philadelphia. There he often bound men hand and foot and carried them whither they would not. "Even in the pulpit the same singular combination appeared. His body was stationary, his voice was hardly modulated, his gesture not much more than a see-saw of the right arm, his features were without play; yet body, voice, arm, and face were so full of flowing, impetuous life and real *unction*, that he was always as captivating and eloquent in his manner of preaching as he was fertile, discerning, and brilliant in matter and style."

He made a deep mark in Brooklyn also, a city which has been famous for its preachers. Fortunately I have a witness here whose word will go far with the reader. It should seem from his account that the Brooklyn experiences of Mr. Alexander were almost Philadelphia over again.

"Many remember," says Prof. Jacobus, "how, in Brooklyn, his sermons held vast audiences spell-bound under the magic of his eloquence. Such a devout afflatus, such fervour and glow of expression and intonation — with such vigour of thought and mastery of appeal! as in his discourses, 'Remember Lot's wife;' "The sacrifices of God are a broken spirit;' 'It doth not yet appear what we shall be.'"

The Rev. Dr. William H. Ruffner, of Virginia, writes:

"I heard him preach many times. Twice only I thought him dull. His expositions at Queenston were wonderfully rich, clear, and comprehensive. But generally the effect of his preaching on me was almost overwhelming. When he would begin to rise in his *crescendo* passages, I would feel as if I had been put in connection with a galvanic battery, and that the stream was getting heavier every moment, and, if there was not a speedy change, I should be thrown over by the power of the charge. Awe and terror, admiration and intellectual delight, a sense of the beautiful, the true, the noble, the triumphant, and feelings of remorse and self-abnegation, were common effects on my mind under his preaching. The sermons that I remember as impressing me most were on the texts, 'He hath not dealt so with any nation;' 'The rich and the poor meet together, &c.' 'Come, for all things are now ready;' 'He that is greatest among you shall be your servant;' 'Behold the Lamb of God.' The latter I heard twice. The first time in the Presbyterian Church in Princeton to a thin audience on a rainy evening; and whilst I felt that it was a powerful discourse, I did not get the full impression of it until I heard it in Lexington, when I saw as I had not seen before the profound philosophy running through it; and toward the last, when he got to shouting the words, 'Behold, behold,' among the rattling dice and glasses of the gambling room, and into the dull ears of the dying reprobate, I felt, and I think the whole audience felt, much as if an angel had sounded a blast from the pulpit."

On the 23d of November, the elder brother writes of the younger: "Two of the most learned German Jews (from Rotterdam) are studying Addison's Isaiah." *

It would appear from the following letter of the commentator himself, that his brother had mentioned the thing to him too, for in the letter he refers with a mixture of pleasure and fear to the "microscopic criticism" of "the Judaic friends" of his correspondent.

It is a letter of unusual learned interest. In it he asks for the best things of Villemain and Guizot.

"November 28th, 1846.

"MY DEAR BROTHER:

"I am glad you have sent an article so massive, timely, and readable, to lead off the new year with. I wish you would do the same with Bush, Woods, and Pond. I am slower than ever to begin my contributions, as I am making, pretty steadily, three lectures a week, besides occasional sermons. I am carrying on three parallel courses—one on Biblical history, one on Biblical criticism, and one on Biblical antiquities. I have now returned to my historical vomit, and should like to consult you on the ways and means of making Dogmengeschichte a distinct part of our course; or rather, on the previous question, whether it is worth while to attempt it. I suspect that my exegetical labours will be limited to correcting and improving my Isaiah. I am flattered by the notice of your Judaic friends, but dread their microscopic criticism. I am acquainted with Luretto only through his French notes on Isaiah, prefixed to the abridged edition of Rosenmüller's Scholia. These are noticed in my Introduction, and repeatedly cited in the Commentary. I am rather afraid than desirous of enlarging my Jesian apparatus, and therefore gratefully decline the offer

* Fam. Let. Vol. II. p. 59.

of your ישאל בכי . Turner has agreed to correct the second volume. Can I get the best things of Villemain and Guizot, without sending to France? I wish you could find out whether the Danes and Swedes have any standard national historians—acknowledged classics, like Guicciardini and Mariana. Such books, with a native dictionary of each language, would content me. I think of confining myself very much to history in all the languages I know.

"My evening recreations are, at present, Thucydides (with Arnold and Blomfield), Eichorn's History of Literature and Meier's Dogmengeschichte. I am much pleased with Meier, who alone has hit upon what I consider a satisfactory method. I will let you have it when you are done with Kleiforth and Schleiermacher. My private pupil enters, and I find it necessary to conclude sans façon.

"Yours ever,

"J. A. A."

Was this great foe of the rational and empirical criticism himself a mere critic, of a higher and safer order? or was he an intellectual originator as well? It is admitted that his mind was fitted for analysis and classification; was it also capable of generalizing or of inventing? These questions have been discussed by many of his admirers, and commonly answered in the affirmative. There are some, however, who incline to the negative of this opinion.

A pupil whose recollections date back to these days, after many pages of discriminating panegyric, expresses himself as follows:

"I do not think his mind was, strictly speaking, of the philosophical and speculative cast, nor of any unusual powers of combination and construction. It was acquisitive and critical, and it was both these in an eminent degree, and in a truly noble style.

"He constructed no theories or system, even in the departments of instruction of which he successively had charge, nor in the department of exegesis in which he published. But in all these branches of learning, he had at once a complete knowledge and a genuine mastery of his field. His faculties of acquisition, retention, and utilizing, were of the most remarkable. They were anything but mechanical. They had the nobilitv of genius. Even such a book as his larger Isaiah, with its massive aggregation of all extant exegetical opinions, could not be called either a *catena* or an eclectic compilation. It has its unity and marked individuality, and standard value of the highest rank. His later commentaries, less learned in their form, let the independence and mastery of his own mind stand out. And then, his critical faculty was of the very soundest kind, combining the strongest natural good sense with the firmest Christian faith. His departments lay among those in which modern criticism and science have been most plausible and prolific in their attacks on the foundations of evangelical orthodoxy; and his broad, rational, and appreciative mind can never be charged with insensibility to the force of those assaults. Yet he never seemed for a moment to feel loosened by them, at any point, from the established views of orthodox Christendom. He *shed*, like a rock, the deluge of rationalistic criticism; and the imperviousness was not that of obstinacy, nor of ignorance, nor of servility to traditional opinion, but of sound sense, complete knowledge, intellectual freedom, and spiritual faith. And if he seemed to lack the gift of construction and organization in proportion to his learning and his faculty for disposing of useless material, or to his critical despatch, it was because he felt the prevailing evangelical views themselves systematic enough.

"His *forte* was, I think, Biblical criticism; and in this, his qualifications as a teacher, as a guide to students, both by word and example, were extraordinary."

This strikingly fair critique demands a few words in the way of comment, which are accordingly offered; and with respectful diffidence, though not with hesitation. The views of the amiable and accomplished writer whose words have just been given are confessedly derived mostly from a distant inspection of his preceptor's class-labours, and his pulpit performances in the chapel, and from his published works. A closer acquaintance with the man in private would undoubtedly have modified those views. The truth is, the writer of the analysis in question seems never to have known Dr. Alexander as he really was when he had cast off the shackles of the recitation-room and the printing-office. He says in another place, "My personal intercourse with Dr. Alexander was so slight that it yields nothing of special interest except in regard to my own plans and labours, particularly in the matter of German translation." He saw him in his study, and enjoyed the charm of his society; but it was only as a student or as a transient visitor at Princeton. He has seen but one side of the great polygon. He is like the knight who swore the shield was of gold, and not of silver.

The contour of Dr. Alexander's abilities, so far as this acute thinker ever had an opportunity of knowing them, could not well have been more accurately or beautifully drawn. He, however, gives but a moiety of the truth. In proof of this, I point with the utmost confidence to the cheerful testimonies of those who were not only, like the present witness, good judges of character, but also Dr. Alexander's intimate personal companions and friends, and some of them his life-long coevals. It is remarkable that, while some of these were struck with the predominance in his mind of the intellectual faculties, popularly so styled, over the fancy, or the gift of emotional eloquence, others were impressed just the other way. But many accounts agree that the most extraordinary thing about this truly extraordinary man was, the remarkable uniform or equal development of *all* his powers. Even his printed sermons have seemed to other critics to show constructive genius; high powers of "combination" and "organization;" call it by what name you will.

By construction I understand *putting together;* which is the opposite of taking to pieces. In this use of the terms, Dr. Alexander was as great in construction as in demolition or resolution. He not only pulled down, but he built up. His grandest sermons have been more than once compared to a Gothic cathedral. The rise and fall of the voice in delivery had much to do with this impression. His sermon on "The Broken Heart," for instance, not only shows the interior of a temple, but *was* the interior of a temple. His sermon on "The City with Foundations," whatever may be its merits or its defects, was a gorgeous piece of richly imaginative painting.

But if, when it is said he was not so great in construction as in analysis, it is meant he has constructed no *theory* or *sys-*

tem, of value commensurate with the results of his merely analytical labours, this may be granted; but it is equally true that, like Bacon, he has dejected the materials for many theories and systems of the highest value, and lavished on every hand the principles which have made their construction easy. This his critic would joyfully assent to. It must not be forgotten, however, how many new and important interpretations of Scripture we owe to him; some of which are of the broadest sweep, and others, though of less scope, are yet of the most sterling value. He has, as it seems to many of us, given us the true theory of Matthew, of Mark, and of the Acts. This, it is thought, was never thoroughly accomplished before. He has, we think, for the first time brought out the true meaning of the Sermon on the Mountain. This is, in the opinion of some, his crowning work as an exegete. He is the originator of the *complex* theory of the Servant of Jehovah in Isaiah, which is now getting to be the accepted view beyond the Atlantic, and, I am told, is likely to prevail among all evangelical scholars. He has, too, in various places and ways shed a new charm and glory over the whole Bible.

But it was in his poetry, his tales, his extravaganzas, his children's books, his magazine articles, some of his letters, and much of his unrestrained and hilarious conversation, or rather table-talk, that Dr. Addison Alexander evinced that he had constructive talents of a high order and of a very unusual degree of excellence. If his namesake Addison, if Swift, if Goldsmith, if Dickens, if De Foe, could be said to have constructive genius, then it seems to me that *he* had it too. Not in the same measure, it may be, but with as much certainty and on kindred evidence. If to write noble stanzas, each instinct with imagination and passion and full of rhythmic music, requires the effort of a constructive artist, then it must be conceded that the subject of this biography was a constructive artist, and on the same grounds that settle the claim of Ariosto or Byron.

It is unquestionable, too, that the name of Dr. Alexander is identified with no new system of divinity, metaphysics, or moral science. Men will not say in reference to him, Alexander's theology, or Alexander's philosophy; as they speak of Edwards's or Taylor's theology, or of Locke's, of Hamilton's, of Kant's, or of Hegel's philosophy. But it does not necessarily follow that he had no ability to construct systems. The true statement would appear to be not that Dr. Addison Alexander had no power to construct, but that he had a dislike for the thing to be constructed. This would, of course, involve a corresponding dislike for the labour of construction; and if he was incapable of anything, it was of working where his mind was not in a state of highly pleasurable excitement. For metaphysics or psychology, except when presenting their simplest outlines, or their most intelligible details, as in Reid or Brown, he had, like one* of the great systematising minds of this century, a certain degree of positive distaste. Nor did circumstances ever force him to conquer this feeling.

The fact referred to cannot be denied or explained away, that he made no new doctrines, but took the evangelical creeds and symbols as he found them; but this he did for the reason assigned by his able critic, viz. that the highest faculties for constructing creeds, if united to sound judgment, would not construct them where they were not needed, and where it was obvious that the most superb deviations from the truth are at last but superb error. I doubt not he could have filled the world with bad systems of theology as new and ingenious as they were false, had he so chosen. A considerable part of his fame arises out of the very fact that he did not do this. He holds on the even tenour of his way amidst all the aberrations of German neology through which he moved. This is one of his chief distinctions.

It is quite true, also, that his mind was not of the "philosophic," *i. e.* "speculative" order; if by *mind* be meant *turn* or *taste*, and not capacity. There is nothing to prove his mental incompetency to the highest philosophic tasks, except his re-

* Auguste Comte. See what is said of his "aversion to metaphysics." Mill's Examination of Hamilton. London, p. 13.

pugnance to this kind of mental labour, and his loathing of the forms of a γνῶσις falsely so called. If he had an incapacity for the toils of speculative inquiry, it was rather, I should fancy, in the heart than in the head; or, to use a figure borrowed from the Edwardean theology, it was a moral rather than a natural inability. He had no patience with nonsense and palpable absurdity. He entertained a supreme disgust for what was evidently and monstrously false and wrong. He abhorred the conclusions of the Gnostic and kindred heresies, and of the pantheistic German psychology; and hence neglected and, it may be, too much despised their elaborate processes of mystical or transcendental reasoning. But he took delight in reading, and comprehended with ease, the writings of the Scotch metaphysicians, and of the philosophic historians, and never wearied of any investigation which lay within the domain of what John Locke calls sound, roundabout sense.

Still it must be admitted that the cast of his mind* was

* Disposed as it was to variation, Mr. Alexander's judgment never fluctuated much on the subject of German transcendentalism. From the opinions expressed in a letter to his brother, J. W. Alexander, under date of Geneva, Aug. 14, 1833, during his first sojourn in Europe, I subjoin a few extracts. It will be noticed that his correspondent was hardly prepared to accept such sweeping conclusions:

"Having disposed of politics, Presbyterianism, psalmody, and sundries, I proceed to German philosophy. I am sorry that I have no light to throw upon your path. I have as yet 'caught none upon my wings,' though at the very gate of Eden, unless I except the sulphureous glimmerings of my poor friend ——, whose very light is darkness. I am sorry to say that the nearer I get to the transcendental Limbo, the stronger becomes my anti-metaphysical prejudice. My common sense is absolutely rampant; and threatens my anschauungsvermögen with extinction. So far as I have yet learned this wisdom, which is not from above, there is nothing in it that can satisfy the bedürfniss which you speak of. The aliment provided to appease that craving is the beautiful *mysticism* of revealed religion. There is one distinction which affects me strongly. The Bible shows us much to make us long for more. Beyond what is revealed there hangs a mystic veil, which recedes as we advance half hoping and half fearing that we shall never see all. This keeps the mind in healthful action, and will probably continue so to keep it, world without end. It is precisely for such progress that our constitution fits us; and in it lies our intellectual happiness. How different is the process of transcendental quackery!

not distinctively of the speculative or even reflective, but of the logical and suggestive kind. In this respect he differed no little from his venerable father, and even from his accomplished brother, both of whom, at their best moments, were never better pleased than when their minds were occupied in high converse with some one or other of the great thinkers who have gone down into the deep and the darkness of unaided human thought. Dr. Archibald Alexander in particular was himself a patient and successful investigator of the phenomena both of psychology and ethics; and the very last article written by Dr. James Alexander for the Repertory was an able reëxamination of the philosophy of the great Arnauld, with special reference to his doctrine of perception, which the review writer thought had been unjustly or inadequately treated of by Sir William Hamilton.

The late Dr. Hewitt, of Bridgeport, Connecticut, on hearing the particulars of his friend's last illness, and of his having written this article within a week, remarked that no one could any longer marvel at his being laid aside, for that the writing

---

Sin affects to rend the veil of truth, and impudently plants herself at the extreme of knowledge, pretending to uncover the foundation-stones of science, and to show us *all at once.* The man who believes this, is no longer capable of rational enjoyment. The majestic stride of intellect . . . . . . is lost forever, and the sublime development of truth in all its symmetry gives place to a huddle of abstractions. So far as sentiment and taste are at all concerned, the partial gleams of sunshine through the pages of the Bible are immeasurably better than the artificial lamp-light of oblivious metaphysics. View the brightest coruscation of the absolutest Ich that ever egotized in German, and how pale it looks beside this one ray from the φῶς ἀπρόσιτον which constitutes God's res[plendent words,] "In Thee is the fountain of life: IN THY LIGHT SHALL WE SEE LIGHT." I grow mystical myself, and perhaps absurd; but I trust you understand me. My dear brother, we are alike in [many things] and in as many differ; in order perhaps that we may bear each other's burdens. . . I have uttered the above *purana* not at all for your instruction or conviction; but I am alone, and want a vent for the crudest fancies, which would otherwise grow acid and impair or disturb my intellectual digestion. German philosophy has served as an emetic."

of that article in that time was enough to kill or craze more than one man in full strength of body.

I am far from being alone in this estimate of Dr. Alexander's artistic as well as scientific powers. Several of his old students have expressed opinions as to his splendid imaginative gifts, and the symmetry of his whole mind, which must be taken as *their* testimony, not mine. One of them writes as follows:

"His imagination was wonderful; and though nothing was out of proportion in his mind, if there was any one faculty that predominated over another, it was this: it was his wonderful imagination; using the term in its highest sense. What Hamilton calls the representative faculties, memory and imagination, were in him preëminent. Yet all the other faculties were in such due proportion, that his intellect was the most complete and symmetrical that I have ever known. I doubt whether, in this respect, the world has ever seen his superior." *

With Dr. Addison Alexander, analysis was but the bond-slave of synthesis. He was, *ex necessitate rei*, a miner or quarry-worker rather than a builder, and yet he expounded with wonderful clearness the true principles of building, and whenever permitted to carry his plans to completion, himself wrought or finished great structures. The old workman on the banks of the Nile was always busy upon small surfaces of stone, hewing, compacting, and polishing; but he thus became the architect of the Pyramids. The generalization of the man of science grows out of a vast induction of particulars. The law of gravitation involves a summary of the minutest phenomena of the universe.

It was on this principle that Dr. Alexander conducted his profound and searching investigations into the domain of Biblical truth, and the bordering territories and kingdoms. He began with particulars; but he never stopped with particulars, unless he was cut short in his process. In his sermons on texts from Isaiah, we see the method which is only indicated in his Commentary carried out approximately to its full ex-

* The Rev. Dr. Rice, of Mobile.

tent. The discourse on Isaiah, lv. 6, 7, well illustrates what I have just said. Every branch of the refined exegetical and analytical process enters into the ramifications of a noble, practical, impressive form of synthesis. The subject and the mode of treatment did not call for flights of imaginative eloquence, but where these seemed to be demanded they were not wanting.

Sometimes he leaves the analytical scaffolding behind him, and mounts up as with the wings of an eagle.

In the rough draught of a sermon,* as yet unpublished, but afterwards written out *in extenso*, on Matt. vi. 33, he thus gives vent to his vehement emotions, and to the thoughts which seem to be bubbling up in his soul. The handwriting, usually so round and plain, in this as in all similar cases becomes gradually more and more difficult to read, until it is almost undecypherable.

"To those who have sought the kingdom, and still seek it, first, i. e., in preference, I apply this text by way of consolation and encouragement:

"Brethren, we live in troublous times—we live in troublous times—in times of tempest and of earthquake. One volcano after another is extinguished, only to be followed by the outbreak of new craters. Fanaticism social and religious has laid hold upon the very corner-stones of church and state, and shaken them till even the vessels in the house of God have felt the shock, and trembled at the altar. Political changes are the order of the day. From beyond the water there are many hollow murmurs of approaching change. The ocean of society presages great events by its perturbed heavings. Old religions and old monarchies begin to nod. Many a crescent wanes, and many a crown grows dim; and many an ancient cedar in the forests of the old world bends and groans in premonition of its fall. And even we, who have no thrones to totter and no sceptres to be broken, bear our part in the convulsion.

"Now, when the foundations are thus out of course, what shall the righteous do?

"To the worldling, the prospect is disconsolate indeed; because he

* It was composed in 1838. Part of the conclusion forms the peroration to his sermon on 1 John iii. 2.

can see nothing but the ruins which surround him. But to the believer's eye, amidst these crumbling ruins there arise new columns more majestic and more beautiful than those of the Acropolis. And amidst arise to view thrones and palaces, and temples, gates and battlements and towers, under whose shadow the strongholds of human power shrink to nothing, and even their melancholy ruins disappear. It is the kingdom of God which thus rises as by magic to the view of the regenerate—for, 'except,' etc. and above its many thrones he sees the throne of Him whose throne is forever and ever, and the sceptre of whose kingdom is a sceptre of righteousness, the Lord of lords and the King of kings.' And now do you ask what shall the righteous do when the foundations shall be out of course? Do you ask what you yourselves shall do when the signs of the times which we behold shall be fulfilled? Cling to these massive pillars; press into yonder temple; bind yourselves with cords to the horns of yonder altar; and at every fresh heave of the ocean or the earth, take the faster hold of His cross and his throne: and you are safe amidst the wreck of matter and the crush of worlds. Though every throne should crumble, and our own boasted system burst with terrible explosion, there is still a kingdom which shall never end; and while the crash of falling empires waxes louder and louder, and then comes fainter till it dies away, the ear of faith, from every mountain top and valley of God's spiritual kingdom, catches first a murmur, then a shout, and then a general burst of voices, like the roll of thunder and the rush of many waters—'Alleluiah! for the Lord God omnipotent reigneth! Jehovah reigneth; let the earth rejoice!'"

The sketch of which this passage forms a part Dr. Alexander copied and delivered at Newark in the very form here given. The original manuscript of this draught, with all its marks of excitement and fiery haste, its abbreviations, its few erasures, and its occasional changes and interlineations, is now in my hands.

No one, from reading this passage alone, or a hundred others of the same description, would ever suspect that its author was nothing but a great analytical scholar, and hardly that he was an analytical scholar at all. One would be far more likely to conjecture that its author was a man characterized by imagination, ardent feeling, and a wonderful power of strong writing, though perhaps without a corresponding faculty of judgment or patient analysis. And yet it is true, as this fine critic says, that his sermons, regarded as an entire collection, are preëminently distinguished by the unequivocal marks and results of analysis and rigid logic.

Referring to this marked trait in his intellectual structure, one of his most ingenious admirers * says, with admirable insight and exactness:

"The same character of his mind distinguished his sermons; and gave them a peculiar interest and power. He rarely, if ever, discussed a doctrine or a subject as such, or constructed a complex systematic discourse. He analyzed and applied the text. He was a great unraveller.† He unravelled the clauses of a text—as in his sermon on 'The grace of God, which bringeth Salvation,' etc. and on 'Seek ye the Lord while He may be found,' etc. He unravelled the ideas of a clause, as in the famous sermon on 'Remember Lot's wife.' He un-unravelled the applications of an idea, as in the sermon on 'All things are now ready;' or, 'It doth not yet appear what we shall be.' And often, again, his sermons were characterized rather by *a gathering together* of the manifold applications of a particular idea, and a setting them in powerful array, as in the sermon on 'The last state of that man is worse than the first.'

"Hence his sermons, though not pretending to any systematic, didactic completeness, were in their way most closely connected, and singularly exhaustive. In fact, climax is characteristic of them; and this not in the way of artful rhetoric and superficial effect, but out of an earnest adherence to the deep, inward connection of thought, and discernment of the vivid applications of it in real life.

"With a powerful imagination, great fertility of illustration, and exuberance of diction, he had not the faintest leaning towards sensation and clap-trap. His thought went too deep, and his temper was too earnest, to tolerate or be imposed on by any sort of sham. As a preacher he unquestionably ranks with such men as Henry Melvill, Archer Butler, and Trench; while his sermons, though they remind one in many respects of Archer Butler's, have yet a strong individuality by the side of these or any others with which it would be fair to associate them. They have the specific power of a continuity, or continuous application or repetition, of force in the same single line; as of the pow-

* The Rev. Edward L. Yeomans, D.D.

† This is one of the best things ever said about Dr. Alexander.

der on the bullet along the barrel of a gun. In this method of impetuously driving home the one truth with which he charged his discourse, I know not his like; and in this, his keen discernment, prolific imagination, steadiness of purpose, strength of will, facility of conception, affluence of language, the very style of his person, and the straightforwardness of his manner and voice in delivery—all found their place. He threw *himself* into his sermons, to a remarkable degree, and that with all the simplicity which characterized him. And his sermons took possession of him, and carried him along, and so carried his hearers irresistibly with him, and lodged themselves deep in the heart. Few who heard him would ever forget what he preached about, or would fail to associate vividly the person and manner of the preacher with the things he preached."

That I may not be suspected of undue bias in this estimate of the symmetrical character of Mr. Alexander's genius, I append here the enthusiastic, but surely not undiscriminating words of another.* He pronounces it emphatically a mistake that Addison Alexander had this or that faculty in high vigour, and in an extraordinary state of cultivation, but at the expense of certain other faculties. He compares the powers of his mind to fiery coursers held in just subjection.

"A remarkable peculiarity of this great man was, not that he had some splendid powers, but that he had the whole cluster of intellectual endowments in such fulness and perfection, and all under the control of strong, overmastering common sense. Intellectually, no man was more truly σώφρων, well-balanced. There was no crack in his judgment. It had the clear, sound ring. His other powers, even when wanton in the fulness of their strength, never broke loose from its sway. His good judgment was never unsettled from its seat; and with a strong grasp, he held all the other powers like spirited, fiery coursers, ever under easy control. In his commentaries, not an instance can be pointed out of the least swaying towards those fantastic capers of the intellect so often cut by learned and even good men, with such palpable want of judgment, in their expositions of the Word of God. Such a mind as his could not be free from the temptations incident to probation in our fallen state; and had it once broken loose from the control of his sound judgment and sturdy

* The Rev. Professor Burrowes, of Easton.

common sense, where might it have stopped, and what mischief might it have caused, in its fiery aberrations? There has been in our church many a heart of thankfulness that the Divine grace which made him what he was preserved that sound and sanctified judgment (a star of the first magnitude) secure against all disturbing influences, and free from all perturbations, even to the last.

"There were resemblances and differences between Mr. Alexander's intellectual traits and those of Jeremy Taylor. In the funeral sermon of Jeremy Taylor, the preacher said that the bishop had 'the reason of a philosopher, the learning of a scholar, the wit of a courtier, the imagination of a poet, and the piety of a saint.'

Much more than this, he thinks, may be said of Dr. Addison Alexander. In the cluster of his great endowments, was "a splendid and exuberant imagination." His fancy, the writer considers as gorgeous as that of Jeremy Taylor; "but the different constitution of Dr. Alexander's mind in other respects, possessing the highest intellectual powers of a very superior degree to those of the bishop," made the products of his genius very different.

What follows is startling for its strength, but is neatly expressed.

"Taylor was a 'fruitful bough by a well, whose branches run over the wall;' a vine, loaded with clusters of fragrant blooms and richest grapes. But when the imagination of Dr. Alexander is allowed to burst into action to aid and reinforce his mental efforts, it reminds me of a cloud rising on a clear night in the tropic seas, coming on with flashes and coruscations of beauty, in fire-works unapproachable by any imitation of man; grand in its dazzling lightnings, and refreshing as 'when Thou, O Lord, didst send a plentiful rain, whereby Thou didst confirm thine inheritance when it was weary.'

"His intellect was comprehensive. Like the god who elaborated the shield of Achilles, he had not only the intellectual strength of muscle for forging out successive folds of the most compact argumentation from thoughts more precious than metals and gold; but also the imagination which could cover these folds with a beauty rich and attractive as the sculpture on that heaven-wrought shield; yet, with the wisdom of that divine artist of Olympus, he called in his imagination only for beautifying and making more attractive the underlying masses of thought. I need only mention the closing part of his sermon on Hebrews, xi. 10, and the close of that on Psalm viii. 1, 9. But why select these? The same spirit pervades the whole. I am not criticising his sermons, or I might show they are among the grandest literary productions in our language. Taking into view, thought, style, and mastery of language, they combine excellences scarcely exhibited by anything in Burke, in Robert Hall, or in Macaulay. No beauties of this kind can be found which are superior to portions of the prose-writings of Milton, and some of the sermons of Addison Alexander. He was 'the greatest of American orientalists and scholars.' Our country has never produced, in church or in state, a man of superior powers and attainments. And it is a precious reflection, that all powers and attainments were consecrated, in defending and unfolding the Scriptures, to the glory of Redeeming Love."

Another hearer* was reminded by his preaching of that of Dr. Thomas Chalmers; whose almost only rival in the modern British pulpit was Robert Hall.

"I was not so fortunate as to hear him preach but once after his piety and theological attainments were mellowed into pulpit performances. The only time I heard him after leaving the Seminary was once when he preached for his brother in Duane street. He then reminded me of a huge locomotive with steam up, and started on the track. He seemed to be *shaking* with the weight of thought and of expression; in which respect he called to my mind the late Dr. Chalmers of Edinburgh. Those who knew him more intimately than I can claim to have done, have testified to the excellence of his character, the depth of his piety, the greatness of his intellect, the wonderful versatility and profoundness of his studies, and to his prodigious memory; and in their estimate of him I fully concur."

The concluding judgment will attract notice:

"I am free to say that when I had the pleasure of knowing him, I then considered him the most learned and intellectual man of his years that I had ever met with; and the years that have passed since then have not changed my opinion. I consider him still as one of the most intellectual and learned men I have ever known."

* The Rev. Dr. Wm. A. Scott, of New York.

A gentleman* who was socially well acquainted with him testifies that the most richly endowed intellect he had ever encountered was that of Dr. Addison Alexander; that his natural gifts were of the highest order, and were all cultivated and developed to the highest degree.

"There are," he says, "comparatively few really *great men.* Of those who truly deserve the distinction, some are entitled to it from the possession of *original powers,* conferred on them by the hand of Providence; others from the thorough training and perfect development of strong and well balanced minds, though destitute of the higher and peculiar gifts of genius; others again from the vast attainments they have made in scholarship, the soundness of their judgments, and the application of their stores of learning. It rarely happens that these different classes are represented by one man; and whenever the combination occurs, we have the highest example of intellectual greatness. If such powers are sanctified by grace, and devoted to the service of God, the character stands complete and commands the admiration of mankind. For native powers, thorough discipline, and extensive learning—for genius, culture, and erudition, Addison Alexander has not been excelled, perhaps not equalled among American divines."

The next letter is to his brother. It is dated Dec. 24th, and relates to various learned authors and the right spelling of the name of an ancient town.

"PRINCETON, December 24th, 1846.

"R. D. B.†

The holidays will be no holidays to me. I must avail myself of them to read Spencer de Legibus, Michaelis on the Law of Moses, Bertheau on ditto, and Bähr's Symbolik before recommencing my lectures after New Year's. In the meantime I am articulating for the Repertory, *malgré moi,* and after that must make a sermon for the chapel next Sunday, when it is my turn to preach there. Your Nineveh arrived safe and is very seasonable. I was greatly mystified by your writing Nin*i*veh all through your MS. You so often have your private reasons for such innovations that I was afraid to change it, and should not have done it after all if I had found any authority for any intermediate form between the French *Ninive* and the English *Nineveh.*"

* The Rev. Dr. B. T. Lacy, of Missouri. † Rev. & Dear Brother.

The commentary on the later prophecies of Isaiah appeared the next year; and in the interval between the publication of the Earlier and the Later Prophecies, Dr. Alexander was employed, as we have seen, in the preparation of his second volume; which came out as a separate and independent work; though the two works must of course be taken together, to form a complete exposition of the prophet. In his preface he says:

This volume is a sequel to the one which appeared about a year ago, under the title of the Earlier Prophecies, the two together forming a continuous commentary on Isaiah. While the same plan has been here retained without alteration, I have aimed at greater uniformity of execution, as well as a more critical selection of materials."

He aims most of his critical shafts in this volume at Dr. Henderson; to whose ability and learning he however pays a handsome compliment. The point in dispute between them was, that the truth of the "exceeding great and precious promises" uttered by Isaiah "is not suspended on the future restoration of the Jews to Palestine;" though the Princeton commentator does not deny such a restoration to be possible or promised elsewhere.

Some of his more critical readers have taken him to task for the slavish literality of his new version. Apparently in allusion to these friendly strictures, he says:

"In this, as well as in the other volume, I may possibly have pushed the rule of rigorous translation to an extreme; but if so, it is an extreme from which recession is much easier and safer than recovery from that of laxity and vagueness. By the course thus taken, I am not without hope that some light may be thrown upon the darker parts of Hebrew grammar, and especially the doctrine of the tenses, which can never be completely solved except by a laborious induction of particulars."

Dr. Alexander read only two sheets of this volume during its progress through the press, and wisely committed the remainder to the expert hands of Mr. W. W. Turner, "to whom so many other works in this department are indebted for the accuracy of their execution."*

He continued to keep steadily in view as his immediate readers, "clergymen and students of theology" considered as the actual or future teachers of the church. "Through them," he says, "I may perhaps indulge the hope of doing something to promote correct opinions, and a taste for exegetical pursuits, as means of intellectual and spiritual culture, even though this should prove to be my last as well as first contribution to the stores of sacred learning."

The tone of modest confidence in his own results which is here exhibited, is in the farthest degree removed from arrogance on the one hand or conscious weakness or timidity on the other.

Dr. Alexander was not altogether singular in believing that there are certain ends that can be accomplished only by the most rigid version of a foreign text, and a version confessedly devoid of every merely literary merit. He once, in my presence, expressed his astonishment to his brother James, that any one should fail to see that he was not trying to rival the incomparable literary excellence of the common English version, but only translating provisionally for purposes of exegesis and with tenacious and wilful adherence to the mere grammatical form of the original text.

He freely conceded the enormous disadvantages of this method for all purposes but the single one he had in view. This he said years afterwards, in his brother's study in Nineteenth street, walking up and down on the carpet and gazing curiously betweentimes at the backs of the volumes on his brother's shelves. His brother remained seated; and appeared to concur with him. The conversation then sought other channels and was very animated. These interviews between the brothers were always seasons of delight to both of them, as well as to any who had the freedom of the apartment where

* For a full account of Mr. Turner's abilities and labours, see Dr. Alexander's article in the Repertory on Nordheimer's Hebrew Grammar.

they were held. The topics were infinitely fluctuating, but the main talk generally settled down upon books, recent debates in the Assembly, what they had last seen or heard that interested them, prominent people in the Church or out of it, the many little things about which the brothers differed but consented to argue, the Princeton *ana*, the smallest family news, but above all the opinions of living European writers, with whom the brothers seemed to have been communing face to face. Sometimes these colloquies were scenes of much innocent merriment. On the occasion I speak of, the younger of the two especially seemed to be in unusually good plight. His face had a glow upon it that made it shine with a species of rosy pleasure; his expressive mouth wreathed itself into playful smiles; his glasses flashed as if there were sparks of fire behind them in those blue orbs which were bathed in the light of a rare intelligence and an equally rare affection and good humour. Everything betokened inward sunshine, and a sense of perfect ease and implicit confidence. The tones of his voice were rapid, eager, higher and mellower than common, and often interrupted by a shout of sudden irrepressible laughter, at some *jeu de mots* or funny description from his brother. The next minute they would both be far away, upon the continent; discussing with gravity the French Chambers, or the British Parliament, or the latest English and American periodicals, or the merits and defects of the last nine days' wonder of literature in Germany. Possibly the theme was the Free Church; Chalmers; the great orators. Or else their thoughts took a wider range still, and embraced the prospects of Christendom and the aspect in which the Scriptures present the latter-day glory. But throughout, the chief speaker was as free and happy as a bird.

When in New York at the house of his youngest brother, Dr. Alexander had full scope for his oral and scribbling tendencies. Here, as in so many other of his resting places, he was kept busy telling stories and writing lives; to the delight of the children. He appeared to have a new system of operations for every house; though the old characters constantly reappeared in his recitals of strange or humorous adventures, very much as Major Pendennis and J. J. Ridley recur in the later writings of Thackeray. His chosen seat was in the corner of a sofa in the back part of the house, and there he would laugh and talk and sing and write by the hour, and sometimes almost by the day.

There are the usual touches of ironical playfulness in the subjoined letter to his Trenton correspondent, in which he promises to be with him by the 20th of June.

"PRINCETON, June 15, 1847 (new style.)

"REV. AND DEAR BROTHER:

"By a rare sagacity or happy accident, you have hit upon the only Sunday which will be at my disposal for at least six weeks. If nothing happens, I propose to commence my visitation of your archdeaconry, on Quasimodo Sunday, profanely called the 20th of June. I advise you to be passively expectant of my coming, as I do not know whether it will be at noon, or in the afternoon, or in the evening, or on Sunday morning; in a private carriage, or in a public conveyance. You will be pleased to learn that your letter, having found its way into the hands of the only 'Rev. Dr. Alexander'* who is recognized in these parts, he was not a little mystified by the tone of the communication, and still more by the allegation of a promise which he could not recollect his having made. The mistake, however, it is thought, will have no permanent injurious effect.

"Yours in the best of bonds,

"Rev. Mr. HALL."

* His father.

CHAPTER XXII.

We have now come to a point of great interest in the history of the retiring scholar. The Rev. Dr. Henry A. Boardman, having taken a voyage to Europe for the benefit of his health, had left his pulpit in Philadelphia vacant. Application was accordingly made to Dr. Addison Alexander to supply his place; which he consented to do for a month, and, after repeated solicitations, during a part of that summer and the whole of the succeeding winter.* He was, of course, not unknown in that city; and it soon came to be noised abroad that the famous Princeton professor was the regular "supply" at the Tenth Church. The expectation thus awakened was not in any sense disappointed. At the second hour for preaching, many of other denominations poured in. The pews were filled early. The aisles were often thronged, and I have heard it said that the passages were sometimes crowded long before the hour for divine service. Sunday after Sunday, true to his appointment, the staid form of the preacher was discerned in the pulpit, and he was presently on his feet, and, with an upward wave of his hand, calling the multitude to prayer. His first sermon in this series was from the text, "Where two or three are gathered together in my name, there am I in the midst of them."

These were still the days of his intellectual prime; and unquestionably they were those of his highest intellectual ascendency. Not that I mean to imply that he could not preach as well before and afterwards, but merely that he had not the same stimulus, and did not. Most of his rich and weighty sermons were prepared, as we have seen, at an earlier date;

* I think his second engagement covered a period of six months; and probably included a large part of the autumn.

but for the same or a similar Philadelphia audience. Whether it was because it was the place of his own birth, and of his father's pastoral labours, I know not; but it was in Philadelphia only, that for consecutive weeks and months he exerted his full strength in the pulpit. His usual efforts in the chapel at Princeton, though often very striking, gave one no conception of the magnetic influence of which he was capable under high excitement. He was very unequal; but there were moments when mighty intellects bowed under him like the pine before the tempest. His chief popularity was among the most intelligent and cultivated classes—the élite of a society of uncommon literary force and polish. But no one was sent empty away. The people all loved to listen to him, and he exulted in the privilege of breaking to them the bread of life.

His brother James, who was recruiting at Long Branch, and had, perhaps, himself never heard "Addison" to advantage, was astonished at the reports that came to him. Writing to his Trenton friend on the 28th of July, he says, "Addison has engaged for another month at Dr. Boardman's;" * and again, after his own return home on the 23d of September, after referring to the Millerites and their great tent on the site of Niblo's Garden, he says, "Addison's popularity in Philadelphia surprises me the more, as his last summer's work here seemed to draw scarcely anybody. The sphere, I admit, is very different. A people engaged solely in trade affords small intellectual ability." † New York, it seems, was not even then the metropolis it is now. And again, on the 5th of the next month, in apparent allusion to the comparative smallness of his brother's audiences in his own city, he writes, "I saw Addison's big congregation in full review." ‡

For whatever reason, the tide of applauding hearers ran after him in the Quaker City, and did not in the hurly-burly of New York.

There were, however, very many in New York who thor-

* Fam. Let. Vol. II. p. 72. † Ibid. Vol. II. p. 74.
‡ Ibid. Vol. II. p. 75.

oughly appreciated him; and I have no doubt the chief reason why large numbers were not gathered there to hear him, and that all were not deeply affected, was that there really was a marked falling-off in the character of his preaching in New York as compared with his efforts in some other places. It may be that this was owing in a measure to his knowledge that in New York, there would be a disposition in certain quarters to pit him against his popular brother; and that this disagreeable conviction chilled the ardour of his feelings. The elder brother reverts to the same topic, November 16. "Addison's popularity is quite extraordinary. I am pleased to think that it urges him to regard more and more the great end of preaching."* This is important testimony; and it is corroborated by the entire circle of extant evidence bearing on this point. The minds of men were exhilarated, as with new wine; but their hearts also were touched, and touched as by the finger of God. Among the sermons which excited most attention, and aroused the deepest feeling, were the one on "Lot's wife," the one on "What I do thou knowest not now," those on the texts, "We know not what we shall be," "The sacrifices of God are a broken spirit," "This is a faithful saying," "Behold, therefore, both the goodness and severity of God," "When thou art converted, strengthen thy brethren," "The word of God is not bound," "What I say unto you I say unto all, watch," "Who is this that is born king of the Jews?" and "He looked for a city which had foundations, whose builder and maker is God."

Dr. Hart says he had good opportunity of judging of his preaching at this time. He often heard him; and remembers well that his sermons drew a large crowd, particularly of gentlemen of high professional standing, such as Judge Kane, Dr. Patterson, and (he might have added) Dr. Chapman—"the very élite of the city."

"For the first few Sundays, we had what were evidently his Seminary sermons—discourses which, with all their brilliancy and power,

* Fam. Let. Vol. II. p. 77.

had the unmistakable professional stamp upon them. But, as the weeks passed by, the stock of this kind was probably getting low. At all events, a marked difference began to appear in the character of the sermons. They began to be more like those which a pastor addresses to his flock. They gave evidence, in their whole tenour, of having been written for the occasion. There was a certain freshness, spontaneousness, and reality about them, quite unlike his previous scholastic performances. He was preaching, instead of sermonizing. There was a still more marked change in his manner of delivery. He became highly animated, almost fiery in his vehemence. I have seen him time after time become so excited as to bring down his hand vehemently upon the pulpit, and to stamp with his feet, so that you could hear it all over the house, and this in the staid old Tenth Presbyterian Church of Philadelphia! His whole internal and external man were swept by the fervour of his emotions; and as he threw himself without reserve into the delivery of his message, he swayed the whole assembly before him as if it had been but one man. There were none of the tricks of oratory about him. He did many things that were not according to the rules. Yet I have never heard more effective preaching than was that of Dr. Addison Alexander during the latter part of his engagement in the Tenth Church. I do believe, if he had given himself to the work of the pastoral office he would have been the prince of American preachers—not even excepting his father, Dr. Archibald Alexander."

The sermons of Dr. Alexander, especially those delivered in Philadelphia, attracted the cultivated women, no less than the men. A lady now resident in Nashville, the daughter of a distinguished statesman of the past era, once remarked to me that, when she heard Professor Addison Alexander, it was a new revelation to her of intellectual power. She writes that, many years ago, she was in the habit of occasionally attending the Rev. Dr. Boardman's church, in Philadelphia. One day, she found a stranger occupying the pulpit. She soon discovered that she was in the presence of a great man:

"He seemed to speak with the *wisdom* of inspiration; his profound knowledge found easy and eloquent expression; while his modest dignity betrayed an unconsciousness of his own superiority." The effect was indescribable. "An impression was made on my mind that can never be forgotten."

This lady was not aware, till the services were over, that she "had been listening to the truly good and great Dr. Addison Alexander." In a private letter, the same lady adds: "He penetrated my soul with an influence which time can never efface."

A lady of Philadelphia, of whose hospitality he once partook during the lifetime of her distinguished husband, writes that she well remembers that visit; and adds that the privilege of entertaining him was so coveted, that he was our guest only on one occasion. "Dr. Alexander was accompanied by his venerable father." The impression which the younger of the two made upon this lady was, "that of a man *all mind*, noticing no one, and desiring to be noticed by no one; yet quietly considerate of those who rendered him any service, however trivial." Great simplicity of manner, and a very quiet demeanour, are among her recollections of "this intellectually great and good man." She has heard one of her connections often speak of Dr. Alexander's "remarkable conversational powers when at ease among his intimates, his sparkling wit, and the rich entertainment he afforded his associates in the freedom of old friendship." The same lady adds her voice to those who have pronounced as to the character of his discourses, and the reception they met with from prominent men of the city. "His preaching, for the most part, gathered intellectual audiences. There was a simplicity and yet a sublimity about his utterances, that seemed to awe his hearers into breathless attention; and often the silent tear would course down the cheek of the strong man. (I have seen it.)" Even infidels were made to bow their heads. "His power over the sceptical mind," this lady thinks, "was very great." She regarded Dr. Addison Alexander "as a preacher for cultivated and intellectual men, not for the masses;" but says his audiences were very large, generally filling all the pews of the church where he preached.

As I have before intimated, the extraordinary impression of his preaching in his native city was not limited to the efforts which grew out of this particular engagement. A gentleman whose judgment will be valued * writes:

"I remember well the last time I had the pleasure of hearing Dr. J. A. Alexander preach. It was in Philadelphia, in the Sixth Presbyterian Church. His subject was 'The Kingdom of God.' Immediately in front of me was seated one of the most brilliant members of the Philadelphia bar, now its senior member. My attention was divided between the preacher and the lawyer. The grandeur and power displayed in the pulpit held in absorbed admiration the intellect accustomed to win its triumphs at the bar. At the close of the service he at once started from his seat, and reaching over two pews to a friend, eagerly enquired, 'Who is that?—Who is that?' "

Another friend says:

"His preaching was appreciated by men of the highest culture in Philadelphia. I have often known my father to send word to Dr. Chapman, Dr. Patterson, and others of like stamp, some of whom seldom went to church, that Dr. Alexander was to preach on a certain evening, and they were always glad to avail themselves of the opportunity of hearing him." †

Some idea of the estimate which was universally placed upon his abilities as a preacher may be had from the following statements of Dr. Beach Jones.

His licensure and ordination to the ministry having taken place after his own graduation, it was not his privilege to hear him preach as one of the Theological faculty. Still, he occasionally enjoyed the opportunity of hearing him, both on special and ordinary occasions; and in the pulpit, as well as everywhere else, he seemed to this friend to tower above his fellows.

"The two published volumes of his sermons convey some idea of the treasures of Divine wisdom and knowledge which he was wont to unfold; the endless variety of his method of constructing his dis-

* The Rev. James W. Dale, D.D. of Media, Penn. the author of "Classic Baptism."

† The Rev. William Harris, of Towanda, Penn.; son of the late Dr. William Harris, of Philadelphia, a distinguished physician and Presbyterian.

courses; his exemption from the fault of repeating himself; his logical vigour; his rich fancy; his faultless rhetoric; his tender pathos; and his manifest faith in all he uttered."

Extraordinary, though, as are the merits of most of his published discourses, none of them, in the judgment of this writer, equals one which has never been printed, and which the Princeton professor delivered at the installation of the Rev. William Henry Green, as Pastor of the Central Church of Philadelphia.

"The sermon was founded on 1 Peter v. 1–4; and combined logical power with rhetorical beauty and thrilling appeal, beyond any discourse which I ever heard. The first part of the sermon was a massive and, as it seemed to me and others, an irrefutable argument for ministerial parity; while the second was a sublime picture of 'the appearing of the Chief Shepherd,' and of 'the crown of glory' reserved for faithful ministers."

No competent judge, so this gentleman thinks, can attentively read his printed sermons without a conviction of the colossal powers and the amazing attainments of the preacher. But no adequate conception of these powers and attainments can be had until it is known that in all probability not one of these sermons was designed by the author for publication; that instead of being painfully elaborated for days and weeks, they were composed and written off with more rapidity than an ordinary writer could even copy them. Such was the discipline of their author's mind, and so complete his mastery of his knowledge, that he could compose and write off a discourse, or a review for a Quarterly, in less time than most men would devote to the mere mechanical work of writing.

The power of Dr. Alexander as a preacher, he considers, lay mainly in the intrinsic richness of his matter.

"He availed himself scarce at all of the ordinary aids of oratory. His voice was indeed musical and resonant; but its intonations were as natural and simple as ordinary conversation. There was in his personal appearance, especially in his majestic head, an air of imperial grandeur, which reminded me and many another of the great Napoleon."

But the writer judged him to be as free from assumed airs of importance, or efforts for effect, as it is possible for a speaker to be. He was sparing in the use of gesture, and always preached as he felt. If his sermon took strong hold on his own feelings, he soon showed it.

"His thorough sincerity and honesty deterred him from assuming a measure of feeling which at the time he did not cherish. I question whether any man ever knew him guilty of that form of hypocrisy which has been wittily described as 'stale indignation, and fervour of a week old.'"

This was one great secret of his power over men.

"I knew him to be sincere; I felt sure that he would resort to no oratorical tricks. I could not but feel the power of thorough honesty, and of a 'faith unfeigned.' I knew that in expounding God's Word he was almost sure of communicating its right meaning, and that in arguing and appealing he would employ no considerations but such as had carried conviction to his own mind."

Dr. Jones then goes on as follows, in reference to the qualities of his diction and his piety:

"The rhetorical beauties of his sermons were not artificial flowers, but the spontaneous products of a teeming fancy. Not even his most masterly sermons smell in the least of oil. His figures are evidently never 'beaten on the anvil,' as was said of another. Like Robert Hall, he never imported his imagery; because it sprang up indigenously from the exuberant soil of his own fertile imagination.

"And the crowning excellence of his preaching was the prominence he habitually gave to the peculiar doctrines of the gospel, the glorious truths of Grace and Redemption, in the messages he delivered. When we consider how multifarious was Dr. Alexander's knowledge, and how easy to him had been the task of entertaining his audiences by discourses on curious and recondite themes, or of dazzling them with mere displays of the sublime and beautiful, and then read what he actually chose to preach, we must feel that he was indeed a herald of 'the glorious gospel of the blessed God,' and that he never in the pulpit lost sight of his high and holy calling."

When Dr. Alexander first began to make a noise in Philadelphia as a learned and eloquent divine, he commonly lodged at hotels. But his many warm personal friends in the city soon persuaded him out of this remorseless habit, and induced him to stay now and then at private houses.*

Yet it should seem that he continued to prefer the independence and security from recognition which he could enjoy only at an inn. He loved to be treated in a carelessly friendly manner; but the hangers-on and the polite Athenians of the city would make a lion of him in spite of all he could do. This he abhorred, and rebelled against. On this point the Rev. Mr. Harris writes:

"One striking trait of Dr. Alexander was his utter detestation of being lionized. He hated to be visited by or introduced to people who came to stare at him as a literary curiosity. I remember hearing my mother bantering him once in regard to this, and proposing to build a back stairway from the pulpit, by which he might avoid the lionizers, who lay in wait for him at the foot of the pulpit stairs. I have heard many amusing anecdotes of how he sometimes avoided and sometimes repelled these Leo Hunters."

There are many of these stories in currency, some of which are true and others, no doubt, false. Dr. Alexander hated to be stopped on his way out of church, and if the dreaded chalice of flattery were unwarily commended to his lips at such moments, he would dash it from him as if it had been the poison of asps, and sometimes say hard things to the person who administered it.

* "The truth is," writes the late Dr. Joseph H. Jones, one of his best friends, "I cannot possibly call to mind much concerning that extraordinary scholar, preacher, and critic, companion and friend, that reads well enough to be printed. I really saw less of Dr. Addison Alexander and knew less than is commonly supposed. He was so retiring in his tastes, preferring the seclusion of a hotel to the parlour of a private family, that he *would* not be my guest very often, much as I desired it. I believe that one of his last letters was written to me requesting me to take his place in the chapel on Sunday. I cannot find it; much to my regret. My brother, Judge Jones, was then at the point of death, and I could not go. He lived but two or three days after my reply; to which he responded, expressing his regret and sympathy. The spirits of both were separated but a short time on their ascent."

Although Philadelphia was the scene of most of his highest efforts in the pulpit, he occasionally held large audiences enchained in other places. A very intelligent lady once asked me about a sermon she had heard him preach in Newark, and which she said affected her profoundly and in such a way that all the attendant circumstances were stamped upon her recollection. She remarked that it excited in her, and in a high degree, the sense of the sublime and the pathetic. It was, I think, the one on, "What I do thou knowest not now;" or perhaps the one on, "Clouds and darkness;" or possibly the one on "Lot's wife." My memory on this point is not clear.

These effects were sometimes produced even upon a New York audience. A gentleman of that city has stated to me that he once heard Professor Addison Alexander in Duane street preach the most eloquent and powerful discourse he had ever listened to from any man. It was from the text which marks one of his most noted sermons: "The sacrifices of God are a broken spirit: a broken and a contrite heart, O God, thou wilt not despise."

But the most extraordinary evidence on this head is contained in the subjoined account, by the Rev. Dr. Charles A. Read, of Richmond, formerly of the Pearl Street Church, New York. A man who could thus bind the soul of a sceptical newspaper reporter must have certainly possessed the true afflatus of the orator:

"Some twenty-five years ago, during my ministry in New York, Dr. Addison Alexander delivered a discourse, by special invitation, at the anniversary of the New York Bible Society, in the old Broadway Tabernacle, near the corner of Broadway and Pearl street. That spacious edifice, which had been converted from a theatre to a house of worship, was densely filled; and I well remember the peculiar solemnity of the occasion, from the commencement to the close of the exercises. About that time the custom of *reporting sermons*, in some of the secular papers of largest circulation, was quite common; and in *that* edifice the professional reporters were accommodated with seats and tables immediately before the pulpit, on occasions of special interest. Among these was one whom I had known as an expert in his profession, serving in the interest of one of the least religious and most widely circulated of the secular papers of the land, himself making no pretension to religion.

"Seated at his table, with paper and pencil before him, he awaited his task, taking no interest apparently in the introductory devotional services, which were peculiarly solemn and impressive. My position afforded a full view of the preacher and the reporter. Dr. Alexander announced his text as from 2 Tim. ii. 9, which the reporter noted down, and *paused*. In clear tones of sweet simplicity, the text — '*The* WORD OF GOD *is* NOT BOUND' — reached every part of the house, and seemed to fall as with a holy spell upon every ear. The reporter's vocation there was *forgotten;* he was '*bound*' by the preacher, as he unfolded the sentiment of the text; and never a word more did he write save the chapter and verse of the text.

"The sermon impressed the vast congregation profoundly; not only by its evangelical spirit and chaste power of thought and diction, but by the unmistakable profound conviction of the importance of the theme on the part of the preacher, and the holy unction which was upon him and which was breathed through him upon the assembly. I will not attempt to give a sketch of the sermon; it is among his published discourses: simple, earnest, thorough in unpretending scholarship, and true to the high purposes of the ministry of the gospel, as well as fitted to the occasion. I am carried back when I read or hear that sentence — 'THE WORD OF GOD IS NOT BOUND' — to that Sabbath evening in the 'Broadway tabernacle;' the speaker's tones are reproduced, and the spirit in which he delivered that message comes over me with fresh power.

"At the close of the service the reporter came hurriedly to the place where I was standing, and, taking me by the arm, said, 'Do you know Dr. Alexander? — I wish an introduction — I came here to report his sermon for our morning issue, but have been too much absorbed to take a single note of it; if he will entrust me with his manuscript it shall be published entire.' The introduction followed, and the complimentary solicitation was with characteristic modesty declined.

"Dr. Alexander was as separate from the class of '*sensation preachers*' in style and aim, as he was superior to them in spirit and qualifications; but his was a power of intellect, an elevation of purpose, and a simple holy charm — as impressed upon my affectionate memory of him — which was adapted to arrest and transfix the attention of sanctified and unsanctified minds."

Among the sermons preached by Mr. Alexander were some which were considered, I am told, of "such superlative merit," that he would not unfrequently be requested to repeat them, for the gratification of those who had not heard them; and in more than one instance the writer whose memoranda I am now using,* has known of his refusing such requests; especially where they were accompanied by complimentary remarks:

"I can recall," he says, "an incident which exemplifies his aversion to flattery and his dislike to display; while at the same time it indicates his tenderness of conscience and his kindliness of feeling.

"During a vacancy in the pastorate of an important church, he, with others, was occasionally invited to supply the pulpit. On one of these occasions an officer of the church waited upon him and obtained a promise to preach on a given Sunday, and at the same time to become his guest. Before leaving, the gentleman added, 'Dr. Alexander, I have heard much of a great sermon of yours on 'Remember Lot's wife;' I want you to preach it to our people.' 'I shall not do it! sir,' was his curt and only reply; and, somewhat chop-fallen, that his flattery had not 'taken,' the gentleman took his leave. At the time and place appointed Dr. A. made his appearance. Nothing was said during the evening about the sermons to be preached the next day: but after his host had ushered him to his bedroom, and just as he was about to bid him good-night, the Doctor said in a quiet way, 'Mr. ——, you mentioned a particular sermon which you should like me to preach. I have brought it, sir;' and he did preach it on the following day. As well as if he had himself disclosed the processes of his mind can those who knew the man understand both his refusal and his consent to preach the discourse referred to. His taste and finer feelings revolted at the flattery bestowed on his 'great sermon.' He shrank from the prospect of preaching before a congregation in which, for days, it had been trumpeted that he was to preach a 'great sermon.' And yet, after reflecting upon the curtness of his refusal, he doubtless felt sorry at having wounded the feeling of a well-meaning, though not over-delicate man, and magnanimously resolved to make the best reparation in his power."

He thus sometimes repelled persons of rare delicacy, who

* Dr. Jones, of Bridgeton.

at subsequent interviews won greatly upon his regards, as well as some who were already his friends.

The reminiscences of Dr. McGill relative to this point and this very period are exactly in place here. He writes:

"The first time I ever saw Dr. J. Addison Alexander, he was in the pulpit of the Tenth Presbyterian Church of Philadelphia (Dr. Boardman's), where he was regularly supplying the congregation in the absence of the pastor, who had gone to Europe for the reinvigoration of his health.

"It was in the afternoon of a warm summer Sabbath [of 1847]. But the church was crowded to overflowing. I had preached in the morning for my friend Dr. Willis Lord, of the Seventh Church, and was languid and uncomfortable in the crowd, so much so as to feel sure that none but a powerful preacher could interest and impress me in the service."

The manner of the speaker in beginning the services was not attractive, and did not altogether prepossess one, on account of a rather hurried movement and the minister's apparent carelessness in reading the Scriptures.

"And the opening prayer itself, though rich and fluent, abundantly indicating both the gift and the grace of prayer, was so condensed and rapid in the transitions, that I was forcibly reminded of John Foster's criticism on Robert Hall in this particular—that he had too much enumeration, and advanced so rapidly as not to afford time enough to kindle the fervour of devotion at any one confession or petition."

Notwithstanding this, the effect of the preparatory exercises was on the whole good; as it left the hearer in readiness "to appreciate any message God would send by such lips, ready, glowing, and accustomed, however fast and impatient to the ears of a stranger."

The text was Psalm xcvii. 2: "Clouds and darkness are round about him; righteousness and judgment are the habitation of his throne," which is one of his great sermons that has never been printed.

"Without the slightest appearance of ambition to impress himself on his audience, and with a total absence of the sensational in the structure, diction, and manner of delivery, every ear was engrossed and every mind carried captive by the massive grandeur of that sermon. It was characteristic of the man; perfectly natural, earnest, and irresistible in logic and eloquence."

The writer adds his testimony to the fact that he was then probably at the height of his popularity as a preacher; and

"Was just opening his eyes to the discovery that he was a public favourite in the pulpit. This was more than he could bear, apparently. Unlike many others, when they begin to realize the admiration of the public gaze, instead of putting on the arts which seek to sustain and increase it, he seemed to renounce the art of oratory from that time, as much as it could be done consistently with the rights of truth and the ordinary dictates of good taste."

The disdain of art was manifest, he says, even at that time, and continued to the end of his life. The writer believes that Dr. Addison Alexander resolutely resigned what he might have reached and held, "the character of the most mighty preacher as well as scholar on our continent." "I never knew any man," he continues, "so little covetous of fame and favour among men. If he could have preached on without being made aware that he was followed by the admiring crowd, he would now be written with Whitefield, Davies, and Mason, among the names which adorn the American pulpit with the greatest achievements of Christian eloquence."

"This recoiling sensibility descended from the pulpit with him, and led him to pass by the multitude of his impressed and profited hearers with indifference of manner which repelled them, exciting feelings of disappointment and even irritation at times. Standing at the door, on the occasion referred to, and awaiting his tardy retirement from the church, that I might obtain an introduction to him, and an opportunity to express the gratification and debt I felt for his discourse, he received me curtly and coldly, so as to seal my lips effectually and render it quite impossible, if I had been so disposed, to offer him the slightest incense of either gratitude or compliment."

He could not forget the sermon, however, and rarely has any discourse he ever heard from him faded from his recollection.

"Earnest power, and profound sensibility, the pertinence and directness of every thought, and every illustration, and withal that perfect mastery of the instrument, language, in which no man has ever excelled him, made him the most attractive to me of all preachers, and has left upon me impressions never to be effaced. Perhaps the exegetic overflow of his mind and its peculiar fondness for running parallel with the sacred text, to note every sense it bears, expressed or implied, abated the synthetic power, with which unity of expression is made in preaching. Perhaps, also, exegesis formed too large a proportion in his discourses often for the popular taste, especially in the later period of his life. But he was never insipid or prosy — never without emotion and imagination, enough to impress any attentive hearer with instruction and delight."

This disposition to check every approach of flattery or even honest praise worked in him to the end.

At no house in Philadelphia was Mr. Alexander more cordially received than at Dr. Harris's, and there were few places he ever visited, where he felt more delightfully at home, or where there were more persons for whom he felt a special kindness.

"My mother," continues Mr. Harris, "recalled one incident, exhibiting a trait of Dr. Addison's character, which I do not think the world at large generally understood, viz., an unconquerable disposition at times to *withdraw into himself*, during which seasons he felt himself to be uncompanionable. It was from coming in contact with him in these cloister periods, that many thought him unapproachable and brusque. You know it was his habit to come to my father's (during the 'Boardman period'), on Saturday to dinner, and to remain until Monday; Saturday afternoon being generally spent in some excursion with my father, from which, by the way, they generally returned in high spirits, and full of anecdote and *badinage* in regard to their adventures. One Saturday, he did not make his appearance, and on my mother's enquiring the cause, the next day at church, he replied that he had 'felt cross,' and did not think himself good company, and therefore had gone to a hotel. My mother told him he must not do so again; that his room was always ready for him; and if he did not feel companionable, he might shut himself up there as in his own study, and we should understand the reason. He always came after that, but I do not know that he ever made use of the privilege of secluding himself. Probably the true genial nature of the man was nowhere, out of his own home-circle, more clearly manifested than at our house. I have known him sit and gossip—yes, gossip—with my mother by the hour, in regard to persons who had been her contemporaries, and whom he knew through his father; while, as I before remarked, he joked with my father, in almost boyish fashion."

I give here a graphic sketch of him, by the hand of one of his pupils.*

"Every enthusiastic student, probably, has his 'hero-worship;' and during my student-life at Princeton, the object of my most reverent homage was DR. ADDISON ALEXANDER. To this hour, I love to cherish even the slightest recollection of him, and he still appears by far the most remarkable man with whom I have ever come into intimate contact. The world saw him afar off; to those who came the nighest he seemed the greatest. To the churches of America, Addison Alexander was chiefly known as the profound Hebraist, and the erudite commentator. To thousands in the Middle States, he was known as one of the foremost preachers of the age. To the privileged few, who were wont to meet him at the hearthstone, he was one of the most brilliant and suggestive of conversers, and one of the most warm-hearted of friends. Two evenings, in which I listened to him as a converser and as a preacher, are so vivid in my memory that I cannot refrain from sketching them.

"But few knew Professor Alexander at the fireside; for, from early boyhood, he was a recluse from promiscuous society. When a lad, he preferred to stretch himself on the carpet, with his book, while his school-fellows were busy with their top or their kite. This modest shyness rather grew than diminished. He is the only man I ever knew to whom popularity was a positive annoyance.

"One of the first evenings I ever spent with him, was during his residence in the 'Breckinridge House,' opposite the Lenox Library. I found him with the notes of his *Isaiah* before him; and as he was wearied with writing in a standing posture at an upright desk, he was ready for a chair and a chat. At that time, his full, rosy cheeks betokened exuberant health. His square, intellectual head (which we students, looking at him from the church-galleries, used to say 'looked like Napoleon's'), would have arrested attention anywhere by its mas-

* "Two Evenings with Professor Alexander." By Rev. T. L. Cuyler, D.D.

siveness. The plaintive, melodious voice, the occasional playful smile, and the singular movement of his eyelid, all the Seminary students of that day will recall in a moment.

"Two hours of that never-to-be-forgotten winter evening rapidly ran away under his brilliant and vivacious talk. His reminiscences of the German Universities, of an amusing journey with a Popish bishop in Italy, and of continental scholars, were mingled with the criticisms of new books, and of the latest caricatures in *Punch*. 'The charm to me, in *Punch*,' said he, 'is, that I always feel that its writers are all men who are *equal to greater things*.' No man enjoyed genuine wit more than Professor Alexander; for his own humour was inexhaustible. Sometimes it found vent through the pages of the Princeton Review, at the expense of poor 'Calvin Colton,' and of the Oxford Tractarians. Sometimes it spent itself in a series of unique little newspapers, executed with his own pen, for the diversion of Dr. Hodge's children. One of these mirth-moving papers, in the style of Thomas Hood, lies before us this morning. It is called '*The Ridge Recorder*, printed at Breckin-Ridge.' It contains, among other things, a ludicrous account a 'terrible *fire* that broke out to-day in the Kisterbock stove;' and an advertisement of a 'Seminary for Chickens,' in the back-yard, where 'Professor Chanticleer' taught *crowing*, and 'Peter Pullet' was the 'Clerk of the Faculty.' With such pleasant recreations did his great intellect refresh itself while producing his magnificent work on *Isaiah*.

"Of that work, he showed me some of the manuscripts. They were written in a round 'back-hand,' with remarkable legibility. Professor Alexander, with his characteristic dislike of self-repetition, sometimes relieved the drudgery of the pen by altering his penmanship. Some of the rough drafts of his Commentary were even written in a *circle* over huge sheets of paper. He once told me that, to avoid the tedium of the recitation-room, he never taught two consecutive classes by the same method entirely; nor did he call the roll two days in exactly the same order. This love of variety he carried into the preparation of his discourses; for we cannot now recall any two that were constructed on the same model.

"We have said that he lived a life of studious seclusion. But when he travelled, he had an eye and an ear for everything. His brother JAMES was not a more observing and entertaining companion. If a Boswell had always been within hearing, he might have preserved a volume of acute and racy observations. Sitting once beside Professor Alexander, in the Senate-Chamber at Washington, he whispered to me, 'Just notice how the presiding officer puts all the bills promptly to vote, on the presumption that all the speaking is to be avoided, if possible. If he were the Moderator of our General Assembly, he would say, 'has any brother any remarks to offer?'

"A more fertile mind was never given to the American pulpit. No man ever saw the bottom of that profound, teeming, inexhaustible intellect. His memory was Herculean. From a single reading, he could commit a whole discourse; and he has been known to repeat a whole class-roll in alphabetical order, although the roll had been called but once in his hearing. Within a few years, the world has lost two great storehouses of knowledge: one was the memory of Lord Macaulay, the other was the memory of Dr. Addison Alexander. Each of these extraordinary men spent those hours in acquiring new thoughts, which men of feebler memories waste in fruitless attempts to recall those things that are wholly forgotten.

"The second evening, which now comes before me, was passed, not beside Dr. Alexander at the fireside, but before him in the pulpit. It was during that winter of 1847 when he supplied the pulpit of the Rev. Dr. Boardman, then travelling in Europe. All Philadelphia flocked to hear him. The most distinguished lawyers of that city were glad to find seats in the aisles, or a standing-place in the crowded vestibule. It was during that season that he delivered nearly all of his most celebrated and powerful discourses. Among them were his sermons on 'The Faithful Saying,' 'the Broken and Contrite Heart,' 'Awake, thou that Sleepest,' 'It doth not yet appear what we shall be,' and 'Remember Lot's wife.' The first-mentioned of these was the most perfect; * but the

* This sermon, as delivered the following year in New York, made a deep impression on the mind of a son of his old preceptor, Dr. Baird. Prof. Henry M. Baird, of the University of the City of New York, writes as follows:

"Dr. Alexander's name was one I often heard in the home of my childhood: for he was a favourite pupil of my father tn the Academy which, for several years after his graduation from the Seminary, he taught in Princeton; and he frequently referred with warm interest to the early indications of that remarkable grasp of intellect which afterwards made him eminent both as a philologist and as a theologian.

"My earliest recollections of Dr. Addison Alexander are connected with a sermon he preached in the Mercer Street Presbyterian Church in the City of New York, on the 6th of February, 1848. It was one of a series of discourses by ministers of promise in several religious denominations. Bishop Janes of the Methodist Episcopal Church, and the Rev. Drs. Adams, Cox, and Tyng, being among the number. The text was one of those salient passages of the New Testament, on which, if I am not mistaken, Dr. Alexander was fond of last one was the most popular. The impressions produced by the matchless discourses of that series can never be effaced. Finer displays of concinnate exegesis, of bold imaginative flights, of soul-moving appeals, of rich, strong, arousing presentation of Calvary and Christ, the Presbyterian pulpit of our day has not heard. His manner, at that period of his life, was exceedingly animated. He was in his splendid prime. His voice often swelled into a volume that rolled through the lobbies of the church, and reached to the passers-by in the street. In pathetic passages, that same voice had the plaintive melody of a lute. The rising inflection with which he was wont to close his sentences will at once occur to many of my readers. This peculiarity was sometimes insensibly imitated by the Seminary students, who betrayed thus their Princeton origin by this rising *Addisonian* inflection. Well would it be, if all the superb attributes of Professor Alexander's ministrations could be transferred to every pulpit in the land! On the evening of which we write, his theme was 'The Broken Heart.' That whole marvellous discourse, with its pictures of the scenes 'behind the veil' where the sacrifices were being offered; with its wailing outcry of contrite spirits; with its melting exhibitions of the soul's penitence and the Saviour's love; all moved before us like one of the inspired panoramas of the Apocalypse. When the sermon was over, a clergyman whispered to me, 'No such preaching as that has been heard since the days of Dr. Mason.'

"It is a thought—oh, how sorrowful to me now!—that the voice which so melted into the hearts of dying men, and rose so lovingly into the ear of Jesus, has been stilled forever on our earth. As I take down the volumes of his printed discourses, and read them over, I can hear that bewitching voice again, and see him once more, as he stood in his fullest inspiration before the hushed and listening assemblies. I hear

taking his stand, rather than upon others of inferior importance or of disputed interpretation. It was that epitome of the Gospel, 1 Tim. i. 15: 'This is a faithful saying, and worthy of all acceptation, that Christ Jesus came into the world to save sinners, of whom I am chief.' It made a deep impression on my mind; so simple was its arrangement, so exhaustive its elucidation of the import of every word, so rich and appropriate the imagery that was introduced to illustrate it. I have often wished to hear or to read it again, and I regret that it could not have found a place among the collected sermons published a few years ago.'

The history of this sermon, from its inception in the mind of its author to the partial disintegration in the MS. would be a remarkable one. It was not inserted among the printed discourses merely because it was in tatters.

again those vehement appeals, those frequent reiterations of the text, and those long-sustained passages, that swept onward so superbly to their climax. All this is now but a fond unfading memory.

"The engraving of his face, as it looked in ruddy and striking beauty, hangs before me. His books stand beside me. As I write these poor words of affectionate tribute to my spiritual benefactor, I look towards my little library, and see two fatal gaps. And I ask myself, who will finish yonder magnificent History, since Macaulay's hand has 'forgot its cunning?' Who will complete yonder affluent and suggestive Commentaries, since ADDISON ALEXANDER has passed from the studies of earth, into the clearer light and loftier knowledge of the heavenly world?"

CHAPTER XXIII.

Dr. Alexander was now on one of his summer excursions. The only trace of him I have, outside of his own correspondence, is in a letter of his brother, of the 28th of July; he writes thus from New York: "Addison is here, on his way to orate at East Windsor." * The journeys he took to New England always pleased him; as the neatness and enterprise of the inhabitants, and the beauty of the country, like the same phenomena beyond the seas, were a refreshing change to him after hard study. His pleasure when at the South, was in the mountain scenery of certain latitudes, and the frank and engaging manners of the people. He was preëminently a citizen of the world in these matters, and not wedded to any geographical zone, or any particular degree of temperature. He loved agreeable towns, fine landscapes, and intellectual, cordial friends wherever he found them.

The Rev. Dr. William Henry Ruffner writes that in 1848 he went to Princeton to be licensed, and during that visit saw "Dr. Addison" at his father's, in company with several ministers of Presbytery, "with whom," he says, "as well as with myself, he conversed with genial piquancy." This surprised and charmed him, as he had never before approached him in one of these bright moods, and he says, "I felt nearer to him afterwards."

There are many whose impressions of Dr. Addison Alexander have been derived from momentary or occasional glimpses, and who have thus totally misconceived his large and fervent nature. Tyndall says, there were times when the "silken ad-

* Fam. Let., Vol. II., p. 86.

jectives," delicate and tender, could not be applied to Faraday; that he had a fiery heart, as well as a humble mind. This, with his true nobleness and simplicity, showed, he thinks, his greatness, and was one cause of his fascination. All this is true as regards the Princeton commentator.*

The following letter to his brother is one of singular interest. In it he urges him to carry out the idea of "a popular theology," which the elder brother had confessed to be needed. "Only think," he says, "of being the popular and juvenile Turretin!" If he will not do this, he must do something. He may elect between a popular Church History and a Life of Christ. The younger brother had too many irons in the fire already, and wanted to get rid of some of them, and was perplexed with doubts about certain points connected with the Gospel story, and would be rejoiced if his brother would take the thing off his hands. He had found the writing of his Isaiah, on the other hand, "a real solace for annoyances." The reader will be likely to consider this a strange anodyne.

"PRINCETON, October 4th, 1848.

"DEAR JAMES:

"Ever since you spoke of a popular theology, I have felt convinced that you ought to undertake it. The plea of incompetency, strikes me only as a reflection on myself and others for attempting anything. Only think of being the popular and juvenile Turretin! If you will not do this, do something else. I have an idea to suggest. My recent

* "You cannot resolve a powerful nature into these elements [sweetness and gentleness], and Faraday's character would have been less admirable than it was, had it not embraced forces and tendencies to which the silken adjectives, 'gentle' and 'tender' would by no means apply. Underneath his sweetness and gentleness, was the heat of a volcano. He was a man of excitable and fiery nature; but through high self-discipline he had converted the fire into a central glow and motive-power of life, instead of permitting it to waste itself in useless passion. 'He that is slow to anger,' saith the sage, 'is greater than the mighty, and he that ruleth his own spirit than he that takes a city.' Faraday was *not* slow to anger, but he completely ruled his own spirit, and thus, though he took no cities, he captivated all hearts,"—Faraday as a Discoverer. By John Tyndall. Appleton & Co., 1868, p. 37.

studies have suggested several plans of books, which I should like to execute. Some of these lie chiefly in my own peculiar line of orientalism, etc. others are equally, if not more, in yours. Any one of these projects would be occupation enough. Their number and variety distracts me. If I could be forestalled in some of them, I could execute the others all the better. From this perplexity, you can relieve me. You may choose between the Life of Christ and the popular Church History. If you will take both off my hands, *tant mieux*. But what I want is, a definite release from one or more of my literary vows. I have no misgiving as to the demand or the success. The Church History would require more laborious preparation. If you will take the Life of Christ, I will place all my collections and notes at your disposal, *i. e.* after finishing my present course. This offer is not a generous one, because I find my views as to the Life of Christ still vague and problematical. I do not feel a drawing to its execution as I do to that of other plans. I sincerely think that you are peculiarly qualified for this specific task. There is one advantage for a heavy job like this, which I think you would appreciate: I found Isaiah, heavy burden as it was, a real solace for annoyances. Please to receive this as a practical and *boná-fide* proposition. Your acceptance of it may materially modify my course of study."

Another letter to the same brother refers to an article in the Repertory, the quarterly list in the same, Dr. Green's call to the Central Church, the History Professorship, Hegel, and his own book on the Acts:

"PRINCETON, ——— 14th, 1848.

"R. D. B.:*

"Finding that you had not corrected the last part of your article, I was obliged to exercise my own discretion as to the questionable passage by leaving out the German words. Dr. Hodge has consented to abolish the short notices, provided we will publish a quarterly list of new publications. My idea of the quarterly list is to give the complete title, place of publication, publisher, form, size, &c. as we do at the beginning of an article; and to make it so far select that it may be something of an honour to appear there. As to classification, I am doubtful. I wish you would begin to take notes for this purpose. I

* R. D. B., in the Addisonian dialect, stands for Reverend and dear Brother.

see no need of confining it to American books. W. H. Green is called to the Central Church [of Philadelphia]; if he goes, I shall immediately resume the Hebrew, and thus have everything in *statu quo* when the Assembly meets. If, without recommendation or solicitation, they appoint me History Professor, I shall be satisfied of my vocation. If they do not, I shall be more content than ever with my old employment.

"I have not had time to begin Hegel till within a few days. What surprises me is that the metaphysical parts do not strike me as absurd or unintelligible, but rather as the presentation of old thoughts under new and strange names. His whole idea of Freedom is to me astonishing. The word always looks to me like a typographical error. What I have read of the historical matter pleases me much. I am now in the fifth chapter of the book upon the Acts."

In the autumn of 1848, the failing health of the venerable Dr. Cuyler, pastor of the Second Presbyterian Church, Philadelphia, admonished his people that he must have assistance, and they applied to Dr. Addison Alexander; who after some hesitation consented to supply the pulpit a part of each Sabbath. He commenced his labours early in November and preached every Sabbath morning for about six months, with great acceptance, although not to the same crowds that greeted him the year before in the Tenth Church.

In the beginning of this year, he commenced the Commentary upon the Book of Psalms, as suggested in the preceding letter; but the work did not appear until the year following. In the subjoined letter to his brother James, he predicts that event, and eulogizes Hengstenberg, whose line of exposition he strictly adhered to in the main:

"Feb. 23d, 1849.

"My dear Brother:

"Baker & Scribner have sent me specimens of type, paper, &c., for my Book of Psalms. Having yielded my own preference for the octavo form to the judgment of the trade, I find it hard to choose between the different duodecimos; if you will do it for me it will be a real service. I have therefore directed them to let you see the samples, and be governed by your judgment. I shall not have room for much quotation. My plan is to convey to the English reader, in the shortest space, the true sense, as determined by the best and latest exegesis.

This I do, when it is possible, by mere translation; if not, by paraphrase; if more is wanted, by brief comment. If I merely brought the substance and results of Hengstenberg's book within the English reader's reach, I should think it an invaluable gift. After much thought I have again resolved to leave the 'practique part' to other hands. I would rather do one thing well than two things badly.

"Ever yours,

J. A. A."

In the following letter he reveals more fully his views and feelings respecting the proposed step of transferring him to the chair of Church History, made vacant by the resignation of Dr. Miller:

"PRINCETON, April 10th, 1849.

"DEAR JAMES:

"I have hitherto abstained from boring you with letters on the Seminary question, and I break my silence now only because the affair has reached a point at which your assistance may be necessary. When my transfer was first thought of, four years ago, I was employed almost entirely in teaching Hebrew and writing on Isaiah. The former has become, from constant repetition, a mechanical employment; and the other, having been prescribed to me, was still more distasteful. The prospect of any change was therefore pleasant; and the proposition had the good effect of forcing me to finish a task which I now look back upon with more astonishment than admiration. But in doing this, a new field opened to my view; and I acquired some skill, as I supposed, in tilling it. The consequence was, that I never felt more inclination to Biblical studies than I did when I got through this tremendous job. Another effect of the new project was, that I acquired the habit of lecturing, and making my instructions more intellectual. They were still, however, purely Biblical; and as I found that this department would afford ample scope for my highest powers and my best resources, I naturally felt less and less desire to undertake a new work which, in order to be well done, should have been begun much earlier, and which would require me to leave the terra firma of inspired truth for the mud and sand of patristical learning, as well as to exchange direct original investigation for the study of second-hand authorities and diluted compilations. This change of feeling was confirmed by Dr. Spring's protestation, in the spring of 1846; and has been growing stronger ever since. Dr. Hodge's views of the relative importance of Church History I think exaggerated; and I doubt very much whether it has been as heartily assented to as he imagines. Still, I cannot draw back if the Church insists upon my going forward; and I have, this day, come to this conclusion with the Doctor. He consents that I shall state officially to the Directors, when they meet in May, and through them to the Assembly, that I not only do not wish the change, but, as a matter of personal choice, should greatly prefer to remain where I am; and that if this statement puts an end to the affair, it shall be finally abandoned. I consent, on my part, to make no resistance, if the Board, notwithstanding this disclosure of my wishes, still persists in recommending my translation, and the General Assembly acts accordingly. Indeed, I should regard this as a clear Providential call to the new station; but only in the case of its being given with a full knowledge of my private inclinations. Now, in order to secure this indispensable condition, it is highly important that the Directors should, as far as possible, be made to see the true state of the case before they meet in May; and as you seem to be placed in a focus of rumours and negotiations on the subject, you can materially aid me by letting others know this fact — that I have no wish for a change, and would unhesitatingly choose to remain *in statu quo*. This I should like to be understood, not as a nolo episcopari, but as an expression of my real sentiments. At the same time, I consider myself bound to let it be known that I shall not refuse the place, if forced upon me after all. With this accompanying qualification I have no objection to the strongest and most explicit statement of my preference for my present place. To whom, when, and how this communication shall be made, I leave to your discretion; only expressing my deliberate preference of oral to graphic promulgation. I am the more disposed to let all this be known, because I have strong reasons for believing that some of your best friends have come into this project on the supposition that I am not satisfied with my position and desire to change it. I do not wish you to step out of your way an inch to make this publication; but only to remove any injunction of reserve or secrecy to which you may feel yourself subjected in this matter.*

"Yours,

"J. A. A."

* Under the date of April 13th, Dr. Archibald Alexander writes to his son James: "The removal of Addison from his professorship to another, never struck me favourably. To be sure, he had spent time enough in teaching the elements of Hebrew; but he has it in his power to comprehend in his course whatever relates to the Bible, and he is now convinced that he had better stay where he is, and let Dr. Miller have an adjunct." He gives it as his judgment

The transfer which he feared was not made at this time, as his brother, the Rev. James W. Alexander, D. D. was appointed to the chair.

During the winter of 1849--1850, he was closely occupied in lecturing to his classes on the Psalms, the Gospels, the Acts, Biblical Criticism, and the Prophecies. In the month of June he went to New York: where he remained during the vacation writing his Commentary on the Psalms.

On the 26th of May, a telegraphic dispatch informed Dr. James Alexander that he was that day elected by the General Assembly at Pittsburg to succeed Dr. Miller. And on Sunday, June the 10th, at the close of service in the morning, he announced to his congregation that he must leave them. There was much weeping. Pastor and people were both greatly overcome. Soon after, he removed to Princeton. On the 20th of June, I find that the younger brother was moving into his chambers in the Seminary building. His restlessness as regarded his rooms could not be quieted.

Dr. James Alexander refers to this change in a letter to Dr. Hall. He could not comprehend his brother's feelings that urged him to these ceaseless revolutions: "Addison (*pro more*) has moved again, and has chambers in the Seminary, lowest floor, front, next to Dr. Hodge's."* He was himself 'moving in' from New York. He went first to his father's, where he remained for six weeks, during the time the house was undergoing repairs. It was in the room at the northwest corner of the Seminary that the younger brother was now piling up the sheets of his book on the Psalms. His window looked out on the green lawn or campus, and beyond the trees and fence upon the street, and beyond that the secluded but exquisitely lovely grounds of Mr. Thomson. During a part

that the comparative importance of the chair of Ecclesiastical History had been magnified beyond reason, and expresses a willingness to acquiesce in any appointment the General Assembly should make. "We cannot tell," he says, "beforehand, who would be a pleasant colleague."

* Fam. Let., Vol. II. p. 100.

of this time I was his private pupil. He was punctual, emphatic, perhaps a little impatient (but always for good cause); but not hard to please. If a paradigm was missed, he would take up the book *ab initio*. He made his private pupils get a small Latin primer of the Greek language by heart. He insisted much on the essential importance of writing as well as reading a dead language. He looked upon all efforts on the part of American boys to *speak* Latin, for instance, as nearly hopeless. A mistake in an exercise seemed to grieve him. He would mourn over it as an indication of mental infirmity. A perfect lesson seemed to exhilarate him like champagne. He loved to recount the little exploits of former pupils. It may seem incredible, but it is literally true that while hearing these recitations, and carrying on these lively dialogues, he was commonly writing on his Psalms. He had few book before him, and I do not remember that I ever saw him rise to consult a lexicon. That stage in his progress had been passed. He was writing as fast as if he were writing a paragraph for a newspaper. I never saw him copy anything, either from himself or others. Once he stopped short in his work, and showed me a letter which he had just received from a friend in Philadelphia; and remarked upon its difficult but elegant abbreviations. He discouraged everything like looking off the book; but mixed a great deal of pleasantry with such strictures. He used to point, when in New York, to a girl getting her lesson at a window, and descant upon the folly of getting it *in that way; i. e.* by a succession of ocular voyages over everything but the page that was lying open in her hands or lap. Yet sometimes he forgot himself, and would talk facetiously and charmingly about the odd or pleasing characters of the place. He suffered me to talk to him as much as I pleased when he was writing, and when I was not under obligation to con my own task. It often occurred to me that his forthcoming volume would necessarily be worthless; and that I should be in some sort to blame for the unexpected failure. The greater portion of the writing, however, was done in New York, in the midst of the street cars and omnibuses, which stimulated him as the sight of a lake or mountain has often stimulated a poet.

His brother James, of course, was deeply interested in his undertaking, though with others he would probably have preferred a purely original exposition. The author changed his plan after getting through the first few Psalms, and his remarks on the verses, which had been somewhat copious, became severely concise. As he advanced, he receded more and more from the guidance of his friend and whilom master, Dr. Hengstenberg.

The first intimations of the book that were given to his life-long correspondent by the New York pastor are the following, of March 19th: "Addison is certainly printing on Psalms. I am glad of it, as no book is more needed." * The New York writer afterwards expresses himself in this fashion. The allusions to Foster, Hall, and his own brother, Addison, are of a striking character: "My taste increases for books which flow straight on, as from an inner source; little erudition, no quotation, no heads or divisions, growing, swelling, &c.: not the less because I am individually of the opposite sort, and tend to mince things up, and put them into patty-pans, with numbers. I got a shove for weeks from reading 'Foster's Estimate of Robert Hall as a Preacher.' Don't fail to read it, especially what he says about Hall's faults. John Howe is the only Puritan writer of the sort I mean. Addison, in one or two of his best sermons, exemplifies my meaning." †

In another letter he says: "Addison has saddled himself with a tremendous job in his book of Psalms, but his working power exceeds anything I ever dreamt of." This was written in August,‡ and I take for granted the energetic scribe was now at work in the city. When his toils were over, he would stroll about at random, sometimes in the fine streets and sometimes in the queer and strange ones. He appeared to be in a high state of enjoyment, and took his usual pleasure in scan-

* Fam. Let. II. p. 94. † Fam. Let. II. p. 95.

‡ Fam. Letters, Vol. II. p. 102. August 28, 1849.

ning the features and gestures of men, women, and children, and in vainly trying to solve the problem of their past and future story. He loved to classify the people of a nation, or a town, by their looks and manners; and to fix them still more accurately by noting their resemblance to others definitely known and vividly remembered.

In the midst of these labours, he was invited to address the young men of the University of Virginia.

> "In 1849 and 1850," writes a friend,* "I tried by correspondence to induce him to deliver one of the lectures in the University course on the 'Evidences,' but he declined; on the ground that when he attempted 'anniversary eloquence' or other oratorical specialties, he always made 'egregious failures;' and when I persisted in my importunities, he made me sorry that I had not accepted his first declinature!"

He did not like to be importuned, and still less to ascend the platform; or even to preach on a preannounced subject. I do not remember that he ever delivered a "popular lecture" in his life. He was really modest in his judgment as to his own fitness for such tasks, and had a fixed aversion to everything like self-obtrusion. It is not always easy to remove preconceptions, but there is certainly a tendency in what follows, from the pen of the Rev. Dr. Leyburn,† towards the obliteration of certain false ideas many continue to have of Dr. Alexander's usual ways and manners when in the society of gentlemen for whom he had a liking. Dr. Leyburn writes:

> "After my leaving college, years passed before I again met the professor. Meanwhile he had not only gained wide renown as a teacher in the Theological Seminary and as an unsurpassed Biblical scholar, but also as a preacher. On my removal to Philadelphia, I found his praises as a preacher on everybody's lips; and to my great gratification, he soon after came down to the city to supply the pulpit of the North Church one Sabbath. He was domiciled during this visit with our common friend, the late Dr. A. W. Mitchell, and the Doctor kindly invited me to spend an evening with him."

* The Rev. Dr. W. H. Ruffner, then Chaplain of the University of Virginia.

† The Rev. Dr. John Leyburn, of Baltimore, formerly of Philadelphia.

He had heard so much, however, as to his shyness and unwillingness to see company, that it was with some apprehension that he accepted the invitation. But all doubt was dissipated when he met him.

"He was cordial, friendly, and most companionable; full of conversation, exceedingly cheerful, and enjoying a good laugh with a zest. I went home delighted with the evening, and feeling how little he was understood by those who only saw him in public and at a distance. One thing which struck me on this occasion, and which I observed in subsequent intercourse, was that, notwithstanding his comparatively recluse life, he was apparently familiar with all that was going on in the church, in particular congregations, and in society generally. He seemed to know men and things as well as if he had been personally associated with them."

He was by no means misanthropical.

"Far from being out of sympathy with the living world, he evidently felt a keen interest in it. Subsequently, whenever I met him I found him ready for a talk, and can truly say that never on any occasion did he show himself to me in any other light than that of a most companionable friend. Overflowing as he was with learning, and instructive as was his conversation on all topics, he was always ready to enter into current events, and seemed even anxious to hear all that was going on."

Dr. James Alexander delivered his introductory lecture at the Seminary on the 4th of September. It was to the second or middle class. He also attended his first preaching exercise, which was with the seniors; and chatted with them about the Chironomian Society of former days, and its champions, "Kirk, Bethune, Vermilye, Collins, Benedict, Lansing, Christmas, Waterbury, and Alexander." He strongly urged the young men not to use notes.

The wind was in the east; the air was raw and irritating. Good old Dr. Miller was now looking very feeble. Prof. James Alexander preached his first sermon in the chapel on the 16th. After it was over his father told him that he spoke too loud.

Of course there was much to please the younger brother in the thought of "James's" return to his old haunts in Steadman street. They were as unlike in many things, and yet as necessary to each other, as two complementary colours. The younger leaned on the intellect and good taste of the elder brother, while the latter felt himself supported by the strong sense and resolute temper of Addison. The mutual admiration and love was truly extraordinary.

The new professor's reading lay much in the Augustinian field, and especially the part pertaining to the controversy with Pelagius. Early in October, he received a letter from Dr. Engles of Philadelphia, requesting him and his brother Addison, in conjunction with Dr. Hodge, to set about a commentary on the New Testament, for the benefit of the Presbyterian Church. "Dirigat Dominus," is the entry in the older brother's diary, "in suam gloriam!"

On Sunday, the 18th of November, the venerable Dr. Alexander, who was himself not long for this world, preached in the Seminary Chapel an extemporaneous sermon from Luke xii. 40, "Be ye therefore ready also." He was calmer than in the old days, but his sons were delightfully reminded of sermons he used to preach many years before, when he was in his prime.

On Tuesday, the 20th, the new professor was inaugurated. There was a large gathering of ministers and friends of the Seminary. Dr. Miller continued to grow weaker and weaker, though he was still able to sit up in his chair. The state of his soul is described as being "very tender and happy; he is waiting till his change comes." * His colleague and successor in the Seminary called upon him about this time, and found him in his study, a room which he seemed greatly to love. He was reclining on an easy chair, with his person half extended. His visitor could not perceive the slightest decay of feeling and intellect, or even of hearing and sight. "If this continues," he records, (quod concedat Deus!) "is it not Euthanasia?" The aged Christian talked some time about the

* Private Journals of the Rev. J. W. Alexander, D. D.

state of the church, and deplored the absence of religious revival in the country. When his friend arose, the old man asked him to lead in prayer; and, as he closed, said, "Remain on your knees, my dear friend!" "He then offered a most touching prayer, thanking God for giving him a colleague, or 'more properly a successor;' spoke of himself as God's 'departing servant;' prayed that God would not forsake him in his old age; and made earnest request for blessings on me. I regarded it as in some sort his parting benediction. He said, 'Lord, now lettest thou thy servant depart in peace, for mine eyes have seen thy salvation!' The prayer was deliberate, and the words well chosen; in two instances he seemed to hesitate about an expression." *

But the time was now approaching when this great light of the intellectual firmament of Princeton was to be extinguished, or rather, let us say, hidden from the view of mortal sin and ignorance. It was evident to all that Dr. Miller was at last sinking. He was very lethargic; and the whole of one side was numb. To a near relative who had come in after a few weeks' absence, he roused himself sufficiently to utter the words "Almost home." He was visited for the last time on Monday, December the 31st, by his new colleague, Dr. James Alexander. He was greatly enfeebled and attenuated. The princely carriage had been broken by a slight paralysis. The power of articulation had also been much impaired. The younger minister had been called in suddenly, and was sensible of having a cold hand at the time he greeted the dying saint, and apologised for it. "Dr. Miller said, 'how do you do? how is your family?' Then, alluding to my momentary apology for my hand, 'Christ's hand is never cold! He has propped me up and led me and comforted me, more than I am able to express, and I wish you affectionately to thank Him for it in my name.'" His visitor knelt down and prayed with him; on which the feelings of the courtly gentleman, by which he had always been distinguished among his contemporaries, seemed

'Private Journals of the Rev. J. W Alexander, D. D.

to work strongly within him, and he said, as if he feared he might have been misunderstood in what he had uttered respecting the cold hand, "Your hand has never been inconveniently cold to me; but the hand of Christ is always warm." Thereupon his visitor withdrew.

He lay very low for some days, but happy, intelligent, pleasant, and at times almost facetious. He breathed his last on the 7th of January, at about eleven o'clock at night. His aged colleague had been with him a few hours previous. Stupor had come on, but he recognized his venerated friend, spoke intelligibly of his condition, and joined in the prayer that was offered at his bedside. The weather was cold. The day before, which was Sunday, Dr. Archibald Alexander, though nearly seventy-eight, preached in his turn at the chapel: Haggai i. 7, "Consider your ways." His voice, matter, and language, were all worthy of his better years. He was fresh and alert, with a beaming face, and, as one said of this effort, had "the greatness of simplicity."

There was much seriousness in the village before the day of prayer for colleges; which was the 28th. The services of this day strengthened and deepened the impression, and greatly widened its area. Dr. Hodge and Dr. Hope spoke with effect in the new chapel. The College was much stirred. The interest at the First Church seemed to be spreading. By the second of March there were thirty or forty inquirers. Prayer-meetings were kept up in the Sophomore recitation-room, and in East and West College, as well as in the lecture-room of the First Church. Sometimes much feeling was manifested. On the Saturday preparatory to the Communion, thirteen persons were baptized, and the names of forty were read out who had been already received by the session. The whole college now became aroused. From one hundred and twenty to two hundred attended the public meetings. Pious students met in their rooms for intercessory prayer. There had been no such time since 1815. Some of the worst men on the roll appeared to be converted.

Dr. Addison Alexander took no active part in these services, but rejoiced to hear of them, and contributed indirectly towards them; and afterwards, on another occasion of religious awakening, his addresses to the young men were greatly prized, and very useful.

CHAPTER XXIV.

The following extract from a very readable letter to his mother, will give an idea of his occupation at this time as a writer of commentaries. It is hard to believe that they were made so fast.

New York, June 10, 1850.

"Honoured Madam (as men used to say a hundred years ago when writing to their mothers):

"I did not write again last week, because they meant to write from 27th Street, and also because William was just coming home. Nor would I have had many interesting incidents to state. My life here, though agreeable, is uniform. The last week passed away like a dream. I spent the whole of every day in writing, from breakfast till late dinner-time, besides correcting proofs at night. I never ran a race with the printer so before. What I gave them in manuscript in the morning, they returned to me in proof at night. This was the next thing to 'composing,' in both senses at the same time; as Dr. Franklin sometimes did. The experiment last week was highly satisfactory. When Saturday night came, I found that we had printed about fifty pages; every word of which was written here. Thus far I find it very wholesome. Notwithstanding my hard work I take a great deal of exercise, and see and hear a great deal to amuse me. I know, indeed, of no situation that would suit my health and inclination better than to live here and make books all the week, and preach as I had opportunity on Sunday."

Here is an extract from another letter of the same period:

"New York, June 15, 1850.

"My Dear Mother:

"I have just finished the twenty-first Psalm, written since I came here, and the whole will be in type this evening. I never worked harder, or enjoyed more recreation. From breakfast to dinner (never earlier than four), I write incessantly. After dinner, I do nothing but amuse myself; chiefly by walking, and riding in the omnibuses; always in a new direction. I meet with many amusing incidents which I rerelate to Sue on my return. She is very kind and cheery. I never spent so pleasant a vacation."

I know not how to insist enough on his deep and childlike affection for his mother. When he thought she was drooping, he was sad; when he saw her happy, he was gay and frolicsome. I will illustrate this by a few extracts from a little *brochure* which he wrote and stitched together expressly for her entertainment. It is intituled,

THE

MOTHER'S MAGAZINE,

AND

MATERNAL ASSOCIATION'S MONTHLY ADVERTISER.

No. 1. July, 1850.

"July 2. * * I wrote from half-past nine till half-past two, and an hour or more after dinner, finishing the 97th and 98th Psalms. In the evening I went up to New York. The omnibus was very full of merchants homeward bound. A tall mulatto, as I thought, got in, and fell back on a little Jew, to whom he apologized with great grace. I afterwards heard him talking Spanish, and found out that he was not a man of colour. It rained fast as I came down in the omnibus, in which, however, there were several ladies. Somewhere near Peteler's, an elderly man and woman, with a younger woman and her child, got in. It is curious to see what small children are dressed up and carried about here, even at night. This one was scarcely bigger than a large doll, but sat on the bench by me, with her little legs stretched out straight before her, and her shining little boots, and snow-white stockings, and visite, and long, white sun-bonnet. She never smiled, except when I tried to make her laugh, but looked with solemn awe at every bright light that we passed. The last passenger who got out before me told the driver to move on a little further, to the door of the ''otel' (Delmonico's); then turned to me and said he liked to get as much for his money as he could, and bade me as affectionate a good-night as if we had been old friends.

"July 3. * * I was working away at the 99th Psalm, when the

waiter brought me Dr. Krebs's card. He was very friendly, and invited me to 'call, dine, drink tea, loaf, and preach next Sunday-week.' This interrupted me somewhat, and compelled me to work longer after dinner than I usually do; as I was anxious to finish the Hundredth Psalm, which I accomplished before dark. I am amused with the curiosity excited by my writing all day at the window. The marble house next door is occupied by foreigners, who watch me a good deal, and then there are babiculars,* both great and small, in Greenwich street, who know not what to make of it. As I came in this evening, the book-keeper gave me a small parcel which had been left for me, and which, he said, they called a *proof*. Ellen was just beginning to distinguish *proof* from copy when I moved down town.

"July 4. I was roused by the usual noises of the glorious Fourth. As I sat in the parlour, —— came and sat by me, and asked if I was not impatient for the noise to be over. He seemed quite disconcerted when I told him no, but said he supposed I liked to see the people enjoy themselves. He seemed to have no idea that I was enjoying *myself*. I made a calculation this morning of the space required for the remainder of the Psalms, and found, to my surprise, that unless I make the third volume still smaller, I must close the second with the Hundredth Psalm, which I completed yesterday. I received a letter to-day from ——, again inviting me to preach a week for him. He still harps upon the old string, about staying at hotels, and in private houses, in reply to which I say: 'You will find it, I trust, much less difficult to provide for my accommodation, than you seem to think it necessary to anticipate. I have had no 'pastoral experience,' but I have preached a good deal in strange places, and have even lodged at private houses.'

"July 5. * * I have suffered more than usual from the heat, because I have been doing nothing. Work is one of the best antidotes to heat I know. Sir Samuel Romilly's Parliamentary Diary interests me very much. Every other night, I hear the most exquisite music almost under my window, for nothing. Instead of the common marches, etc. they play the finest operatic music, overtures, etc. After sunset, the most delicious breeze blows from the bay. Good-night.

"July 10. * * I finished the 103d Psalm, and began the 104th. These are delightful Psalms. I am glad that the last part of my labour is so pleasant. I corrected the last proof-sheet of the second volume. As I was coming down Broadway, there was a very little man before me, dressed in the height of the fashion, walking with another of ordi-

* A jesting word of his own invention.

nary size. In crossing Canal street, a high wind carried away a black lace veil from somebody in front. The little man ran, 'fit to break his neck,' snatched it from under the feet of an omnibus-horse, and presented it gracefully to the owner, who, turning round to thank him, proved to be a splendidly-dressed black woman. I pitied the generous little fellow when the people laughed. As to health and spirits, I was never better. I am quite exhilarated by the prospect of soon finishing my work. How pleasant it is to have something, and especially something rather hard to do. That reminds me of a sermon I heard Edward Smith * preach yesterday in his own church, from 2 Thess. iii. 10, on labour, considered first as a curse, and second as a blessing; on the true dignity of workingmen, when pious, well-informed, etc.; and the sin and folly of excessive toil merely for gain, and without these attendant advantages. His style is clear, strong, and accurate, without excess of ornament. His voice is not so pleasant as it was when I heard him speak the valedictory, two years before I entered college. I have never heard him speak in public since."

Sir Robert Peel was dead; and the event was a topic of frequent conversation with Dr. Alexander. He often wondered who would be his successor, and pitched alternately upon this man and that man as the probable recipient of the dead man's place, if not of his honours. He was excessively fond of noting coincidences; and he had a remarkable one now in the deaths of Sir Robert Peel and President Zachary Taylor. He was fond of dwelling upon the fact that so many of the British statesmen of rank and abilities are University-bred men, and some of them (as were Macaulay and Cornwall Lewis) very distinguished scholars. He often spoke of the classical knowledge and tastes of such men as Pitt, Fox, Burke, Windham, Brougham, Gladstone, and the Stanleys, father and son. He delighted, also, to recall the fact that Henry Martyn was a Senior Wrangler, and that some of the best of the old practical writers, English and Scotch, were accomplished Hebraists. I remember his mentioning Flavel and Boston as examples. He thought well of college distinctions, and believed it to be

* The Rev. Edward D. Smith, D.D., of New York.

a mistake, even in this country, that the men thus honoured did not afterwards fulfil their early promise.

His habits about books differed much from his brother's; who was exquisitely careful of his volumes, and never touched a margin but to adorn it. Dr. Addison Alexander, on the other hand, though neat in all things was yet indifferent about the preservation of his books; and he sometimes disfigured the page with his bold erasures and rapid markings. He was very cruel in some of these marginalia; and very comical in others. He marked equally where he liked and where he disliked. Sometimes one cannot tell why he uses the pencil. His eye was ruthlessly turned to the construction of sentences, and he never spared the offender. He is very hard in this way upon some famous writers. He was too clean and sensible in his tastes to cut the leaves of a new book with the butter knife, as De Quincey avers that Wordsworth did at Windermere, but he thought nothing of tearing the leaves out altogether. I have been reminded, when considering this trait, of Alison's description of Napoleon in the coach reading the new books as they came out, and flinging them in whole or in parcels out of the window. I have an English copy of Alexander on Isaiah, a beautiful specimen of foreign presswork, which he has interlarded everywhere with large pencil marks, and literally torn to pieces for *copy!* I presume that at least fifty pages at the beginning are clean gone, and the edges of the mutilated pages show signs of haste and violence. This was when he was getting out his abridged edition. He was made up of pleasant contradictions: the covers of his books were very precious to him, and he was very partial to a sumptuous and, strange to say, a uniform binding. The same fiery impetuosity and recklessness which governed Bonaparte must at times have actuated him.

À propos of his criticisms along the margin, he seldom let a book go through his hands and come out of them unscathed. He could never make much in this way out of Macaulay and Edward Everett. Of the last he said that he showed the scholar in every line he had ever printed; and that if he had devoted himself to the more permanent forms of literature, he would have achieved a more enviable reputation as a writer. I am informed by a friend that a volume might easily be made out of these marginal annotations; most of which may be read by any one visiting the Lenox Library at Princeton, where Dr. Alexander's books are now permanently shelved. He tells us that his Bengel is especially rich in these treasures.*

Another hint of his movements occurs in the Forty Years' Correspondence. The elder brother watched the younger one very scrupulously when he was rounding off a volume. "Addison's present duties keep him reading the text of the Bible, with versions, &c. from morning till night." This was a delightful occupation to him. These were regions where his own half-forgotten foot-prints were abundant. The quaint old English writers had the charm for him that Scott's romances had for the generation of young people that was co-

* The Rev. Wm. Harris of Towanda. One of the books he most admired and loved to read, Boston's Fourfold State, is almost slashed to pieces with pencil strokes. Nearly all the characteristic and deeply spiritual parts, the original ideas, the laughable oddities, and the frequent mistakes, are thus pointed out. I have before me the first volume of his copy of Dr. Abel Stevens's History of Methodism; which was another book he greatly liked, but has treated in much the same fashion. The index is copiously annotated in this way. The body of the work is fairly sprinkled over with heavy pencillings; some of them designed to indicate something wrong or unusual in the style; others to denote approval, astonishment, admiration, or even denial; others again simply to call his attention to something that had struck him as noteworthy. Here and there occurs a sentence, or merely a syllable, in the way of running commentary. Sometimes he erases a letter: and in various ways he corrects what are obvious misprints or *lapsus calami*. Nothing of this sort, not even the smallest, seems to have escaped him. Marks of interrogation and exclamation are frequent. He invariably marks the Websterian spelling in words like "theater." Some things he marks evidently because they are repeated often. Many of his scratches seem to be merely mnemonic or referential. Sometimes nearly the whole of a page is enclosed in a sweeping bracket. Occasionally a whole page is thus enclosed. Sometimes he adds a hand in the margin. Once he writes, "Don't skip any of this." He often italicises mere dates or statements of local interest. It would be impossible to give examples without leaving erroneous impressions as to his system.

eval with his boyhood. I have seen him laugh till the tears came in his eyes over their odd turns; and the rose of pleasure would bloom again in his cheek as he went from his desk to his friend to make him a partner in his joy. Need I say that that friend was often his new colleague? And there was no difference in their feelings here. Professor James Alexander once more records among his reasons for not leaving Princeton again, his "delightful house, and the company of his brother Addison."

At the beginning of the session Dr. Addison Alexander returned to Princeton, and lectured during the winter upon Biblical History, the Messianic Prophecies, and Gospel History. An extract from his journal will exhibit the nature of his studies at this time:

"Nov. 27th. Lectured to the Second Class on Luke. Read Zech. ii. in Hebrew and English, Chaldee and Syriac, Greek and Latin; the German versions of Luther and De Wette, and the exposition of the same by Lowth, Schulten, Michaelis, Gill, Rosenmüller, Hitzig, Maurer, Hengstenberg. Read Guizot's Histoire de la Civilization Française. Wrote additions to my paper on the Odyssey.* Corrected proofs of my paper in the Magazine. Read Edinburgh Review for 1807."

In December the elder brother proceeded to the University of Virginia, and delivered his discourse in the series of lectures on the Evidences of Christianity, before the young men and the maturer minds of that institution. His subject was the Character of Christ, and it was handled with the utmost delicacy and tenderness. It has been pronounced a gem in this respect. The argument preceded those of Young and Bushnell. When he came back he plunged once more into the sea of professional labours and vicissitudes. He knew care and sorrow and perplexity, and has covered the pages of his diaries for this period with confessions, thanksgivings, and supplications, written partly in English, partly in Latin, and partly in stenography. It was a struggle for him to leave Princeton in the

* In the Princeton Magazine.

first instance. It was a greater struggle to return to it. He was soon to be called to make up his mind to leave it. This last step was not taken without a violent shock to all his newly rooted affections; but was no doubt ordered in mercy and wisdom.

It was in 1850 that the thoughts of the three brothers Alexander were turned to the project of a new literary magazine, to be edited by one of themselves and to be largely filled with their own ephemeral productions.*

There was no lack of material already waiting for the printer. Their portfolios were overstocked with essays, dialogues, satirical squibs, bits of Latin criticism, popular philosophy, and indescribable burlesques of every quality. The editor and main projector, the Hon. William C. Alexander, wrote an article for it styled "A Trip to the Levant," describing with rare minuteness a real voyage of a real man-of-war, and with a technical precision that afterwards greatly astonished his friend Commodore Kearney, whose log he had been

* On March 2, 1850, the elder brother writes to Dr. Hall: "My brother William is about to set up the Princeton Magazine, pp. 48, monthly. Of course we shall all help. It will not exclude scientific, classical, erudite, sportive, or Jersey articles. Probably a number out three weeks hence. 'Princeton in 1801' will open it, a reminiscence of my father." Fam. L. II. p. 112.

Referring to this venture, the editor of the Familiar Letters, in a foot note, makes the statements which are here subjoined:

"Twelve numbers of this magazine appeared in 1850, after which it was discontinued. The brothers James and Addison made it the repository of many of their desultory effusions. The hand of the former is seen in such subjects as 'Education among Merchants,' 'The Prospects of the Mechanic,' 'The Workingman's Aim,' 'Wordsworth,' 'Le Pays Latin,' 'Books and Business,' 'Aesthetics,' 'Minor Works of Dr. Johnson,' 'Machinery and Labour,' 'The Physiognomy of Houses,' 'Letters on the Early Latin Writers,' 'Roadside Architecture.' The sportive and ironical wit of the younger brother is seen in most of the humorous pieces with which the magazine abounds. Among these is the satirical poem which soon attracted extensive notice, 'The Reconstruction of Society.' In a letter to the editor of these letters, from the late Mr. Walsh (Paris, Nov. 12th, 1850), that eminent scholar wrote: 'The promise of the youth of the brothers Alexander seems to have been fulfilled. The magazine abounds with matter which I read with keen relish.'" Fam. L. II, p. 112.

using. Dr. Archibald Alexander wrote about Patrick Henry and the olden times. Dr. James Alexander contributed some of his most delightful literary recreations in the way of gossiping criticism, and one or two fine pieces of dignified humour.* The pieces on classical subjects are mostly from his pen, though the one on the Odyssey is by his brother Addi-

* Among these I may mention the lively pieces entitled Merry Men and Visit to The Somerset Farmer.

The following is the list of Dr. Addison Alexander's contributions:

A Private Letter from a Public Letter-Writer.
Reconstruction of Society.
Freedom of Speech. Nos. 1 and 2.
Utilitarian Poetry.
Monosyllabics.
South Smithfield Correspondence. Nos. 1 and 2.
The Complaint.
Economy of Thought.
School of Legislation.
Some People.
Economy of Words.
Dialogue.
The Tailor's Strike.
Persian Proverbs.
Discoveries at Dinner.
Ham and Eggs.
Mother-Country and Father-Land.
Nil Admirari.
Seeing the World.
Old Commencement.
Something New.
The Persian Language.
Counsellor Phillips.
Pedagogics. Nos. 1 and 2.
The Odyssey. Nos. 1 and 2.
Gentlemanly.

The Magazine was written by members of the family (principally by J. W. A.) with occasional articles by an outsider. The volume contained one hundred and twelve articles. Eighty-three articles were written in the family. To these may be added sixty-one notices of new books. These notices were almost exclusively from the pen of the editor.

son. Dr. Addison Alexander wrote in every style, but commonly in the broadest irony.

The work made its appearance in the autumn of this year, was issued monthly, and continued just a year. It had a poor sale, and its worth was never recognized till it was out of print. There is now a demand for old files of the periodical on the part of literary connoisseurs and antiquaries, and the friends of its chief contributors. The editor also had regular and efficient aid from other quarters; and now and then some friend would rally to its assistance with a pleasant article. I believe the general opinion is that its flag was struck without dishonour.

In the month of December Dr. James Alexander was unanimously recalled to Duane Street Church in New York. After setting apart the 24th for prayer and fasting, I find him on the 29th decided to go, provided the new church which they proposed building should be out of debt. Here the rejoicing, anxious, fearing, troubled, jaded, broken pastor spent the remainder of his life. The Directors of the Seminary met in February following, and passed eulogistic and very cordial resolutions. The attendance was large, and there was great unanimity of action.

In the beginning of the year 1851, Dr. Addison Alexander projected his book on Primitive Church Offices; and during that winter he lectured in the Seminary one hundred and fifty-five times, viz.: seventy lectures on the Acts, fifty-seven on New Testament History, and twenty-eight on Old Testament History.

The following note to Dr. Hall is largely made up of incorrect or current phrases. It however contains an affectionate reference to the retiring professor, and in a playful way assumes that his correspondent is applying for the place:

"PRINCETON, May 3d, 1851.

"REVEREND DEAR BROTHER:

"Your esteemed favour of yesterday came to hand and its contents are duly noted. In reply I beg leave to state that the second Sunday (or eleventh day) of May falls in our annual examination; which is always a season of special interest and effort in our midst, so that none of us can usually leave home; but in this case, our beloved brother, the outgoing Professor of Ecclesiastical History and Church Government, and Sacred Rhetoric, wishing to be with his past and future flock, the quondam Cedar Street and ex-Duane Street Church, New York, N. Y., I arranged the order of examination so as to relieve him of all service on the Saturday and Monday, by taking his share of these days to myself; from which you will at once perceive that I cannot be expected to supply your sacred desk on the ensuing Sabbath, the promise of remuneration and the prospect of your company at tea to the contrary notwithstanding. If this explanation should be deemed insufficient, I beg leave to inform you that I have others still more cogent, but too tedious to mention.

"As to the Professorship, I regret that I have nothing encouraging to say; and I feel a delicacy in suggesting that pastoral experience alone is hardly a sufficient qualification for the vacant office. I will certainly do what I can to promote your wishes, but alas! I fear it will be little.

I remain, dear Brother,

In the best of bonds,

fraternally yours,

J. A. ALEXANDER."

Professor James Alexander was now fixed in his determination, with God's blessing, to cross the Atlantic and visit Europe in the spring. The time soon slipped by, and on the 22d of May he sailed in one of the mail steamers for Liverpool. He was gone about six months.

The time now drew near that the venerable Dr. Archibald Alexander should die and return to his dust. He had enjoyed better health in the last few years than ever before; but now the strength that had for nearly eighty years supported him was rapidly failing. A great change had lately taken place in his appearance. He had grown thin and weak; and talked with increasing solemnity of his declining age and the prospect of his speedy removal from this world. The first person I heard speak very despondingly of his situation was his son Addison, who in the most feeling manner and with a moving tone that reminded me of some of his pathetic bursts in the pulpit, said one day to a near relative not living at the house, that he did not think persons were generally aware how grave his father's seizure was, and how little hope there was of his recovery. The thought seemed to pierce his heart with anguish; though there was no sign of dismay or querulousness. He spoke like a strong man who had made up his mind to take up a burden which might prove greater than he could bear.

Dr. James Alexander arrived at New York, in the U. S. mail steamer Atlantic, on the 15th of October; and after a day's rest in the city, took a seat in the railway carriage for Princeton, where he found his aged father lying ill, and very near his end. During his absence, a member of his own family had been removed by death. He records, "What a dream of pleasure in being in the bosom of my family! One is not; but Jessie is with the Lord." On Thursday, the 16th, he saw his father; who was reclining on a sofa in the study. He was much thinner and weaker than his son expected to see him, and yet put him strangely in mind of his younger days. He took the hand of the returned traveller, and gave thanks to God for preserving him, and bringing him back to see him.*

There was an air of unearthly authority about his face and manner, which was remarked upon by all who conversed with him. A private interview with him in his bed-room, made an indelible impression upon one in particular, whose course in life he accurately marked out, and to whom he spoke in a strain of wonderful eloquence. Yet he made all the needful provision for the future comfort of his family, with even more than his accustomed sagacity and business-like attention to little things. After settling his own worldly affairs, he talked freely with his son, and with all his usual acumen, of God's work and people abroad; after which, finding his strength was exhausted, he took his hand and dismissed him. He was clear, distinct, and decided, and spoke with an air of unusual command. His visitor "still could not believe he was dying." On

* See Life of Dr. Alexander, p. 604, for particulars which need not to be repeated here.

Friday, the 17th, Dr. Alexander walked down stairs to his sofa in the study, where he was seen by his son at intervals during the day, and gave him a message for Dr. Smyth. But his debility became so great that, finding he could no longer walk, he insisted on being carried up to his chamber. This was done by Mr. Cleghorn, of the Seminary, and one or two others, "who placed his dear, shrunken form on a mattrass." He said he should never come down; and he never did. He was greatly refreshed with ice-water, but refused to take much nourishment. A distressing hiccough had supervened on other bad symptoms. He expressed his undoubting confidence of his acceptance through the Redeemer. His last hours were a season of tranquillity and peace. The balance of his reason was never once affected. On the 22d, about six o'clock in the morning, he breathed his last, so gently that the precise moment of his departure was not ascertained. As in the case of his colleague, Dr. Miller, his son records: "This is the Euthanasia. Blessed be God for Jesus Christ!" As death approached, the countenance became more and more like what it was in former days. To the last, there continued to be a kind of marble comeliness about the features.

The Synod of New Jersey was assembled at Princeton, at the time of Dr. Alexander's decease, and adopted a respectful and affectionate minute appropriate to the occasion. The funeral took place on Friday the 24th. It was fine autumn weather; and an immense throng moved towards the old grave-yard on Witherspoon street. Such a concourse was seldom known in Princeton. Three synods were sitting near enough to get the tidings. The whole Synod of New Jersey walked. The Presbytery of New Brunswick acted as pall-bearers. A large body of his students and other friends were present. A number of ministers filled the spaces about and in the pulpit, and some sat on the floor. The prayers were by Dr. Murray and Dr. Plumer. The sermon was preached by Dr. John McDowell, from Rev. xiv. 13. Dr. Magie made a brief address at the grave, and pronounced the benediction. The autumnal sun was just going down in the rich West, when the remains were lowered into the earth, and little Jessie's (the only daughter of Dr. James Alexander) grave was still fresh in the same portion of the New Cemetery. It was, as was stated at the time, "a funeral without gloom, which bore the thoughts quite to the verge of heaven. The light of the resurrection and of immortality seemed to dispel the shadows of death and the grave, and the spectators of the scene could say, and no doubt did say, 'Let me die the death of the righteous, and let my last end be like his!'" * But there was one present whose grief seemed inconsolable. It was Dr. Addison Alexander; the giant of intellectual prowess, the terror and admiration of the classrooms. He stood weeping like a child.

"I observed him," says one,† "in the funeral procession, and during the exercises in the church. He sat motionless; his countenance expressive of the deepest grief; until the singing of the hymn

"Unveil thy bosom, faithful tomb."

At the close of the second stanza, his whole frame became violently agitated, and several convulsive sobs were heard over the whole house. With a mighty effort he controlled the emotion, and in a few moments he was calm and motionless.

"My stay in Princeton on that occasion was brief, and I did not presume to intrude upon the sacredness of his grief."

It was not long after that he composed the beautiful lines which are given below, and which were labelled on the outside of the envelope that contained them, "Medicine for Lucy;" and within—

"LINES 'TO A FATHERLESS GIRL.'

"You asked me, Lucy, to express
My feelings towards the fatherless,
And I consented so to do;

* See a contemporary account quoted in the life of Dr. Alexander, p. 625.

† Rev. B. T. Lacy.

But ere I could redeem my word—
The solemn tidings you had heard—
  I was without a father, too.

Believe not the calumnious tongue,
Which says that none except the young
  Are sensible of such distress.
Though many years have o'er me passed,
And though the next may be the last,
  I feel that I am fatherless.

The breaking of that 'golden bowl'
Has caused to gush within my soul
  A spring of sympathy with you.
I know, with all my mind and heart,
What once I only knew in part;
  For I have lost a father too.

Though you are young, and I am old,
Your feelings warm, and mine too cold,
  I need a comforter no less.
But while I now with you can grieve,
With you I likewise can believe
  That God will help the fatherless.

And if his care extends to me,
How strong must his compassions be
  Towards gentler natures in distress.
The mercy that will not neglect
The strong man, surely will protect
  The child, and that child fatherless.

Woe to the sinner that 'offends'
The 'little ones' whom God befriends,
  And whom the Saviour will 'confess!'
Woe to the wretch who can deceive,
Or would intentionally grieve,
  The orphans and the fatherless!

But no! thou hast a Father still,
Who can defend his child, and will
  Her rights maintain, her wrongs redress.

The 'witness of the spirit' gives
Assurance that thy Father lives.
Lucy, thou art not fatherless!

What is this life of cares and tears,
If He in smiles to thee appears.
Through Christ's dear passion reconciled?
Each pang and shock while here we roam,
Is but a gentle summons home—
The Father calling for his child.

Sooner or later, on his breast,
Thou shalt enjoy unbroken rest,
Beyond the reach of earth's alarms;
Sooner or later, thou shalt win
The prize of perfect peace within
Thy Father's 'everlasting arms.'

Meantime, be cheerful and be bold,
Dear lamb of the Good Shepherd's fold.
He loves his 'little ones' to bless.
Though all forsake thee, He will not;
Though desolation be thy lot,
He will not leave thee fatherless."

PRINCETON, November 10, 1851.

A friend from Virginia refers very kindly to an interview he had with Dr. Addison Alexander a few months after his father's death; in the "Seminary House," of which he had now become the occupant.

"He was then head of the house. He received me cordially at the door; took me into his study, which he had now removed into the house; invited me to remain to dinner, which I did; and during the hours I remained, was kind, social, and attentive. I saw unmistakable evidences of deep sorrow for the loss of his father."

His hospitality was sincere and gratifying to his many guests. He seemed to feel that he was called upon to take his father's place in these matters, so far as he or any one was able to take the place of such a man, even in what may seem so small a thing; for Dr. Archibald Alexander was one of the most charming hosts in the land, and his death made a void in the social circle, no less than in the councils and business of the Church, which it would be hard to fill. But his son did his part manfully, and with becoming grace and cheerfulness; and many left his door, from this time impressed with the fact that the mantle of the father had fallen upon the shoulders of the son, who stood ready, like the prophet who had seen the chariot of fire, to cleave the waters of American prejudice and intolerance, and to pour salt into the fountains of German error and skepticism. He was now reading as much and writing as much as was customary with him in former years when not actually working on a commentary.

CHAPTER XXV.

ALL was again turmoil with the kind people of Duane street. The new pastor was installed on the 12th of November. The congregation were worshipping in the Chapel of the University, but were contemplating a building higher up-town. They afterwards constructed and entered the building at the corner of Fifth Avenue and Nineteenth street, which still stands there, and has latterly enjoyed the ministrations of N. L. Rice, D.D. and afterwards of John Hall, D.D. of Dublin, who is now their beloved and honoured pastor.

The following letter to Dr. Hall of Trenton speaks of an extraordinary structure which Dr. Addison Alexander had set up in his study:

"PRINCETON, 1852.

"MY DEAR SIR:

"Having been providentially deprived of the enjoyment which I anticipated from a visit to your interesting little place, I do not feel at liberty to name another day at once. When 'the way is clear,' I will put myself in communication with you. If I should not be able to come down this winter, I will try to do so in the spring or summer. As to the table, I will see what can be done for you. I am sorry that it made such an impression, as you may be disappointed. The invention is designed for a limited class. James hopes to have one, and the railroad office has already secured several. Besides its other merits, it has a deep symbolical and mystical import; as I use it for a standing-desk in the morning, a sitting-desk in the afternoon, and a flat table at night. It constantly reminds me of the sphinx and Oedipus. *Verbum sat.*

"You may find me in the room which I occupied ten years ago: the north-west room on the ground-floor of my father's house.

"With strong faith in the solidarity of the peoples,

"I am, etc.

"JOSEPH ADDISON ALEXANDER."

The next is one of his bookish and scholar-like letters to his brother James:

"March 17th, 1852.

"My Dear Brother:

"I have this day finished an attentive, but not critical, perusal of the Pentateuch in the Septuagint version, constantly comparing the original. This course of reading, which I began January 27, 1851, I think of continuing, not so much with a view to the investigation of the Old Testament, in reference to which I think the value of the Seventy but small, as to the study of the New Testament, the style and religious phraseology of which were formed upon this model. In the hope of being suffered to devote myself hereafter to New-Testament studies, I have also recommenced the cursory but careful reading of the classics; to note coincidences with Scripture and other sources of illustration. I take the authors in the alphabetical order of my Tauchnitz collection. I have lately read every word of Æschines and Æschylus. I always thought the former a delightful writer. Long represents Cicero and Quintilian as making him equal, if not superior, to Demosthenes. Why is one so easy to a modern reader, and the other so hard? Æschylus pleases me no more than formerly; perhaps because I understand so little. The best things I retain are some magnificent descriptive phrases. One advantage of the Tauchnitz volumes is, that I can carry them about with me, and read them even in travelling, without exciting suspicion.

"Richard Armstrong of the Sandwich Islands, has written to my mother to share his private property with her, if in want."

The following, to his brother, touches upon the proposed changes in the Seminary, an article of his father's, and its similarity to something in the Noctes Ambrosianæ, the Sanscrit and Turkish languages, the Septuagint, Targums, &c., Mariana, the Baptist controversy, Biblical History, a suggested plan of lectures, etc. etc. etc.

"April 22d, 1852.

"My Dear Brother:

"My mind is now at ease as to my professorship. I am quite willing to remain for the present as I am. I observe a remarkable coincidence between lib. VI. cap. 1 of the Noctes, and one of my father's latest papers on moral philosophy. See if a word should not be added there to forestall the objection from the happiness of heaven, which has no pain mixed with it. Another coincidence. In Sanscrit nineteen, twenty-nine, thirty-nine, &c. may be expressed, as in Latin, by *una*, twenty, &c.; but the *una* has nothing to do with *one* but means *less*. I am renewing my youth as to study, and especially of languages. Sanscrit and Turkish, which I have repeatedly failed to learn since I returned from Europe, are becoming quite familiar. I have all the old irons in the fire—Septuagint—Targum — Peshito —Vulgate — Classics — Guericke — Mariana — Buchanan — Rapin — Schiller — Abulfeda — and Draper's Chemistry! I have hit upon a grand plan for unifying Biblical History and Antiquities next year. This is one thing that reconciles me to the *status quo*. The Greek *labas* is not the text but the pretext. Halley reminds me of the 'Baptist article.' His wit exceeds his other powers, which are high. I am struck with a scholarlike accuracy not common in English Independents. One is almost sorry Carson did not live to get his due. I like what he says about βαπτίζω, but dissent, in toto, from his synagogue theory. I have a book in petto on this subject, but nobody would read it. My new plan of lectures will carry me over the whole ground again. Suppose we get up a course of lectures like Halley & Co.'s! they might be delivered in your church or chapel, and then published."

The reports of Dr. Addison Alexander's memory have not been much exaggerated. As has been said elsewhere in this book, his occasional "memoriter" efforts in the pulpit were apt to be mistaken for extemporaneous. I think it was so in the case referred to below by Prof. Cameron; and that I remember the discourse. It was delivered during this year, and soon after his great affliction:

"The first sermon that Dr. 'Addison' preached after his father's death was *extempore*, or rather without the manuscript. It happened in this way. The evening was not very favourable, the audience was small, and the minister who was to preach in the First Church did not come. After waiting for some time one of the elders arose, approached Dr. A. and requested him to preach, but he declined. Several others were asked and in like manner begged to be excused. Presently Prof. Duffield and I observed Dr. Addison changing his position, &c. and looking round as if intimating that he would preach if again called upon. We intimated this to the elder, and upon a renewal of the request he ascended the pulpit and preached with an earnestness, an unction, and a power that I never heard him surpass. It seemed as if his recent affliction in the death of his father, that great and good man, had stirred his nature to its utmost depths, or had brought him into closer contact with that other and unseen world. This occurred in November, 1851."

Much has been said, during the course of this narrative, of Dr. Alexander's love of what I may style *local novelty*. On this subject he was probably more amusingly whimsical and capricious than any one that ever lived. *À propos* of this, a friend * writes:

"Mrs. Alexander will tell you how upon one occasion of house cleaning she proposed to clean and arrange his study. He consented, and disappeared from the scene as gentlemen are too happy to do upon such occasions. She took note of everything, its position, &c. and carefully superintending the whole matter, restored everything to the *precise place* that it had previously occupied. She thought he would be very much pleased with the arrangement; but when he returned home and was ushered into his study, he exclaimed in the most plaintive manner and with a tone of disappointment, 'Why, you have everything just as it was!'"

His brother Henry says he rejoiced to let *him* make plans for new arrangements of the books.

His library, which to many would have been a desert, was Dr. Alexander's paradise. He loved to sit near a window and look out upon the foliage and soft turf of what was once his father's yard; and when the weather was warm to throw up the sash, and smell the flowers, and drink in the cool breeze which was almost always shivering in the aspen at the side gate near the Seminary, and which often shook the branches of the great larch that shadowed the front walk. This walk was of brick and was bordered with beautiful and fragrant plants. In the spring the grass was full of white and blue violets, and a little later of yellow buttercups. The air was full of the melody of birds. The swallows, in the early spring, never seemed to tire of circling about the chimneys and eaves. The blue-bird and robin were annual visitants. A wren built

* The Rev. H. C. Cameron, Professor of Greek in the College of New Jersey.

its nest year after year, in a cavity caused by the displacement of a brick in the red wall over Dr. Archibald Alexander's study door: the sash-door which opened upon the path leading to the Seminary. The summer thrush yearly made its home in the thick coverts, and the turtle-dove mourned upon the branches in the opposite grounds of Mr. Thomson. It may be the Princeton air and Princeton sunsets are not as fine as I have elsewhere painted them. However this may be, he thought so.

But these odours, sights, and sounds seldom allured the sedentary scholar from his favourite employments; they but served to refresh his senses, and to lend a new charm to the romantic pages of some Persian or Italian poet, and to invigorate his intellectual powers for the grapple with some Briarean language which he had never before encountered, but which he was now resolved to master.

He was exceedingly fond of taking notice of the various groups and couples of pedestrians that passed by the gate, and the school children and especially the school girls as they went to and from school. He knew them all: knew their names, ages, individual peculiarities; indeed every thing that could be known about them. He loved to look too at the lazy carts and market wagons, as well as the men on horseback, and the rumbling pleasure carriages, as they swept by his door; and in the winter he was a delighted spectator of the sleighs and loved to hear the merry jingle of the bells. The servants on the road with their baskets and parcels, the crier ringing his bell for the *vendue*, the young people of the town or strangers from the country, strolling through the village on a holiday, the veriest beggars and trampers, afforded him endless diversion. But all this was the merest pastime. It did not tempt him from his toil. And his toil was after all his highest satisfaction. His books, his pens and inkstand, the journal, the black portfolio with its treasures of white unruled paper, the hours of deep intellectual repose among his volumes, the days of labour, the nights of ease and meditation: these were his chief entertainment. He was a man of the closet. There was a fountain of hope and cheerfulness within him that never ran dry. He was constitutionally an optimist. His morbid feelings were the exception, and did not usually arise until he came in contact with some one between whom and himself there was at the moment no congeniality of tastes and sympathies. He was as sensitive as the steel filings to the touch of the magnet. Some people greatly attracted him, and others violently and suddenly repelled him, and often unaccountably. He was said to repel them; but the repulsion was often just as much or even more the other way. When *he* repelled it was often when he could not help it, and exerted no conscious much less malicious force. It was a kind of diamagnetism. He shrank from some men instinctively. They were often good men, excellent men, men of talents and attainments. This made no difference. It was the old story about Dr. Fell:

> "I do not love thee, Dr. Fell;
> You ask me why, I cannot tell."

No one was more ready to acknowledge and admire the virtues of some of these very persons. What most affected him in this way was a sort of cringing humiliation of manner which some people put on when they saw him. He was also driven within his inmost castle of reserve, and sometimes of curt disdain, by the foolish persistence of conceit, pretension, and upstart sauciness. There are brazen, impudent people in the world who like nothing better than to impose themselves upon men of soft, yielding dispositions. Dr. Alexander was not to be so easily daunted. When attacked in this way he swiftly opened every loop-hole and poured upon the assailant a merciless and deadly fire of small arms. The drums of the enemy were instantly silenced, or were only heard in the distance beating a retreat. The enemy was at last fain to acknowledge his overwhelming superiority. It was useless to contend with forked lightnings. Sometimes he cut people up most dreadfully and often without really intending it. He was quick and sudden in his anger, but he relented immediately. Sometimes he was sorry by the time the words were out of his mouth, and the very tones of his voice became subdued and mollified.

The gentleman* whose words I quoted a while ago, goes on to say of the younger brother and the subject of this memoir:

"During my pastorate in Philadelphia [1851–1853], I saw Dr. Addison Alexander several times. A visit I paid to him in his study was one of the most delightful I ever enjoyed. Throughout the interview he treated me as an equal and almost as a confidential friend. I then for the first time saw into the depths of his Christian feeling, felt the power of his conversational abilities, and saw that he had a heart full of kindness and human sympathy. For the first time, I *loved* Addison Alexander."

Ah, how many could have said the same if they had only known him a little more closely, and been a little more forbearing as regards his infirmities! He was as gentle as he was strong, and yearned more and more as he grew older for human sympathy.

During the month of July, Dr. Alexander was travelling through New England and New York; a tour undertaken and gone through wholly for the benefit and comfort of his sorrowing mother, who accompanied him. Wherever she wished to go, he went. Whatever she wished to have, if it was possible to procure it, he provided. Never was tender devotion to a mother more conspicuously shown than by Addison Alexander.

On the 6th, Dr. James Alexander was called to Princeton, "little knowing," as he says himself, "what he was sent for." On getting out of the carriage he found the house still, and entering the study he was shocked to see his mother lying in a state of alarming weakness on the same sofa from which his father had been carried the previous October. She looked pale and haggard, but rose on her son's entrance, and during the afternoon sat with the family, drank tea, and engaged in conversation. That evening she was forced to go to bed. In the morning she dressed herself and walked across the passage

* Dr. W. H. Ruffner.

up stairs to the room over her son Addison's study. This was her last effort. She sank rapidly during the day, and at noon fell into a gentle sleep from which she was never aroused. She breathed away her spirit at five minutes before nine P. M. Several members of her family were standing by, and one of her sons was kneeling in prayer. There was no convulsion of her person, and there has seldom been an instance of a more tranquil or painless death.

During the winter of 1852 Dr. Alexander was absorbed in the study of Ecclesiastical History; having been appointed to the chair vacated by his brother; his journals contain nothing but first drafts of lectures on this subject.

Among all his vacillations of feeling he remained fixed in his aversion to this chair, though after entering upon his duties he tried, and not without success, to throw into his instructions something of the old fire and enthusiasm. But his exultation was high and refreshing, when he was permitted to return to his Biblical lectures, and could apply all his powers to the art and science of interpretation.

Such a December for mildness was never known in the latitude of Princeton. Hardly any cold weather had yet been felt. Dr. James Alexander's work entitled "Consolation," was published on the 15th. The next day he preached at Newtown before the Long Island Bible Society. On the 19th the new church was dedicated at the corner of Fifth avenue and Nineteenth street. Dr. Plumer preached. At night the pews were sold, and the church was officially pronounced free from debt. On the 21st the first service was held in the new lecture room, and the beloved pastor resumed a course of lectures on the life of Christ.

The following letter to his brother James opens the year 1853:

"PRINCETON, January 5th, 1853.

"MY DEAR BROTHER:

"Is there any book besides the great costly collections that gives a good idea of the ancient liturgies? I do not mean in the way of history or description merely, but in that of actual exemplification. If you should ever have the means of purchasing any of the great collections for us, I hope you will begin with the councils and liturgies.

"I think of beginning to execute a plan, formed many years ago, of making a collection of the Fathers for my own use. If at all complete, it would always be valuable property, and might enrich some public library. What I should want would be serviceable editions, whether fine or not. I hardly know how to choose between the old standard editions and the more convenient modern ones.

"I am reading Allen's History of Denmark (Paa Dansk), which I imported several years ago, but could then make nothing of it. Having, in the meantime, followed Locke's rule, by reading the four Gospels, Acts and Revelation; also Rask's Grammar; I find, to my surprise, that I can read Allen very fluently with a dictionary. The book is a prize-composition, very highly praised. Prefixed, is a very copious apparatus of historical and archæological bibliography. It is like getting into a new world, to read the names of scholars and immense works of which I had never heard before. The Danes appear to have kept pace with all the German movements in advance. I am suffering for want of a book to write, being paralyzed by infirmity of choice. I am not at all ambitious in the matter, being only anxious to discover how my gifts and materials could be employed most usefully. I am more and more satisfied, that a man must make Church History either everything or nothing; he must either be a whaler or angler of the pettiest and pitifullest kind.

"Hast read the Nestorian girls' anniversary speech in one of the Missionary papers? How different from the Sandwich Islanders on the same page! The Sandwich Islanders are officially struck off the roll of heathen lands and foreign missions. How well I remember the first colony, and the news of Tamahamaha's iconoclasm! There seems to be a new turn in the mission to the Jews in Northern Europe. I hope it will soon be understood that the study of the Talmud by our own missionaries is sheer loss of time. The best view of prophecy and Old Testament History I know is in Owen's Exercitations."

The extract below is from a letter to the same, dated January, 1853:

"Have you seen the correspondence between Gladstone and McCaul? I never saw the supercilious better done. The English universities seem likely to be overhauled. Disraeli's speech on Wellington is probably the most un-English ever spoken in St. Stephen's, without counting the plagiarism from Thiers. The Jew is unmistakable in all he does. We have just heard the dreadful news about poor Pierce's only child. What a συγκυρία! There seems to be little danger now of his being exalted above measure. How can I get a complete Roman Liturgy as used in this country? I mean the sacerdotal part—Missal, Ritual, Breviary, and what not. We are all as well as usual.

"Yours,

"J. A. ALEXANDER."

The next is to his brother Samuel, and describes several of the New Haven preachers:

NEW HAVEN, March 28, 1853.

"REV. AND DEAR BROTHER:

I left home on Saturday at half-past ten, and reached this place at half-past six. I am staying, as you will see by the envelope, at the New Haven Hotel, a capital house of the best New England kind; new, clean, quiet, and genteel, with an excellent table, and excellent servants. I attended the College-chapel yesterday morning, and heard a stranger preach a very striking sermon (with more law than Gospel in it), from the last clause of Jer. iii.: 5. Doctrine: every sinner acts as badly as he can. In the afternoon I heard another striking sermon from Dr. Bacon, on Heb. ix: 27. I intended to hear Cleveland, but he did not preach himself. Although he is old-school, Dr. Taylor says he is the best preacher in New Haven. At night, I found the whole population streaming to one of the churches in the public square, and in a short time it was jammed like commencement. At the door I heard that Gough was to speak, and went in, but afterwards learned that he was not present. So I had to sit (on a bench in the aisle) through a 'statement of facts' and two or three temperance addresses, before I could get out in the wake of some fainting females. I hope to be at home to-night. You owe the unexpected pleasure of this letter partly to my vivid recollections of our visit to New Haven, and the Park House, which was denounced last night as one of the worst rum-holes; and partly to my wish to know where you got that wide-ruled paper in Philadelphia, as I want some more of the same kind. It was very warm when I arrived here, but it afterwards turned very cold. At your next visit I advise you to try this house.

"Ever yours,

"J. A. ALEXANDER."

Some extracts from his journals will give an insight into his studies at this period:

"*March* 18. Began Koch on 1st Thess. Lectured to the first class (from Kurtz), on 1750–1814. Read Job in the LXX., and 1 Samuel in the Vulgate; Old Red Sandstone; Alford and Baumgarten on Acts, xix; Thucydides; Allen's Danish History; Stevens's Lectures on France.

"*March* 21. LXX. Job xxi.; Vulgate, 1 Samuel viii.; Koch on 1 Thess.; Old Red Sandstone; Studied Mark xiv.; Mariana Historia de España; began to write questions on the Gospel History; read the service for Monday before Easter in the Hebrew (Christian) prayer-book; lectured to the third class on Mark xiv.; Stevens's Lecture on the Fronde; Thucydides."

The following interesting letter on the subject of Interpretation is to his brother James:

"March 31st, 1853.

"MY DEAR BROTHER:

"I wave (or waive) the etiquette of waiting for an answer, as I find it a relief to vent my thoughts in some safe quarter. Whatever may be the issue of the present movement, one thing is certain, that I never felt so much complacency in any plan or prospect of employment, since I first became connected with the Seminary. Even when I have been most contented and resigned, I have never felt anything like enthusiasm for my work here. Besides other reasons, some of which you know as well as I do, this has arisen from my business having always had some disagreeable adjuncts, and some painful feelings of responsibility for things in which I did not feel sufficient interest to do them well. But now, for the first time, Providence seems really to open the prospect of employment precisely suited to my taste, and so far as I can judge, my talents, my previous studies, and whatever reputation I may thus far have acquired. I cannot desire anything better than to teach Interpretation, without the preceding drudgery, as a science, as an art, and as a function of the ministry. While all the professors will interpret Scripture for grammatical, historical, doctrinal, and theological purposes, my task, according to the present plan, would be to teach the student *to interpret Scripture for himself* hereafter, as the only sure source of sound and sufficient matter for his popular instructions.

"This view of the matter seems to strip off the scholastic character which offends some minds, by connecting the study, in the closest manner, with the active duties of the pastoral office. At the same time, it leaves it all its learning, etc., for Interpretation must be studied as an art requiring knowledge, judgment, taste, skill, and experience, just as much as any other course on fine arts; and yet this art is not empirical, but founded upon science, *i. e.*, governed by established laws and principles. All this seems to me to give a substantive individuality to Interpretation as a distinct branch of study and instruction. My idea as to execution is, to teach the subject in a threefold method: I. In theory, or by precept, presenting dogmatically the principles of hermeneutics, with historical illustrations. II. By example, applying my principles to actual exposition in exegetical lectures. III. By practice, accustoming the student to interpret for himself, under the direction of the teacher. I am very much taken with this view of the matter, and prefer it greatly to a mere New Testament professorship, not merely on the grounds which my father used to urge against such a division, but because there is a loud demand from friends and foes for more systematic attention to the subject of prophetical Interpretation, which would be excluded from my field upon the other plan. Since I wrote, therefore, I have convinced myself that the mention of apologetics in my title would destroy the unity of my department, and impose a disagreeable responsibility. My present notion is, to borrow a formula from the faculty of medicine, which would not be an unmeaning one in the case—'The Theory and Practice (or Principles and Practice) of Interpretation.'

"Affectionately yours,

"J. A. A."

His correspondence with his publishers was brisk and active, but is mainly of a business character. It, however, throws some light on the workings of his mind when preparing his different books, and also upon his variable, emphatic, impulsive, original character. They are almost void of wit or humour; but abound in touches of good taste, strong sense, benevolence, delicacy of feeling, and a strange mixture of simplicity and worldly wisdom. They are, moreover, as frank as candour itself.

The following was written a month before his second Atlantic voyage, and shows that he was thinking of publishing his travels:

"PRINCETON, April 20th, 1853.

"DEAR SIR:

"It is now quite probable that I shall go abroad next month, and if so, it is my intention to prepare at least one volume for the press, with the materials thus procured. The three plans which have occurred to me are: (1.) a visit to the universities of Europe; (2.) an account of the great preachers; (3.) an amalgamation of my old journals with the new, under some such title as 'Europe Revisited, after an interval of Twenty Years.' I may, if my life and health are spared, carry out all these plans; but one of them I fully expect to execute. My principal motive in determining to do this is, to furnish the expenses of the voyage itself; and it is on this subject that I now address you. I am willing to engage to furnish, within six months after my return (*Deo volente*), at least one volume, equal in amount of matter to the largest of the Psalms, of as popular a character as I can make it, and to sell the copyright beforehand. The style, price, mode of printing, etc., would then be, of course, at the discretion of the publisher. As my main object is to raise money, I am under the necessity of giving it to the highest bidder. Instead of inviting competition, however, which would be ridiculously arrogant, I begin by giving you the offer, and shall make it to no other, if you think it worth your while to close with it, on terms that will at all answer my immediate purpose. I set no price myself, because I have no idea of the risks and chances which must constitute the elements of calculation. My own estimate of such a book's success is not very high, and I should therefore, probably, be better off in your hands than my own. Will you be so good, then, as to state the highest sum which you would think it right to offer for the copyright of such a book as I have described? My proposition does not necessarily involve any actual advance or prepayment, but only an assurance that my expenses will be reimbursed, although, of course, any accommodation of that kind would make the arrangement more desirable to me. In order to provide for all contingencies, I should like to stipulate that, if I should in any way be hindered from producing the precise book, or kind of book, proposed at present, I will furnish, within the same time, a work of some other kind, equal in commercial value, yourself being the judge. If you choose to confer with Henry on the subject, you can do so; but I wish to hear from you directly, when you have made up your mind either to make an offer or decline it. I need not add that I have no time to lose.

"Sincerely yours,

"J. A. ALEXANDER.

"MR. SCRIBNER."

Mr. Scribner quickly answered this letter, acceding to all that had been asked; but before its arrival Dr. Alexander had changed his plan, and thanks Mr. Scribner in the following letter for his liberality and promptness:

"PRINCETON, April 26th, 1853.

"DEAR SIR:

"I expected to acknowledge your last letter in person, but was obliged to leave New York without seeing you. I write now to say that, while I fully appreciate the liberality and promptness of your offer, I have determined to decline making any engagement of the kind at present. This determination has been partly occasioned by suggestions of your own, as to the conditions of success in works of that class, but chiefly by my finding that such an arrangement will not be necessary to enable me to go abroad; and this being the case, I should enjoy my visit far more, unencumbered by a sense of obligation to make something out of it. If I should be able and disposed, on my return, to make a book, you shall be among the first to hear of it. I am glad that you and Dr. Schaff have come to an understanding mutually satisfactory.

"Truly yours,

"JOS. ADDISON ALEXANDER.

"MR. SCRIBNER."

Dr. Alexander having determined to spend the summer of 1853 in Europe, completed his arrangements and was now ready for his departure, and looked forward eagerly to a renewal of the pleasures he had snatched in the same way and from the same objects, just twenty years before. During that trip he was commonly alone, or nearly alone. This time he was to be accompanied, to his great satisfaction, by his friend and former pupil, the Rev. C. W. Hodge of Princeton. The intercourse between them was throughout, familiar and affectionate, wholly unembarrassed and often highly amusing. The excitements preliminary to the getting off were soon over, and everything was on tip-toe for the journey.

On Wednesday, May 18th, the light-hearted travellers sailed from New York in the steamship Asia, and after a pleasant voyage landed at Liverpool on Sunday the 29th.

Dr. Alexander's journals during this short visit are deeply interesting and on most accounts well worthy of being published entire. But the limited space at my disposal will only allow me, as in the journal of his former visit, to make brief extracts here and there, leaving much to be supplied by the wit or knowledge of the reader. The Guide Books have by this time superseded the use of elaborate diaries.

During this flying visit he spent two days in Liverpool, seven days in Edinburgh, two days at Melrose and Abbotsford, six days in London, six days at Oxford and Cambridge, and seventeen days in Paris. From thence he visited in order Nancy, Basel, Heidelberg, Mannheim, Mayence, Cologne, Arnheim, Utrecht, Amsterdam, Rotterdam, Haarlem, Leyden, The Hague, Antwerp, Ghent, Bruges, and Ostend. On the 2d of August he crossed over to Dover, and spent a week in London. He then made a flying visit to Dublin, going thence to Manchester, and making his last stop at Liverpool; from which port he sailed on the 20th for America, in the Europa, arriving at Boston on the 31st.

My object will be to select such portions of this epistolary chronicle as may seem to me to possess the greatest intrinsic value, or else to afford the best lights in which to view *the man*—his strong and peculiar intellect; his almost perpetual vivacity of spirits; his learning; his command of English; his power of description; his quick discernment of character; his dislike of sameness; his contempt of many fashionable usages, maxims, and opinions; his whimsical tastes; his fancy for odd people, startling adventures, queer expressions and street signs; his passionate love of children, and fondness for courts and public spectacles; his delight in attending different churches and comparing different preachers; his quick and impulsive sympathies; his rare humour; his sterling common-sense and orthodoxy; and his devout piety.

The travellers landed at Liverpool on the 29th of May. The diverting account one of them gives of his exploit in getting down the side of the vessel, with another man's hat on, ought not to be skipped. After a detailed exhibition of the difficulties he had to encounter, Dr. Alexander continues as follows:

"Down this almost perpendicular descent, I was among the first to venture. Hard as it would have been at any time, it was rendered doubly so by a circumstance, of which we never think without laughing."

His old hat, poor enough when he set out, had been reduced to a ruinous condition by repeated onsets on the part of some of those who had been suffering from sea-sickness.

"My cap was too large for me and very odd-looking, especially since the oilcloth cover had been blown into the sea upon the first or second day, and, notwithstanding efforts to rescue it, borne by an east wind toward its native shores. As ——'s cap was very nice, and he preferred it, he proposed that I should wear his new hat till we got to Liverpool. This could only be done by perching it on the crown of my head, from which the wind threatened every moment to remove it. The problem now was to prevent its flight and at the same time to effect an almost vertical descent over the ship's side. With one hand on my hat (or rather not mine) and the other on the slight rail, I began a descent which can only be compared to that of Righi. All that I know is that I found myself soon after at the bottom with my borrowed hat in *statu quo*. It was now quite a treat to see the rest descend."

From what the reader may recollect of his habit on the former occasion, and from the hint just thrown out, it is hardly necessary for me to say that Dr. Alexander lost no time in hearing some of the famous preachers. The first he had the pleasure of listening to was Dr. McNeile. For this purpose he had recourse to

"Princess Park, a beautiful enclosure, on the edge of which, facing a wide street or road leading out into the country, is St. Paul's Church. The people were already streaming in, and continued so to do until the sermon began, by which time the church was full. It is ugly inside, with an unpleasant mixture of the modern and antique, the plain and ornamental. The service was read by two monkish youths, and McNeill then preached from Song Sol. v. 16, expounding the whole chapter to that verse. The doctrines and sentiments were excellent, the mode of treatment delicate and skilful, language correct and plain, manner self-possessed and dignified, voice powerful and sweet though not always used well; but what most surprised me was the absence of all power, either logical or rhetorical. The whole thing was tame, and if heard from a stranger would have gained no attention and left no impression. Perhaps it was not a fair sample, but the audience seemed perfectly enraptured. I am glad to have heard McNeile, as no man can judge of preaching for another; with my present impressions, I would not go across the street to hear him again."

His next essay was to hear Dr. Candlish, and was equally successful. The whole account is so remarkable for its vehement emotion and graphic description, that I shall give it without abridgment. He always after this regarded Candlish as the greatest preacher he ever heard. What follows was of course written in Edinburgh and on the Lord's Day:

"This morning a profound sabbatical stillness reigned throughout the city. We did not get our breakfast until 9, and at 10 we sallied forth, and as we walked through the whole length of Princess street, found it almost empty. At Free St. George's we went into a kind of dwelling house behind or beneath the church, and learned from a man who was washing a basin for the vestry, that Dr. Candlish was to preach 'all day,' and that the doors would be open a quarter before eleven. We walked up under the brow of the castle rock to Free St. John's where we learned to our regret that Dr. Guthrie was out of town, and that Dr. Hanna (no doubt the son-in-law and biographer of Chalmers), was to preach 'all day.' Determined to make sure of Candlish, we went back in some haste. The whole scene was now changed. The profound repose was broken by the clangor of church-bells, especially the great one of St. Giles's (the old cathedral) and the fine new one of Victoria Hall. The streets, too, were literally full of people. At St. George's a decent man admitted me into his pew, and showed me how to put my hat upon the book-board. The church is wide and nearly square; quite plain, the galleries very spacious; the pulpit small and slight; under it sat the precentor; a handsome black-haired man in a gown. The whole congregation sang; with less spirit but more sweetness and apparent culture than the Scotch congregations in America. The 60th chapter of Isaiah was read after the prayer, then another psalm, then the Lord's Prayer, then the sermon. For several years past I have expected less from Candlish than I once did, and had grown almost indifferent to hearing him, so that I should have been less disappointed at his absence than at Dr. Guthrie's. This predisposition was increased by his appearance, which is indescribably grotesque and even mean. I cannot convey a faint idea of it better than by faithfully recording the identical impression which it made upon me, or rather the image which it conjured up, and which was that of a sickly boy, just roused from sleep, and without any washing or combing—his eyes scarcely open and his hair disordered—forced into the ugliest and clumsiest black gown you can imagine, dragged into the pulpit and compelled to preach. The illusion was kept up by what seemed to be incessant efforts to get his gown off, or to button his clothes under it, with occasional pulls at his hair as if it was a wig which he had just discovered to be hind part before, and was pettishly trying to reverse or throw away. Now and then too a white handkerchief would come out in a kind of whirlwind and go back again without performing any office. Add to all this that one shoulder was held as if by a painful effort a foot higher than the other, and the neck quite nullified, and you have no exaggerated picture of the preacher's personal appearance. As to speech, imagine the funniest burlesque of the Scotch sing-song and the broadest Scotch pronunciation of some common words, such as *waun* (one), *naw* (no), *Hawly Gawst*, &c., with a voice rather husky in its best estate and sometimes a mere rattling in the throat; and you have the impression made upon my ear as well as my eye. He read the first three verses of the eleventh chapter of 2d Corinthians, and repeated as his text the third. He read every word of his sermon from a small MS. in the pulpit Bible, never looking at the congregation, but once in every sentence raising his eye to some fixed point or turning it on vacancy. He began by pointing out the contrast in the passage between Christ's simplicity and Satan's subtlety, as exemplified in Eve's case. God gave one sufficient reason for not eating. Satan gave several for eating. This he generalized; truth and simplicity are satisfied with one good reason; craft and falsehood must have many; as if many weaknesses equal one strength. Theme: The simplicity of Christ, as shown in five particulars: 1st. His atoning work; 2d. The free offer of salvation; 3d. The completeness of his people in him; 4th. Their growth in grace by following Him; 5th. The expectation of his second coming. Though much of the exterior above described struck me as probably a caricature of Chalmers, I soon found that he did not imitate the style of his great model. The composition was masterly; both strong and beautiful; no Scotticisms; no provincialisms; no violations of taste, except perhaps an occasional excess of ingenious and pointed antithesis. As to substance, the first head was a most captivating view of the old doctrine of Atonement, as a simple scheme opposed to the complexities of error. The second was more experimental. Under this he accumulated all the difficulties men feel as to election, ability, the unpardonable sin, insufficient conviction, faith, love, hope, &c. There was something fearful in this part of the discourse. I shuddered, as he enumerated the terrible contingencies. I never can forget the strange, unearthly drawl with which he said, 'You may not be one of the elect; you may not be sorry enough; you may not be willing enough; you may not be able enough; you may have committed the unpardonable sin.' But when to these (as the subtleties of Satan) he opposed the simple truth that Christ had died and God was in earnest in offering salvation; and exhorted us to let God take care of his own attributes, and to look at the Atonement not from his side but from ours; not to debate with Satan or wait for the solution of all puzzles, but simply believe what Christ has said, and do what he requires; it was like coming out of an English railway tunnel into the paradise of an English landscape. And then, when he appealed to the experience of the convert, and described the escape of the poor soul from the knotted meshes of the devil's snare to the 'simplicity that is in Christ,' I was completely overcome. I shook with violent agitation; and I don't know how I could have sat still if my eyes had not relieved me. But I passed entirely unnoticed. Many were in the same condition, and the rest were unconsciously bent forward to catch every word. During the height of this excitement the preacher's ugliness and awkwardness was not forgotten or unobserved. They seemed to be constantly increasing, but by some strange process to enhance the effect of the discourse which they had threatened to make quite ridiculous. In the crisis or acme of the eloquence his gown fell half off; his right arm was at liberty; and he assumed the look of a demoniac fighting with a fiend. His gestures were those of conflict with one immediately before him thrusting and struggling. It reminded me of Burley's fencing* in Old Mortality. At the end of this part of the discourse he relapsed into his 'first manner:' and although the third was admirable too, I was only preparing to be shocked (in the electric sense) again, when he abruptly shut the book and said, 'The rest must be deferred.' After the prayer he read one or two notices, threw them behind him, and pronounced the benediction. The members of

* See Old Mortality, vol. II. pp. 297, 298. Parker, 1836.

the congregation seemed to sit till the strangers had withdrawn. It was cheering to see such a crowd pouring out from such a sermon. On rejoining ——, I found him scarcely less excited than myself; and without knowing whither we were going we strolled off in a direction opposite to that of our hotel. We got into the southern suburbs; and as the interval was only until 2 o'clock, we took a cup of coffee at a coffee-house, in a little private room of the old fashion; made a few inquiries about churches, and returned to Free St. George's. Here we waited in the lobby as before; saw Candlish come out of his vestry near us and ascend the pulpit, preceded by the sexton carrying the book, and followed by the gowned precentor. He read his text; the same as in the morning; and without the least allusion to the previous service, repeated word for word the introduction to his sermon as if he was preaching it again to a different congregation. In like manner he repeated most distinctly the five heads of the discourse several times, so that no one could forget them: summing up in a few sentences the three heads which he had already handled. He then took up the fourth, which was comparatively short, but excellent and striking in a high degree, and then came to the last; the simplicity of the Christian doctrine of the Second Advent. This had greatly awakened my curiosity when announced in the morning, and I trembled for the preacher; but my fears were groundless. His treatment of this topic was as wise as it was eloquent. I admired what he did not say as much as what he said. The idea he presented was that of a great picture, the outline of which is distinctly drawn in Scripture and distinctly visible to all alike. The disputed matters are the filling up. He said nothing to conciliate or offend the Millennarian. He admitted the lawfulness and use of such investigation, but denied that they belong to the great outline which the hand of God himself has traced, and which he now retraced before us with transcendent skill and power, introducing himself as the spectator; under various characters: a convicted sinner; a heart-broken mourner, &c. &c. and telling what it is that sustains his hope—not this; not that; but Christ, Christ alone; apart from all accessories; independent of all revolutions, earthquakes, catastrophes; one insulated, solitary figure, standing amidst the wreck of empires and of worlds: not the church; not the ministry; not a new state of society &c. &c:—not that (he shrieked in the most thrilling way) not that at all; but Christ in his simplicity—none but Christ! It is to him that I look forward; that I am approaching; I have caught up *with him;* I am caught up *to* him; with them that sleep in Jesus; in the clouds; in the air; into heaven; to be ever with the Lord! Judging merely by the actual effect upon myself, without regard to rules or the judgment of others, this was certainly one of the grandest bursts of eloquence that I have ever heard. If Chalmers was as much above this man in actual power as he is in fame, he was almost superhuman. It was some relief from the tension of this winding-up to find it followed by a threefold application to the careless, the anxious, the believing hearer. The first was masterly: characterized by a solemn irony, well suited to impress supercilious sinners. Instead of warning them *now* against the subtlety of Satan, he told them Satan did not think it worth his while to practise arts on *them:* he reserved his craft for those who had escaped, or were escaping, from his toils; with the careless sinner he used great simplicity: not many lies, but one lie not even a new one, but the same old lie that had seduced Eve and its tens of thousands since: 'Ye shall not surely die.' The other applications were brief but excellent; though not so striking as the other, being rather a gradual descent from the previous elevation. In any ordinary sermon even this part might have made the preacher's fortune. I have given this account, with all its seeming extravagance, for the very reason that I do not wish to let my first impressions be corrected and cooled down by subsequent reflection; but to preserve them just as they are; for my *own* future use, as well as for your present entertainment."

Such a lover of Scottish history and dialect, of course, could not fail to meet with objects of interest everywhere in the land of the Douglas and the Covenanters, and of Jeanie Deans and Edie Ochiltree. The references he makes to the old legends are, however, not of a nature to justify quotation. The pithy sayings of the Scotch peasantry are more worthy of preservation. At Melrose Abbey, he fell in with a shrewd, satirical old guide; and overheard a sentence or two from a lady, which had better have been left unsaid.

"I was amused at the straightforward, common-sense way in which our cicerone answered a lady of the party. He also took her down from her stilts in reference to the nobility. She spoke familiarly of the Duke of Buccleuch. He asked her if she knew him. She said, with a stammer, that she knew where he lived. The old man said the duke had so many dwellings it was hard to know them all. Seeing Lord Somerville's name upon a vault, the lady said (as if it was the name of an acquaintance) 'Ah! is Lord Somerville buried here?' The old man, with a dry laugh, said, 'Lord Somerville is no buried at all, but when he dies he has a recht to lie here.' In short, he was an admirable type of the sturdy, sensible, free-spoken Scotchman."

After a brief but pleasant jaunt among the scenes immortalized by Burns and Scott, he returned, with but little reluctance to England.

Of course, he went to hear the late beloved and honoured Dr. Hamilton, of Regent Square, London; and he was much pleased with the sermon. The whole account is worthy of perusal.

"The church in Regent Square was built for Edward Irving, and is a neat, plain building of the Gothic sort. The door-keeper told us he could not give us seats till the service began, but he thought there was plenty of room in the gallery. We accordingly ascended, and were shown by a female pew-opener into a very good front seat. The house below was well filled, but not crowded. The congregation seemed to be entirely Scotch. We thought at first a stranger was to preach, but soon saw that it was the sexton ushering the minister into the pulpit. I was greatly pleased with Hamilton's appearance. The portraits flatter him very little. While his presence is naturally an impressive one, he wins respect by his look of unfeigned seriousness and modesty. He read a chapter, just as we do, without note or comment. His sermon was a lecture on the stilling of the storm; precisely like his books, and not at all improved by the delivery. Its great defect was some peculiarity of utterance that made a large part wholly unintelligible. His voice is deep and guttural. He did not read by any means so closely as Candlish; but looked at and addressed the congregation, sometimes uttering several sentences without referring to his green-covered MS. After a brief but interesting summary of the narrative, he remarked upon it as illustrating the character both of the disciples and the Master. The most striking points were, the difference between faith and physical courage, as exemplified in Peter's walking on the water; and the apparent hardship in Christ's treatment of the twelve, who were sent away alone in a storm, and permitted to share neither in the rest of the five thousand, nor in the prayers of Christ. In this connection, he made use of a magnificent figure, which Wordsworth might have envied; in his own line, too; for it was that of the eagle stirring up her nest; the apparent hardship, as it seems to the spectator, on some Highland precipice or Alpine cliff, of forcing the poor eaglets from the eyrie where they have so long been fostered, over the verge of the abyss in which sure destruction seems to await them, till the parent bird, with a sweep of its pinions, like a flash of lightning, passes beneath, and bears them up to heaven! This was intended to illustrate our Lord's method of preparing the apostles for their future work. But by far the finest part of the discourse was the conclusion: in which he brought out the old use of the passage as an emblem of the trials of the Church; tracing the points of correspondence with great beauty both of thought and language, and especially describing with extraordinary graphic power, the dangers of the Church in our day, when the Master seems asleep upon a pillow, or absent from the vessel altogether, and where every effort to do good, or remove evil, is but a single stroke of the oar when the wind is contrary, and the sea tempestuous; but when the night is darkest, and the weather worst, a form is seen walking on the waters (this was wrought up very beautifully), sometimes dreaded as a spectre by the Church itself; but the moment his foot treads the deck, the waves fall flat, the wind is hushed; even the world acknowledges the presence of the Master, and straightway they are at the land whither they went. "Let us pray"! Comparisons are odious; but I must say that, with all its beauty, this discourse of Hamilton's was far below Candlish's, in all respects, even in literary merit: for, though more exuberant in figures, it was not in such good taste; while as to argument and doctrine and experimental power, effect upon the conscience and religious feelings (judging, of course, by my own experience) it was child's play in comparison. I say this the more freely, because all my prepossessions were in Hamilton's favour; and I liked the man as soon as I saw him: whereas, Candlish's exterior created a repugnance which all my admiration of his preaching has not wholly overcome."

The mention of Hamilton naturally calls up the name of another distinguished London minister and pulpit-celebrity, Dr. Cumming; whom he also heard with pleasure, and whom he thus describes:

"I inquired repeatedly the way to Dr. Cumming's church, of which I had entirely forgotten the locality. One stupid policeman said it was close by; but on following his directions, I found myself in *Doctors' Commons*. Another thought it must be *Strand-ways*, an expression new to me, though very English. At length I asked a policeman of superior rank, and of a portly presence, whom I took to be a Scotchman, whether he could direct me to the National Scotch Church. He was just beginning to say No, when I added, Dr. Cumming's. 'Oh, yes!' said he, 'I can direct you to Dr. Cumming's church; I was not aware that it was called the National Scotch Church.' He then directed me to Crown Court, Drury Lane, the entrance to the court being directly opposite the colonnade of Drury-Lane Theatre. Here I found a small, oblong court, surrounded on three sides by high brick houses, and on the fourth by an odd-looking, old stone church, with a profusion of small arched windows, irregularly placed, some above, and some in clusters. Here I found several waiting, more than an hour before the time of service. When I came back, the number was increased, and while I stood there the court actually filled up, so that it would hold no more. A policeman in attendance said that all these were strangers, waiting for the opening of the doors, at the commencement of the service; the seat-holders being admitted at a door in Drury Lane, except those who had seats in the gallery, and who were all the time passing through the crowd in Crown Court, being admitted by a Scotch sexton, with a very cunning look, who seemed to recognize every individual seat-holder, and to expel every stranger. His authority was enforced by a second policeman, who stood near him, while the first walked up and down through the crowd. At length, the doors were opened, and a great rush followed. The aisles were soon filled, and the vacant places in the pews, to one of which I was admitted. The church is of a singular form, being nearly semicircular, with the pulpit in the centre (of the diameter), the curved part having galleries. Cumming has tried to assimilate the Presbyterian worship to the Episcopal; but, I think, with no advantage. They sing standing, and pray kneeling or sitting. He seemed to read his prayers, which contained occasional snatches from the liturgy. Choir for precentor. He has a very flashy look; bare neck, elaborate triangular black whiskers, gold spectacles; very sweet voice, and great suavity of elocution. Read and expounded Mark xv; preached on v. 5. Very orthodox on divinity of Christ; but disparaged theology and doctrinal preaching, and metaphysics. Extempore-colloquial; sometimes very beautiful; occasional sarcasm against apostolical succession; priests had regular succession, yet crucified Christ! Let worshippers of succession now beware, lest they crucify the Son of God afresh, and teach the people to prefer a Barnabas to a Jesus. He called Popery the religion of the crucifix, and not of the cross. Some original ideas as to Judas and Pilate: the motive of their conduct, suspicion or belief of Christ's divinity. He urged the impossibility of such a character as Christ's being invented by the evangelist.

Many points of coincidence with James's lecture at the University of Virginia; but some things *ad captandum*. At times very eloquent, but commonly too English, or Scotch. He introduced several Greek phrases. I am glad to have heard him, but have no wish to hear him again."

If the American traveller had been himself a retired member of the bar, his interest could not well have been greater than it actually was in everything pertaining to courts of justice, judges, barristers, juries, witnesses, and legal formalities. Here is an account of one of his visits to Westminster Hall, and the Courts of Common Pleas, Exchequer, and Queen's Bench; with his impressions of Jervis, Talfourd, Pollock, and Lord Campbell:

"Walking any longer being out of the question, I went into Westminster Hall; and seeing the wigged barristers running about, entered the Court of Common Pleas, where I saw Sir John Jervis, Talfourd, and two other judges, on the bench. I afterwards visited the Court of Exchequer, where Sir Frederick Pollock and three others were presiding; then the Queen's Bench, where Lord Campbell was pronouncing a decision, in which his colleagues all concurred successively. These court-rooms have been rebuilt since I was here. They would all be thought small, if not mean, with us. They are lighted entirely by sky-lights, and wainscotted with oak. The judges sit behind a little altar-shaped mahogany desk, on a long, red sofa. Beneath them is a row of clerks and other officers, in wigs and gowns. Beneath these, in all the courts, was a row of shabby-looking men, much below the average of English neatness and respectability, who seemed to be interested in the causes, and occasionally spoke to the counsel. Could they be attorneys? The judges' gowns are the most ridiculous you can imagine. They look like blue nankeen greatcoats, with long capes, worn over old calico bed-gowns. The lawyers' gowns are of some coarse black stuff, without any kind of ornament. I never saw a finer collection of intelligent and healthy faces than these barristers. I was also pleased to sit and hear their English. The colloquial proceedings, which I like to read in the reports, I now had *vivâ voce*. The great object of the judges seems to be, to prevent speechification, and get at the truth as soon as possible. Scarcely a sentence was uttered without interruption from the bench. The encounter of wits was very interesting. Now and then, there was a general laugh from bench and bar. The judges, notwithstanding their old-women's dress, have a noble judicial presence. I heard several motions for new trials, and the statement of the judge who had presided, with his answer to the arguments of counsel. The mutual courtesy is admirable, even in exciting disputes; one of which, on this occasion, was somewhat personal in its character. From the Tower we proceeded through Eastcheap, to the West End, where I proceeded to my favourite resort, Westminster Hall, to which I find my steps continually turning. I first went up into the Parliament House, and found a crowd about the Committee Room; where the investigation of the Liverpool election is still dragging its slow length along. Seeing a man prohibited from entering by the ubiquitous police, I returned to the Hall, and going into the Court of Common Pleas, found it crowded to excess. A jury-trial was in progress, before Judge Talfourd. The case was uninteresting in itself (something about building a distillery) but all judicial proceedings interest me, especially in England. I had now an opportunity of observing the old English method of examining and cross-examining a witness. The examiner stands, and his associate sitting by him takes the notes. The attorney sits behind and suggests questions. Great mirth was occasioned by the testimony of a Scotch distiller, who turned the laugh against Sergeant Shea repeatedly; as did an architectural surveyor, who testified that no skill was required for the making of certain wooden bolts. 'What!' said Shea; 'no more skill than for the making of a wash-tub?' 'Not so much,' was the reply. But Shea revenged himself on both of them, in summing up; the finest specimen of English elocution I have yet heard. It was masterly indeed, and I would not have missed it for a guinea. The effect upon the jury could be seen with the naked eye; or, at the most, with spectacles. The moment Shea concluded, Talfourd began his charge, and a greater contrast cannot be imagined. Extremely rapid, mincing, and affected, especially in the excess to which he carries the English stammer, with a great deal of the coxcomb and the bon-vivant combined in his appearance, he impresses me as little *vivâ voce* as on paper. The jury did not leave the box, but literally put their heads together, and agreed upon their verdict in a moment. I then went into the Court of Exchequer; where precisely the same kind of thing was going on before another judge whose name I did not learn. And I had a sample of the famous method of brow-beating witnesses which once prevailed here. The cross-examining counsel bellowed in the most threatening manner, and with the most ferocious look, without appearing to accomplish anything. The judge seemed thoroughly disgusted and ashamed while this was going on: twisting his handkerchief impatiently round his hands; pretending to sleep, etc. etc. This was another thing which I would not willingly have missed, though perfectly ridiculous. The opposing counsel was a very handsome man; which, indeed, is very generally true of all these barristers: while the attorneys are by far the shabbiest class (not paupers) I have seen in England."

With all his love of music, and especially of vocal music, Dr. Alexander seldom went to hear any of the public singers in his own country. He did so, however, now and then, in London and elsewhere in Europe, and on one occasion had the satisfaction of witnessing a wonderful performance on the organ. Here are his own words:

"We went to a concert at Exeter Hall. The performers were eighty Germans, from Cologne, amateurs, who have been singing here with great applause. Among them was a famous organist from Dresden, who performed a masterpiece of Bach, and one of Handel (the Hallelujah Chorus again.) His execution was wonderful, especially with his feet, which seemed all the time to be skating; but his performance was nothing to that of the others, without any instrumental accompaniment whatever, a new and grand proof of what the human voice can do, not so much in the way of loudness as in that of sweetness. The subdued tone of these fourscore strong voices, was almost celestial, and yet perfectly distinct. The breath of angels scarcely could be sweeter. Two pieces of Mendelssohn which they performed were in themselves transporting. The applause was rapturous. Several of the pieces were repeated."

I give the following account of another visit he made to Westminster Hall and the law courts. Part of the description is very graphic:

"I found jury trials going on in the three courts; before the three chief judges, Lord Campbell, Sir Frederick Pollock, and Sir John Jervis. The last is more of an American than any public speaker I have heard. He is very excitable and impatient. When a lawyer wanted to prove something yesterday, he screamed that it could not be proved; it was physically impossible; repeating it several times over at the top of his voice; stepping down to the jury-box and showing the paper in question to the jury, asking them whether the fact alleged was not physically impossible. To-day there was an interesting trial before him of a breach of promise case; Miss Caroline White and Captain Peel. The plaintiff's sister testified that everything was ready for the wedding. The counsel asked her whether the wedding breakfast was not ordered and the trousseau purchased. This roused Jervis, who contemptuously asked what they meant by a trousseau; and whether everybody that was married must have diamonds and all that; adding in a way that caused a general roar, 'When I get married, I don't do that way.' Chief Baron Pollock (a very intellectual but haughty-looking man) lost his patience with a lawyer for examining a servant-woman too minutely about the dimensions and arrangements of a house. After trying ineffectually to arrest it, the judge startled everybody present by asking the woman in a voice of thunder, 'Are you a house-surveyor?' 'No, my lord, I am a servant of all work.' This question and answer convulsed the bar and jury."

Among the more striking of the preachers whom he heard in London was the famous Mr. Binney.* From a notice on the outside of the chapel, the American visitor inferred that great attention was there paid to psalmody:

"A new tune-book is just published, with pieces harmonized by Lowell Mason, Turle, Novello, and others, and a preface by Binney. There is no choir, but simply a precentor. For the first time I heard a prose passage chanted by a large congregation. What excuse have the seceders for turning David's Psalms into doggerel rhyme? Binney is a man of imposing presence; tall, large-framed, with a bald and shining forehead. His voice is deep, but not full or agreeable; and when he is excited, it is harsh and guttural. He not only did not read his sermon, but he could not; for it was so dark, before he got half through, that I could scarcely see him. He repudiated all ornament, and indeed all style: affecting the colloquial laconic to excess; uttering a few words at a time, with many pauses and emphatic repetitions. His subject was the parable of the marriage supper in Luke xiv. with the preliminary circumstances. His exposition was able, his illustration striking and original. The way in which he dealt with our Lord's directions to invite only the poor, showed sense and independence. Instead of quibbling, he acknowledged the difficulty; but appealed to the common sense of men in general, which never understands the passage strictly. 'Does any man believe that I or any interpreter of

* A good idea of this gentleman's style may be had from a little book entitled, "Make the Most of Both Worlds."

Scripture am to tell the Lord Mayor of London, that he can never entertain his friends and equals at dinner?' He adopted the solution, that the feasts to which our Lord referred were abuses of a charitable institution designed expressly for the poor. Of this he gave a striking illustration. 'From time immemorial, the Archbishop of Canterbury, on certain Saturday evenings in the year, has kept open house. All have access to him and may enjoy his hospitality without distinction of ranks, or rather with a preference to the poor and humble. Now, suppose some Archbishop had converted this into a social entertainment of his own friends and equals in position: might I not say to him, Don't do this; don't invite your friends at these times, which are specially appointed for the humble classes; without meaning to forbid his entertaining his personal acquaintances and friends at other times and in another way?' He talked a great deal about 'minor morals,' manners, selfish and ungenerous conduct in little things. This struck me rather oddly in connection with the treatment of strangers in the Presbyterian and Independent Churches here. While he was expounding Christ's directions about taking the lowest places, I could not help thinking of the many who were excluded from any place at all until after the 'second prayer.' I know of nothing in which our American usages compare more advantageously with those of Europe, than in this very particular. Binney's manner, although striking, is not pleasant. There is too much irony; in the ancient sense; and too much latent sarcasm in his whole discourse, as indicated by his frequent smile, a very bitter smile to my eye. There is, however, no appearance of affectation or of an effort at theatrical effects, but abundant evidence of strength of mind."

On Tuesday, June 11th, he went to St. Margaret's Church, Lothbury, to hear Melvill lecture. He heard him, and was delighted even beyond all his expectations. The discourse is given in full among the preacher's published efforts entitled "Golden Lectures." He ranks Melvill next to Candlish. No subsequent sermon from another ever modified his judgment of the uncouth Scotchman.

"We entered the church," he records, "and were shown by the pew-opener to a very eligible seat. We found the service just begun, by a stout, gray-haired man, of no very prepossessing aspect, who seemed abstracted from the words which he was reading, or rather repeating from memory, and looked constantly about, as if he saw something that surprised him, or was scanning the appearance of persons in different parts of the congregation. He would sometimes fix his eye for a minute on a particular quarter of the gallery, without the slightest interruption of his reading which, with this exception, and in point of elocution and expression, was exceedingly well done. So disagreeable, however, was the general impression made upon me by the reader's manner, that I felt convinced, and whispered to my friend, that this must be a curate. My only fear was that he was to preach: but this was in a great degree allayed by the increase of the congregation, which, before the close of the prayers, quite filled the church, no small one. When I saw the same person in the pulpit, my heart sank within me; but how great was my surprise when he began to read in the most admirable manner! but, strange to say, without raising his eyes once so far as I could see, from the manuscript before him, a most beautiful and spiritual sermon on Ps. cxix. 116; full of scriptural truth and poetical imagery, adopting as his plan the apostolic exposition of the text: 1. Tribulation worketh patience; 2. Patience, experience; 3. Experience, hope. The whole was captivating, but the last few sentences were grand, in which he brought out the idea, that the day must soon come, when he and all his hearers would feel the Psalmist's first petition to be useless—when instead of saying, 'Uphold me that I may live,' we can only say, 'Uphold me that I may *die*'; but even then the last petition would remain as appropriate as ever; and with strong assurance the expiring saint may cry, 'Let me not be ashamed of my hope!' I did not ask the preacher's name; for if it was not Melvill, it was something better. The discourse pleased me more than any of his printed ones; perhaps because it was so admirably read, a circumstance which I had not expected. The audience was breathless with attention. What a sight upon a week-day morning in the heart of the old city, surrounded by a labyrinth of warehouses and banks! It reminded me of Chalmers's Thursday morning lectures in the Tron Church at Glasgow, when the merchants used to rush from the Exchange to hear him. I have not attempted to give any analysis of his discourse, which, although highly edifying and instructive, derived its great charm from the original and striking images with which it was adorned, and which I cannot reproduce. It pleased me greatly more than any sermon I have heard, excepting those of Candlish; and with these it is not easy to compare it, because Candlish had the vast advantage of a great Christian doctrine, as the basis of his practical appeals and the ground of his pictorial illustrations. Partly on this account, but not alone, he still stands forth upon the surface of my memory, as equal in elegance and eloquence to any of the rest, and in doctrinal richness and intellectual force superior to them all. It is a satisfactory reflection, that while my parliamentary designs have failed almost entirely, I have been unexpectedly successful in my preaching projects—having heard every preacher in London that I wished or hoped to hear, and several in addition."

He heard a strange discourse at St. Mary's, Cambridge, at a portion of which one of the masters in the pit laughed; and not without strong provocation.

"The sermon (on Isaiah viii. 20) seemed to be the first of a series of apologetic lectures (like the Boyle and Bampton) and was very orthodox and antigeological. The preacher coughed so much and in such a canine manner, that I could have fancied myself in Allhallow's Barking. The one master in the pit laughed at the sermon, especially when a vacuum was said to be a rock on which men suffered shipwreck."

On the first of July he crossed the English channel, and after the usual experiences, and a few adventures of the kind that befall nearly every tourist, found himself once more in Paris. Nothing seemed to strike him with greater force than the pertinacity of the *commissionaires*, and the true gentility of the common people. He greatly preferred the English, however, on the score of personal cleanliness. For a while he was highly entertained in the imperial city; chiefly with observing the changes that had been introduced since his former sojourn. But he became tired long before the month was out, and hailed as a relief the utter contrast presented by some of the chief cities of Germany and Holland.

On the 3d of July, he went after breakfast to the Oratoire, under a vague impression that he might hear either Cocquerel or Monod. Finding it shut at 10 o'clock, and no one in the neighbourhood to give information, he proceeded to Nôtre Dame and saw the Archbishop perform high mass. Hastening back at 11½ to the Oratoire, he "found the precentor reading prayers." He afterwards heard an excellent sermon on the 20th Psalm, especially the verse "Be wise, &c" The de livery, he says, was excellent. The audience increased gradually till the house was full. They still sang Clement Marot's psalms and the old song tunes adapted to them. "I asked the beadle who that was. 'M. Monod.' 'Adolphe?' 'Oui, monsieur, Adolphe.' So I have heard another of the preachers whom I had upon my list."

He thus portrays another of the well known preachers of the French Capital:

"M. Cocquerel preaches at the church in the Rue de Grenelle. I crossed the Seine upon the Pont des Arts, and with the help of two policemen found the place I wanted. It is in a very fine street, near several departments of the government, including those of the Interior and of Public Instruction. The church bears a strong resemblance to the Oratoire; like which it is elliptical in form, and has pews or rather chambers in the wall, like the old German churches. As at the Oratoire last Sunday, the congregation constantly increased until the church was crowded; some coming in at the very end of the sermon. The scriptures, psalms, and stated prayers were read by a precentor, a very young-looking man in gown and bands. Cocquerel preached from Mark v. 14, 16. He is a red-faced, gray-haired man, of no very pleasing aspect; a powerful but grimacing and theatrical speaker, very colloquial and very declamatory. His sermon was a glorification of true Protestantism (*i. e.* rational Christianity, freedom of thought, &c.) with many reflections on the doctrines of grace; no doubt as preached by his colleague, Adolphe Monod, whose elocution I prefer as much as his doctrines. To my own surprise I have now heard every preacher that I cared to hear in London and Paris."

But he was yet to hear still another who was worth listening to with deep attention. On the 17th of July he found his way to the Salle Taitbout,

"which revived many of my ancient recollections, as the place where I attended public worship most frequently on my former visit to Paris. The people sit on chairs, as in the Catholic churches. A black-haired, white-cravated man gave me two tracts, and said he supposed I was a foreigner. He afterwards handed me a hymn-book. The room, which is not very large, was quite full before the sermon began. The preacher was rather a young-looking man who might have passed for an American. He had a disagreeable way of praying with his eyes open and rolling up the whites thereof. But his sermon was a very able and edifying one, and in some parts powerful. The text was 1 John i. 8; the theme: The various ways in which men may deny that they are sinners: 1. By denying the essential distinction between right and wrong; 2. By calling good evil and evil good; 3. By owning the reality of sin but denying its consequences; 4. By owning it in general and denying it in particular; 5. By owning it in particular, but making the good outweigh it. The last head was particularly striking and original. I was the more impressed with the whole discourse from the resemblance of the plan to one of mine on Jer. ii. 26. The expression was often very forcible and happy. The elocution would have been fine if he had kept his body still and spoken more deliberately. The most impressive part was on making God a liar. God brings man to the foot of the cross, and from the height of it says to him, 'Thou art a sinner.' Man's reply is, 'Mensonge!' 'Nothing but grace can save thee;' 'Mensonge!' And so to all the doctrines and offers of the Gospel, the unconverted sinner's answer is still, 'Mensonge! Mensonge! Mensonge!' The application to believers was equally searching. Several of the hearers wept. One sobbed aloud. The sermon was of the best kind known in America. I asked the preacher's name. M. Pressensé. I had often read of him."

Nothing delighted him when travelling so much as the study of character. On the Rhine boat he indulged himself in this way to his heart's content. After a description of the various people aboard, he gives us the following detailed and racy account of an amusing pair of Englishmen—a doctor and a naval or military officer:

"I derived great amusement from another pair of Englishmen. One was a short, clean-shaved, gray-haired man, in a home-made sort of black dress coat and trousers, who had obviously left home without the slightest change of costume. I took him at first for a country parson, but learned from the talk, and the inscription on his trunks, that he was a physician. He was a perfect specimen of a blunt, positive, straightforward, sensible, prejudiced John Bull. His companion was a man of more refinement and gentility, but equally John Bullish; with a dash of frankness and insouciance which led me to regard him as a sailor, even before I saw upon a trunk adjoining the doctor's, the name of 'Captain ——.' Perhaps, however, he was of the army, and the doctor an army surgeon; as I heard them throw out several military allusions. The diverting part of their behaviour was that, although quite free from all obtrusiveness, or airs of any kind, and wholly intent upon their own enjoyment, they acted precisely as if all the people on the boat were English. The doctor especially, who was much less a man of the world than his companion, and, indeed, a very decided humourist, would stop the first person that he met on deck and ask him or her, without a moment's hesitation, any question that occurred to him, and when he got a German answer would say, 'Eh, Eh?' in a tone of great surprise, as if he wondered what those foreigners were doing there. In one case particularly, he convulsed me by running up to two heavy-looking German peasant boys, who had probably never seen a Dampfschiff before, and asking them, in English, in the most earnest, peremptory tone, 'What is the boat stopping for, eh, eh?' I should not have been half so much amused at all this, if the men had seemed conscious of the fun themselves; but the idea of anything ludicrous about it, or of anything except the inconvenience attending it, seemed never to occur to them. I was quite surprised at the frequency with which they lighted upon people who could understand them, and according to the universal law in all such cases, perfectly willing to talk broken English to the best of their ability. Among the persons whom they thus encountered were two French or German ladies, of a faded-stylish look, who heard them mumbling over a map of the river, and volunteered to give them information. The Englishmen received the remarks with great civility, and several times went back to ask them questions. More than once, as I passed near them, I heard the doctor's 'Eh, Eh?' like the 'What, What?' of George the Third, as described by Madame d'Arblay.* But the richest exhibition of the two John Bulls was at the *table d'hôte*. Soon after we set sail (or rather steam), a man went round inquiring who would wish to dine. I expected the table to be set in the cabin, and foreboded a great loss in point of prospect. But about half-past twelve, a great commotion took place upon deck, occasioned by the setting of the table there."

One is reminded by the following dialogue between a French priest and a German abbé (for the most part in dog-Latin), of "Father Tom and the Pope:"

* The reader will be reminded, too, of the couplet:

"When lo! the monarch, in his usual way,
Like lightning spoke, What's this? What's this? what, what?'"

Peter Pindar's Works, p. 16, 1835.

"Among the passengers I had early observed a man in a peculiar dress, which I remembered to be that of an abbé—an ugly and conceited, but distingué-looking man, who talked to all the upper sort of Germans, especially the ladies, and read poetry with and to the wife of the Tyroler before mentioned. At one of the stations where we stopped, there came on board an elderly French priest, in the usual ugly garb, and rather squalid-looking, but with an intelligent countenance, and with all the bonhommie and easy manners of his nation. The two ecclesiastics were naturally drawn together, but it happened; curiously enough, that the one knew no French and the other no German: which must be a very rare occurrence here among men of any education. I happened to be by when the French priest accosted the German, by asking him whether a building on the high bank we were passing was a 'convent.' The other, understanding his gesture, replied at once in Latin, '*Monasterium est.*' I pricked up my ears, for I had long wished to hear a Latin conversation. After several other questions and answers about places in sight, the Frenchman said something to the German in a low voice, whereupon the latter called to a waiter to bring the gentleman a flask of Burgundy. They then took seats together at the table near me, and I listened eagerly to their discourse, which was made intelligible by the deliberation with which they were forced to speak, especially the Frenchman, who appeared quite unaccustomed to it, though he showed a scholarlike acquaintance with the language. The German spoke more glibly, but in a lower voice. While they were waiting for the wine, the Frenchman said, with pathos 'J'ai soif!' then recollecting himself, added, 'Sitio!' The dialogue was rendered the more comic by his thus continually lapsing into French, and then, by an effort, bringing out another scrap of Latin. Having half filled his own glass, and then his neighbour's, according to the etiquette of drinking, he struck the glasses together. 'Multos annos!' quoth the German. Answer: 'Idem!' It was plain that the German did not like the drink, and tried to shirk it by officiously filling his companion's glass; but the old man would not let him off, crying, 'Bibe, bibe!' till he had to yield. Meantime, this drinking scene, which looked like a picture of Gerard Dow, or Teniers, began to draw attention. The two figures were themselves quite striking—the German in a long black coat and shovel hat; the Frenchman in the hideous black petticoat and girdle, with a shabby-looking skull-cap; both seated at a table on the open deck. Some of the passengers seemed to wonder merely at the unknown tongue; but others gathered round with more intelligence. A man whom I had taken for a Scotch or Irish clergyman, with a youth who seemed to be his pupil, was attracted by the Latin, and they both came and silently took seats behind. A group of young men, whom I took to be Bonn students, stood close by, laughing and conversing freely on the scene before them. The German appeared conscious of the notice they attracted, and endeavoured to escape it by remaining silent, or replying briefly and in an undertone. But the fine old Frenchman was not only wholly unsuspicious, but continued to draw the other out by making him repeat his observations more distinctly. For reply to some muttered observation of the German, he said aloud, 'Sanè convivium, seu aqua fermentata, sufficit ad restaurandum hominem; sed vinum bonum est ad confortandum!' The German was now obliged to order a bottle of wine, although the mirth of the students was thereby much increased. On tasting it, the Frenchman rubbed his breast, saying, 'Bonum, bonum est!' He then asked whether it was 'Vinum Rheni?' and informed his friend that, in his country, they had 'Vinum rubrum bonum, excellentissimum, ex provinciâ Burgundiâ ortum, et in Campaniâ vinum album celeberrimum.' When he wanted to pay for his wine, he was in a great quandary; and asked the other, in French, the value of the German coins. The other, in a low voice, asked him to speak Latin. 'Oui, oui!' said he hastily and pulling out a handful of kreutzers, and their multiples, 'non cognosco hanc monetam: quot nummos mihi est solvendum?' The other fluently but almost inaudibly explained to him the value of the coins; to which the poor old fellow answered, 'Oui, oui, oui, oui!' then again forgetting himself, 'et ea?—pardon! et istud?' After their compotations were concluded, they went back to their geography. 'Estne ecclesia quam videmus hîc?' 'Non est ecclesia, sed arx, castellum.' With respect to a church which did appear soon afterwards, the German told a story in a low voice, which the Frenchman did not understand until he had forced him to repeat it. All that I heard was, that 'In tempore reformationis, episcopus hujus ecclesiæ Lutheranus factus est et duxit uxorem;' and then something about 'Omnes successores—,' at which the old priest expressed great disgust. Anon he said, 'Ecce urbs magna!' 'Bona est, ah! Bona est.' 'Quot millia habitantium habet?' 'Quindecim.' 'Omns sunt Catholici?' 'Non: mixti.' The bells of Bonn were chiming very sweetly as we passed. 'Campane sonant!' and then they joined in some devout remarks about the 'Angelus' and the sacrament. The Frenchman related the following piece of news: 'Sacerdos Seminarii Sancti iter faciebat in Rheno. Saccum continentem vestimenta et alia aliquis vidit, eripuit, et fugit. Regressus est post raptorem, et mansit ad recuperandum saccum.' He also asked the other about his employment; who answered something with respect to a 'beneficium in familiâ mea;' to which the priest replied, 'Apud nos beneficia ecclesiastica non existunt.' He had previously said that the 'Regio Belgiaca, quæ est meâ, non producit vinum; multum frumentum, sed nullum vinum:' to which his friend replied that *his* country produced both. As we touched at Bonn, the German said, 'Ecce multitudo astantium!' and they both went towards the gang-board, and I heard no more. The Latin expressions above given are, I think, exact."

He was unaffectedly charmed with the Low Countries: especially at the first blush.

"The Hollanders," he records, "are more like Americans than any people I have seen in Europe; and their language is more like English in its tone and accent. Again and again, since I entered Holland, I have taken it for English, at a little distance; which I never did with French or German. Its intonations are as much like ours as the Scotch or Irish. It is also very soft and musical, so that when you hear it close at hand, it sounds like German spoken by an Englishman, with a suppression of the harsh sounds."

What a pleasing glimpse of his heart we have in the following!

"However strange the old folks may appear in any place, the babies all seem to know me. One pretty little creature held its hand out to be shaken; and all seem ready to respond to the least hint by smile or look. The adults look rather heavy, but the children all seem bright and lively. I am amused with the practice of giving a familiar but respectful nod to passers by. I have received it myself from persons of all ages."

From Ostend he sailed to Dover, reaching the chalk cliffs before night of the 31st of July, and was presently ensconced in his chambers in London; where he fell in with another admirable Scotch preacher.

I return to the record:

"When I got to Upper George Street, Portman Square, I saw no church, and was about to take a cab to Hamilton's, but happily inquired first of two policemen, who replied together, 'Yes; a Scotch Church just a little further on, behind the trees.' And sure enough, I found a portico and large door in the front of what appeared to be a row of private houses. The people were beginning to pour in, and soon filled (without crowding) a good-sized, handsome hall, with pews and galleries, lighted from above, like the Salle Taitbout, in Paris, and the Bank of England here. The sexton took me to an empty pew far forward, and requested me to occupy the inner end. He afterwards brought in another man, and then a man and woman; who took their seats as they came in, without disturbing me. The singing was conducted by a precentor, but with a kind of choir in the circular pew, as I saw in the Free Church at Montreal. They sang standing; which, of all the apings of Episcopacy, is to me the most unpleasant. The prayer was a delightful treat—an exquisite Scotch prayer of the best kind, worth a volume of St. Chrysostom's Collects. The sermon was upon Isai. xxxii: 2, very much in Hamilton's style, abounding in poetical descriptions, more correct, but less original; with a good substratum of sound doctrine and experimental truth, but without argument or formal exposition. It seemed to me to be no fair sample of the preacher's gifts, but probably a sermon intended for the dog-days. Its chief merit, unlike most Scotch sermons, lay in the delivery; which was, at the same time, elegant and powerful. The preacher, unless my eye deceived me, is a very handsome man, in face and figure; with a voice of extraordinary sweetness, strength, and flexibility, perfectly audible even in a whisper and susceptible of endless modulation without any seeming effort. I never saw such freedom and energy of action in the reading of a manuscript. Indeed, as to much of the discourse, I could not find out whether it was written or extempore. With such advantages of voice and person, with so fine an elocution, and so little brogue, he would be very popular across the water. I was going to make sure of his identity before I came away, when the man who had sat next me asked if I attended there always. 'No; I am a stranger.' 'Did you never hear Mr. Chalmers before?' 'I never did.' 'He is a good preacher.' 'Yes.' 'And an excellent man.' This was not a member of his congregation, but a person brought in by the sexton. My attention was somewhat diverted from the sermon, by a lively little blue-eyed, white-haired, red-cheeked, earnest-looking boy, about four years old, in the adjoining pew, with a respectable Scotchman."

On the 20th of August, Dr. Alexander (who had been rejoined by his friend Mr. Hodge) sailed from Liverpool in the steamer Europa, and arrived in Boston on the 31st of the same month. From the capital of New England it was but a short journey home, where he was received with open arms.

Thus was accomplished his second and final trip to Europe; and thus a pleasure long coveted, and once tasted, but never to be again repeated, was enjoyed with nearly the old zest; and the delight which springs from hope and ends in fruition, was succeeded, as before, by the happiness which lives in memory and grows pensive in retrospection.

CHAPTER XXVI.

We now stand, as it were, upon a bright summit in Dr. Alexander's history. From this point his life shelves down—alas, too abruptly—into sweet glades among the hills and tranquil waters; and then, beyond all, among mysterious shadows that shall never be lifted in this world.

Long absence from his accustomed tasks seemed only to whet his appetite for books and solitude. His journeyings in Europe proved a spur to his diligence at home. He threw himself into his studies with greater zeal than ever. He again turned a deaf ear and an impassive heart to the allurements of society. Like the Greek stripling, he bounded over the course with new impulse as he beheld the goal, which had receded for awhile, once more approaching him. Even the least harmful of the guiles of dreamy indolence he could now trample beneath his feet with fresh disdain. Indeed, I cannot help thinking that out of his cloistered silence he might utter with new meaning and a hearty approval of their sentiments, the verses entitled "Farewell to the World," which Ben Jonson puts into the mouth of a "gentlewoman virtuous and noble."

Dr. Alexander fell in again about this time with an old pupil,* to whom we are indebted for the particulars which follow:

"I saw him again in 1853, just before the meeting of the General Assembly at Philadelphia. I had at that time a great deal of conversation with him on the subject of the Seminary and theological train-

* Dr. J. H. Rice, of Mobile.

ing generally. Whenever I met with him I was more and more astonished at the vast range of his learning and the perfect ease with which his mind embraced and comprehended the most difficult subjects. He had in a wonderful degree that most uncommon faculty commonly called common sense. He seemed to me to be as wise as he was learned. He understood the politics of the church as well as he did the Hebrew grammar."

A single fact will illustrate his marvellous facility of acquisition; and this I get from Dr. Jones, of Bridgeton. Not long before his death, one of his brothers, residing under the same roof, was from home for six or eight weeks. To fill the void occasioned by his absence, Dr. Alexander determined to enter upon the study of two entirely new languages, one of them being the *Danish*. By the time of his brother's return, he had so far mastered both these languages as to be able to read dramas and novels in each of them.

Dr. James Alexander spent the summer partly at Sharon Springs and partly at Newport; from which place he returned to New York early in September, and was soon busy over the pages of Montaigne, Fénélon, Quintilian, and Plato—also in his wonted laborious pastoral duties. In October the news was received that the venerable Mrs. Graham of Lexington, a sister of Dr. Archibald Alexander, was dead; and in November the same tidings came with regard to her brother Major John Alexander. He was the last male survivor of the old Rockbridge household. They were both excellent Christian people, and both admirable exemplifications of the Scotch-Irish type of intellect and manners. The former had soft dark eyes and a sedate, reflective mind of high capacity. The latter was robust, ruddy, impulsive, kind-hearted, and fearless—a thorough Saxon. Though not like one another, they were both in some respects like their brother of Princeton. The tidings from Lexington brought sorrow to the hearts of all the friends.

We now turn again to the old roof-tree, where Dr. Addison Alexander was hard at work on Church History. His records relate chiefly to that subject. The statements he makes are sometimes of a nature which render them valuable to Biblical students. I accordingly ask the reader to return with me to the journals, which are unbroken from this time on; but as one day was so much like another, selections here and there will answer every purpose. I begin with a

"Plan for 1853 and 1854 (ἐὰν ὁ κύριος θελήσῃ). First Class. Lectures on Church History, twice a week with recitations. Second Class. 1. Thorough exegetical study of the Acts of the Apostles. 2. First part of lectures on Church History as above. Third Class. 1. Lectures and lessons on Old Testament History. 2. Lectures and lessons on Connection of the Old and New Testament. 3. Thorough exegetical study of the Gospels."

"Nov. 2.—Lectured to the first class on the heathen reaction under Julian, the Donatists' schism, and the Apollinarian heresy. Received a letter from the Rev. Dr. Macdonnell, Provost of Trinity College, Dublin, which I answered. Wrote ten quarto pages of my Introduction to the Sacred History. Read Hefele's Prolegomena to Barnabas and Clement."

"Nov. 23.—Lectured to the First Class on the theologians of the Fifth Century. Read Gibbon and Kurtz on the reign of Justinian. Prepared notes for my next lecture. Finished Hagenbach's lectures on the Church of the First Three Centuries, which I began October 30. Continued Clement and Thucydides. Received from Westermann copies of Lange's Church History, Noack's Dogmengeschichte, and Neander on James and John. Received from Dr. Schaff a specimen (in MS.) of his proposed smaller work on Church History."

On December the 2d, I find that he finished Mark in Campbell's version; lectured to the First Class on Gregory and his times; read Hackett, Alford, Baumgarten, Schaff, and Conybeare and Howson on Acts xix.; read the Epistle of Ignatius to the Romans; continued Cicero Pro Roscio, Hoffmann, and Thucydides. On the last day of the same month he finished the Acts with the Second Class; continued Eadie on Ephesians, Hamilton on the Philosophy of Perception, Hoffmann's Syriac Grammar, Allen's History of Denmark, Keil's Introduction to the Old Testament, and Buttman's Greek Grammar. He also finished the Shepherd of Hermas and the whole collection of Apostolical Fathers, in Hefele's edition, which he had begun on the first day of November. He likewise finished Thucydides, which he had begun in 1849, and had been reading ever since, though not without many interruptions. "Herodotus," he says, "I read through when quite a youth. I propose to take up the Hellenica of Xenophon. In reading Thucydides, especially the last books, I have noted many parallel or illustrative expressions on the margin of my Knapp's Greek Testament." He also this week closed two courses of lectures: one on the Old Testament History, and one on the Acts of the Apostles.

These labours did not restrain him from going off to preach. His brother in New York often asked him, and delighted to hear him. On the 4th of December, the latter writes: "Addison preached a grand sermon for me yesterday. He is very unequal."* The elder brother was wont to say that "Addison" was becoming too exegetical in his sermons, for the popular taste. This was natural, but, he thought, needed to be somewhat guarded against. I have heard him remark that "Addison" had an unaccountable contempt for the more florid and animated discourses of the kind he used to preach in Philadelphia, and was consequently getting to think that his forte was the lecture-room and not the pulpit. But now and then in what seemed their ashes lived his wonted fires; which would once more blaze, and roar, and burn.

Among the students whose names appear upon the general catalogue for the period 1849 and 1850, was Dr. Wm. C. Cattell, President of Lafayette College; who has kindly furnished his reminiscences of Dr. Alexander. After referring to his "brilliant genius and prodigious learning," and "the magnetism of his very presence in the class-room," of which it is impossible, he thinks, to convey to others any adequate impression, President Cattell proceeds to speak of a trait of his character which was not so generally known even to his pupils:

* Fam. Letters, Vol. II. p. 193.

"During the three years that I was in the regular classes of the Seminary, I shared fully in the enthusiasm of all the students who were under his instruction; but after I was graduated, and remained a fourth year to pursue my studies as a 'Resident Licentiate,' Dr. Alexander invited me to spend three evenings a week with him in the study of Hebrew. Those who remember how much interest he threw around this difficult language even in a large class of fifty or sixty students, can judge of my privilege to sit by his side for hours in his own study, examining the Hebrew text line by line, and word by word; and certainly the impression made upon me in the class-room of his wonderful erudition, was only deepened during these interviews. But in the long talks we had after the books were closed, and which embraced so many subjects and so many people that we both knew, I also learned what a great loving *heart* he had. I cannot, of course, give you any particulars of these delightful talks, but I am glad of the opportunity of placing upon record what his family and intimate friends well knew, but which, owing to his recluse habits, so few of his students ever knew, that he was as patient and kind and sympathizing as a woman; and when, afterwards, I met him in Europe, he still seemed not merely the brilliant and learned professor, but also the genial, thoughtful, and loving friend."

His final record for the year is characteristic, and on the whole does not breathe a feeling of dissatisfaction. When time flies with a man he is commonly happy. His memory for dates was always called into exercise at these conjunctures. "This year has passed with great rapidity. I can hardly believe that I spent three months of it at sea and in Europe. I closed the month of May at Liverpool, June at Dover, July at Ostend, August at Halifax."

The diary for this year offers little that is specially noteworthy:

"New Year's Day, 1854. Heard Dr. Hodge preach in the chapel (Rom. i. 16). Continued Eadie on Ephesians. Resumed the reading of the original SS. with ancient versions. Began 1. Ecclesiastes in Hebrew and Greek (having finished Proverbs shortly before I sailed for Europe). 2. 1 Kings in Hebrew and Latin (having finished 2 Samuel May 15th). 3. Deuteronomy in Hebrew and Chaldee; which I began but laid aside a year ago. (N. B. I have read these three versions regularly from the beginning of the Old Testament.) 4. Mark in Greek and Syriac. Made a few remarks at Conference, and heard a powerful discourse from Dr. Hodge on time considered as a talent."

Two days after, he explained the course of study to the Second Class; and continued the prosecution of his private studies on the same plan. He read 1 Kings ii, in Hebrew and Latin, and Eadie on Ephesians ii. He prepared a paper on the tenth century. He continued Hoffmann's Syriac Grammar and Allen's History of Denmark. He finished Hamilton on the Philosophy of Perception. He continued Kiel's Introduction. He began Justin Martyr's Address to the Greeks, which he had translated for the Repertory in his youth; also Xenophon's Hellenica. He also returned to his boyish pursuits, and read the first sura of the Koran in Arabic. (He had accomplished the whole book twenty-five years before.) The perusal of Deuteronomy iii. in Hebrew, brought the day's tasks to a close.

"Feb. 2. Lectured to the third Class on the chronology of the Gospels. Continued Eadie on Ephesians, Caspari's Arabic Grammar, Keil's Einleitung ins Alte Test., the Koran in Arabic with Kasimirski's version, Canticles in Greek, and Mark in Syriac. Finished the second book of Xenophon's Hellenica. Read Lord Brougham's admirable speech on the Reform Bill (1831). Began a list of the grammatical forms actually used in the Greek Testament."

He was in the habit at this time of having a book open before him while he shaved. His brother James had perhaps suggested this, as one of his own practices for many years.

"April 28. Finished Eadie on Ephesians; which has been my 'shaving-book' for several months: also the vulgate version of 2 Kings (begun Jan. 1). Examined the First Class on Church History."

How full his mind always was of fresh matter and new impressions, it is unnecessary to state. He wrought in gold and silver and precious stones. He was not content to build his structures out of wood, hay, and stubble; he so erected his pillars and entablatures as to bid defiance to the deluge of flame which he knew would one day devour most of the labours of this generation.

On one of the early days of June the two brothers met at Princeton, and had one of their delightful reunions. The elder one then proceeded to Trenton, and thence to Easton, returning home by the Central Railroad of New Jersey. The air, the chat by the way, the scenery, were all that is refreshing. He spent the chief part of the summer again at Newport; in absolute repose of mind and body, as he declares. In the early part of September he went once or twice to the picturesque undulations and sylvan solitudes of the county of Sussex in New Jersey, amidst the spurs of the Blue Ridge, where he had left the members of his household. He was, however, very ill in October; and suffered excruciating pains. During the paroxysms he had extraordinary experience of the Divine mercies. He records, "I can only express it by saying, the experience was *steeped* in pain." His strength on recovering from this attack was remarkable. I do not think he ever had another of these nephritic seizures. He was again in Princeton early in December; and pronounces it "a delightful visit to the dearest spot on earth." After speaking of the "indescribable pleasure" with which he listened to a lecture from Professor Guyot, he adds: "But most of all I received stimulation in my Biblical studies from my brother Addison. I ought to go often, if it were only for the benefit which I derive from the last of these." After a short visit to Trenton, he returned home to find every thing going on prosperously and happily. On the 21st he records: "Letters from Addison; I lament his discontent in his present situation." This discontent arose out of the professor's strong and growing conviction that he was not in the right chair; that he was specially suited by his tastes and capacities not to church history, but to the scientific exposition of the Bible, to its literature and archæology and philology, and to the training of interpreters of a new school.

The Life of Dr. Archibald Alexander, by his eldest son, which was now finished and set afloat, was received with extraordinary favour. It was a heavy task and a sore trial to the author. His own opinion of its merits was very low.

The autumn journal of Dr. Addison Alexander is as usual little more than an epitome of his studies. I find that on the 26th of September he examined the Second Class, and lectured on Acts i. He also studied church history in various books, and continued the reading of Polybius in Greek, Allen in Danish, Genesis in Hebrew, and Matthew in Greek. Having the Spanish fever on him again, he this day resumed Mariana's "Historia de España;" the fifth book of which he had finished just before he went to Europe. He also made a dash at French and Italian, and completed "Joinville's Histoire de St. Louis," which he had laid aside in January, and alternating between the two languages, finished Sarpi's "Istoria del Concilio Tridentino," which he had laid aside just four months before.

"Nov. 2. Lectured to the Third Class on the early missions and persecutions. Prepared questions and a lecture for to-morrow. Resumed the Gospel of Luke in Syriac, which I laid aside on the 7th of May. Continued Exodus in Hebrew; Joshua in Chaldee; John and Eusebius in Greek; Joinville in French; Mariana in Spanish; Olshausen and Kurtz in German. Reëxamined Gibbon, Hallam, and Koeppen, with a view to my lecture on the Middle Ages."

I only give specimens, taken here and there.

"Nov. 15. Examined the First Class on the Crusades and Military Orders, and lectured on the interpretation of the Apocalypse. Continued Leviticus in Hebrew; Acts, Ezekiel, and Polybius in Greek; Chronicles and Buchanan in Latin; Kurtz and Wiltsch in German; Pallavicini in Italian. Began the Gospel of John in Dutch and Polish."

The record for the next day is almost the same, only adding the reading of the Gospel of John in Swedish and Portuguese.

"Dec. 4. Lectured to the Third Class on the civil institutions of the Law. Attended the monthly concert. Finished Leviticus again in Hebrew. Resumed my commentary on the Acts. Continued Acts,

Ezekiel, and Polybius in Greek; Buchanan, Chronicles, Uhlemann, in Latin; Olshausen (Romans) and Ewald (Hebrew Syntax) in German; John in Dutch; Allen in Danish; Mariana in Spanish. Began to premeditate a sermon on 'The stone which the builders rejected.'"

The following letter to his brother Samuel tells of a comical adventure he had; describes one sermon, and alludes to another. It is written on a sheet of two and a half inches by twelve.

"PRINCETON, Nov. 28, 1854.

"DEAR SAMUEL:

"I was glad to hear from you and Janetta, as I felt anxious as to her exposure. I had a very pleasant trip to Philadelphia, where I put up at the United States Hotel, being lodged in a large room facing the United States Bank. The house is like Jones's at its best estate; in one respect better; namely, you hear no servants' voices, and no noise at the bar. Bridges, you know, is dead. I believe the United States Hotel is kept by McClellan who was steward at Jones's. As funny an incident occurred at Ogden's as the one at Bloodgood's. I stopped there on my way to the hotel, and found the younger Ogden with a gentleman. I asked if anything had been left there for me. 'No.' I then said, 'Your brother is not in?' 'Oh yes! I will call him. Here he is, Doctor!' Through the darkness of the shop I saw a form approaching, very unlike Henry Ogden; and on nearing me, it proved to be a black boy! The stranger, who appeared to be a good deal mystified, told Mr. Ogden I had asked for his brother. 'Oh!' said he, 'I thought you asked for our boy and wanted to send him somewhere.'

"I heard Wylie, in the fine new Covenanting Church which Duff consecrated, expound Psalm xxxi. and Genesis xix.; two full length sermons in one diet. He compared the Know-Nothing or Native American proscription to the people of Sodom saying, This fellow came in and will needs be a judge. From Lot's treatment of the angels, he deduced the duty of sitting in the city gate to watch for strangers and protect them from temptation and imposition; not literally, but by joining an association lately formed for that purpose. Perhaps it was the Young Men's Christian Association! for he afterwards invited his young men to go and hear young Tyng preach at the Epiphany. As I went down Walnut street at night, Tom Hall ran after me and asked me when I was to preach; as he and his sister were following me up. His mother is much better. I stopped at St. Mary's Church at night for a few minutes, and heard a musical service, probably a mass for the dead. The church was crowded.

"Do you know that the regiment which repulsed the Russians in the late attack, was the one we saw at Montreal ten years ago? Professor Guyot is lecturing at College. I had a letter from Scribner last night, urging me to finish Acts."

A travelling clergyman who had been in Princeton in the winter, had been compelled to leave behind him one of the swift and elegant little sleighs called "cutters." Some time afterwards, he wrote an elaborate letter to the professor of ecclesiastical history, requesting him to sell the cutter and bestow the proceeds of the sale upon any distressed minister of his acquaintance. He thereupon sat down and penned the following laughable note to Dr. Hall, inclosing the long letter about the cutter.

"PRINCETON, Dec. 9, 1854.

"MY DEAR SIR:

"I received your affecting letter, and regret that I can do so little to relieve you. If the use or proceeds of my cutter would be of any service, I need not say how greatly your acceptance of it would oblige

"Your sincere friend,

"REV. DR. HALL. J. A. ALEXANDER."

What became of the cutter I do not know. The professor at Princeton never applied for it, and the troubles of the Trenton pastor had to be relieved in some other way.

A little more than three weeks later, to wit, on Dec. 28th, I find he lectured to the Second Class on the Carthaginian school of theology; read and abstracted Ewald, Stuart, Elliott, De Wette, Hengstenberg, and Ebrard, on Rev. i. 9; continued Numbers in Hebrew; Judges in Chaldee; Luke in Syriac; John in Swedish; 1 John and Polybius in Greek; Buchanan in Latin; Psalm cl. ii. in Coptic; Mariana in Spanish; Allen in Danish; and Thiers in French. He also ran over several articles by Low in English.

The letter following is one to Dr. Philip Schaff, and will be read with interest. It will be seen that Dr. Schaff had asked him to assist him in preparing a work on Church History.

"PRINCETON, Dec. 29, 1854.

"REV. AND DEAR SIR:

"I congratulate you on your pleasant journey and your safe return. I will take an early opportunity of depositing your manuscript with Mr. Scribner, who had previously requested me to do so. I have little hope of being able to engage in any joint task of the kind you mention. My present judgment is in favour of your finishing your larger work, or some considerable part of it, before attempting a compendium. One immediate want of such a book would be supplied, as you suggest, by a good translation of Kurtz's Handbuch. This, I think, will be undertaken by Dr. Schaefer of Easton, who has done the Heilige Geschichte in a very admirable manner. The demand is so urgent that I do not feel at liberty to wait for books as yet unwritten, however satisfactory they might be when completed. With my best wishes for your personal welfare and professional success, I remain, with great regard,

Your friend and servant,

PROF. SCHAFF." ADDISON ALEXANDER.

"P. S. I am just renewing my subscription to the Kirchenfreund, in the hope that you will furnish it with some of the results of your late visit to the old world."

Dr. Alexander was a warm admirer of the talents, attainments, and piety of Professor Schaff, and thought him better fitted than any man in America to write the great popular work on Church History which has always been desired by the mass of educated Christian readers.

His social habits were the same as formerly, with the exception that he was less apt to displease, and more sure to delight and fascinate his visitors. He still, however, lived among his books and manuscripts.

The following sketch is from the pen of the Rev. Dr. B. M. Smith, Professor of Biblical and Oriental Literature in Union Theological Seminary, Va.:

"Of course, no one capable of appreciating his profound and extensive learning could withhold due admiration for him, or fail to feel assured that he would, in time, make valuable contributions to the Biblical literature, and to other parts of theological science. But his recluse habits and aversion to the usual forms of social intercourse produced the impression, that his sphere of knowledge and his tastes were exclusively literary, or, to use a common expression, that he was a 'book-worm.'"

His subsequent career as a highly acceptable and popular preacher had not entirely removed this impression from the writer's mind, when he was again unexpectedly thrown in his company. The impressions produced by this second interview were in the highest degree gratifying and delightful. In the winter of 1854, while in Princeton, on business for the Board of Publication, he called at the house, not only not expecting to see Dr. Addison Alexander, but, so far as he had thought of the matter, rather predetermined not to see him. When taking his leave he was invited by one of the family into his study. He at once promptly, and very firmly, but courteously declined; alleging that he was not acquainted with him, and that doubtless, his engagements were too pressing to allow him to see a casual visitor with no special business and no claims on his attention. The invitation, however, was so earnestly pressed, that he felt he could no longer refuse without apparent rudeness; and suffered himself to be almost forced into the room, with the expressed intention of stopping but a "few minutes." His reliance on the friend who introduced him, for support during the awkward encounter, was speedily cut off by the withdrawal of that person after announcing his name at the door. But his apprehensions were soon quieted.

"Never," he remarks "was I more agreeably disappointed. The most cherished friendof twenty years' standing would hardly have extended to me a more cordial welcome. After a few minutes' conversation about common friends in Virginia, we insensibly glided into a comparison of views on those subjects which would naturally interest the minds of clergymen; especially such as related to the study of the scriptures and the training of ministers. I use the phrase 'comparison of views' simply for want of a better. It was rather an interchange of suggestions by me of a leading nature, and full expressions of opinion by him. On these topics I not only found him possessed of extensive and valuable information, but as communicative as I had supposed he would be reticent. I was prepared to hear from him the most thoroughly digested opinions on all subjects connected with the study of the scriptures, to commentaries, lexicons, grammars and other aids to interpretation; and also on those parts of ministerial training which lie within the lines of scholastic arrangements; but I was surprised to find that on subjects of Bible study of more general bearing, and on those parts of ministerial training which are unconnected with the course of a theological seminary, he was equally at home, and his views were most eminently practical. He evinced the possession and exercise of that rare talent, so eminently conspicuous in the character of his father, for at once seizing on the salient points of any matter of interest and, by a kind of instinct or strong common sense, at once reaching sound conclusions."

During that and subsequent interviews, the conviction fast grew in his mind, that so far from being a mere scholar or recluse, who knew little, and cared for less, outside of his study and lecture-room, he was the most eminently practical man he ever knew; thoroughly informed on all topics of current interest in the religious and political world, and even as minutely informed on the state of our Church, as if he had made it the leading object of his investigations.

"His knowledge of the ministers in various regions, my own included, was as accurate as if he had made the study of the men his business. Entirely removed from the influence of petty considerations and personal prejudices, his powers of discrimination enabled him to form very just estimates of the character and conduct of the men who passed under his observation."

A few weeks after Dr. Smith's first visit, he went to Princeton to attend a meeting of New Brunswick Presbytery. He found Dr. Addison Alexander a member, and contrary to all his preconceptions, nearly as active a member as any present. It was a new and interesting view of his character as a minister; as he had been led to suppose him indifferent to such engagements, and had imagined that if he attended the meetings, it would be only as a matter of duty and as a silent voter.

"When I parted with him after my first visit, which you may well infer, was by no means limited to 'a few minutes,' he made me promise, on all future occasions, to make his house my home, while in P. I did so; and never was I made to feel more at my ease, or entertained with more evident cordiality."

Dr. Smith then gives a résumé of his final conclusions:

"I may sum up the particulars of the impressions made on my mind by his acquaintance by saying, that, on subjects on which we look to books for information, I found his communications more than a substitute, and it mattered not what might be the subject; on those, in respect of which we deem the extended observation and experience of practical men most desirable, his views were of the highest value for comprehensiveness, perspicuity, and sound sense; while on topics which afford occasion for entertainment and amusement, no professed wit or humourist could so gratify a listener. Indeed, of his powers of humour, including good-natured satire, no reader of his essays and his commentary on Isaiah needs to be informed. On reading any of his works, which are among my table-books, I am often so forcibly reminded of his sound discriminating views and humorous remarks as expressed in conversation, that I feel very much as if I had been sitting with him in his study."

Such was his versatility, the extent of his curiosity on all matters of interest and use, the extraordinary retentiveness of his memory, his good sense, and his remarkable practical turn, that it has often occurred to this writer that whatever pursuit he had seen fit to adopt, whether law, medicine, agriculture, commerce, manufactures, or political science and life, he would have met with eminent success.

"Excuse one remark, rather aside from the plan of this communication. In reading his 'Explanations' of Scripture, I have been struck with the clearness and conclusiveness with which his most thoroughly critical and profound interpretations of Scripture sustain the distinguishing peculiarities of Calvinism. And while he examines and dissects the text according to the sound laws of criticism, and most unflinchingly pushes his investigations of the 'letter' of the Bible, in the proper use of all the discoveries of modern Biblical criticism, he never forgets that it is the word of God he handles. With a childlike faith and the most humble reverence of one who never had heard the purity or the integrity of the text questioned, he yet pursues the most extensive and minute investigations of mere critical discussions. That a man of his independent habits of thought, his apparently inexhaustible resources of knowledge, and his extended and infinitesimal research, leads his readers to stronger confidence in the Divine authority of the Scriptures, is no slight contribution to the ever accumulating mass of evidence by which the faith of God's people is sustained, and the efforts of all sorts of infidelity, in the church and out of it, are confounded."

It has been the privilege of Dr. Smith to know, with some very good opportunities of forming intelligent estimates of character, some of the most eminent scholars, both in theology and other departments of science, in the United States and in Europe, and it is his deliberate and careful conclusion, that he never met one who so completely filled his idea of the accomplished professor and teacher, the keen and subtle casuist, the skilful interpreter of Scripture, the Christian gentleman, the pious and humble expositor and vindicator "of the ways of God to man." That the reputation of Dr. Alexander has not been more general in our church is due, he suspects, to two facts:

" One, that he was as modest as he was learned, and the other, that many of the men of this generation, who give tone to public opinion, either had not the opportunity to know him, or the ability to appreciate him."

The following letter is interesting as showing what his feeling was with regard to a popular Church History:

"PRINCETON, Dec. 1, 1854.

"DEAR SIR:

"I have not abandoned the Acts, but am slowly adding to the manuscript; although I have not yet decided as to size and shape. When I do so, you shall know it. You are the best judge as to the expediency of publishing on the subject of Church history: though neither of the works you name will answer the immediate demand. I am tired of translations and impatient to see something written in English. If we must have translations, I prefer Kurtz to Hase. Dr. Schaefer, of Easton, thinks of Englishing the former. Dr. Schaff could make the only book we want, if he would write for English and American and not for German readers. But two years is a long time to wait, unless he publishes in parts or numbers. If I continue to teach this subject, which is doubtful, I shall be glad to get assistance sooner. The manuscript of which you speak is ready to be forwarded. I wish to know, however, whether I shall wait for a safe private opportunity, which may not occur soon, or forward it by mail at your risk.

"Yours truly,

"MR. SCRIBNER. J. A. ALEXANDER."

It is an indication of the fairness of the views given in these volumes, that they are not those merely of Americans, or of those who have been strangers to the best European scholars, teachers, and pulpit notorieties; but also of men who have sat under the Gamaliels of the Old World. Dr. Smith was reminded, by his lectures on geography, of Ritter in his day the acknowledged prince of continental geographers. President Sears could not determine whether Professor Addison Alexander, or the venerated Tholuck of Halle, was the better scholar, knew the greater number of languages, had the larger stock of curious general knowledge, or had the more elastic and vivacious mind. Professor Hepburn, as we shall presently see, greatly preferred the lectures of the American professor on Biblical History to those of Hengstenberg himself. Dr. Scott has dared to speak of Dr. Alexander's preaching in the same connection with that of Dr. Chalmers of Edinburgh. I now refer with pleasure to the words of the Rev. James Little of Florida, formerly a student of Queen's College, Belfast. Mr. Little writes:

"My first distinct and personal knowledge of Dr. J. A. Alexander was gained in the fall of 1854. In that year, during my summer vacation in Queen's College, Belfast, I visited the United States, and found myself a member of Nassau Hall before the vacation had expired. I had indeed heard and known something of Dr. Alexander before that time, for his fame and some of his learned writings had reached the Old World. But in my mind his reputation was to a considerable extent included in, and blended with, that of the family to which he belonged, and had not taken that distinct individual form which it soon after did. My impressions of him, on reaching the venerable library and theological metropolis of American Presbyterianism in which he lived, were akin to those of a traveller approaching a country whose mountains, lakes, and rivers he has never seen, but concerning which fame has spoken much; having something of the vague and indistinct in them, which on closer examination, becomes distinct, definite, and satisfactory. Thus did the vagueness and indistinctness of my notions of Dr. Alexander's reputation pass away, and my impressions of his great talents and wonderful learning become definite and clearly fixed.

"This high yet distinct impression was forced upon me from every point of view I had of him. It was common among all (literate and illiterate) where he lived. The students of the College, among whom I daily mingled, entertained the most profound respect for his learning, talents, and genius, and thronged to hear all his public discourses. Such respect is not, I believe, permanently entertained for and bestowed on any save those who possess the qualities which inspire it. But I came nearer to him, saw, and heard him. I was introduced to him and heard him preach some of his most popular and powerful sermons. The clearness of his thought, the exactness of his language, his masterly elucidation and enforcement of truth, united with an ardent and impetuous eloquence which like an irresistable torrent rushed over and bore down everything opposing, forever fixed him in my mind as a genuine and inimitable originality—a preacher of the order of which Melchizedec was a priest; as among, and yet different from, the greatest preachers of Edinburgh, London, Paris, or Geneva, whom I had then, or have since, heard."

What he was in his relations with his colleagues in the Seminary, may be inferred from the following affectionate statements of the Reverend Dr. Alexander T. McGill, who knew him intimately and for a number of years. He writes:

"It is a melancholy pleasure to recall now the personal and private relations between Dr. Alexander and myself as colleagues and friends. I would record it as the highest gratification of my life, so far as honour from man could be appreciated, that, through more than five years of intimate intercourse, I could possess the confidence and esteem and increasing love of one so keenly discriminating in his judgment of men, as well as learned beyond all his contemporaries, here and elsewhere. If I could venture to boast of friendship, or needed to shield myself from the malevolent reproaches and cruel disparagement of others, I would be contented to rest my defence on the solitary fact, that the searching eye and honest heart of this great man drew me to himself, with confiding estimation, which seemed to increase to the last hour of his life."

Nothing has struck me more forcibly in preparing these memorials of the departed scholar and commentator, than the difficulty of reconciling the popular impressions as to his coldness and severity of feeling, with such an impassioned tumult of sensibility as he pours out in some of his sermons, with the pathetic turn he has given to several touching sentences in his books, with the loving friendliness which often struggles through a cloud of irony in his letters, and above all, with the vehement regard for him which he succeeded in implanting in the bosoms of some of his acquaintances and fellow-labourers. Says Dr. McGill:

"There was never the slightest interruption of good will and fraternal affection, from the first to the last day of our coöperation, as professors and friends. On the contrary, it was only increasing radiation, manifested on every possible occasion. Often he came to my study, with overflowing mind and heart, to cheer me in my labours, appreciate my plans, talk over his own, confer about the interests of the Seminary, and the character of the students. No one was ever more welcome in his visits. He seemed to know everybody and everything."

He often ran over to the study of Dr. Hodge or of Dr. Green in the same way, and unless perplexed with some private care or matter of public business, he was as chatty as any of them and often left a beam of sunshine behind him.

No man, says Dr. Hodge, was ever more free from vanity.

"He was of necessity conscious of his strength. But as an adult man knows that he is stronger than a child, but neither prides himself on that superiority nor seeks to display it, so it was with him. It was an admitted fact, which he never seemed to think of, and never dreamed of exhibiting."

These words are not less honourable to Dr. Hodge than

accurately true of Dr. Alexander. He loved the retreats of letters and philosophy, and the faces of his chosen friends, with but occasional glimpses of the giddy world, whose shows, mannerisms, hypocrisies, applause, and intercourse he very greatly despised.

But his heart beat warmly for his respected associates, one of whom * says of him:

"Loyal, loving, and magnanimous, delicate and courteous and just and truthful—words fail me to express my estimation of his value as a personal friend; and I felt the world to be a solitude, outside of my own family, when the grave closed on his precious remains. The severe dignity, which a superficial acquaintance with him so often recoiled from, was anything but indifference to the sensibilities and sympathies of others. Indeed, it required but a short time of intercourse to see that the origin of his peculiar shyness was the very opposite of proud and cold disdain for any class or condition in society."

No one had more abundant opportunities of knowing the solitary professor than Dr. Charles Hodge; for whom the subject of this memoir cherished a strong personal affection. He writes that as Dr. Archibald Alexander came to Princeton as professor in the Theological Seminary, in the spring of 1812, and as that was the year in which he himself entered college, it so happened that it was his lot to live in the same village with Dr. Addison Alexander forty-eight years. During the greater part of that time he was intimately associated with him.

"He was elected a professor in the Seminary by the General Assembly of 1836; so that from that time until his death, in 1860, I was his colleague. From this long-continued and intimate connection, it may be assumed that I knew him well, as a man, a teacher, and as a minister of the gospel. It may also be supposed that I have much to say about him. This, however, is not the fact. The retrospect of a calm academic life is very much like looking over a wide plain, or the wider ocean. The prospect may be very extended, but the prominent objects are few. He indeed made a deep impression on all who knew

* Dr. McGill.

him. We all felt his superiority. There was a continued sense of the power, greatness, and goodness of the man, which secured deference to all he said, and a willingness to recognize the ascendency which was so obviously his due. Such ascendency was never claimed, and never seemed to be consciously exercised. It was nevertheless constantly felt and cheerfully conceded."

CHAPTER XXVII.

It is a relief to turn now and then from the excessive labours of the student to those of the pastor. If there is a certain sameness in the employments of the younger brother, who above all things coveted change, there was variety enough in the small daily incidents of the life of the city minister, who hated transition and innovation, and who prayed for rest—peaceful quiet, unperturbed by distractions a routine unbroken by exciting novelties. I can only touch lightly and then pass on. I find Dr. James Alexander lecturing one Sabbath night early in February to his young men on Augustin, one of his prime favourites among saints and authors, and one among whose writings he was thoroughly at home. Those scholarlike addresses were often indescribably fascinating. No one had a better idea of Augustin's biography and opinions, and few could tell the sweet story of Monica more effectively. His brother Addison also liked Augustin, and sometimes quoted his sayings, as in the note to his exposition of Matt. xvi: 18, where he says of a certain view of the passage, "This is no new opinion, having been advocated by one of the earliest of the fathers, and the greatest of the popes." He then gives the famous words of Augustin and of Hildebrand. Dr. Alexander was very fond of such pithy sentences, and was commonly able to trace them to their several authors. He loved to repeat happy proverbs; and to dwell upon Rabbinical stories and picturesque ecclesiastical traditions. He did not, however, attach much importance to these. He was much addicted to the use of felicitous Latin phrases; but in the Princeton Magazine has ridiculed the piebald way in which foreign words and idioms are introduced into such books as Lady Blessington's novels. He was very scrupulous about the purity of his English, and many of his letters to Dr. Hall are ingeniously made up of Americanisms and current but respectable slang. He retained his early repugnance to commas and italics, and made as little use of them as possible. He had a wonderful way of digesting a long paragraph, when reviewing a book, and of putting it into a short sentence of his own. He seldom quotes the *ipsissima verba* of the writers he mentions in his commentaries. He gives their gist and spirit.

His work on the Acts was now nearly ripe for the printer; that is, he had it mapped out in his mind, and had begun to write down his comments in a blank book. He wanted now to tear the leaves out and send them to press at once.

In the letter given below he offers his new book to Mr. Scribner, on certain hard conditions which are specified.

"PRINCETON, April 4, 1855.

"DEAR SIR:

"I propose to print my work on the Acts in one octavo volume, of the size and general appearance of 'Da Costa's Four Witnesses,' printed by Ballantyne at Edinburgh but reissued here by Carter. I am ready to go to press immediately, provided I can interrupt the printing and resume it at my own convenience. This is an indispensable condition; as I cannot bind myself to stay at home or in New York all summer. Another condition is, that the first proofs must be read by a person competent to correct Latin, Greek, and Hebrew accurately, not by one who learns the alphabet for the occasion; a clean proof to be regularly sent to me, for general revision. My third and last condition is, that I must have a specimen, not only of the type, but of the ink and presswork, upon which I think much more depends than on the paper in determining the general appearance of the volume. Why may not a sheet or half sheet be worked off precisely as the whole will be when completed? I state my terms thus positively to afford you the opportunity of declining to accept them, if you do not like them. I do not consider you at all bound by anything that has passed between us, to go on with this work now, especially as some of the arrangements upon which I have insisted are opposed to your own taste and judgment. I only beg that you will answer yea or nay, as I have no time or inclination to discuss the subject.

"Yours sincerely,

"MR. SCRIBNER. J. A. ALEXANDER."

A letter like the following is worth getting. It contains an anecdote from Pallavicino.

"PRINCETON, March 19th, 1855.

"MY DEAR BROTHER:

"The books came safe to hand, but not having been opened yet, escaped my recollection. I should still be glad to have the opportunity of viewing such remittances before they are deposited in bank. I congratulate you on the change of weather. Pallavicino gives a Spanish anecdote which may interest you. On the 17th of April, 1536, Charles V. addressed the Pope and Cardinals in full consistory at Rome, '*in lingua castigliana per lo spazio d'un' ora*,' winding up with his famous declaration, that it would be better for the world if he and Francis I. could end their long strife by a single combat. Hereupon the French ambassador at Rome who, with all the court, was present, begged leave of his holiness to ask his majesty for a copy of his speech, '*non intendendo egli perpettamente l'idioma spagnuolo*,' yet desiring to make a true report to his master. The Emperor replied, with some warmth, that his speech was not addressed to the French king, but to the Pope and Cardinals, and that if he wished to send it to the former, he would do it through the French envoy at his own court, '*che intendeva ottimamente spagnuolo*.' The next day, both the French ambassadors demanded of the Emperor whether he had meant to challenge their master to a duel, and received for answer that he did not give such challenges in the presence of his holiness, &c. &c. &c. &c.

"Polybius is wonderfully modern and certainly the inventor of 'Philosophy of History.' He says that history without the ΔΙΑ ΤΙ, the ΠΩΣ, and the ΤΙΝΟΣ ΧΑΡΙΝ, may be an ΑΓΩΝΙΣΜΑ, but is no ΜΑΘΗΜΑ. He also refers to a certain class of writers, I suppose like Gulliver and Crusoe, as ΤΟΙΣΑΞΙ ΟΠΙΣΤΩΣ ΨΕΥΔΟΜΕΝΟΙΣ. The Notes and Queries in Norton's Literary Gazette are getting to be quite interesting. Four hundred dollars have been raised in Princeton for the outburnt students, besides a hundred-dollar bill from New York. Mezzofanti was a marvel. Did you ever read the scene in Ben Jonson's Poetaster, where an author vomits up his hard words? It is really Aristophanic, and the only thing in all Ben worthy of remembrance."

On Saturday, the 28th, the two brothers were to be seen riding together in the cars between Princeton and New York. What they talked about on this particular occasion, I do not know; but I will venture to say that they had a joyous time of it. They often differed, and sometimes had vehement discussions. One point on which they differed was that of style. What the core of the dispute was, I never certainly learned, but inferred from a word or two dropped by the elder brother, that it was partly as to the propriety of adhering steadfastly to Saxon forms, and of avoiding a rhythmical construction of sentences. Their own styles were very dissimilar. The elder writer was the more carefully terse and fastidiously elegant in his diction, the younger the more copious, varied, and natural. The one preferred the language of courtly precision, the other the language of the Bible and of common life. So far as they went to the classics for their models, it always seemed to me that the former found his pattern in the concise Roman writers and the latter in the energetic and musical Greeks. On many themes their manner is much the same, and some of their articles in the Repertory can be distinguished as to their authorship only by very sharp eyes.

Some time during the month of May Dr. Addison Alexander took a trip to Richmond, and lodged in the family of one of its esteemed pastors. Here he enjoyed himself in a social way as he had seldom done before during his manhood, without the households of his very near kindred.

The pleasing letter given below was penned in the house of Dr. Moore. It is to one of his own brothers and gives a very amiable view of the man who wrote it.

"RICHMOND, May 19, 1855.

"REV. AND DEAR BROTHER:

"Why did you not come to Virginia with me, as you promised? I have found it more agreeable than ever. I spent the last Lord's-day in Washington, and the next day at the house of John and Phœbe Wilson, where I met Gurley. I have been since Tuesday last a guest, or rather a member of the family, in this delightful house, which seems to me a perfect model of elegant simplicity and comfort, without the slightest ceremony or display. Dr. and Mrs. Moore are the perfection of unobtrusive kindness, and their children that of life and freedom with the best of manners. I preached on Wednesday evening to a large and brilliant-looking company, and am waiting to perform the same duty on the morrow, after which I hope to journey Blueridge-and-Augusta-wards. I do not want to go to Prince Edward, although very near by railroad, while the College is in session. I may come back here from Augusta, and run to Hampden Sidney, Petersburg, and even Raleigh, before sailing for New York. I have received visits from William Maxwell, William Love, and Moses Hoge,(with whom I dined yesterday.) We have heard nothing yet from the General Assembly. Moore is editing the Watchman and Observer during Gildersleeve's absence. I am reading over his popular commentary on the Minor Prophets, which Carter is to publish, and which, methinks, will be a very useful book. They are suffering from drought here, and abhor the sun. If you write, address me at Staunton, and after that at Waynesboro. I have no news to send, except that I have written to Princeton and New York.

"Yours truly,

"Rev. S. D. Alexander. J. A. Alexander."

For the reasons expressed in the foregoing letter, the writer conducted himself in the family of Dr. Moore very much as he would have done in his own; but with even more obvious cordiality and vivacity than in scenes to which he was more accustomed. His whole heart seemed to be drawn out towards his old host and pupil.

Dr. Moore's own account of these visits is, therefore, worthy of the closest scrutiny. The incident about "Dokyana," is very characteristic and pleasant. He writes:

"You ask me to give you a full account of his character in social life, on the ground that you know he visited in my family at least as unreservedly as he did anywhere else except among his own kindred, if not more so. I fear that I can give you much less satisfaction on this point than this statement might authorize you to expect; for the simple reason that there was nothing peculiar in his habits or conduct, in this respect. Indeed, being what I have already described him, there ought not to have been any special peculiarity, distinguishing him from any other intelligent Christian gentleman. Those who would have expected something different, would do so on the ground of supposed eccentricities of genius, and those stories about his peculiar feelings and conduct in regard to society which were so rife when I was in the Seminary. Indeed, I confess that I had some of this feeling myself, and invited him to visit me with some apprehension, knowing how generally he avoided private families in travelling, and how little he mingled in general society, and fearing that we might not be able to make things pleasant to him. But never was I more delightfully relieved of apprehension, and never has there been a guest in my house who was more completely one of the family, and whose presence blended more perfectly with the quiet flow of domestic life.

"Before his first visit there was a feeling of awe and restraint that seemed inevitable in regard to one supposed to be so peculiar and so apart from common minds; but he had not been in the house a day when all that wore off, never to return. And this was not because there was any seeming effort on his part to let himself down to the level of other minds, but because he seemed unconscious of any elevation above them. He was so simple, natural, and genial, that he forgot he was a great man, and nothing in his manner or conduct ever reminded us of it. We saw at once that he did not wish to be lionized, or have any parade over him of any kind; and we made none; and it is to this mainly that I refer the pleasure he seemed to have in visiting us. We made no more change in our habits for him than we should have done for the nearest, humblest, and most intimate relative; and he saw that he was not putting us out of our even course of life, but was with us as a beloved addition to the family circle, and this was what exactly suited him. He had no peculiar habits or tastes to be studied, that we could perceive, but fell in with the simple routine of our home-life just as if he had been accustomed to it always. Indeed, I have since regretted that he had not been disposed to think and to speak more of himself than he was, for as I look back I remember some little facts that attracted no attention at the time, but which I now see to have been the stealthy symptoms of the incipiency of that insidious disease which afterwards carried him to a premature grave. But they were so trivial that I did not think of them at the time, and he was so utterly indisposed to make himself the subject of thought or care, that had I noticed them, I should probably have hesitated to press them on his attention.

"Were I to designate his character as a guest in a single phrase, it would be that he was as simple, natural, and gentle as an unspoiled, unaffected child. He would amuse himself with the children by pronouncing Arabic and Chinese words, and getting them to repeat them after him; would invent plays for them, and tell them stories. He once taught them an alphabet of characters to be used for secret correspondence, very simple and easily learned by a child, which he recalled once to their recollection in a characteristic manner. The youngest child, who could just talk, was only able to express his name by the vocable 'Dokyana,' which he adopted afterwards as his designation in talking with the children. The first day he arrived on one of his visits, she came down to see him, and when asked on her return to the nursery what he said to her, replied that 'Dokyana thought she was a sweet little thing,' presuming that his estimate of her was the same that was told her by others every day. He was amused at her report of his first impressions, but told her he must wait to see whether this was the fact; and the trivial incident was forgotten by us all very soon. But after he went to Lexington, I received a large envelope directed to myself; and opening it found one directed to the oldest child, inside of which was another to the next one; and so on to the youngest, in which was a paper written in this square character to which I have referred, which, on examining the key, I found to be, 'Yes, Dokyana does think that F—— is a sweet little thing.' This little incident will show the pains he often took to amuse children, and his fertility of invention.

"On another occasion, one of the children was sick and was lying in the room adjoining his. We missed him for a good while down-stairs, when some one going up to see about the sick child found Dr. Alexander lying beside him on the bed, telling him stories. These little incidents will perhaps illustrate, better than more elaborate details, that beautiful simplicity and childlike character of his mind, which made him so delightful an inmate of our household. There was no putting on of interest or any mere show of any kind, but all was so natural and simple, that it was evidently the genuine outflow of an honest, loving heart.

"It was in my intercourse with him in the privacy of my study that I learned to value him as I now do, for he talked with complete unreserve of everything, even of his private matters, that enabled me to see the unveiled nature of the man. And I found in him a noble and generous manliness, and at the same time a keen and accurate knowledge of men, some of whom I had more opportunities of knowing than he had, and yet found that I did not know them any more accurately. It was in these frank and unreserved communications that I saw his genuine and unaffected humility, and I can truly say, that I have never met a man with a tithe of his intellect and culture more entirely free from all pretension, and more utterly insensible to the value of any difference between him and other minds.

After leaving Richmond, Dr. Alexander crossed the mountains, visiting among his relations of the valley. He dallied longest in Lexington and Staunton, and the immediate vicinity of these places. He was delighted with his visit to his uncle's, Major John Alexander, near Lexington. In the following interesting letter he gives his impressions of "Clifton" to his brother Henry.

"CLIFTON,* June 9th, 1855.

"DEAR HENRY:

"I would give more than a trifle if you and yours could be in this delicious spot, even for a single day. A noble farm stretching as far as you can see, with every variety of prospect; ploughed ground, corn-fields, meadows, woodland, hill, and dale; a river running by the front gate, with a lofty cliff beyond it; splendid horses, droves of cattle, turkeys, geese, ducks, chickens, dogs, and negro children: trees and groves in perfection, with a flower garden for those who have a taste in that way: a commodious country house, without the slightest decoration, but with every comfort: a table, at once plentiful and elegant; the best of wheat and corn-bread, perfectly fresh butter, oceans of milk and ice-water: and above all, a family extremely kind, without appearing to be in the least disturbed or interrupted by your presence—these are some of the attractions which belong to this delightful residence. Another is the thought that it belongs not only to your friends, but to your nearest kindred and to those who bear your own name. I am constantly surprised to hear visitors say Mrs. Miss, and Mr. Alexander. I could spend my whole vacation here with perfect satisfaction, but am constantly disturbed in my enjoyment by the recollection that I have to go to so many other places. One consolation is, that I shall probably be just as sorry to leave them. I ought to have mentioned that the house is full of books, with all the latest Magazines, &c. J. A. is one of the most sharp-witted, well-read fellows I have ever met with. My faculties are rather quickened than benumbed by idling here. I am to preach to-morrow for my old friend Ramsey at New Monmouth Church. Then I must go to Colonel Reid's, and Major Preston's, and Archy Alexander's, and I know not where else. Almost all our relations in Rockbridge are well off, and live in some degree of style. The view of Lexington from the hill behind this house is one of the most beautiful I ever saw. The House Mountain is superb. The scenery described in the first chapter of the "Life" is here seen in perfection.

* The residence of his uncle, Major John Alexander.

I should like to see Charley and Netty running about among these trees. From the front porch you descend by a dozen stone steps to a green bank, and from that, by grassy terraces, to the road and river."

I am glad to be able to give here the impressions of his cousin, J. McD. Alexander of the Natural Bridge, then an inmate of the family at Clifton.

He writes that his recollection of him is exceedingly pleasant, but at the same time so shadowy that there is scarcely anything of a tangible character that he can recall. He remembers with perfect distinctness the impression that he had of him before the learned professor came, and that that impression was completely changed by the association he then had with him. He went to Staunton to meet and bring him to Lexington, and on the trip was surprised and delighted at "his extreme sociability, affability, or whatever you may choose to call it." He entertained him the whole way home by "the variety and versatility of his talk, and that too about things that are not to be found in books." The only thing he positively remembers was a description of the appearance and surroundings of one of the quadrangles of some one of the Colleges at Cambridge or Oxford.

"While he was in Lexington," he goes on to say, "I took him to Kerr's Creek, to see the house of Mr. John T. McKee, where Dr. Alexander commenced his life as a preacher; the very room was still extant when we were there, and he was deeply moved by the sight of it; I doubt if I ever saw him so completely *silent*, as he was when there, or after he came away. He also on that occasion paid a visit to the Rev. Dr. Ramsey, who was at that time preaching at Monmouth and lived within a half mile of Mr. McKee's. I was exceedingly struck with the reverence and devotion that Dr. Ramsey expressed and seemed to feel for him; and this, coming from him, made a profound impression upon me. I tell you all this just to show you what was the amount of opportunity I had to see and know him when in this county, and at the same time to indicate the sort of influence he had upon me."

There is nothing further from the truth, so far as Mr. Alexander's knowledge is concerned, than the idea that has been believed and propagated, that he was ungenial.

"His whole intercourse with our family, and with everybody else, especially with the children, shows that every such imputation was utterly foreign to his whole nature. I believe it is universally true that every child with whom he ever became familiar has the liveliest recollection of his stories and, of course, the pleasantest memory of him."

Among those who fell in with Dr. Alexander in Lexington at this time, was the Rev. Dr. R. L. Dabney, of Union Theological Seminary, Virginia, whose name needs no introduction from me, and whose commendation is never flattery. He writes:

"I never met the Rev. Addison Alexander until his last visit to Lexington, Virginia. There I spent parts of two days in the same house with him, and heard him preach twice. I found his sermons characterized by very thorough and evidently faithful preparation, scholarly finish of style, and fine, discriminating acumen in the criticism and exposition of scriptural propositions. I may say, once for all, that these have always struck me as the prominent traits of his critical writings, with (also) laborious, painstaking diligence, and profound reverence for the very words of Scripture.

"You are perfectly aware, of course, that gossipping people had given him a name for great and sometimes morbid reserve. I found him a truly unobtrusive and retiring man; but he met every civil advance towards social intercourse with modest courtesy; and I had much sober, but agreeable converse with him, in which I was impressed with his excellent good sense. While his manner was what I have described, he still left the impression on me of one who had a profound contempt for pretence, conceit, flunkeyism, and impertinence, and who, if these were obtruded, would be likely to mark his disapprobation either by his silence, or by some quiet sarcasm. But not a trace of this appeared towards any one during these agreeable interviews.

"I remember that during the evening sermon, a lively summer shower came up. This enabled me to test a peculiarity of his voice and utterance. This was the remarkable continuity of the vowel sounds of his words and syllables. He spoke rather rapidly, and I noticed that it was only at the ends of periods, or such like pauses, that the pattering of the rain on the pavement without could be heard between his words. Yet the articulation of consonants was remarkably clear and distinct, and I do not believe one syllable was lost to sensitive ears by any confusion of utterance."

The testimony of "his old friend Ramsey" is equally important, and will be attractive to the general reader. On his preceptor's first visit to the Valley of Virginia, Dr. Ramsey was preaching at New Monmouth Church on Kerr's Creek, of which he had just become the pastor. He had seen Dr. Alexander in Lexington, and invited him out to his little country church to preach for him. He had said he could not do so then, but should probably visit the Valley the next summer, and might then do so. The next summer, when he came to his relatives near Lexington, he sent Dr. Ramsey a note saying he would, if convenient, fulfil the promise of the year before, and preach for him the next sabbath. This was more than his friend expected, and he gladly welcomed him. He was himself living then, he says, in a small log-house of the rudest kind and quite old (the church were then building a parsonage), unplastered, of course, except the "chinking and daubing" between the logs. The study and bed-room was the up-stairs part, the roof coming down at the sides to within about two feet of the floor, with two little four-pane windows. All this attracted the notice of his visitor. "When he had clambered up the old, rickety stairs and seated himself, and looked out of the window upon the grand old mountains towering above (it was just at the foot of the House Mountain),* he expressed himself as being deeply interested and much delighted."

After dinner, his kind host took him over to the house of good old father McKee, only a few hundred yards off, and into "the very room where his own father had first opened his lips to proclaim the gospel of Christ." There was much there to cause silent meditation. "The room was unaltered, except that the fire-place had been changed to the other side

* One of the most curious and beautiful mountains in all Virginia. For an exact description of it, and for Dr. Archibald Alexander's childish fancies about it, see "Life of Dr. A. Alexander," p. 26.

of it. After sitting down in silence a few minutes, he said, 'This is deeply interesting,' and then relapsed into silence, while I conversed with some of the family and left him to pursue his own more valuable musings."

After that visit to the Valley, the writer never saw him again.

He preached for him the sermon on Phil. iv. 13: "I can do all things through Christ which strengtheneth me," which is found in the volumes, since published, of his printed discourses. Though the people were not accustomed to hearing sermons read, and many were prejudiced against this practice, and notwithstanding he read from a large and crumpled manuscript, "yet he *so* read, with such perfect naturalness, that every word was understood and received, and that all present were both delighted and profited: the attention of everybody seemed to be riveted to the very end."

The author of these accounts then regretted, and has often regretted since, that his visitor did not write and publish more for the people. "He had, it seemed to me, very great ability to state the most difficult questions, and treat the most difficult subjects so that the very statement was an argument." His power of expression, his mastery of the English language, and the compass of his mind, enabled him to do this as almost no other man could. None, certainly, that he ever knew, could even approach him in this respect.

Dr. Ramsey ventured to suggest to him, with some earnestness, the preparation of a Church History for our people, a work, he thought, more needed than almost anything else, and that no man was so well qualified to write; but the professor seemed as usual to think that it could be better done by others, and, at any rate, he was then engaged in the preparation of his commentaries on the Gospels, which would take all his time. Dr. Ramsey also proposed his preparing a work for the churches, on the "Jewish Tabernacle, and the Ceremonial Law, as the divine, visible picture of the Gospel, and specially adapted to make its abstrusest doctrines plain to the popular mind."

He had enjoyed while at the Seminary the advantage of using some manuscript notes of his on Leviticus,* written merely as memoranda in his study of the book, from which Dr. R. had gained more light than from all other commentaries combined, in regard to the laws of sacrifice. "The analyses of the first few chapters, though perhaps, if printed, they could be put on a couple of pages, was to me worth more than anything I had seen, or have ever seen since."

He agreed that such a work was needed, but said that Professor Green would probably prepare one on the subject, and that Professor Green had given it a good deal of study.

While Dr. Alexander never "talked shop," he was, of course, at home in those topics which specially and professionally interested his former pupil; but much of the conversation was on minor matters which have been forgotten by the survivor.

Another witness of this period is the Rev. Joseph R. Wilson, D.D., formerly pastor of the Presbyterian church in Staunton, now of Augusta, Ga. When Dr. Alexander first visited Staunton, Dr. Wilson was at a loss how to treat him, and hesitated to call upon him, not knowing, indeed, how to approach one of whom he "had been kept in such wholesome fear at Princeton." Awed by his greatness and impressed by his unapproachableness, he thought an interview with him must be an almost impracticable affair, from the lack of something to say on his own part. He nevertheless did call, and resolved to treat him as he would any other gentleman, by engaging him in conversation upon the ordinary topics of the day. The result was remarkable. "He received me," he says, "with great courtesy, and seeing I was disposed not to make 'a great man' of him (a treatment which he abhorred with the honest sensitiveness of true greatness), we got on swimmingly together," and he never heard any common man more

* There are several volumes of these notes, or else copies of the same, still extant, and the opinion in which they are held by Dr. Ramsey is entertained by others. One of these is in my possession.

eloquent upon the weather, the crops, the little interests of the community, and the every-day affairs of life, than he was.

Mrs. McClung* has told him, that at her house, where he spent most of his time in the company of that venerable lady and other relatives, he would stand by the hour at some window that overlooked the street, and engage his mind in watching everybody that passed, noticing every turn of things, and making comments upon every individual, whenever any peculiarity of gait or dress or manner enabled him to utter a comment that could picture it to those within. He then appeared as if his whole being was absorbed in mere minute observation, and as if all scholarly thoughts were as foreign to his mind as they are to the merest boy.

These visits to Staunton and Lexington left an indelible impression upon the mind of the guest as well as of his entertainers. The change of scene, and the delightful unaffected hospitality seemed for the time to make a boy of him. When in Staunton, among his kinsfolk, who knew all about him and yet were not afraid of him, and treated him like anybody else, except that they were freer with him than with many people, and loved him more sincerely and evidently, and admired him with a peculiar and generous feeling of delight and wonder, he shook off all the trammels of academic habit and personal idiosyncrasy, forgot all his morbid antipathies and aversions, so far as he may be said to have really had any, and began to enjoy life with a new and almost painful zest. He was from this time, in some particulars, a wiser, and on certain accounts, a happier man. He never afterwards shut himself up with so absolute a rigour as he had done in former days. He mingled more than he had done before in familiar social gatherings, and seemed to relish with unusual pleasure the society of persons who had but little title to his friendship. This change was remarked by every one on his return to Princeton.

In the Valley of Virginia, and in the city of Richmond,

* The youngest sister of Dr. Archibald Alexander.

however, as well as in Philadelphia, Trenton, and some other places, he continued to preserve the freshness of his youth, and to expatiate with the buoyancy of a boy of ten years old, through strange and almost untrodden fields of what was to him and others the most delightful, because the most refined yet unconstrained "foregathering." Even when most at his ease, however, he had no great fondness for general society. He vastly preferred a small circle or accidental group of chosen spirits. He was nowhere more thoroughly understood and appreciated than among his Scotch-Irish connections and cultivated friends of Rockbridge and Augusta. It was here, above most other places, as Dr. Wilson intimates, that Dr. Alexander was, by force of his genius, his common sense, his good feeling, and perfect candour, as well as of a certain special gift of fascination, one of the most *taking* men in the world; illustrating now and then most admirably the truth of Cowper's sagacious lines,

> "Discourse may want an animated *No*,
> To brush the surface and to make it flow."

Dr. Alexander was himself distinctly conscious of this necessity, and was often tired to death in the company of *assentative* people. The practice of always chiming in with, and echoing back the sentiment of others, is felicitously ridiculed in one of his unpublished minor works, in an article entitled "Polite Conversation," which is very characteristic of him.*

* The first speaker is a sort of caricature of himself: "*A.* A fine day, sir. *B.* A very agreeable morning, sir. *A.* The Spring is very forward. *B.* I am struck with the unusual advancement of the season. *A.* I am afraid the warm weather is not very healthy. *B.* I have been apprehensive myself of some unwholesome effects from the extraordinary mildness of the temperature. *A.* Are you fond of warm weather? *B.* I am very partial to a great degree of heat. *A.* I prefer cold. *B.* I have also a preference for winter. *A.* You like both best. *B.* Yes, I give the preference to each. *A.* I have observed that some men have no mind of their own. *B.* It has occurred to me that there are persons who are not possessed of any intellect peculiar to themselves. *A.* I do not like to be always agreed with. *B.* It is certainly very disagreeable

I resume the thread of Dr. Wilson's pleasing reminiscences:

"Were I to attempt a delineation of the man, as the features of his wonderful character are impressed upon my memory, I should certainly fail. I can truthfully declare, however, that of all the men of mark I have ever met, he had, in my opinion, no superior. What struck me most of all was the extreme self-forgetfulness which he always exhibited, notwithstanding he must have been aware of the high, the commanding position he occupied in the eyes of the whole Church, both as an unequalled preacher and a profound and varied scholar. Of this position he seemed to possess no consciousness whatsoever. He never sought to *impress* you with his greatness, because he did not appear to be aware of its existence. He felt no superiority over others, and therefore assumed none; but under the circumstances this non-assumption it was that made his superiority the more manifest. Another feature of his character struck and deeply interested me. I allude to his simple, unadorned, straight-forward piety. He appeared conscious of being one of God's humblest children; and accordingly it was more refreshing than I can tell, to hear him converse on experimental religion, and more edifying than I can describe, to follow him in his prayers at the throne of grace: whilst his preaching was all that the most unlettered believer as well as that the most gifted Christian could desire, in its explanations and illustrations of truth; especially when he extemporized his sermons, which you know he often did."

The accounts of Dr. Wilson and Dr. Ramsey are fully substantiated by that of J. A. Waddell, Esq., which I now give. Mr. Waddell's was one of those quiet Christian homes where Dr. Alexander loved to unbend, and to leave all traces of the learned teacher and commentator far behind him. Mr. Waddell writes:

"It seemed to me that he knew everything, and could do anything the human mind was capable of, and that nothing cost him an effort. His sermons always impressed me as among the grandest compositions in the language, and since they have been printed, I have often won-

to experience perpetual coincidence of sentiment. *A.* Some people do not practise what they preach. *B.* The professional services of some are not in harmony with their discourses. *A.* What do you mean by that, sir? *B.* I was thinking what I could intend by such an observation," &c., &c.

dered they did not attract more attention. As he pronounced some of them from the pulpit in this place, his audience hung upon his lips and appeared to drink in every word. The announcement that he was to preach, never failed to attract a large congregation, at whatever hour."

Mr. Waddell believes the universal sentiment in Staunton to be that his sermons, for every excellence of thought and style, were unrivalled. He does not remember to have heard him more than once preach without a manuscript before him. On that occasion, Dr. Alexander attended a night-meeting with no expectation of preaching, and there were comparatively few persons present. He spoke, however, with as much fluency as if he were reading; and in hardly any respect was his discourse inferior to his more formal efforts.

"I heard at one time—and indeed he told me so himself—that he contemplated writing a history of the Church, or of the Christian religion; and I anticipated the appearance of the work with much impatience. When subsequently his commentaries came out from time to time, I felt disappointed at finding that he was spending his time and labour upon what I imagined were works of minor importance compared with the other. In my ignorance, I thought that nothing valuable remained to be accomplished in the way of Scripture interpretation; and upon reading a little now and then in the commentaries I did not find them interesting. It was not till I began to study them, that I discovered their incomparable excellence; and it was not so much the learning and research displayed by him, as the common-sense interpretations that excited my surprise. In reading his expositions, the thought is apt to occur frequently: 'I wonder *I* did not think of that.'"

The writer's recollections of the man and the companion are of the most affectionate and delightful nature.

"I may speak of him as a man, but must restrain myself from expressing all that I felt towards him. Although I had seen him on two occasions at Princeton, before he came to Virginia, I thought of him as a person of great intellect and learning, but unsocial in his habits and feelings. At Princeton, however, he was absorbed in the duties of his office: here he was free and acted as his nature prompted. You know he made three visits to Staunton, and always staid at my house. I therefore saw him morning, noon, and night; and the more I saw him the more I not only wondered at his greatness, but admired and loved him. Sometimes when with him I was almost carried away with delight, and positively felt like throwing my arms around him and embracing him. He never sought to make an impression of his superior wisdom, and was far removed as possible from dogmatism, egotism, and everything that is disagreeable in social intercourse. His manner was always polite, but as unaffected and simple as a child's. It was evident that his heart overflowed with sympathy and genuine kind feeling.

"At that time, as you know, there were several little girls in my family; and they associated with him on the most familiar terms, leaning upon him and climbing on his shoulders. It is impossible for me to describe his inimitable mode of entertaining children. I particularly remember one morning, when he had the girls I have mentioned around him amusing them and himself in his peculiar manner. He first undertook to teach one of them to write in an 'unknown language;' and after she succeeded in getting a correct sentence, he called for a piece of paper to write a certificate of her proficiency. Then he related a story of his own invention, personating the various characters in his manner and the tones of his voice, and the children shouted so loud as to be heard over the neighbourhood. Other children gathered in the street opposite the house, full of astonishment at the unusual uproar. He seemed to enjoy the sport as much as the little girls, and was not in the least disturbed by one of them, who was perhaps crowded out by the others, so far forgetting herself as to go behind him and climb upon his back, so as to lean over his shoulder!"

The man who is here portrayed could hardly be your cynic, misanthrope, cobwebbed antiquary, or harsh censor of his fellow-mortals. He was certainly no mere repository of knowledge or armoury of glittering but cold intellectual power. He was evidently, at the time referred to, a gentle, playful, conversable, and even tender being; with a warm heart beating in his bosom; a man wholly unspoiled by books and scholastic habits; a person of the rarest faculty of making himself vastly agreeable, although somewhat shy in company; a man who loved guileless, unaffected children, and who was loved by them in return: yet one who had his moments of abstracted silence and mysterious reserve. He could chill the very heart of those who purposely annoyed him. He would not be intruded upon. He felt the raw air. He knew the changes of the temperature by changes in his feelings. He could kindle a friendship that sometimes mounted to the heights of enthusiasm. He could adapt himself to new scenes and associations. He was a keen observer of manners and people, and of sights and customs. In the pulpit he was Boanerges—a son of thunder.

Among the gentlemen of Staunton who had the pleasure of hearing him was the Hon. John B. Baldwin, whose ability to judge in the premises no one will call in question. He says* that it would be a very low statement of the matter to testify that Dr. Alexander's sermons made a favourable impression on him: they were the most remarkable and attractive he ever listened to. The thoughts were fresh and original, and the fine scholarship, for which he had been prepared, was undoubtedly present but was exquisitely concealed. He never once stopped to ask himself what he thought of the manner, which was altogether appropriate and interesting. In his personal appearance the preacher reminded him strongly of Mrs. McClung, his aunt, of whom Col. Baldwin speaks in terms of high respect and regard. That is to say, Dr. Alexander was getting to look more and more like his father. There was a strange admixture in him, as has been noticed elsewhere, of the Alexander and the Waddel.

* I am sorry that the accidental loss of Col. Baldwin's manuscript compels me to give the substance and not the words of what he wrote.

CHAPTER XXVIII.

But it is time for us to go back with the traveller to Princeton, and hear the news of Commencement. His former connection with Nassau Hall had not been forgotten by Dr. James Alexander. The young men of the College Societies were disappointed this year as regarded their Commencement Orator, who unexpectedly, and at a very late hour, declined. In the emergency they applied to Dr. Alexander of New York; who consented to fill the gap, and at the time appointed made the address. It was, of course, very hastily prepared, but was a graceful and felicitous composition, and was widely commended.

His brother Addison was now settled at his desk again, or rather his table. The red standing desk he once affected, and several black swinging ones which succeeded it, had been long ago abandoned.

Here are some entries from his journal:

"Aug. 9. Began the Greek Testament again in Tischendorf's edition (Leip., 1839.) Continued 2 Sam. in Hebrew, and in the Chaldee paraphrase (suspended last spring). Resumed the Syriac version of Luke (ch. xx.). Read the London *Times*. Resumed the Abulfeda in Arabic and Ahn's Dutch Grammar. Continued Acts. Visited by Charles and Henry Baird. Henry enters to-day upon his office as a teacher of ancient and modern Greek in the College; he will also complete his theological studies in the Seminary. Besides spending most of their early years in France and Switzerland, Charles has resided as a chaplain at Rome, and Henry as a student at Athens."

On the 5th of September he wrote two sheets in addition to an old Introductory lecture. The amount and diversity of his reading was as great as ever. This day he went through 2 Samuel xxi. in Hebrew and Chaldee, Esther in Latin, and Matthew xxiv. in Greek. He still amused himself with Spanish history; and this day began the 9th book of Mariana. Even Dutch grammar had its attractions for him, since his second voyage to Europe, and this day he found diversion in an extract from Stijl (on Charles V.) in Ahn's Dutch Grammar. He also continued Bernhardy's Greek Syntax, Abulfeda in Arabic, and Edwards's History of Redemption. He also finished the Epistles of Horace, and continued Tischendorf's Prolegomena, Eusebius, and the Letters of Sydney Smith. The two volumes of Lady Holland are full of his pencil marks. The wise and witty Englishman kept him almost choked with laughter.

"Lord's day, October 14. Heard Dr. Hodge in the Seminary Chapel (Matthew xxviii. 19). Conference (2 Cor. ii. 15). Read the morning service of the Church of England, with the Psalms, lessons, Gospel and Epistle, in French. Continued Luke in Greek; Doddridge's Exposition; Boston's Four-fold State; Fisher's Catechism; Hahn on Job; consulted Calvin, Grotius, Pool, Wetstein, Wolf, Whitby, Henry, Doddridge, Scott, Bloomfield, Trollope, Rosenmüller, Bengel, Olshausen, Meyer, de Wette, von Gerlach, Alford on 2 Corinthians ii.: 15—and the same with the addition of Kuinoel, Campbell, Fritzsche, Ripley, Ebrard and Tholuck on Matthew vi. 9 and Luke xi. 1."

On the 31st of the same month, he lectured to the First Class on the Controversies of the Middle Ages, and continued 1 Kings in Hebrew and Chaldee; John in Syriac and Greek; Sarpi in Italian; Allen in Danish; Ahn's Dutch Grammar; Hahn and Schlottmann on Job; Doddridge's Exposition; Boston's Four-fold State; Schmitz's Ancient History; Horace's Odes; and Polybius in Greek. On this day he made the following record: "Talked to Professor Green about opening classes in the Oriental languages. I think of teaching Syriac. I am now lecturing twice a week on Mediæval Church history, twice a week on Apostolical history, and once a week on Old Testament history."

He had no lectures on the first of November, but read in private Doddridge's Exposition; John xi. in Greek (Tischendorf's edition); Boston's Four-fold State; Horace's Odes; 1 Kings xviii. in the Targum of Jonathan; in Arabic, Abulfeda's account of Alexander the Great; in Spanish, Mariana's Historia de España, let. xi. cap. 2; in Dutch, part of a poem by Spandau, appended to Ahn's Grammar; in French, Froissart, liv. I, caps. 109 and 110; in Latin, Melancthon's Loci Communes, *De Lege;* in English, Schmitz's Manual of Ancient History (Carthage and Sicily); Journal of Missions for November. He spent an hour with his private class, after which he read Neander, Schaff, Thiersch, Lange, and Baumgarten on Acts viii.: read Job xiv. in Hebrew, Greek, Latin, German, and English, with the notes of Hahn and Schlottmann. He also read Hengstenberg's Kirchenzeitung for December, 1851. The same day he is refreshed by letters from two of his warmest friends, one of whom had been his pupil.

"Received and answered a letter from my old friend, Dr. William Harris, inviting me to preach for him in Penn Square Church next Sunday night. Received a letter from my friend, Dr. T. V. Moore, of Richmond, inviting me to contribute to a paper about to be established under the auspices of the Synod of Virginia as a substitute for Gildersleeve's."

Dr. Alexander was gratified by the evidences which multiplied upon him that his labour as a commentator on the Prophetical Scriptures had not been in vain. I subjoin a letter from the Hon. and Rev. Samuel Waldegrave, then rector of Basford St. Martin, Wilts, which pleased him very much. It was followed up, a few years later, by one which accompanied a presentation copy of the noble author's striking Bampton Lectures on the Millennium, in which he acknowledges he was much aided by the perusal of Alexander on Isaiah. Dr. James Alexander attempted to see Dr. Waldegrave in 1857, but was not so fortunate. He was, however, honoured with the card of the Earl of Waldegrave, his father

"BASFORD ST. MARTIN, near SALISBURY,
"July 30, 1855.

"MY DEAR SIR:

"If you will do me the favour of referring to your own name in the Index of Authors cited in the accompanying volume, you will soon learn how much and how reasonably I desire your acceptance of my work.

"The opinions you have so ably stated and illustrated in your invaluable commentary on Isaiah were not altogether foreign to my own mind. But I confess that I derived much confidence and instruction from your labours when, after my Lectures had been preached, and before they were printed, I had the advantage of studying your pages. I have not, I trust, made more use of those pages than you will deem to be quite warrantable. Meanwhile, will you join with me in praying that so far as my book is in harmony with the mind of the Spirit, it may be of some use to the one Church of God?

"Should you favour me with a reply, I need scarcely say how much I should value your faithful criticisms.

"Yours, dear sir,
"With very sincere respect,
"SAMUEL WALDEGRAVE."

From the following letter to Mr. Scribner, it would seem that Dr. Alexander was thinking of reprinting his essays in the Repertory:

"PRINCETON, Nov. 8th, 1855.

"DEAR SIR:

"I am lecturing on Acts on a new plan, which will probably modify the character of the book, if ever published. I cannot, therefore, go to press immediately or very soon. But as I have disappointed you so often in this matter, and as the Essays, in their printed form, have proved a failure, I am inclined to accede to your last proposal, if we can agree upon the terms. You remember, no doubt, that the volume, as originally planned, was to have been published on the same conditions with the Psalms, and it was only when I stopped short and withheld my name, that I relinquished any interest in it. As the proposition to collect my articles has been made in another quarter, I should be under the necessity of copyrighting the new volume, and either selling you the copyright or making an arrangement similar to our existing one. With this understanding I am willing to proceed at once, provided the new part can be made to match the old exactly as to type and paper. The last page would have to be reprinted, as well as the title and contents. I should probably add one or two unpublished articles. If you determine to go on, you will have to procure copies of the Repertory from the publisher in Philadelphia. Let me know your decision, and on what terms you are willing to undertake the publication. Yours,

"J. A. ALEXANDER.

'MR. SCRIBNER."

The next letter to his publisher implies that his mind was in a state of vacillation between a volume of essays and a commentary. He had grown weary of his work on Acts, and had stopped the furnaces.

"PRINCETON, Jan. 8th, 1856.

"DEAR SIR:

"You have given me so much time to think about the Essays, that (as usual) I have changed my mind, and should be glad to get rid of the engagement, even on the condition of going at the Acts again. The only way to keep me to my purpose in these matters, is to begin printing. I am always glad, however, to get off, as I can never satisfy myself as to the form in which the thing is to be done. If you have gone so far in this case as to make a change of plan injurious to your interests, I will of course go on. If not, I leave it to your choice, which work shall be proceeded with.

"Yours,

"MR. SCRIBNER. J. A. ALEXANDER."

The fertility of his invention was enormous. Here is one of his numberless plans as laid before Mr. Scribner:

"PRINCETON, Jan. 14th, 1856.

"DEAR SIR:

"One reason that I feel disposed to take up Acts * again is, that I have thought of a new plan which will, I think, facilitate its execution and perhaps increase its value. It was originally suggested to me by

* Some time about 1852, he had formed the purpose of writing a critical commentary upon the book of Acts, on the plan of his work on Isaiah; but did not actually enter upon his work until after his return from Europe in 1853, and the work was put to press in the winter of 1855, and he had actually stereotyped about 100 pages, when the whole plan was changed."

a proposition of Mr. Wiley to complete the small edition of Isaiah by a third volume, to contain what was omitted in the other two. This was of course out of the question, but it afterwards occurred to me, that the end might be accomplished by preparing a new volume, to contain the critical matter and the history of the interpretation. Thus the first two volumes would form a complete commentary for general use, while the third would add what is interesting chiefly to the professional and learned reader. This course I have agreed to take in reference to the Isaiah, and if I find the first experiment successful, am disposed to write the other book upon the same plan ab initio. The advantage to myself would be, that I could write more rapidly and with more spirit, if not obliged to pause at every step and criticise the views of others. The advantage to the public would be that no abridgment would be necessary, the work being both of a popular and learned character. The plan would be to put it in three volumes like the Psalms, the first two completing the analysis and exposition of the whole book, and the third containing the additional notes upon the Greek text as above described. By printing fewer of the third volume, you could furnish the first two as a complete work to such purchasers as wished it, and all three to any who preferred it. Another advantage of this plan is, that the first two volumes could appear as soon as finished, and the third be prepared at my leisure. I do not know how this will strike you as a business operation. If you think well of it, I will begin as soon as I have tried my hand on the Isaiah. I propose to print the second volume first, as I have grown sick of recounting the first part so often, and am now going over the last part with my class. If I get this part done, I can soon complete the first, as it is in fact already written, and would only require some change of form. The two volumes would then appear together. Let me have your candid judgment on this point.

"Yours in haste,

"J. A. Alexander."

The letter subjoined is in the usual vein of business-like badinage.

"Princeton, March 17th, 1856.

"My Dear Sir:

"On looking at my calendar, I find that I have cruelly deceived you; and I hasten to nip your hopes in the bud, lest their withering when full-blown should be more than you can bear. When I spoke of April as a holiday month, I forgot to tell you that the first Sabbath thereof is my regular day here; and that as to the second, I had been invited by the Rev. Dr. Thomson, of New York, to wind up his yearly or half-yearly sacramental service with an evening sermon, and although I declined making any positive engagement for a day so distant, I am not quite sure that he has let me off. The same stern, uncompromising principle forbids my promising to be in Trenton on the only remaining Sunday of that month (27th). It is true that the 30th of March is unappropriated, but as Dr. H. is to be with you on the 23d, and I do not approve of young ministers having help on two successive Sabbaths, I am forced to deny you that indulgence. The upshot of the whole thing is, that the private visitation must be indefinitely postponed. Allow me, my dear sir, to express my satisfaction that our long correspondence on this interesting subject will be preserved in your biography, and to suggest that in filing this communication, it would be well to add an annotation to the names of Dr. H. and A., explaining who they were. Yours truly,

"J. A. ALEXANDER.

"REV. DR. HALL."

On Lord's day, April the 13th, the fifty-second anniversary of his brother's baptism, Dr. Addison Alexander preached for him in his church on Nineteenth street. It was his famous sermon from the text "Remember Lot's wife." "The impression," writes the city pastor, "was very great." There was much seriousness prevailing in the congregation. Within a few days the elder brother had heard of several cases of awakening, some of which were those of aged persons.

The exordium to this sermon has always seemed to me one of the most startling and impressive in print; and as delivered by the author in the days of his fiery vehemence, the whole sermon was one which was stamped upon the soul of every hearer as if it were red hot iron. It was, I think, the most popularly effective of his discourses, though not at all more imaginative and masterly than many others. There was something about it that was unique, solemn, and awful.

The history of the exegetical books of Dr. Alexander must always possess an interest to the student of his writings, and to those who seek information as to his habits and motives.

I return, here, without apology to the journal, which after

after all is our main reliance as to all questions respecting the daily habits and scholarlike erudition of the subject of this memoir, as it may be to some also a source of interest.

"February 1, 1856. No lectures. Read Lange on the Pauline Epistles. Resumed the preparation of my book on the Acts, and, also, of a new edition of my Isaiah.

"April 5. Examined the Third class on the interval between the Old and New Testament, closing the course of Old Testament History begun September 17. Received a letter from the Hon. and Rev. Samuel Waldegrave in answer to mine of February 25; and from Dr. Buchanan of Edinburgh a copy of his work on 'Faith in God, and Atheism.' Finished Proverbs in Hebrew and Latin, begun January 19.

"May 12. Finished Keil on Joshua, which I have been reading since the 14th of January; also the Ecclesiastical History.

"May 13. Finished the 10th book of Mariana's Historia de España which I began December 21; also, the Targum of Jonathan on Jeremiah, which I began December 12. Finished also, the rewriting of my notes on the 1st chap. of Acts.

"May 14. Finished the Greek Testament again, with Tischendorf's variations, which I have been reading since the 9th of August. Compared notes with Dr. Hodge about our Commentary. Corrected my notes on Acts i. for the press."

Sad news came in March from Virginia. The venerable Dr. Benjamin H. Rice, who had some years previously removed to Prince Edward county in his native State, was suddenly attacked with paralysis while in the pulpit of the College Church at Hampden Sidney, on the 7th of January, and died on the 24th of February. He was the brother-in-law of Dr. Archibald Alexander, and in his best days, and in his happy moments, one of the most effective of extemporaneous preachers. Dr. Rice was a more popular speaker in Virginia than even his more celebrated brother, John H. Rice, D.D., the bosom friend of Dr. Speece and Dr. Archibald Alexander. He was greatly beloved, and exceedingly useful as a pastor; and his piety was made up of the qualities of manly vigour and a delightful, almost womanly, delicacy and tenderness.

The next letter to his publisher in New York contains an interesting statement about the commentator's mode of working:

"PRINCETON, February 16, 1856.

"DEAR SIR:

"I sent you by this morning's mail a new analysis of ch. i., on the plan which I intend to pursue hereafter, together with a continuation of the commentary to the end of the 8th verse. I am enabled to contract these introductory remarks, without omitting any valuable matter, by reserving a minute historical analysis of the whole book for the general introduction. This I expect to prepare with a direct view to its use here as a text book in my own department; and had thought of proposing to strike off some copies of the introduction by itself, for the use of students. I am now satisfied, however, that the commentary cannot be completed by the time that we had fixed, and it has therefore occurred to me to make a suggestion, which you may possibly think it for your interest, as well as mine, to act upon. Although I should prefer, on some accounts, to write the introduction last, yet as I have the materials prepared, and have repeatedly gone over the whole subject, there would be no difficulty in preparing that part first; and this I think I could engage to do before the meeting of the Assembly. It might then be printed as an 'Introduction to the Acts of the Apostles,' a form which I have often thought of giving to the whole work, and might be followed, either by the commentary, or at first by similar introductions to the Old Testament and Gospel history; for all of which I have the materials collected, and for all which there would be a steady demand here as class-books, and not improbably in some other Seminaries also. These publications would prepare the way for commentaries on the single books to which they might be then prefixed as introductions. I have no reason to prefer this plan, except that it would furnish me with text-books sooner, and enable you to publish in the Spring, which is forbidden in the other case, by the amount of manual as well as mental labour requisite to carry out my plan. I may add, that introductions to the books of scripture are in great demand. I have often been requested to prepare one on the Psalms, as I had partly promised in the preface. I do not press this in the least; and should not have proposed it, if I had not thought it due to you to give you the refusal of a plan which you may possibly prefer. If not, I am prepared to go ahead upon the old one just as fast as possible, but wholly unpledged as to time, and with very little hope of being able to complete the work in three, or even in six months.

"I am, &c.,

"J. A. ALEXANDER.

"MR. SCRIBNER.

The next is to his brother James; and is written with great rapidity, without the slightest partition between the words. It is a literary curiosity:

"PRINCETON, February 22, 1856.

"MY DEAR BROTHER:

"The more I think of your idea about Moses and Elijah, Acts iii. 22, the more I like it. I have sought in vain for any trace of it in books, and as it thus belongs to you exclusively, I crave permission to immortalize you as its author in a forthcoming work of great ability. It would perhaps have been more elegant to do it without asking you, but I would rather sacrifice the éclat and surprise of such a coup de force to the certainty that it would not be disagreeable. I need not say that in addition to the justice of this recognition, it will give me no small satisfaction to connect your name with mine on so legitimate and proper an occasion. As the copy is now ready down to that verse, I am under the necessity of asking for as speedy a reply to this flattering proposal as your avocations and engagements allow. Your hints as to the plan arrived exactly in the nick of time, confirming the conclusions which I had just reached myself after many vacillations. I received last night a note from Gaussen, of Geneva, enclosing a list of about forty books on French Church History, prepared by Merle D'Aubigné, or his order, including works in German, French, and English, with minute specifications as to date and plan of publication. The manuscript is partly in coarse French, and partly in a fine and minute, but most legible German hand. If you can get as many more from Pressensé our library will be complete. I am strangely fascinated by old Doddridge's Exposition; although I want to kick him at times for making the Apostles, and one infinitely greater, talk the dialect of English nonconformity at the period of its deepest, I mean shallowest, namby-pambyism. Do look at the paraphrase of Peter's answer in John xiii. 9, and think of the Apostle talking about intellectual and executive powers in 'such a circumstance,' as Doddridge always says himself!"

The following is one of a dozen letters on the subject of the title-page and press-work of his Acts:

"PRINCETON, March 14th, 1856.

"DEAR SIR:

"I wrote upon the margin of the proof when I received it, but will add a few lines here. My own taste is satisfied with the last arrangement of the dashes. The inconvenience that you spoke of can be obviated by a little care. As to the heading, I am not so much pleased with the new one as displeased with the old, which still has a mean appearance. The admirers of English books think the American printers are too much afraid of large type in their titles. Acts is so short a word that it requires to be printed large. I should like the antique style on page nine very well, but perhaps it would not match the body of the page sufficiently. The ordinary small type (Acts) of sufficient size might do as well. I wish you to decide this without sending back to me again. If you think the Roman figures (I or i) would look better at the top (I mean for chapters) you can introduce them. I have the copy for the first chapter now written out, and am going to correct it. I will then send it on, and no more till the second is complete. I propose to finish it by chapters. When you have decided about the heading you can let me have more proof, but I am in no hurry.

Yours,

"MR. SCRIBNER. J. A. ALEXANDER."

Dr. Hodge offers the following explanation of his frequent changes:

"He could not bear to teach the same thing over and over, or in the same way. He was constantly changing his methods, and yet such was his skill and power that each new method seemed better than that which had gone before. He occupied three chairs successively in this institution. He was first professor of Hebrew and Old Testament Literature; then of Ecclesiastical History; then of the Language and Literature of the New Testament. His impatience of sameness was a great inconvenience to him. He would often begin to write on some subject and get tired of it and throw it aside. Or having written for a while on one plan, he would change it for another. He wrote the first part of his commentary on the Acts of the Apostles several times over; first on one plan and then on another. He said the only way he could do anything, was to begin to print, and thus feel himself forced to keep ahead of the press. In this way he got through his Isaiah. The whole of the second volume of his commentary on that prophet was written during one summer vacation. He occupied the house of his brother James in New York, the family being absent. His habit was to rise early, get a slight breakfast, and then sit steadily at his work until 5 p.m. At that hour he dined, and then would get in an omnibus and ride to the end of the route and back; and go to another line and keep riding about the city until 10 p.m.; and find himself after a good night's rest refreshed for the labour of another day."

The subjoined letter to Mr. Scribner, shows where he got the germ of his smaller commentaries, and what he thought of the new proposal.

"PRINCETON, April 16th, 1856.

"DEAR SIR:

"Dr. Hodge has just made a proposition, which I think of the highest importance, not only to myself, but to the public, and in which you may be interested also, for which reason I communicate it *confidentially and on my own responsibility*. He invites me to unite with him in writing a series of notes upon the whole New Testament, not for professional and educated readers merely, but for a much larger and continually growing class—the same for which Barnes, Bush & Co. have written. The idea is, that we divide the labour but share the responsibility, each being answerable for the whole, while each prepares his own part, that is, he the doctrinal and epistolary, and I the historical and prophetical. I can imagine no way in which we could both exert more influence than this, nor any that would probably be more advantageous in a commercial point of view. Now the Doctor's plan is to begin at once and carry on the work in parallel lines, publishing probably two volumes at a time, *i.e.*, one from each of us. But my book already in the press seems to be an insurmountable objection to my undertaking it; first, because it would forestall a part of the proposed work in a different form; and secondly, because it will require too much time for its completion. On these two grounds, I should consider myself bound to decline the invitation at once, if I did not think it right to allow you the opportunity of choosing between these two plans, so far as I can give it. If I decline, Dr. Hodge will either give up the whole thing, or do the whole himself (which is exceedingly improbable), or make the proposition to some other person. I confess, that if we had not made the beginning (or rather a dozen) I would much rather undertake a task of that kind, especially as I find that at the rate I am now going the book is likely to be boundless and endless. I propose, however, to reduce its scale and quicken its progress when I settle down to it in my vacation.

This is by far the most attractive proposition that has yet come to my knowledge, both for authors, publishers, and the public, especially as Dr. Hodge himself considers it entirely compatible with works of a more learned kind hereafter on the separate books of the New Testament. An *early* and frank answer will oblige,

"Yours,

"MR. SCRIBNER. J. A. ALEXANDER."

In answer to the preceding letter, Mr. Scribner with his accustomed liberality, proposed to cancel the sheets of the larger Acts which had already been stereotyped, and accept the new proposition. Here is Dr. Alexander's answer:

"NEW YORK, April 28th, 1856.

"DEAR SIR:

"Not finding you at home, I am obliged to say in writing what I meant to say by word of mouth. Your estimate of the larger work on Acts is so extremely high, that I cannot consent to your making such a sacrifice for my accommodation. I shall, therefore, hold myself in readiness to execute our contract by completing that work, either now or at a later day, as you may choose. This will, of course, put an end to all comparison of claims and questions about compensation, and place you upon precisely the same footing with all others in relation to the new work. No further communication will be necessary until I have sent you the final agreement between Dr. Hodge and myself.

"Yours,

"MR. SCRIBNER. J. A. ALEXANDER."

Dr. McGill expresses himself as follows, in reference to his strange union of mobility and steadfastness.

"The great activity of his mind was given also to changing of methods more frequently than comported with the greatest benefit of teaching. He was a man of genius, far more than of method; and could never content himself long with even the best methods which his fertile mind contrived. For the sake of change itself, and the pleasure of novelty to his own mind, he seemed to baffle the forecast of the plodding student continually in the plans he pursued and advised, though sure to captivate the interest of learners notwithstanding their preference for the cast-off methods which had delighted the classes before them. No man of his generation was so remarkable for the immovable tenacity with which he held the old formulas of truth in our standards, combined with ever-varying modes and sides, to which he kept shifting his own views, and the views of his pupils. And all this, without philosophical speculation of mind merely, for which he had no respect, but even contempt, in seats of sacred learning."

Many of his pupils could see and feel all this, and were as much pleased as amazed at the benefit they derived from their whimsical master.

The new commentary came out early in this year, a popular not a critical exposition, and in the reduced proportions that made it correspond with the series of volumes issued, and to be issued, by Dr. Hodge. Many have never ceased to pour forth lamentations that Dr. Alexander did not carry out his original intention of writing a critical rather than a popular work. In that case we should have never known the extent of his versatility and his charming power of communicating what he knew, and yet of hiding the source of his information. The work on the Psalms was not only concise, and bare of citation, but almost meagre. The later commentaries of Dr. Alexander, I mean the ones on the New Testament, have almost the brevity and the vivid peculiarity of Calvin. The Isaiah could boast his logic, his erudition, and his orthodoxy, but in comparison with his later works lacked the wonderful sententious completeness and power of statement, and the high popular elegance of the great Genevan. These are to be found, if anywhere, only in the Acts and books on the Gospels.

It has always struck me as a very absurd notion that Alexander on either of the first two Gospels, or on the Acts, was any less learned than Alexander on Isaiah. The difference, as it appears to me, was that between a builder who leaves his scaffold up and one who takes it down. The more extensively one reads beyond the covers of Dr. Alexander's books on the Acts and the Gospels, the more deeply, I am told, is one impressed with that masterly control of the materials which could enable the author to bring in the views of so vast a body of writers in various languages, analyze them, group them, refute them, or make them his own, and yet scarcely hint at the existence or qualities of the individual writers in question. He had a way of extracting the pith of a page or a chapter, and cramming it into a sentence, a clause, and sometimes an epithet. He could also bundle up the substance of a shelf of authors in a paragraph. His adjectives are a study of comprehension and precision. They are often allusive, and point to traits of mind or character in particular writers whom he had been reading, but whom he does not name or otherwise indicate. Thackeray said a man's knowledge might be gauged by his ability to *see* the covert allusions of Macaulay, which, he says, are crowded almost as thick as his words. In like manner, I conceive, the larger and more discursive a man's reading, the more he will admire and value Dr. Addison Alexander's Acts and Gospels. But though when put side by side with his Isaiah, these smaller works may seem unembarrassed by formal citations or circumstantial details of any kind, it is really astonishing how many books, events, historical characters, traits of feeling, and minor things he has expressly referred to in these little compact volumes. The Bible he knew as even he knew nothing else. The Rabbinical and classical authors were at his fingers' ends. The references were seldom, if ever, made at second hand. He read over the principal Greek authors, and took notes on them with a view to these very labours. And in like manner he read the Targums, the fathers, and the chef-d'œuvres and curious performances of modern literature. For the same purpose he often treasured up what he saw in the newspapers and other effusions of the periodical press, and what he met with in his own consciousness and in the intercourse of daily life.

On this point Dr. Beach Jones has written very forcibly. He says that there was in Dr. Alexander no parade of learning or talent; and continues:

"If his great Commentary on Isaiah seems by the citation of so many critical authorities and variant opinions, to furnish an exception to this remark, it is only an apparent exception. The design and plan of that great work rendered necessary the exhibition of critical erudition beyond what would otherwise have suited his taste. His expositions of the Acts of the Apostles, and of the Gospels of Mark and Matthew indicate the actual taste of the man. Scholars can see in every part of these commentaries proofs of amazing erudition, as well as of the profoundest and nicest scholarship; and even unprofessional readers become convinced that the author must have possessed vast resources. Yet it would be difficult to point to any similar production where so much learning is presupposed and implied; and where so little is displayed. We have the ripest fruits of consummate scholarship, but no parade of the means and processes by which they were produced. One of the first scholars and greatest minds in this country was once contrasting the commentaries of Professor Alexander with those of another distinguished author in the same department, and illustrated the difference by the following expressive figure: 'When ——— has done his work, you find yourself up to your knees in shavings. When Dr. A. has finished his, you don't see a chip.' This absence of 'chips,' I have no doubt, has prevented many from estimating at their real value the three commentaries last mentioned. There is so little appearance of effort, and so entire an absence of the parade of learning, that superficial students have thereby underrated both the workman and his work. Scholars most versed in the field cultivated by Prof. Alexander are the men who most readily concede to him superlative merit. The highest published eulogium I ever knew pronounced upon the Exposition of Mark was a *critique* contained in a foreign periodical, in which the writer, apparently a professional scholar, pronounces the work incomparably the best ever written."

Every word of this statement is true. The Mark and the Matthew, and to a great extent also, the Acts, show on inspection a granitic formation covered with herbage and revived with springs of water. These fields are irrigated throughout, not only from Siloa's brook, but from the wells of English undefiled. The commentaries in question are perhaps their author's noblest monument. They afford an exquisite light to the scholar, but may also be read with profit and pleasure by men who have not the means of estimating their true rank and value. As to the relative merits of these later books it is hard to decide. Probably most readers would pronounce for his "Mark." His Matthew is a torso; but contains discussions which perhaps he has not equalled elsewhere. A competent judge of such matters gives it as his opinion that the most interesting, and, as he thinks, generally valuable of his commentaries, is his book on the Acts, "which," he says, "is for me the best commentary I ever read."

This was the book which he now placed upon the counters, and introduced into his class-room. I was a student at the time in the Theological Seminary, and can testify to the thoroughness with which the professor did his work. The massive page seemed to brighten and soften under the influence of his invaluable running comments on his own text.

Let us now try to picture to ourselves what he was at this period in the privacy, contentment, and unaffected ease of his own dwelling. He had everything around him to make him comfortable, and to minister to his various cravings. He rose neither very early nor late, but was absolutely regular in the discharge of his religious duties in the family. Punctuality was the law of the house. At the striking of the clock, the bell would ring for prayers; and on the cessation of the sound, the door of Mr. Alexander's study, which was the front room on the right, would open suddenly and its occupant would issue from it and repair to the sitting-room in the rear of the house, which is known to all old students as having been the study of Dr. Archibald Alexander in the days during which that venerable man spent his life in one room, and during the latter part of the time in one chair. That chair was still standing on its short rockers in the middle of that same room, near a centre-table on which were placed the Bible and a hymn-book. The family had gathered by the time he entered, and Mr. Alexander would at once move his hand swiftly among the leaves of the old brown volume which he had used so long, select or find the passage of Scripture he wished to read, and then go through it in a dry, measured tone, and with great rapidity, holding the book up before him in both hands very near his eyes, with his head slightly bent forward and his eyes looking upward over his spectacles. One who knew him could see that there was nothing perfunctory in his manner. When his glasses where removed, his eyes recoiled from the light, and had a very unusual appearance. The power in his face often struck me more then than at common times. He was very near-sighted, but his vision was very strong. Like William Beckford, he might have been said to have the eyes of an eagle. He read without glasses in the twilight, and never complained of soreness or weariness in the organ. He could go to a window and read when no one else could see a letter. Having read the chapter, he would close the book, say "let us pray," and be upon his knees, and sometimes well advanced in his petitions, before the rest were all fully aware that he had reached this part of the service. The same or nearly the same rapidity of utterance characterized him here as before. Yet with all the rapidity, though there was no sanctimony, there was no irreverence. The duty was performed in a spirit of child-like simplicity. The quickness with which one word followed another would be the first thing to strike a stranger, and the next would be the perfect fluency of the speaker and his marvellous command of language.

It was impossible that the thoughts of a listener should not be directed sometimes from the spiritual exercise, to notice and reflect upon this. The difference between Mr. Alexander and nearly all others in this respect was the difference between that which cannot easily be improved, and that which is less or more faulty. I never knew him to hesitate for a word, or to break the current which was rushing on with such even velocity for any other purpose than to cough or clear his throat when he had a cold. I never knew him to recall a word or syllable once uttered; and yet months of elaboration could not well have added polish or terseness or a more exquisite propriety to a single sentence. The happiest pages of his commentaries will give some notion of the character of the language I refer to. Every word was in its right place, and was the very word of the whole English vocabulary to express the precise shade of thought. There was something of the same rhythmical and dactylic peculiarity that is observable in his sermons. And yet these wonderful words were poured out with an ease that resembled negligence, though the close observer could not fail to discern traces of consummate previous preparation for these tasks. The prayers themselves were models of all that is beautiful and edifying in such transcripts of Christian experience. They were withal as exact and massive as his Isaiah. There was a happy blending of sameness and variety—a mixture of simplicity and refinement—that it would be impossible to describe. There were certain favourite phrases and petitions, sometimes in the form of scripture texts, which were constantly recurring; but with so many modulations, that the recurrence was always agreeable both to the mind and the ear. One of these phrases was, "Let the wickedness of the wicked come to an end." Another was, "Deliver us from the extremes of despondency and presumption." The sentences were commonly short, and very uncomplicated in structure. Yet often a technical term was used, where its avoidance would have seemed an affectation. This was especially so in the case of the prayers at the opening of each lecture.

In prayer, the manner, which had been unimpressive during the reading of the chapter, became mellowed and soft, and sometimes very sweet and subduing. Even in the reading of the chapter the tones of his voice would sometimes accommodate themselves to a glowing narrative, or a bold and graphic prophesy, or an exultant Psalm. There was something grand about the way he often read such books as Isaiah and Nahum. There was a swell in the voice, and a sonorous chanting music in the tone, which, with the knowledge and admirable emphasis of the reader, brought out the force of the original as nothing else could do.

As soon as the word "Amen" had been pronounced, Mr. Alexander was at once in rapid motion towards the door of his study, and was there secluded till breakfast. He always had some special intellectual work for these odd moments, which he could attend to at no other time. He always said that he could keep up his acquaintance with all the languages he had ever learned by reading a sentence in each every day. At one time he devoted a half hour before dinner to this purpose, most agreeably to himself and with entire satisfaction as regarded the results. It was one evidence of his great memory. His journals show how he spent the hours which were regularly devoted to study. He would then seldom leave his room; but if he did, it was commonly with a bright face and with some cheerful question or delighted comment on what he had been reading, or some laughing jest or recollection. He would often step out into the entry to express the pleasure he had derived from the society of some rare but congenial visitor. When no one was visiting in the family, his habit as to talk and social demonstration at the table was variable. At ordinary times he was lively and chatty. He would sometimes talk incessantly for twenty minutes at a stretch, while others perhaps were disposed to remain silent. He was as free as a bird as to the topics on which he descanted. Sometimes it was altogether about various articles of food, English and American fashions as to meals, waiters, courses, &c. Sometimes it was about the books or newspapers he was reading. More commonly it was about every-day people and things, in which wide range of subjects he manifested an interest that never seemed to flag. Sometimes a brisk dialogue or general conversation would spring up, in which he would uniformly join and commonly take the chief part. What struck me most in these daily outpourings of his, was the conclusive evidence which they furnished of *his impulsiveness*, when he felt entirely at home. There were now and then, too, the scintillations of genius. There were times when he would be silent and in drooping spirits. Sometimes he would be as gay as a school-boy just let out from school. There were seasons when he seemed to crave the stimulus of opposition, and he would seek a pleasant intellectual combat, in which, it is needless to say, he was very apt to come off victor. Not always, however. Professional knowledge would sometimes interpose an invincible and unexpected check to the march of his logic. He would then give up the point, and invent a dozen new arguments in a twinkling, or else change the subject altogether. Sometimes it was plain that his simple object was to elicit truth, and that his objections were only intended to draw out others whom he thought better informed. He would then delight to be confuted, and freely express the joy with which he found himself instructed.

This talk at table, in his own house, was something unlike all his other talk. It was often more like monologue than any he ever would consent to engage in under other circumstances. It was without restraint of diffidence or reluctance, of whatever origin whether morbid or otherwise. He seemed to be thinking aloud. There were times when he sparkled with lambent repartee and wit. His blue eye then twinkled with a serene and jubilant intelligence. The conscious gleam of that eye when a good thing had been uttered, put one in mind of Thackeray at his lectures on the English Humourists. There was in it a shrewd, dry intelligence; of the sagacious Anglo-Saxon Scotch-Irish sort, mingled with an expression that must have been inspired by the very genius of fun and drollery. He never looked more intellectually brilliant than at such moments. His countenance then befitted the *ci-devant* editor of the "Patriot," and the correspondent from "South Smithville," and might have been painted beside those of Æsop, Molière, and Cervantes. At other times he was terribly sarcastic. His talent for caustic rejoinder was unequalled. This was usually at the expense of persons or classes of people mentioned in the course of conversation. The spleen he vented at any casual notice taken of braggadocios, upstarts in literature, and plausible charlatans of every kind, was at such times vitriolic. I well remember the prodigious burst of satirical wrath with which he heard that some small pretender was denominated a "genius," and the noble warmth with which he recognized the true men who justly wear that title. He was very fond of applying the term himself to the controlling or original minds of Church History, good and bad, especially the men of action as distinguished from mere scholars; such men as Hildebrand, Innocent, Bernard, Luther, Farel, John Knox. But the general tone of his remarks was either instructively grave and rich with native common-sense and a learning he could not wholly suppress, or else marked by an almost boyish playfulness and mirthful ebullition of spirits. When the weather was dreary, one could tell at once, from a certain listlessness and dejection of manner, in what quarter the wind was setting. He seemed to give himself more margin in the way of leisure immediately after tea than at any time during the day. He would also sit rocking idly in his chair, and drumming with his hands on the smooth wooden elbow, after evening prayers. After drinking tea, the family would resort to the sitting-room, which was still called "the study," and which still retained much of the old library look, and would indulge for half an hour or more in general conversation. Some of these evenings were intellectual and social feasts of the highest order. Commonly the talk ran high on the political news of the hour, or the petty details of personal village incident.

Nothing, however, even at night, could long detain him from his books, or rather his reviews and newspapers; for there is reason to believe that at this time he occupied the larger part of his evenings in recreating his mind over the daily bulletin of home news, or some one or more of the English or continental journals. He was *au courant* in all matters of contemporary literature, and especially the British and foreign chit-chat.

He took (as is well known) very little exercise, except when he was travelling. He however appreciated its essential importance. He had a way of pacing slowly up and down a tan-bark path surrounding his front yard, lined with lilac bushes; generally with a book in his hand, and with his head bent upon his breast. He looked up frequently, and nothing that was going on escaped his observation. Sometimes he carried a chair to one of the two mounds which are still in the spring embosomed in glossy green leaves and purple periwinkles. Here, after the bushes were grown, he was fairly encircled by the bloom; and here he loved to read, and to tell stories to the children. One who saw him passing rapidly from the oratory with his hat on, between five and six in the evening, would be struck with a certain air of neatness, reserve, good breeding, and determination. His short gray hair, gold spectacles, trim overcoat (of olive green), and smooth beaver, with his hurried gait, struck an admiring awe into many beholders. The crowded entries never offered any impediment to him. He moved right on like a bullet to its mark, and everything gave way before him. Ten chances to one he was in a genial mood, and the next moment would be laughing and talking with the family at home. Sometimes a student of bolder temperament than his comrades would overtake him, before he got out of the Seminary, and put some question to him. He loved to be thus accosted, and if the student did not disgust him by conceit or sycophancy, he was always richly repaid for his supposed audacity. He had two methods of correcting the faults which he remarked in his friends. One was by sarcasm that was absolutely blighting. This was seldom resorted to unless the error lay deep or threatened to prove obstinate if not incurable. I do not think he commonly intended to hit as hard as he did: but he was scarcely aware of the terrible edge of his own weapon. He would cut a man's side open, to relieve him of a festering briar. Or, to change the figure, he hurled rocks at the fly that troubled his friend's slumbers. The other and more usual method was by taking him aside, and dealing with him in the way of faithful but gentle remonstrance. He was fond of breaking up bad habits in small things in this way. He once drew a young relative to him, and said with the most insinuating sweetness that he had noticed he said "commenced *to* do a thing," instead of "*began* to do it," or "commenced *doing* it." The fault, he said, was one that was getting to be very prevalent in America, but was one of those little things that are worth correcting. His young kinsman was thankful for the lesson, and profited by it.

Much has been said about the way he changed his books and study apparatus. At this time he had a very long, narrow, massive table, with Gothic legs, and covered with green morocco. This table occupied various places in the room, but was generally on the north side. He changed his chairs (not only in the Seminary, but in his study) and his position at this table. Sometimes he sat opposite the middle part, with his face fronting towards the road; sometimes he sat to the right or left of this point, or on the other side of the table, or even at one of the ends. On this table there were nearly always a large clear-glass inkstand, an ivory paper-cutter and folder, a bunch of quills or a box of Mitchell's J pens, a black portfolio with plenty of loose sheets and blotting-paper, his manuscript journal or lecture book, the Hexapla, the New Testament in Syriac, Aben-Ezra or Jarchi, one or other of the Targums, the latest commentaries on the Gospels, some recent work of literature, Bagster's Greek Testament, and the English Bible. There was never any litter on the table or in the room. There was an air of comfort and neatness about everything. A cheerful fire of coals was generally glowing in the grate. The walls were covered everywhere with books, which were nearly all bound in the same style in half calf or rich morocco backs not ribbed but indented. The lower tier of shelves was crammed with enormous folios. There were the Talmud, the whole Rabbinical literature, the oldest versions, the great paraphrases. There, too, were the early chronicles of England, in which he greatly delighted. For one of so much modern feeling, he had a true scholar's love for a folio. Higher up were his lexicons, grammars, thesauruses, geographies, atlases, chronological tables, learned helps of every kind. Higher up still were works of travel, books on art, commentaries, sermons, works on practical religion, University textbooks, belles-lettres, biography, volumes of choice poetry, the masterpieces of literature in many languages, theological books, metaphysical books, romances, most of the Tauchnitz or Teubner classics, other editions of favourite classics, picture books, books of humour, books of every sort and size; piled away in the strangest confusion, with no regard except to their appearance. It was astonishing that such a lover of system and such a master of analysis should not have had a better arrangement for his volumes: but so it was. The sameness even of good order was here intolerable to him. Sometimes he would *shuffle* his whole library. If any one came in to borrow a book, he was always very kind and generous, and would say, "You may have it if you can find it. I can't and don't pretend to." He ceased towards the last to be so particular about his bindings. He did not have much sympathy with the mere bibliographer, but he was himself on many points of interest a walking Dibdin. He cared much more for the good reading that was in a book than for anything that could be said or known about it. While he did not have his brother's tenderness for Baskervilles and Elzevirs, he was notwithstanding very open to the influence of good white paper, good black type, good broad margins, substantial covers, and a creditable title-page. He was fastidious to the point of nicety about his letterpress.

When any one knocked at his door, he said "Come in" in a very vigorous and sometimes rather dissatisfied manner; with a peculiar prolongation of the tone. The pitch and sound were nearly those of the C tuning-fork. When his visitor entered, he turned his head to see him, and if he was not uncommonly busy, and was not bored by the intrusion, greeted him with amiable and natural politeness. He did not usually rise himself, but inclined his head and in a kind voice requested his visitor to "take a seat." He would then commonly turn his chair round towards the fire, and before long would probably be upon his legs. Sometimes he was curt and short. This was very seldom the case where he was not provoked by people who had not common sense enough to know how to behave themselves in his presence. He would show in an instant whether he liked the call or not. The rule was, that he was affable, free and easy, full of interesting talk, and in many cases enthusiastically joyous and friendly, and to the last degree fascinating. No matter how the interview commenced, this was usually the way it ended; especially if the visitor took no umbrage at the sincerity of his manners, and illustrated in his own person the qualities of the agreeable gentleman. Whoever had good reason for coming were welcomed. Those who came to cringe, or stare, or compliment, were rebuffed. With very slight exceptions, Dr. Alexander's treatment of those who went to see him was very much like that they would have received from others, save that few others had so perfectly at command and could so unconsciously exercise the art and charm of conversation. Not a few have been perfectly carried away with these hit-or-miss interviews, and have cherished the memory of those snatched half hours as among their most precious recollections.

He had a way of talking, or rather reading, to himself, when he was engaged in study, and also of humming tunes. His favourite device was to apply the edge of a folder to his mouth, and whistle or blow tunes upon it. He did the same with stiff paper. The tune he was fondest of, at least for these purposes, was a very singular and pretty one which he is thought to have made himself, and which he had adapted to the words, "O for a blast of that dread horn." The tune was so ingeniously contrived that it brought in every note in the scale. If children came to see him, he hardly ever failed to sing them the Persian air (how sweet and graceful a one, many well remember) "Sa-ki-biar badeh." He is shrewdly suspected of having made this likewise.

He often paced the floor of his study, reading or glancing about over his shelves. This he seemed to do for exercise, or as a relief from the sitting posture. He was then visible from the street, and excited many curious wishes in the breasts of the gossips, who all the world over covet a position beside the great man's *valet de chambre*. The students of the College and Seminary many of them regarded him as they might have done the statues of Memnon. He was an impressive stony riddle to them, breaking into music under the sunbeams of a polyglot literature. Others looked upon him as an astronomer walking in solitary rapture among stars and constellations. The simple truth was he was just like other people in most of his tastes and feelings, and like them too in most of his domestic habits; with this marked difference, that he appreciated the shortness of life, and heartily enjoyed the work on which he had resolved to spend the strength and affluent resources with which heaven had gifted him.

Let me give an example of one of the casual encounters he sometimes had with the students. Late one afternoon, with a "hod" of wood on his shoulder, a very young gentleman was whistling a lively tune and keeping time with his feet as he ascended the stairs in the first story. Having gone about half way up to the first landing (making a shuffling and patting noise on each step as he went), looking up to see whose feet those were on the top step, he received a great shock of surprise at beholding Dr. Addison Alexander standing at the first turn of the steps, patiently awaiting his movements—which were quite rapid enough, although for the reason mentioned he was making very little headway.

> "To retreat," he says, "was my only thought, and the movement was made in regular *crawfish* style, until my back was against the bulletin board.* There I stood, hod piled high with wood still on my shoulder, expecting nothing but a reproof for my undignified and boyish conduct; but as he reached the floor, with as bright and pleasant a countenance as ever shone on mortal, he said: 'Good evening, Mr. ——, I believe you are always in good spirits. I am glad of it, sir.'"

As the dreaded scholar passed out towards his father's, the eyes of the vexed yet amazed and delighted student pursued him, though the pupil stood motionless at the foot of the stairs, thinking to himself that the professor was a most extraordinary man and that it was very strange that so many people, especially students, should think him austere. By

* In the middle of the entry on the first floor.

this and other little kindnesses he made friends of the young man for life. Nor was he the only one who carried off with him these sentiments of personal love and gratitude. He is forever enshrined in the hearts of many who are now themselves ornaments of the Presbyterian Church.

CHAPTER XXIX.

Dr. Alexander's visits to his brothers in New York were now more frequent than ever. At this time he had the additional inducement of the expected concourse of able ministers and ruling elders who this spring were to dignify the city with their presence, and entertain and impress it with their discussions.

Sunday, May the eleventh, was the communion at Nineteenth Street. In the evening the pastor preached at the installation of his brother, the Rev. S. D. Alexander. The Assembly-men were beginning to come in. Dr. James Alexander's weekly lectures to his congregation were now at the zenith of their popularity, from which they never declined. The house on Eighteenth Street was full of company. The Supreme Court of the Church was opened with a great sermon by the Rev. Dr. N. L. Rice, from the text "Preach the Word."

The Assembly was dissolved about 10 p.m., of Wednesday the 28th. "The general impression" Dr. James Alexander records, "is that there has never been a more harmonious, judicious, and respectable body, or a more grave, courteous, wise, affectionate, and pious, moderator."

The subject of these biographical sketches was now in the city, and though very much secluded, managed to hear some of the notabilities. He had the satisfaction of listening to Dr. Thornwell's surpassing effort on the subject of Foreign Missions, and tranquilly admired it. He compared the structure of the discourse to that of the French preachers of the school of Massillon. He had had his expectations much raised, and was not as much carried away as some others were.* He however applauded the masterly handling of the theme. He was

* Dr. Thornwell used to say that the Isaiah was a "mine" of learning.

very capricious in his likes and dislikes, or rather in the vehemence or lukewarmness of his emotions, while listening to a sermon. An ordinary man would, in some moods, excite him to ecstasy, while the most elaborate efforts of the celebrated preacher would often fail to impress his feelings. He could only be taken by surprise.

The other Assembly was meeting at the same time, at Dr. Adams's Church, and I accompanied, or met with him, there more than once. He sat in the corner of one of the galleries. The great debate on slavery, which resulted in the secession the following year of the Southern Presbyteries, interested him vastly. Among the strong speakers in this body, were Dr. Asa D. Smith, and Dr. Joel Parker, of New York; Dr. Ross, of Huntsville; Judge Jessup, and others, whose names were not communicated to me. Dr. Beman was present, and I think Dr. Cox, but I do not think that either took much part in the heated controversy.

It was probably soon after the adjournment of the two Assemblies, that Dr. Dabney of Virginia was again in company with Dr. Alexander, and spent a day in his house at Princeton. This was the last time they ever met. The interview was a most agreeable one. Dr. Dabney writes:

"He received me with quiet, but genuine kindness. I ascertained that he was suffering with an aching tooth, and was much struck with the self-sacrificing spirit in which he declined to retire (as I urged him), and knowing that I had but the one day which I could possibly spend, devoted himself to my entertainment, without betraying his annoying pain in any manner. Our talk was chiefly of matters pertaining to our own profession and the Church. I ascertained that he was a man who thought for himself, and had original views, many of them far from harmonious with prevalent and fashionable ecclesiasticism.

"I was much struck with the fact that one who was so much a man of the closet as he, should have so much practical knowledge of society and human nature. During the day I remarked, that there seemed to be a great difficulty in combining practical knowledge of men and affairs with thorough scholarship, in our young men; because the study which secured the latter necessarily shut them out of the publicity which taught the former. He very quietly replied, that there was a way by which the recluse in his study might acquire a correct knowledge of human nature; by the study of his Bible and his own heart. I have no doubt that this remark gave the key to his own character, as concerned this trait of it. There was a remarkable absence of egotism and dogmatism, for one who must have been conscious of powers and acquirements, and who had been so much complimented and applauded. This, unhappily for me, happily for him, was my last interview; for 'the good man was taken away from the evil to come.'"

The early part of this summer Dr. Alexander spent in travelling. He left Princeton on the 12th of June, and I find him in Washington on the 16th, where he spent a day or two, dividing his time between the Court of Claims and the Senate and House of Representatives. Returning to New York on the 20th, he proceeded directly to New England, spending Sunday, the 22d, in Boston where he heard N. Adams, D.D., preach, and Sunday, the 29th, in New Haven, listening to Prof. Fisher, Dr. Bacon, and Dr. Winslow. He returned to New York on the 30th, stopping at Blancard's on the Fourth Avenue, where he insisted on a front room, that commanded the picturesque hubbub of the highway. This, he said, was a large part of the pleasure he had when in town, seeing and hearing what was passing. Here he spent the months of July and August, chiefly absorbed in writing his commentary.

But on this occasion he must have sometimes drawn up his chair to his brother James's table, for the latter informs Dr. Hall, July 28th, "Addison is writing on Acts in my study, and printing too." * His love of freshness and novelty prompted him to exchange one place for the other frequently, and his diary is sometimes made up of the list of the different hotels where he often took his meals. On the 31st he writes from Fourth Avenue † to the Rev. C. W. Hodge of Princeton, the letter which is placed below. This letter sufficiently implies that it was here his main work was done. His habit, it seems, was to write from six to eight hours a day, in full view of the cars and omnibuses, on the ground-floor of Blancard's private

* Fam. Letters, Vol. II. p. 227.

† This was in the study of his brother, Rev. S. D. Alexander.

boarding-house. His meals were either brought to his room, or he went abroad to get them. The letter is graphic and pleasant. The object of the writer was to obtain certainty about a Greek word.

"238 Fourth Avenue, N. Y., July 31st, 1856.

"My Dear Friend:

"As I hear you are in Princeton, and I fear still at leisure, I make bold to occupy your thoughts with a small commission, which I hope you will find neither troublesome nor uncongenial. Without further preface, what I want is this, to know with tolerable certainty, whether the Greek word ἰδιώτης, which occurs in Acts ix. 13 ever has the sense of its derivation *idiot* or *ideot* in English. I can find no trace of such a use in any of the ordinary lexicons, but do not like to assert a negative on their authority. All that I would ask of you, and that of course only if entirely convenient, is to look at Stephens's Thesaurus for me. If it is not there, I shall be pretty safe in saying that it is not anywhere. I am led by my work here into many philological inquiries which cannot be put into a popular comment, save as bare results, but which may serve some useful purpose at another time. I write from six to eight hours per diem, in a situation which would drive you mad, or make you as seasick as you were that day between Dover and Calais —I mean at a front window on the level of Fourth Avenue, with all the cars and omnibuses in full blast day and night. It is the noisiest place I ever occupied, except Madame Le Clèse's lodgings in the Rue Neuve Saint Roch. I find it agrees well, however, both with my health, and with my work which is advancing slowly but a mile ahead of the poor printers. Did your father get the plate-proofs which I ordered for him? I think the volume will look very well, although I care less and less *for typographical* appearance. This I know, will shock you. Accept this gentle criticism as my payment in advance for the favour I have asked, and believe me to be ever,

"Most sincerely yours,

"Rev. C. W. Hodge. J. A. Alexander."

He was at home by the first of September, as I learn from the following record. The subject which now took up most of his time was the chequered story of Christianity.

"September 18. Lectured to all the classes on the Ancient and Mediæval Church historians. Walked. Reduced my two first lectures (those of last week) to a written form, making seventy-three paragraphs. This I propose to do every week, after delivering the lecture once from notes, and then examining three classes separately on them. Wrote on Acts vii. 19."

These lectures, in the abbreviated form of the first draught, were subsequently printed in a volume of posthumous essays on Church History and New Testament Literature, which was put forth by Mr. Scribner.

The admirable remarks of Professor Hepburn, of Miami University, will be interesting to all old students of this course:

"During my Seminary course, Dr. Alexander lectured upon Old Testament History, the Harmony of the Gospels, the book of Acts, and on Ecclesiastical History. He interpolated, as I believe was his custom, special courses of lectures;—one on Joshua and another on the book of Revelation. The course on Old Testament History was the most popular, and I think was Dr. Alexander's favourite course. He told me that he intended to prepare a text-book on that subject; I fear he has left no portion of the work in a condition fit for publication. Many of his views on these subjects, in fact the summary of many of his lectures, are contained in some of his articles in the Repertory.

"It was characteristic of his whole course of lectures that they were not so much intended to impart full, detailed information on the subjects discussed as to recommend methods of study, to give suggestions for the prosecution of the study hereafter. This he continually stated to us. His views of teaching history were substantially those of Professor Smyth of Cambridge, of whose Lectures on Modern History he once said in class, 'I owe more to that book than to any other one book, as to method in historical study.' He urged upon the students to use the material given them in this course in their pulpit preparations, remarking that it seemed that most of the students after spending years at the Seminary in study, when they went to preaching fell back upon something or other which they learned before entering. He laid great stress on the fact that in Scripture the historical form of presenting the truth is so prevalent, and urged that this divine model should be more observed in preaching.

"He did not often recommend books to us. He once said to me, that he never recommended a work to the students which he did not regard as entirely evangelical. I remember his once remarking in class that it was a paradox of his, that he preferred an inferior book by a great man to a better book by an inferior one. Edwards's History of Redemption was one most highly commended by him. He stated that he had when young read the work and thought it a good kind of book, but without being specially struck with its merits; but that lately, after having read largely in all the languages of which he was master, he had taken up the work again, and was surprised to find in it what he had been seeking for in such remote quarters.

"The lectures delivered in class-room were models of their kind. They never failed to keep the attention even of the more negligent, and to impress themselves on the memory. They were not written. He stated once that he held that there was a great difference between spoken and written style, and proceeded to illustrate his views by reading us some of his lectures on Church History as he wrote them after delivery. The difference was marked. In the ordinary lecture I never failed to secure every thought—but so condensed was this specimen read, that although familiar with the matter from previous lectures, I had to abandon my attempt to take notes.

"He was fond of making experiments. One that he made for a few weeks has not been without its results. In our first year, when as yet we were unacquainted with Hebrew, he instituted a series of lectures on the book of Joshua, for the purpose of seeing whether he could give to those unacquainted with the original language (making the English text the basis of the lecture) the results of a critical study of the book in the original. I do not know how he was pleased with the results of his experiment; I suspect not very well. A few years after, Dr. Broadus, who was one of the Committee for organizing the Baptist Theological Seminary at Greenville, S. C., inquired of me what I thought of the possibility of communicating to a class ignorant of Greek and Hebrew the results of exegetical study of the Scriptures. I gave him at full length an account of Dr. Alexander's experiment. He was delighted to hear it, and told me some months afterwards that he had laid it before the Committee, who also were pleased with it, and intended to introduce the feature into their Seminary. By their Catalogue which I received afterwards from Dr. Broadus, I see that critical lectures on the Old and New Testament with English text as basis, constitutes a part of the course.

"I wish I could have communicated this to Dr. Alexander. He was always pleased to hear of the results of his labours outside of the Seminary. I once told him I had taken a class in my country church through his course of Old Testament History. He said that it always gratified him to hear of such experiments. That his only mode of becoming useful in a more extended sphere, was through those who understood him and could popularize what they had received from him. We went on then to discuss text-books for this study, He criticized a number, and then added, "Well, sir, I will write you one;" and then proceeded to explain, by saying that he had long intended to prepare such a book for his classes, and would be glad to have it used, as I proposed, in popular instruction in Bible classes."

The October weather was fine. Dr. Addison Alexander left New York on the 30th. The city was on the eve of the national election. Dr. James Alexander prays, "May God turn all to the good of our great yet sinful country! Amen." He had dark forebodings for the future, having always, like his father, predicted that the quarrel between the North and South would probably turn out to be irreconcilable. He felt that the atmosphere was charged with war. He however prayed ardently for peace. His brother Addison seldom referred to the subject of politics, but like his more despondent brother, had devoted himself to the interests of that "kingdom which is not of this world," and which amidst all the commotions of earthly change and revolution, can "never be moved."

In the following letter to his brother Samuel, he talks of more journeying and more writing:

"PRINCETON, Oct. 23, 1856.

"REV. AND DEAR SAMUEL:

"I expect to finish my first course of lectures this week, and to give next week to the classes for revision, and to myself for change of air, &c. I cannot determine whether I will merely change my place and spend the week in New York, writing Acts, or whether I will take a journey. What do you think of visiting Quebec and Montreal with me? If you cannot do this, what do you think of my spending next week at the Family Hotel? Is my old room still vacant, and will Blancard let me have it and my board at the old price? Whether I hear from you or not, I expect to be in town on Saturday—perhaps at No. 30 West 18th Street—and shall probably bring my box of books, and then determine whether I will stay in New York or go further. If I do this I may send my books to your house, and will thank you to let them lodge in one of your rooms till the question is determined. I should not like to stop Acts for a week, if the printers were not so far behind me. I have had no proof this week, though I expected one every day. I make no complaint, however, as I do not wish them to go faster.

"Accept the assurance of my high consideration.

"J. A. ALEXANDER."

Dr. James Alexander went to Princeton on the 16th of December to attend the meeting of the College Trustees, and returned the next day. During this visit, his brother Addison, whose mind was astoundingly fertile in new projects, proposed to him a plan of authorship which embraced the scheme of writing and printing a succession of letters, "which," writes the elder brother, "in humble reliance on Providence, I think of attempting." I never heard of his actually doing so. How little did his people suspect that he had but three years more to live! His light was now flaming near the socket, and its lustre was transient and delusive. Oh! how we should all prize the possibilities of to-day, if we did but forecast the certainties of to-morrow.

Meanwhile Dr. Addison Alexander was moving steadily on in his various courses of technical and discursive reading. I give an extract or two from the journal. They reveal the fact that he was as usual studying various foreign languages, and reading Acts, Genesis and Mark, in a course of scriptural exegesis.

"December 9. Read the Scriptures in Arabic, Portuguese, Swedish, and English. Began the 11th book of Mariana's Historia de España. Lectured to the 2d class on Acts ii. 1–9. Began Acts xi. (writing). Continued Brandt, Gibbon, and the Edinburgh Review.

"December 30. Read Chrysostom, Ammonius, Cyril, Erasmus, Calvin, Grotius, Bengel, Lightfoot, Whitby, Gill, Rosenmüller, Olshausen, Meyer, De Wette, Baumgarten, Neander, Schaff, Lange, Bloomfield, Humphrey, Hackett, Alford, Trollope, Barnes and Ripley on Acts xiv. Genesis in Arabic, Matthew in Portuguese, Mark in Swedish."

The year had been well spent, and was now ended.

We have scarce a glimpse of him from the beginning of the year 1857 until May. He was, as his journal shows, continuing his immense circuits in literature and Biblical science. As the spring opened, he became anxious to transfer his papers to New York.

The following letter to Mr. Scribner is all that can be recovered of his labours during this winter. He was at this time deep in his commentary, and in the study of the Apocalypse; both of which are referred to in the letter.

"PRINCETON, Jan. 26th, 1857.

"DEAR SIR:

"I have made considerable progress in my second volume, and as soon as I have filled the book in which I am now writing, will send it on. In the meantime, please to order, by the next steamer, a copy of the 'Voyage and Shipwreck of St. Paul,' by Smith of Jordanhill, which I shall need in writing on the last chapter. I have heretofore used a copy of the first edition, presented by the author to my brother when in Scotland, but I see that the work has been reprinted with some new discoveries. I should like also to obtain a sight of Lord Lyttleton before I finish. Perhaps a standing order on your English correspondent, or on some importing house at home, would bring it here in time, if it is actually published. I wish to ascertain the author of a book called "Hypoia, or Thoughts on a Spiritual Understanding of the Apocalypse," a large octavo published by Leavitt, Trow & Co. in 1844. The copyright is in the name of John R. Hurd, but whether he is the author I am not aware and should be glad to know. I presume, that by inquiring either up or down stairs, you can easily obtain the information, and thereby oblige,

"Yours truly,

"J. A. ALEXANDER."

The little volume of the elder brother entitled the "American Sunday School and its Adjuncts," was now in the hands of the booksellers and their customers. It is addressed to teachers, and is chiefly aimed at the correction of certain practical evils. The foreign newspapers were deeply studied by the younger brother. Now and then he saw what startled and often pleased him. At this time he noticed (what few other Americans would have noticed) that there was a wholesome change going on among the English bishoprics. His brother to whom he mentioned it, brings the matter before Dr. Hall. "Addison calls my attention to the remarkable revolution, which, under the Palmerston rule, is going on in the English Sees, in favour of evangelicalism. Both Archbishops and three leading bishops are now on that side." *

The overtasked brain and nerves of the city pastor, however, needed rest rather than stimulus. His throat also began to cause him profound uneasiness. In this state of things he often called upon his brother for help. Late in April he writes, "Addison preached for me yesterday, though I think I could have preached once myself." † The trouble grew, until matters came to a crisis, and the sorrowful and heavy-laden minister had to stop work for a time.

Professor Alexander was now lecturing on the history contained in the later part of the historical scriptures, and the prophets of the Exile and the Restoration; as may be gathered from the following extract:

> "March 25.—Lectured to the third class on the Babylonish Conquest and Captivity, the Restoration and the foreign Domination. Closing the course in Old Testament History pro hâc vice. Read Acts xxi. in Syriac, Latin, and old English versions—wrote on verses 1–8."

His lectures on Biblical History can be only guessed at from the volume of published notes, which are a mere epitome. A better idea of them, in some respects, may be culled from parts of his commentaries and from some of his later articles in the Repertory. They showed a wonderful acquaintance with the facts and structure of the scriptural books, and of collateral authorities, and were given in the most nervous style of graphic extemporaneous English. The classes were delighted with them; having, indeed, but one ground of complaint against their teacher, and that was, that he so often changed his plans. But he had his reasons for his movements, which many of them did not understand.

* Fam. Let. II. p. 234.

† Ibid II. p. 235.

Professor Hepburn says, "I have always regretted that Dr. Alexander gave himself so exclusively to Exegesis. He would no doubt condemn such a sentiment. I observed while studying under him that it was hard for him to leave the interpretation of Scripture, for the other parts of his course. He gave two years to Bible History, the second year being given entirely to Exegesis (on Acts), and endeavoured to crowd the whole of Ecclesiastical History into one year. In addition he gave several short special courses on portions of Scripture, as on Joshua, and on Revelation.

"There was one peculiarity about him, which you may have noticed—the students often complained of it, and I have heard the same complaint from many who have read his Isaiah—that is, that he frequently gives, as I have heard it expressed, 'Every one's opinion on the passage, except his own.' Some of Neander's pupils have told me that he was frequently guilty of the same. But is it a fault? I have been told that Neander, while so reticent often in his public lectures, was very free in expressing his views in private. I suspect this was true also of Dr. Alexander. This reserve was, however, very characteristic of him; he passed over many subjects without indicating his views, yet on all, he held very decided ones; *e.g.* on Church Government and on Ordination of Ruling Elders."

I learn from the next entry in his journal, that he was still busily engaged upon the Acts.

"May 14.—Read Acts xxviii. in the Peshito, Vulgate, Luther, Meyer, De Wette, Erasmus, Calvin, Wolf, Bengel, Wetstein, Lightfoot, Lardner, Winer, Bloomfield, Olshausen, Von Gerlach, Humphrey, Hackett, Trollope, and Lyttleton."

The class got the benefit of these studies, and when his book was published had it for a text-book. At one time he examined them on the Harmony of the Gospels, using Dr. Robinson's convenient synoptical arrangement of the Evangelists in Greek. The lessons were vastly interesting, but were soon discontinued. He used to ask questions in Etymology and construction, just as if he had been handling a Greek classic. His questions in Biblical History were written down and copied by the students, and were plain enough for the older scholars in a Sunday school. To miss them was disgraceful, and sometimes incurred a reprimand. In general he was meek and tolerant.

In New York, matters were much as formerly. Dr. James Alexander's people had been for some time talking of sending their pastor to Europe. The step was now determined upon, and a liberal provision for the trip was voted by the congregation. This proposal was the more agreeable to him, as it included his wife and youngest child, both of whom needed rest and healing. His own bronchial cough had become very troublesome and even a little alarming. The Session acted promptly in the matter, and the Trustees unanimously agreed to give the ailing pastor a vacation till the cool weather. His consent to the arrangement was after all a reluctant one. He did not like the thought of intermitting his labours for any but the most serious cause, and his sensitive spirit shrank from the generosity of his friends and parishioners. He nevertheless fell in with the wishes of his best advisers.

Meanwhile he took a sea-voyage to Virginia, in the steamer Roanoke. He touched at City Point, and visited Petersburg, Richmond, and the University. The interval between his return and his sailing, which took place after the middle of May, was spent in shopping and preparations. The passage across the Atlantic was taken under Captain Scott, and was very beneficial to him.

At the beginning of the vacation of 1857, the subject of this memoir went to New York, intending to write a book on Old Testament History. His journal will give the result of these expectations:

"June 1.—Began my book on Old Testament history.
"June 2.—Broke down.
"June 3.—Resumed my experiment.
"June 4.—Broke down again.
"June 16.—Began a book on Mark; wrote i. 1–4.
"Aug. 29.—Finished Mark between one and two o'clock. Collapse.

"Aug. 31.—Revised four chapters of Mark." *

An account of Dr. Alexander as a teacher, given by one of his pupils, † is here inserted.

"There are a great many who by no means agree with me in pronouncing Dr. Alexander a great teacher. Those who deny his merits as a teacher refer invariably to his course on Ecclesiastical History. It was the fashion in the Seminary to complain of that course. 'Dr. Alexander was so fickle'—that, I believe, was the word. He did change his method frequently with our class: he commenced the course with a general view of the various modes of treating Church History, criticizing all. Mosheim's he regarded as most defective (the centurial method). He gave us then his own, commenced on it, soon abandoned it, and ended by falling back on Mosheim's centurial method. I had no sympathy with this clamour about his frequent changes, and was as ready to hear of a new method as Dr. Alexander was to give it: my experience since has shown me still more how senseless it was. The fact is that the proper method of teaching history remains to be discovered. No method adopted in the limited time allowed the study in our country, has satisfied either instructor or pupil. Dr. Alexander was continually studying methods of instruction. He frequently mentioned and criticized different methods in class. He thought once of introducing Gieseler as a text-book. Had he done so, the disgust of the majority with his course would have increased a thousand-fold. The conclusion he came to when lecturing to us was, that a course of history in a literary institution can give only the method of study—directions for the prosecution of the study afterwards. Besides this difficulty inherent in the subject, he had an additional one to contend with, in the limited time allotted the subject. His strong predilection for Biblical studies led him to devote a larger proportion of time to them, and he found himself compelled to finish eighteen centuries in one year's course. This was all the more embar-

* The following table gives the time occupied in writing each chapter of Mark:

"Wrote Mark, Chap. i. June 18–24; Chap. ii. June 25–29; Chap. iii. June 30–July 4; Chap. iv. July 7–10; Chap. v. July 11–14; Chap. vi. July 15–18; Chap. vii. July 21–23; Chap. viii. July 24, 25; Chap. ix. July 27–31; Chap. x. Aug. 3–5; Chap. xi. Aug. 6–8; Chap. xii. Aug. 10, 11; Chap. xiii. Aug. 14, 15; Chap. xiv. Aug. 19–22; Chap. xv. Aug. 25, 26; Chap. xvi. Aug. 28, 29.

† Professor Hepburn.

rassing, as he disapproved of severing so completely as is usually done, Church history from profane. He frequently expressed these views in class. If I remember, they are also contained in an article in the Repertory.

"If Dr. Alexander failed as a teacher of history, he had for companions every other professor of the same science in our country. I do not think he failed. He did not give a detailed outline of the facts of modern history, such as the students could commit to memory and repeat at examination before Presbytery; but those who received and improved his instructions as he intended they should be received and improved, he gave an impulse to study, and furnished directions for study, of far more value than all the information he could have packed in a three years' course. If we are to judge of a teacher's success by this test, the strength and permanence of the impulse he gives to the minds which have yielded themselves to his influence, then can we pronounce Dr. Alexander a great teacher. I believe, though, that he himself was never satisfied with this department, and was even in our day anxious to get rid of it. The chairs were, if I am not mistaken, reorganized shortly before his death, and to him more congenial studies were assigned.

"I received the impression from Dr. Alexander's instructions that he had no respect for abstract speculation, for metaphysical discussions either in history, theology, or language. At any rate, he evidently thought the place for such discussions was not in a preparatory course of education. He expressed himself slightingly of what is called the Philosophy of History. The name, at any rate, he did not like. So in the study of languages, it was a means not an end."

The following letter to Dr. Schaff asks for the names of some German authors on Church History:

"New York, July 14, 1857.

"Rev. and Dear Sir:

"Wishing to prepare a course of lectures on the rise and progress of existing churches, I find myself at fault in reference to the national Protestant establishments of Germany. As to some of them, I meet with no descriptions or titles of special histories, while in the case of others I experience the embarrassment of riches. As my object is to ascertain as few names as would answer my immediate purpose, I cannot rely upon the ordinary bibliographical authorities, much less upon the information of booksellers. Even where no special history exists,

I should be glad to learn the fact from some one who can speak upon the subject *ex cathedrâ*. In this emergency I turn of course to you, without apology for troubling you, but with a particular request that you will give yourself as little trouble as you can in shedding light upon my darkness. I have no hope of ever being able to return the favour *in specie*, but can promise my sincere thanks for any help you can give me. What I want is simply a few names of books or authors to be afterwards procured from Germany, or information that there are none in any given case, which is the next best thing to getting them. I presume that Dr. Schaeffer has consulted you in reference to the new edition of Kurtz's smaller work. I could not conscientiously advise him to attempt the translation of the book in its enlarged form, but should not regret to learn that he had been encouraged so to do from other quarters. I am, however, more and more persuaded that no German history, in its crude state, will answer for this country, but that books of this kind must be manufactured for us and among us. In default of such helps, I am tempted to dispense with text-books, in the ordinary sense of the expression, and to content myself with lectures and reference to the standard works of Gieseler and Neander. Whether this is all that we require to elevate the standard of instruction, and if not, what more can be accomplished in the way of supplying the deficiency, are questions which I beg you to consider seriously; and once more remain,

"With great respect,

"Your friend and servant,

"DR. SCHAFF. J. A. ALEXANDER."

I was living in the same house with Dr. Alexander during a part of this summer, and was an attentive observer of his ways. His brother's family were in Europe, and we had the range of the building to ourselves. It was hot weather, and any time between breakfast and dinner I was sure to find him in his brother's study with his coat off, and the indispensable pitcher of ice-water by his side, writing on his Commentary. The long table was partly covered with manuscript, and his hand was going like a race-horse. I seldom disturbed him: never, unless it was necessary for me to enter the room to get a book or ask a question. He never said anything about his work except in reply to such queries. We took our meals in different quarters of the city. One day I encountered him at the front door just as he was sallying out after his morning's task was over. He asked me where I was going, and I said, "To dinner." "Then," said he, "we are aiming at the same object. Suppose you go and take your dinner with me!" I saw he was in a fine humour, so nothing loth I acceded to the proposal, and we made our way to the dining-room of the * * * House, on the Fifth Avenue, then one of the most sumptuous and recherché of the New York *salles*. The small round tables were covered with the whitest damask, and ornamented with the most weighty silver. The company was aristocratically select, and as silent as the images of Thebes or Persepolis. The day before, it is likely he had supplied his needs at one of the cheapest of the restaurants down town. The foreign ministers and clergymen in white cravats and roundabouts, who condescended to carry the joints, glided noiselessly about, and placed before each stranger the customary French roll, pat of butter, and decanter of Croton water. Soft breadths of purple twilight gleamed in the distance. We sat down under the south wall, and hung up our hats on the rack. It was evident to me at once that he was in one of his best moods. His face was genial and bright, and his eyes twinkled like the pendants of the chandeliers. He charged me, and insisted on it, that I should order what I pleased. He himself partook heartily of what was set before him, and talked with uninterrupted volubility. I never saw him appear to greater advantage. Sometimes his face had the fine Napoleonic look that it often wore when in repose: there was the light and fire of genius in it. He struck me as having again the dew of his youth. He seemed reluctant to leave his seat, and talked some time with his hat on his head before he would turn towards the door. Of his own accord he carried me among the German Universities, and gave me pen-and-ink portraits of the Berlin and Halle professors. He drew a ludicrous picture of Neander on his way to the lecture-room with great coat over his study-gown and a slipper on one foot, and actually delivering a lecture to the wall. He had not seen the great Church historian in any of these displays, but like all others had heard of them. He laughed, he chatted, and jested, like a man who was supremely contented. He compared the European and American modes of education, giving the palm to the former, but pointing out many deficiencies even in the European system. He also rambled away on other matters, and Coleridge himself could not have communicated more instruction and delight; though it would have been in the Orinoko style of private eloquence which is commended by De Quincey, and was carefully shunned by Dr. Alexander. We walked home a different way from the one by which we had come, and in a short time he was once more pouring the overflowings of his mind into his book. We both relapsed as if by instinct into the former silence.

I have since thought that he had probably solved some great difficulty or made some extraordinary advance in his labours that day, and that this is the true explanation of his uncommon spirits and of the brilliant conversational outburst to which I have referred. He seemed to understand that there was no danger of his being invaded at ordinary times, and I never afterwards broke in upon his seclusion unless he himself gave the signal which invited me to do so. Then I followed the bent of his humour, and enjoyed with all the greater zest the cream of his rich talk and delightful badinage. Yet he was so shy, that a strange glance or an unconsidered word might scare him into his studious reserve again. He was sometimes as mysterious, if not as dark, as Milton's cloud, but like it, was forever turning a silver lining on the night.

In another letter to Dr. Schaff, he refers to a proposed work by the former, and urges him to adapt it to American readers.

"PRINCETON, Sept. 15th, 1857.

"REV. AND DEAR SIR:

"I ought to have thanked you long ago for your obliging answer to my troublesome inquiries, and your friendly though unnecessary warning against wasting time and money on the infinitesimal Church histories of Germany, as to which I am content to share your *docta ignorantia*. My question ought to have been more distinctly limited to the leading national establishments. With respect to your proposed work, I can only say that I have always thought such a book peculiarly desirable, and you peculiarly qualified to write it, and am still convinced that if, in addition to its intellectual and literary merit—which I take for granted—it maintains the good old Protestant principles avowed in several of your earlier publications, there can be no doubt of its proving eminently popular and useful. I have nothing to suggest as to its plan or execution, beyond what I have intimated heretofore in reference to the barrenness of all German histories on the subject of English and American theology; the inexpediency of substituting foreign modes of printing and arrangement for those with which our public is familiar; and the danger of your English being made *too good*, by the sacrifice of all original expression to the mere conventionalities of hackneyed usage. Sincerely wishing that you may be able to provide us with a text-book universally acceptable,

"I am, &c.,

"Rev. Dr. Schaff. J. A. Alexander."

Two days after he writes to Dr. Hall:

"Princeton, Sept. 17th, 1857.

"I am much encouraged by your first impressions of my book, and *interested in the test to which you are about to put it.* As I have a volume on one of the Gospels nearly ready for the press, I should really be thankful for suggestions even as to small external matters, mode of printing and arrangement, exegetical formulas, reference to authors, use of Greek, &c. I could settle all this for myself on merely literary grounds, but want the help of 'PASTORS and Teachers' in determining what will suit the greatest number, without defrauding the class for which I write especially, viz., that of ministers and students. Very truly yours,

"J. A. Alexander.

"Rev. Dr. Hall."

I return to the journal.

"Sept. 30. Lecture to the Seniors on the Origin of Churches since the Reformation; and to the Juniors on the Noachic Period. Since the beginning of this month I have finished the revision of my book on Mark, written during the last summer; written one sermon (on Mark i. 1.) and one article for the Biblical Repertory (a review of Smith's Gieseler). I have preached eight times; four old sermons, one new written one, and three new unwritten ones (on passages of Mark which I have lately studied)."

He had also begun six courses of instruction in the Seminary, and had already given five lectures on Old Testament History, four on Apostolic History, four on Introduction to Ecclesiastical History, and four on the Origin of Existing Churches, and three on Ecclesiastical Biography; making a total of twenty-three.

Dr. James Alexander arrived in the Baltic, Capt. Comstock, on the 25th of October. They touched the wharf at five, and the minister was among his "bairns" by seven. The trip had apparently done him good, and he was in ecstacies to be once more at home. Many friends rejoiced with him. "Through God's infinite mercies," as the invalid pastor writes himself, he "returned from his foreign journey on the one hundred and fiftieth day, in the steamship Baltic, which touched the wharf about 7 P. M. of the Sabbath, Oct. 25." One of his brothers and one of his sons were ready to receive him. Another son and two more brothers awaited him at the house. The whole party was in improved health and spirits. It was a season of high gratulation and pleasure. Hands were warmly clasped, bosoms were pressed, and laughter struggled vainly with tears. "Hope bright, but to be overcast!" "It was," records the happy traveller, "almost like a foretaste of heavenly rest, when from the dark and dingy and uneasy ship I came to our sweet, clean, light, cheerful home, and after six months' absence sat down among the beaming faces of those who loved us."

The night of the city pastor's return was made memorable by the presence and unusual brilliancy of his brother Addison. The family were soon gathered in the back parlor, and the brothers were both of them in the highest gale of animation. The budget of travel was unfolded, and recollections and descriptions of every kind, pious wishes, playful sallies, prompt demurrers, keen exposures of folly, generous bursts of feeling, scraps of criticism, bits of politics, learned allusions and fine *bon mots*, followed each other in quick succession, like the flashes of sheet lightning over the summer heavens. The laughter excited was now and then almost boisterous. Most of the intercourse, however, though highly enthusiastic, was very grave and sober. Ah, when shall such talk be heard again in the like circumstances! O that it could have been taken down with a pen of iron, and preserved like that of Johnson! O for an hour of these intellectual and theological convivia! The mutual contact seemed to brighten the wits of both. Nothing that either of the brothers has left in print can take the place of their joyous, ever copious, ever instructive, ever inimitable dialogue! It is gone forever. *Lateat scintillula forsan.* The rest is a mere echo.

A return to the memorials of the younger brother, carries us back to the middle of autumn. The following may serve as a specimen of these records:

"Oct. 28.—Examined the Senior Class on Acts viii.: 1–9. Finished Daniel in Hebrew, Greek, Latin, and German; at the same time finishing the Vulgate version of the Old Testament, which I have been reading in course but with many interruptions since the first of February, 1852. Resumed Ezekiel in Hebrew and Chaldee, which I laid aside on leaving home last spring."

"Oct. 31.—Lectured to the Second Class (and many of the others) on Ecclesiastical Biography, closing the course for the present. Examined the Juniors on the Ante-Mosaic History, and lectured on the Mosaic Legislation."

"Since the end of the last month I have preached eight times:—seven unwritten sermons, and one partially so. I have lectured six times on the Life of Christ; five times on Old Testament History; three times on Ecclesiastical Biography; four times on the History of the Church of Rome; and four times on the Periodology of Ecclesiastical History. I have finished my exposition of Luke ii.: 36–52, and my reading of the Vulgate (6, 7). I have read the concluding part of Hengstenberg's Christology."

"Dec. 1.—No lecture. Walked. Read Ezekiel xxv. in Chaldee. Read Gieseler, on the History of the Reformed Churches and made notes thereon. *Laid aside Luke and took up Matthew.* Read Erasmus, Calvin, Kuinoel, and Robinson, on parts of Matthew i. Coverdale's Bible, Genesis x. and Matthew i. Hansard, 1828."

"During the year, I have lectured in the Seminary one hundred and fifty times, and examined classes without lecture thirty times—spoken at Conference and Monthly Concerts, twelve times—preached here and elsewhere, thirty-two times—heard others preach, seventy-five times—written a commentary on the last fifteen chapters of Acts, on the whole of Mark, and on the first chapter of Matthew. Read a multitude of authors on these parts of Scripture—also Smith, of Jordanhill, on St. Paul's Shipwreck (second edition and second time). Smith's Students' Gibbon; several commentaries on the book of Revelation—besides parts of other books, completed or begun within the year. I have visited New York twenty times (besides spending the whole summer there); Philadelphia, seven times; and Trenton, four times."

It is not commonly supposed that his preaching was productive of much visible good if measured by external signs. The testimony now to be given upon this point is valuable.

"I think it was in 1856," writes Professor Cameron, "there was considerable religious interest in the College, and a wish was expressed that Dr. Addison should preach. I accordingly paid him a visit, stated to him the condition of affairs in the College, the religious interest among our students, &c. and concluded by requesting him to preach for us on the next Sabbath. He declined: but I would not take a refusal, and urged him to come. He advised me to get Dr. Hodge; as much better qualified than himself for the peculiar circumstances then prevailing in the College, as his religious life had begun there,* as he therefore understood the matter better, could sympathize more with them in their actual state of feeling than himself, and thus could exert a better and more powerful influence than he. I confess I began to despair of success; when at last I ventured to remark, 'Doctor, excuse me if I say I think *you underrate your influence with our students.*' This seemed to decide him, for he consented to preach, excused himself from a partial engagement in Trenton, and was at our College Chapel on Sunday. He preached one of his great sermons, that on the Gospel Feast, 'Come, for all things are now ready.' Our students hung upon his words, and I know of at least one minister of the Gospel who traces his conversion, under the providence of God, to that sermon. He had not preached in the Chapel for some years, but was so much gratified that he expressed his pleasure and remarked, to our agreeable surprise, as he was going away, that he would be happy to come down and preach again if desired."

* That is, as a student.

Dr. Alexander himself often spoke mournfully of the barrenness of his ministry. Yet here we read of a minister of the Gospel converted through his instrumentality, and if the truth were known, it would probably appear that in the great day many will "arise up and call him blessed." His sermons were singularly fitted to awaken the deepest conviction in the most intelligent minds. Many such heard him who cared to hear no other. During the exercises which attended the inauguration of President McCosh, a lady present remarked to a friend that a sermon of Dr. J. A. Alexander in Philadelphia had been the means of her salvation.

CHAPTER XXX.

We now go once more to the pages of Dr. Alexander's journal, which exhibits the same wonderful industry and a greater concentration of power upon one point than almost ever before.

"Jan. 31, 1858. During this month I have lectured twenty times, with a short examination on each lecture. I have examined four times (without lecture) on my exposition of Acts. I have preached twice, besides speaking once at Conference and once at Monthly Concert. I have also written on the second chapter of Matthew and begun the third. I have heard nine sermons from other preachers. I have finished Pinnock's Analysis of English Church History, and the first volume of Middleton's Cicero."

Nothing could restrain the propensity of this incessant student towards the indulgence of a harmless quizzical humour, such as has often been illustrated in these pages. The main conduit for these effusions was his correspondence with Dr. Hall. Trifling as most of the letters are in themselves, they yet show the kindliness and real humanity of his feelings, and abound in laughable exaggerations, jocose censures, mysterious allusions, and whimsical irony. They continue to relate chiefly to ministerial proposals and arrangements, and are not devoid of a certain aroma of fine clerical suavity, which pervades even those which are couched in terms of pompous hierarchical pretension.

He was off, as usual, during part of the summer. I find from his journal that, on the 9th of June, he sailed for Virginia in the steamer Roanoke. His aim was Norfolk and Richmond. He says he saw Norfolk, touched at Portsmouth, and visited Richmond, Staunton, and Waynesboro'. While in Augusta, he fell in with his sister, who returned with him as far as New Jersey. Dr. Alexander himself proceeded, viâ Washington, Baltimore, and Philadelphia, as far as New York; where I find him, at a somewhat later date, busy correcting the proof-sheets of his Mark. On the 12th of the following month he returned to Princeton, after an absence of two months; where he records that he ascertained a great improvement in the arrangements of his house and study. He was still following the printers. The Introduction, which he had begun to write July 21, he finished on the 23d. In the meanwhile he was pursuing his usual studies. On the 16th of August he completed his labours upon Mark, and records: "(g. f. f. s.)." The day following he set out on a journey to Canada; passing through Saratoga. He returned from this trip August the 30th.

The subjoined letter is about the trip to Richmond.

"RICHMOND, May 17th, 1858.

"MY DEAR SISTER:

"I need not say that I was received here with cordiality—almost with joy. I have been very stationary since I came. I never more enjoyed the *dolce far niente*. Dr. Moore took me to the cemetery and other points of interest yesterday. Last night I preached at his weekly lecture to a crowded room. The singing was delightful. This is really a charming family. I ought to be most thankful for such friends. I received your letter yesterday at dinner time, and while at tea, another, directed by your hand, which made me fear that something was amiss, until I found it was from F. A. P. about that everlasting Doomed Man. I am glad that you are getting on so well, and hope you do not overwork yourself. Do not put my long table by the front windows, but along one of the book-cases.

I give an extract from another letter to his sister describing more fully his visit to Dr. Moore's:

"WASHINGTON, May 21st, 1858.

"MY DEAREST JANE:

"If you have enjoyed yourself as much as I have since we parted, I have nothing to desire or regret for either. I had a very pleasant journey to Richmond. I saw the great sight of the African Church, and heard the greater sounds. They sang "Turn, sinner, turn," which impressed me more than any singing I ever heard. At night I preached for Moore, and again on Monday and Tuesday nights. I was made as comfortable as possible at Moore's. He seems to understand my very whims intuitively, and prevents everything that would be unpleasant."

While in Staunton, Dr. Alexander had not neglected to see much of his venerable aunt, Mrs. McClung, who has since entered into the heavenly rest. Just here I am permitted to take the following extracts from a touching letter which Dr. Moore wrote at the time of this event to Mrs. William Maxwell of Staunton. It is fitting that the words of the two friends should be placed side by side.

"I see by my papers of this morning that dear old mother McClung has gone to her rest. I am not surprised to see it, and yet I feel saddened to think that this blessed tie binding to the past is snapped. She was linked, by so many associations, to my dearest and most revered friends of other years, that the love I felt for them seemed to centre on her.

"As I gazed in that placid face, with its deep and searching eyes, and listened to that voice so strangely tuned to the very pitch and intonation of her matchless brother, my Princeton days and Princeton friends always came thronging around me; and as I sat again at the feet of that man whom I shall ever regard as the wisest man I ever met, and listened to the electric flashes of Addison's wit and learning, and enjoyed the silver flow of James's ripened scholarship and piety; I lived over again those days, the brightness and value of which I have only learned in these times of degeneracy and wrong.

"I loved to look at her face, even aside from those associations; for the seal of God seemed to be in her forehead—its motto "Peace" being imprinted there in letters of a light not born of earth.

"Dear old mother in Israel! She never knew what a sweet homily her face often was to me, and how much good she did me by her warm and hearty greeting."

The author of the following letter wilfully confounds his correspondent with one of his namesakes.

"New York, Oct. 4, 1858.

"My Dear Sir:

"Having been absent from my post on Friday, Saturday, and Sunday in fulfilment of an old engagement on the North Shore of Long Island, I do not feel at liberty to leave the dear young brethren to themselves for one or two more days this week, and shall therefore rely upon your intercessions to make my apology acceptable to the Venerable Company which meets to-morrow, as well as to yourself and Mrs. Hall, for declining your respective hospitalities. Should I be able to attend the higher court of review and control, I have agreed to tarry, tabernacle, make my home, and occupy the prophet's chamber with an old friend and classmate, in your neighbourhood, who, though belonging to another liberal profession, is a great friend to the clergy, or at least to some of them. This will enable you to house a greater number of Synodical guests without putting more than two or three in a bed. As to the other delicate matter upon which you have consulted me, I regret that I shall not have the opportunity of personal communication thereabout, and I hesitate to write about it too explicitly. I can only say, therefore, that I would not advise a public confession in the great congregation, nor even in the Presbytery with closed doors, but rather an auricular communication to some eminently spiritual father or brother, such as ——— or ———, through whom it might afterwards be made as public as would be desirable and safe for you and all the interested parties. By this means scandal might be wholly, or in a great degree, avoided, and your ministry continued in some secluded spot with tolerable comfort. With my best thanks for your hospitality, &c., Yours,

"J. A. Alexander.

"Rev. Dr. Hall."

The publication of his works on the Acts and the 2d Gospel called forth many expressions of delight from discriminating judges of what had been done, and what was needed, in this department of Biblical exposition.

The posthumous appearance of his work on Matthew heightened this feeling of admiration.

The Commentary on Mark came out in the early part of October. It was judged by not a few competent minds to be the best treatise he had as yet produced on Scripture subjects. Among these was his own brother James. Writing to the commentator soon after, he indulges in the following strain of refined critical praise:

"October 14, 1858.

"I pronounce this [his Commentary on Mark] by far your best work. It is eminently readable. It contains episodical passages very agreeable to a purist in language. Especially have you hit off the rendering into happy equivalents in sound English. The diction is better than in any of your opera. Two qualities are quite unusual: 1. You place the reader (and this more than any expositor known to me) near the standpunct of a Greek scholar; and 2. You give vividness to the narrative and remove the integument, or rusty coating, of custom and daily use."

This letter, the recipient was wont to say, was in his estimation, the highest compliment ever paid him.

What is here said of the surprising success which has attended the efforts of Dr. Alexander to make the English reader acquainted with the living meaning of the Hebrew and Greek orignals, has often been said by others, and will probably continue to be said so long as this species of talent continues to be noticed and prized. The correspondence of idioms is sometimes so exact, and yet seemingly unsought, that the translated sentences or phrases communicate a pleasure as sudden and delightful as that of wit. The version is commonly quite liberal, and yet the transfusion of the thought is often perfect. The mastery of both languages that is evinced in all such cases, is something that might appear beforehand to be unattainable. Nothing in Dr. Alexander has ever more astonished me than his seemingly universal knowledge of *idioms* and *words*, and the fluency and deftness with which he used them. The same thing excited the surprise of Dr. Tholuck when Dr. Alexander was in Halle.

Light has been thrown on this narrative from time to time by those who were personal acquaintance of the subject of these memoirs. I am indebted just here to the recollections of his brother the Rev. Dr. Samuel D. Alexander of New York, whose intimate and constant association with him at this time lends great weight to the following words:

"The greater part of the commentaries on the Psalms, the Acts, and Mark, were written in New York. During the winter, amidst the pressure of professional labour, he found time to read and digest all known commentaries on the book in hand; and then, when his vacation began, he would proceed to New York, leaving his books behind him, and in his room in a hotel or in my study, would write from eight o'clock in the morning until five in the afternoon. Of course, human nature could not endure this long stretch of intense mental action. So at intervals he would throw down his pen and take up some book of light literature, which he would read for twenty or thirty minutes, and then resume his pen. Dickens, especially his Sketches, was his favourite in these moments. In my library I have a collection of the early history of the different States of the Union and early travels in America, and in looking over these books, which amount to a hundred or a hundred and fifty volumes, I find his marks in nearly all of them; showing that in the intervals of labour he had beguiled himself in this way.

"Sometimes, on some hot day in August, I would find him at his table with his coat off, toiling away at his work. One day in particular, I remember, he had been for several hours considering a most difficult passage, and as I entered he threw down his pen saying, with a glow upon his face that I shall never forget, 'Well, this is the most delightful and exciting occupation that I can conceive of, it is better than any novel that I ever read.'

"It was just this exalted delight that stimulated him in all his work. At times this spirit would flag; and I have known him to cease from writing for two or three days, spending the time in walking the streets, or looking over the volumes in some of the libraries; and then the work would suddenly begin again with new ardour.

"The table at which he wrote, was generally placed at a window in my study looking out upon one of the noisiest streets in the city, but he has often told me, that when engaged in writing, he was absolutely deaf to the noise of cars and omnibuses that were continually passing. In Princeton, while preparing his subject, I have seen thirty commentaries open before him at once. But in New York he would have nothing but his Hebrew Bible and Greek Testament: and I have never seen him use a Lexicon at these times. I once asked him, 'How can you get along without your commentaries on these difficult points?' He answered, 'I know what they all have said.'

"On one occasion he was talking to me about some most obscure point in a passage, mentioning the different explanations that had been given of it, and stating the reasons why he considered them all unsound, when suddenly he said, 'I have it!' and seizing his pen, wrote down a clear and natural explanation of the doubtful passage.

"He never put pen to paper on the Lord's day; never even read on subjects connected with the work in hand: but employed his time in reading hymns and devotional works, and while in New York attended church three times a day. He heard all the ministers then settled here, prominent and obscure, but I never heard him once make an unfavourable criticism. One Sunday, coming in from church, he said, 'I heard Mr. ——, preach on the First Psalm: he used my exposition very fully; that is what I like; that is what I write my commentaries for."

Among his many ardent admirers was the Rev. Paul Eugene Stevenson, of Paterson, N. J., who has kindly contributed the following genial account of the last interview he ever had with him.

"On the evening preceding the morning of my departure, he had told me, of his own accord, that he meant to take a trip and visit me at my house. As I rose, with a lamp in my hand, to retire, and standing near the door of his study was about to bid him good-night, he said, 'Well; the docket is not yet exhausted: we will take it up again: this is only an adjournment.' 'Yes,' I replied, carrying out his pleasant figure, 'Adjourned, to meet at the house of the Rev. Mr. ———, at ———!' 'Agreed!' was his animated answer. How little we know of the future. How, little I thought, when greeting him in the Synod and at once noticing how gray he had grown, that he was whitening and ripening for a near translation to the society of heaven!"

The new year opened with vernal softness. The laborious city pastor reckoned these spring-like days among his choicest mercies. He, too, was nearing his goal, which he was destined to reach before the blazing chariot of his younger brother was wrecked in mid course.

On the 17th of January, Dr. Addison Alexander preached for his brother James in the morning, and Dr. James Alexander for his brother Samuel in the afternoon. The brothers James and Addison sat together in the Nineteenth street pulpit. The former of these records that he felt the solemnity of sitting in the pulpit with one brother in the morning and with the other in the afternoon. He also gave vent to a wish or sigh, that he could preach with more simplicity and nature —less of the conventional, less regard for rule, less care for criticism, less notice of the literary element, less regard for custom, more as Calvin, as Luther, as Paul preached. "As life runs on," he says, "I feel the seriousness of my situation as a minister, but oh, how little improvement! Oh, my ascended Lord and Master! be pleased to anoint me afresh for my ministry, send me some new and special grace, and cast me not aside as a useless instrument: for Christ's sake. Amen."

This fear was becoming an increasing anxiety to him. He had a dread of growing old and worthless, and of being incapacitated for the service of his Master.

Dr. Addison Alexander spent New Year's day, and several days succeeding, in New York.

This is his entry for Saturday, January the 2d.

"Wrote (at 238 Fourth avenue) on Matt. ii. 1-4. At night went with J. A. and S. D. A. to the Thalberg Festival at the Academy of Music. Heard several pieces of Beethoven performed by the orchestra, solos by Thalberg, Vieuxtemps, Formes, Caradori, D'Angri, and Brignoli, and Mozart's Requiem by the choir and orchestra. Lodged at the Clinton Place Hotel."

On the 4th, he lodged at the Dey Street House.

On the 5th, he was in his place in the lecture-room, making his class acquainted with the Persian, Macedonian, and Hasmonean dynasties, and in his study reading Calvin and Hetherington.

It was my privilege, from the autumn of 1855 to the spring of 1858, to attend the regular instructions of Dr. Addison Alexander in the Seminary, and it gives me pleasure to testify to the singular union of impartiality and kindness which marked his treatment of me. His lectures on Biblical and Church History delighted and stimulated his classes to a degree that I could hardly exaggerate. The only objection they ever raised to his plans was their excessive and bewildering diversity; and I once signed and presented a round-robin requesting him to adhere to one of them to which the class had become accustomed. This he received with complacent courtesy, and pursued the scheme suggested.

During the early months of the spring of 1858, he was lecturing to different classes on the Gospels and on Apostolic History, and on Scottish Church History (using Hetherington as a text-book); reading books in various languages, including Swedish and Portuguese, on Matthew, and many more on Church History and philology; writing some on Matthew; reading such books as Middleton's Cicero, St. Simon's Memoirs, Hansard's Debates, Mirkhoud in Persian, Fürst's smaller Hebrew lexicon, the Koran in Arabic, with Maricci, Coverdale, and Jonathan, a good deal in German, and unknown quantities in English books; besides roaming over an indefinite number of periodicals and pamphlets in various languages. Among his linguistic studies were parts of Wilkinson's Greek Testament (London, 1855) and of the 4th edition of Liddell & Scott's lexicon (Oxford, 1855); also parts of dictionaries in Latin, German, Dutch, Flemish, French, and Persian. He perused for the second time a number of writers on Mark, with a view to his introductory. The book he most loved to talk about at this time was the "Voyage and Shipwreck of St. Paul," by Smith of Jordanhill; which helped him greatly in his commentary, and excited his admiration as the performance of one who was at once a scholar and a nautical expert. He also read a great deal in many works on *einleitung*, and especially archæology.

This grand sweep of research in many fields and various languages was continued with but slight intermission, except where interrupted by illness, to the day of his death; and was made to bear mightily upon his proper work of Biblical instruction.

The mind of a strong and healthy man, of good parts and many acquirements, would, it is likely, be sometimes baffled in the attempt to trace out the innumerable footprints of this extraordinary adventurer through his daily readings.

Yet at the time we have now arrived at, though thin, he

looked well, was full of spring and vivacity, and found time for many a gay bout with his friends and many a peal of hearty laughter.

I find him in the month of February writing in his commentary on the First Gospel, and enchanted with Erasmus's Paraphrase of the Gospels, which he pronounces to be " more than the Life of Christ by Cicero." This he does in the following striking letter to his brother in New York:

" PRINCETON, Feb. 20, 1858.

" MY DEAR BROTHER:

" I am slowly advancing with St. Matthew. The reading is delightful: the writing, less so. The richest treat of all, when I have fagged through every commentary (Pool's included), is to read the exquisite paraphrase of Erasmus, which is more than the Life of Christ by Cicero. There is a classicality, without a tinge of modern affectation, that is perfectly delicious as to style; and then the taste, the sense, the elegant insinuation of the finest exegetical ideas, without one violation of the narrative or periphrastic form! In depth and orthodoxy, he is, of course, not Calvin, but neither Calvin nor anybody else, before or after, could have made such a paraphrase. It ought to be used as a Latin classic in our schools and Presbyterial examinations. I know not how much of my admiration is occasioned by the printer; as my copy is from Froben's press, and dated 1535. How much is crowded into this one sentence as the exemplary design of Christ's temptation: '*Vicit illum Christus ut nobis ostenderet vici posse et vincendi rationem; docuit nobis; vicit non sibi per nos eundem victurus.*' What a lesson this would furnish on the forms of 'vinco;' and how truly antique is the lusus verborum! Now, for a sample of rhetorical embellishment, but exquisitely simple—speaking of what follows our Lord's baptism, Desiderius saith: 'NON MEMINIT BETHLEHEM, NON REPETIT NAZARETH, NON REDIT AD MATREM AUT NUTRICEM, SED IMPETU RAPTUQUE SPIRITU VETERUM PROPHETARUM EXEMPLOQUE MORUM DESERTA PETIT.' Still better is the following on Christ's coming to John's baptism: '*Per medias peccatorum turmas is qui solus ommium nullâ peccati labe contactus fuerat, imo qui solus tolleret peccata mundi velut peccator, adit Joannem ad baptismum: flagitat qui solus baptismum sanctificat.*' And again, in answer to the question why he underwent the rite at all: '*sic baptizatus est, ut circumcisus, ut purificatus in templo cum matre, ut flagel-*

latus, ut crucifixus, nobis haec omnia passus est non sibi.' Nothing strikes me more than his simple and perspicuous constructions. which are low enough for any school-boy to parse, and yet too high for any pedagogue to imitate. I admire, also, his entire freedom from the late Dutch and German affectation of avoiding scriptural expressions when scriptural ideas are to be conveyed. He never calls baptism tincture in a sacred font, nor uses any of those hideous elegancies which Kuinoel, et id genus omne, choke you with on every page. Should this 'cram' have the same effect, I plead your own example in excuse, as I have often been refreshed with the overflowings of your recent lectures. (Lesen nicht Vorlesung.) I shall be glad to follow you in your St. Simonian reminiscences. I fear you will not find the Abbé Le Dieu quite so racy. But then you have the Seneschal de Joinville yet before you—that naïve but noble knight who told St. Louis he would rather commit thirty mortal sins than have the leprosy.

"To the Rev. JAMES W. ALEXANDER, D.D."

CHAPTER XXXI.

We may well pause here and take a look backwards and forwards. The half century covered by the career I am sketching was now almost complete. The intellectual labours of Dr. Alexander had been interrupted only during his journeys from home, and not always then. He had been scarcely ever ill, and his zeal and capacity for work had been such as to excite wonder in the breasts of his most accomplished pupils, and indeed all who came near him. His talents were singular and commanding. Versatility and mobility of mind were the law of his being. His attainments were by this time so numerous, varied, exact, and thorough, and his readiness in using them was so remarkable, that I know not in what terms to speak of them, and am glad to believe this will not be expected of me. He was withal an humble, pious, childlike worshipper of the man Christ Jesus, and had laid all the trophies of his far-sought learning at His feet. Enough, perhaps, has already been said on these points for effect upon the mind of the inquisitive reader, but I desire to accumulate the evidence.

His harsher qualities, if they may be called such, were at the time we have now reached much softened and toned down, and if not in all respects so dazzling a character as in the days of his youth and early manhood, he was a more simple-hearted and lovable one. But it could not be denied that with this change there was also observable a diminution of his wonderful physical strength, though not in the vivacity of his animal spirits. There was the old light in his eye, and the bees, according to the pleasing fancy of the Greek, still visited his lips; but his complexion, though still delicate, and in moments of excitement tinged with colour, was becoming pale, and his immense bulk had been gradually reduced to something like ordinary proportions. Friends who looked back to former periods, when he was in the flush of his golden prime, were shocked at the change in his appearance, though his habitual associates did not take much notice of it. One of his old pupils encountered him on Broadway, and was fairly startled at his looks. His rosy cheek and massive rotundity of person were gone. An eminent physician and distinguished professor of medicine has since told me that he saw him about this time and was impressed just in this way. His experience, he says, taught him, moreover, that so marked and steady a decline in weight in one who was naturally corpulent, sadly betokened some grave organic lesion. The diagnosis was not erroneous, as events have since proved.

The incautious student was now very near the bottom of the hill, but though he sometimes suspected that all was not well with him, he did not seem to know it. He toiled on as earnestly and uninterruptedly as ever. Little did he think, in the midst of his fascinating study labours, that they were to be so soon abruptly suspended and then merged in the active and ceaseless rest of heaven!

Professor Jacobus and Dr. T. V. Moore have much to say, the one of "his Napoleonic rapidity" in the recitation-room, and the other of his magnetic delivery in the pulpit. The latter gives us the following description (which he derived from another) of his manner of preaching. Speaking of his sermons, he writes:

"A distinguished minister of our church who heard one of them ("The Word of God is not bound") said he seemed to him in the discourse, like an immense locomotive rushing along and laying its own track as it ran."*

* An anonymous writer, from Owensboro', Kentucky, in the Free Christian Commonwealth for Dec. 17, 1868, in a letter belonging to a series which is entitled "Reminiscences of Princeton," after speaking in the most exalted terms of Dr. Addison Alexander's genius and learning, and power as a preacher and commentator and writer, says of the massive introduction to his first great work: "Although written when comparatively young, his intro-

Accumulation of evidence as to his brilliant talents is no longer wanting. I may, however, call in two or three more witnesses to the stand. The Rev. James Turner Leftwich, of Alexandria, Virginia, a grandson of the celebrated "Father Turner" that burning and shining light in the Presbyterian pulpit of a former day, has furnished the following additional testimony on several points already brought out in these memoirs:

"I heard Dr. Alexander preach only a few times, and though my impressions of him are vivid, still they are of that general character which would impart no interest" to an account of them. "His rapid sentences; his style, flowing lucid as a mountain brook, and yet deep and noiseless as a river; his wonderful expositions, laying the passage open in its interior recesses; his masterly grasp of the inspired thought, in its multitudinous, most delicate, and far-reaching relations; his voice, melting into the inmost souls of his hearers; his affections, kindling at times almost like those of a seraph, the sweep and edge of his appeals: who that has ever had opportunity to know this prince in Israel will ever forget these characteristics of his preaching? The void created by his death will remain long unfilled."

The versatility of the man in everything calling for brightness of mind, mastered knowledge, ready wit, dazzling retort, pathetic or imaginative eloquence, feats of memory or *tours de force* of intellectual genius in any form, has amazed everybody. Of him it could be written as of Buckingham (whom he resembled in nothing else, unless it was his fickle fancies):

"Some of their chiefs were princes of the land;
In the first ranks of these did Zimri stand;
A man so various that he seemed to be
Not one, but all mankind's epitome."

Such encomium is, I think, not extravagant. He verily seemed to know everything. There were a few subjects that he shunned, or treated somewhat cavalierly, and all others he appeared to have mastered. He was like Whewell, in the

duction to his commentary on Isaiah deserves to be ranked among the few great prolegomena of the world."

range of his tastes and his resources. His articles in the Princeton Review are, after all, perhaps chiefly noticeable for the breadth and nicety of the acquisitions without which they could never have been produced, and the consummate ease and good taste with which those acquisitions are made to contribute to the instruction of the reader.

Professor Cameron, of Princeton, gives the following account of a notable day with him in the cars. Hundreds can remember similar conversation.

"There is particularly one day of my intercourse with Dr. Alexander, which is marked with chalk, (*Cressâ ne careat pulchra dies notâ*). This was Sept. the 13th, 1851. Dr. Alexander happened to be at the dépôt, then on the canal bank, and while we were waiting for the arrival of the train, I approached him and asked him the precise meaning of the word *Urevangelium*. He very kindly informed me, comparing it with *Urgeschichte*, &c., and then remarked, 'I observed that you used that word in your recitation the other day: I did not employ it in my lecture!' 'No, doctor,' I replied, 'but you used it in an article which you wrote some time since, upon the Gospel History, and published in the Repertory.' He seemed pleased to find that his students were not satisfied with simply hearing his lectures, but were incited to further investigation. We talked for some little time, until the arrival of the cars. When we entered the train I was about to take a seat in a distant part of the car and was astonished to hear him invite me to take a seat beside him.

"We naturally got upon the subject of Theological Seminaries, European Universities, and American Colleges, the advantages of studying Theology at home and abroad, &c. He gave me an account of his own experience in Germany; the mode of life among the students, which he said, would not generally suit young Americans; compared the German and English Universities, &c. He said he was in Germany only a short time and did not approve much of studying Theology in Germany, and remarked that Dr. Hodge, who had spent two years there, condemned the custom more strongly than he did."

He expressed a very favourable view of the English Universities.

The same gentleman was always well received by him in his study.

"I never went to see him unless for some good reason, and I always remained longer than I intended. As soon as I had despatched the object for which I came, I would rise to leave, but he often requested me to remain, and would keep up the conversation until the last minute. I have frequently stood like a school-boy, holding the knob of the door, unable to get away without rudeness, because he had not finished talking: or he would come and lean against one door-post while I was at the other.

"Sometimes you would find him standing at his little desk, writing rapidly; then again at his table with many books open before him or upon the floor; sometimes seated by the open fire, which he seemed to like when he had a friend to talk to, or at the desk which I think your father gave him, and which, if I mistake not, could be raised or lowered at pleasure.

"I cannot forget the kindly manner, the warm pressure of the hand, the cordial welcome I always received from him, and how he would sit beside the cheerful fire of Cannel coal (I never knew him to use any other fuel), and talk of books, of men, of students, &c."

He must say that in an acquaintance of ten years, and with an opportunity of judging such as students do not generally enjoy, he never found him other than kind and considerate to an unusual degree, putting one completely at one's ease if one were disposed to treat him as one gentleman should and does treat another.

He was never brusque or crusty to those who evidently sought him out from a reasonable motive. A member of his very latest classes* recalls to mind an interview he had with him on the subject of the Reviews of Great Britain. His simple wish was to know the exact status of the London Quarterly at that time. Dr. Alexander immediately begged him to be seated, and proceeded to say that he was paying very little attention to the Reviews, and to give the reason why; and then poured forth, for an hour, the most minute and comprehensive information about all the Reviews, stating the circumstances of their origin, the schools of thought they severally represented, their chief contributors from the beginning, and their past influence. The writer listened in astonishment,

* The Rev. Wm. C. Stitt, of New York, formerly of Maryland

and left fully determined never in future to hesitate to approach the kind professor on any subject on which he wanted light.

A kinswoman writes, that she has often heard a gentleman of great intelligence, who was in the habit of visiting at her house, remark, when Dr. Alexander "was 'carrying on' in such a funny way for the amusement of the children, that he for his own part always felt as if the *mind* of the great scholar was at work upon some profound subject, and only the physical man was at play."

But this was far from being the case. He entered into his recreations with as much heartiness as into his studies.

I remember meeting him myself once in Staunton, and the delight and admiration his visit awakened. One reason of this (which has been faintly hinted above) was his flow of animal spirits, and irresistible glee and drollery. He was certainly, at times, one of the most amusing men in private that has appeared since the days of the incomparable jester of Combe Florey. Yet, unlike the wise wit of Holland House, he never for an instant sank his character as a sincere and dignified minister of Jesus Christ. His unquestioned piety did not forbid a spirit of lightsome and innocent gaiety. The impression his religious character made upon one of his most intelligent visitors was, that it was remarkable for its *depth* and *earnestness*. He seemed to have fathomed, in his own experience, all the practical exercises of the unregenerate and of the regenerate heart. A profound reverence pervaded all his public services, and governed him in all sacred things. He could never tolerate lightness or irreverence, even in remote connection with religious matters. His great circumspection in this respect was the more remarkable, from the fact that his natural disposition turned readily into the channels of wit and humour.

"He gave evidences, especially in his intercourse with children, and in some playful freaks of his pen, which have been preserved by his friends, that he possessed a vein of fancy, which if indulged would have made him distinguished among the most celebrated and popular humourists of the age."

The possession of this rare talent, in such an extrordinary degree, involved, he thinks, the necessity for much self-control, and required the exertion of a strong will and much watchfulness to subdue the disposition to the limited measure in which he indulged it.

> "Some of us who knew and admired his powers in these respects as well as in others, cannot but regret the severe restrictions he imposed, and believe that, without indulging the license of Dean Swift, or even Sydney Smith, he might have left much to enliven and amuse, without detracting from the dignity of his reputation, or from the serious and instructive character of his severer and more learned productions."

But if he did not choose to *print* much of this nature, his common talk at home, with children, and especially with his brother James, and his humorous friend the Trenton pastor, abounded in quips, and jests, happy turns, and pranks of wit, and every sort of delightful, rational fun. The same disposition, as we have seen, occasionally breaks out, and even runs riot, in his familiar correspondence. This is a side of his character that some may not regard with special favour. But it is precisely this union of high intellectual abilities and attainments with a rare vein of *humour*, which has made such reputations as those of Montaigne, Le Sage, and Fuller.

A. A. Rice, M.D., of Wyoming, Ky., observes justly:

> "If you would put the man before the world as he was, it will be but the truth if you say, that for keen wit and genial humour he was surpassed by none, and equalled by few, who were so great as he in other directions."

Joseph Addison Alexander was indeed a Coryphæus of literature and a Mercury of eloquence. And yet

> "A merrier man
> Within the limits of becoming mirth,
> I never spent an hour's talk withal."

Dr. Rice, gives the account which follows of the most elaborate of the thousand-and-one mystifying jokes which Dr. Alexander ever practised upon his friend of Trenton. The document here referred to was lately in my possession; but is of too personal a character to bear publication, though the subject of the amusing portrait once kindly consented that so characteristic a production, and one so full of laughable ingenuity, should be committed to print. The Kentucky writer says:

"The last time I ever saw him, which was at his own house in Princeton in the spring of 1853, he was amusing himself with a little joke upon the Rev. Dr. Hall, of Trenton. Dr. Hall had said that he thought his own name was a very uncommon one, in fact doubting whether there was another man of that name to be found. Upon this Addison undertook to write the 'Life of Hall, with vouchers;' and picking up advertisements from old newspapers, lists of names, catalogues of colleges, &c. &c., which contained the name 'John Hall,' cut them out, pasted them at the bottom of the sheet, and then proceeded to write the Life as upon the supposition that there was only one man John Hall, and that the Rev. John Hall his friend. When he had filled a sheet he would walk into the sitting-room—it used to be his father's study, where the family were sitting—drop the paper on the table, and walk out without a word as to what he left. We would then take it up and enjoy it. I should not be surprised if Dr. Hall had the Life of Hall even now. It was a *jeu d'esprit* well worth preserving."

The same friend communicates the following additional illustration of his droll humours:

"Shortly after his return from Europe, my mother was urging him to give her some account of his travels abroad, which he declined doing at the time, but said that he would write for her a minute and particular account that should leave nothing untold that she could possibly wish to know. A few days afterwards, he sent her a MS. on an immense folio sheet nearly as large as a newspaper, and closely written, in which he commenced with his leaving his father's house in order to go to the post office to get a letter, the reception of which decided the time of his starting for Europe. The whole of the paper was filled, and yet at the close he had got no farther than to the post-office."

The writer of the words given above, who knew Dr. Alexander from a boy (or rather while himself a boy), furnishes still another example of his "whimsicalities." He says:

"Considering his retired mode of life, and the little intercourse he had with the inhabitants of the village, his knowledge of all the little gossip of the place, minute and particular, was perfectly amazing. After our family had moved back to Virginia, a letter was received from Princeton directed to 'The Hon. Matthew C. Rice, care of the Rev. B. H. Rice, D.D.' which we all knew to be in Addison's handwriting, and was without doubt intended for a member of the family who had been from her very infancy a very great favourite of his. It was filled with the sayings and doings of her former companions at Princeton, and such minute accounts of changes, the gossip, and the small talk of the town, as would be most interesting to her and indeed to us all. The doubt would sometimes arise in my mind whether it was not all the creation of his own brain; as it seemed almost an impossibility for him, living as he did, to have learned all that he wrote, even if he had given himself up to that line of inquiry: but on either supposition the letter was a striking evidence of his amazing versatility of talent. This letter ended with a sentence half finished and without signature of any kind. After a few weeks another, came, directed as before, beginning with the rest of the sentence that was left unfinished in the former epistle, and filled with the same sort of news; the very perfection of what a friendly letter ought to be, and ending with the first part of a word. These letters came for some months; and at last he signed at the bottom of the last page a perfectly indecipherable hieroglyphic for a name, and then they came no more. My sister Martha had at one time enough of his writings in this style to make quite a volume; all written for her amusement and edification."

This (which I get from Mr. Cameron) is much like him:

It once befell that they were speaking of an author of high position and no little reputation, who had just published an important work; the professor remarked:

"There is much in it that is valuable, but I would not give a sixpence for *an original* idea of his."

Here is another of his *mots*, which has been preserved by one who was evidently one of his pupils:

His propensity towards facetious and satirical epigram was sometimes indulged in the lecture-room. A writer in one of the late numbers of the Princeton Review is responsible for the following: "Speaking to his class on this theme, (the nature of the office of the ministry) he once said, 'The pastor is sent to feed the flock of Christ, but some men only drive the sheep about and fleece them.'" *

He laughed heartily, but with perfect good nature, at the blunders people sometimes made when trying in vain to be thought learned.

"Any one who recalls the keen sense of the ludicrous displayed in his review of 'Colton on Episcopacy,' published in the Biblical Repertory for 1836, will readily understand his amusement when, as he was preparing for a voyage to Europe, he was asked by a would-be literary man whether he intended to visit *Allgemeine* while in Germany. Dr. A. had heard of the Allgemeine Zeitung, but not of the city where his friend evidently supposed it to be published. He often related the joke with the greatest relish." †

The truth is, he had as much of the spirit of mere *camaradie* as anybody; and was only restrained by diffidence, by odd humour, by long habit, by much work, by deep sorrows, from showing it more generally. When aroused his wit flew like foam-flakes, or like a gay streamer before the wind.

Even the expressions of his unaffected humility were sometimes oddly streaked with wit. The terse point of some of his sayings could not be made finer than it is.

At a time when the Pre-Millennial Advent was exciting unusual interest in the church, one of his former pupils expressed to Dr. Alexander his desire and that of others, that he would take up the discussion of the subject in the Biblical Repertory. "Well," said he, "I have myself been thinking that the Repertory should engage in the discussion: and I have told Dr. Hodge, that if he will break ground, I will follow: for you know, *he frames our constitutions, and we make the laws.*"

* See an article on "The Pastorate for the Times," in the Princeton Review for January, 1868, p. 102.

† I am indebted for this to the Rev. Dr. Hugh N. Wilson, of New Jersey, who was one of Dr. Alexander's most admired pupils in the Seminary, and a member of one of his most enthusiastic private classes in Arabic.

"On another occasion, having heard a rumour that he had discontinued all work upon his commentary on Matthew, I wrote him, inquiring whether this were so, and urging him, in case he had laid aside his work, to resume it. He replied that he had ceased writing because he had lost his zest for the work, and that it had been a maxim with his father (whom he always religiously revered) never to prosecute such work unless *con amore;* that he had prepared a portion of the commentary, and had accumulated large materials for more of it which he would cheerfully hand over to me, to be put in order to be completed by myself. That this offer was made in perfect good faith, I never for a moment doubted; while I regarded it as the most emphatic proof of his humility, that he should deem me fit to finish a work begun by himself. I would as soon have contracted to complete the Cathedral of Cologne, as to finish a commentary begun by such a scholar and such a writer as Addison Alexander. I therefore repeated my solicitations that he would resume his work; and have since had reason to believe that my letters were one means of securing a commentary which, had he written no other, will place him among the very first critics of any age or of any land."

The strange combination of intellectual gifts which has given so great a traditionary, as well as historic, eminence to the name of Joseph Addison Alexander, had its signature upon his rosy face and sparkling eye, and has been discerned, as they at least fancy, by some even in the imperfect engravings that have been made of him. A writer in the "Christian Observer," published in Richmond Va., who is understood to be the Rev. T. W. Hooper, of Christiansburg, in a pleasant description of some of the portraits hanging in his own study, thus hits off that of the Princeton scholar and humourist:

"The next picture is Dr. Addison Alexander. It seems to me that the face is a little too round and full, for my recollection of him—though I never saw him but once; and then the wonderful power of his imagination, and his peculiar aptness of language, and beauty of conception, made me lose sight of everything but the sermon, with whose gushing eloquence I was enraptured. The countenance itself is a study; a riddle; an enigma. At one time, you see the shade that must have rested there when he wrote, 'There is a time, we know not when.' And again there is the merry twinkle, and quaint humour, that must have played there, when, in *Wistar's Magazine*,* I think he called it—he wrote that scathing burlesque on 'Illustrations;' closing with a fictitious tale about some man who proposed to illustrate the Shorter Catechism, but who found an impossibility in discovering an illustration that would suit the first question and answer."

The picture of the elder of the two Alexanders, by the same genial pencil, may well be added.

"The next is James W. Alexander, D.D., one of the kindest, noblest, most benevolent-looking countenances that I ever saw. It does me good to look at him; and I feel as if I would give almost anything to have conversed with him one day. I consider his 'Thoughts on Preaching,' almost invaluable, and his 'Forty Years' Familiar Letters' is certainly one of the most delightfully entertaining and instructive books that I ever read."

This animated and affectionate tribute from a comparative stranger has brought up many cheerful and delightful recollections in the mind of the present biographer; some of them dating back to a very early period in his own life; when the family circle was unbroken; when the hoar hairs and uncertain steps of Dr. Archibald Alexander might be seen at well-known hours near his sash-door, as he muffled himself more closely in his warm cloak and directed his course towards the oratory; when the household all poured into a common room in the evenings, and the happy mirth of the mother of his children could not be restrained, as she turned her soft, liquid eye upon the laughing group, saw her husband shaking in his chair, and listened to the wit, the learning, the acumen, and the harmless jollity of her sons.

Those days have not been succeeded by better ones. The sunshine of that vernal noontide has been invaded by clouds.

* Mr. Hooper has since informed me that he was mistaken (as I had apprized him) in thinking that this piece is to be found in Wistar's Magazine. Upon refreshing his memory, he says that the gentleman from whom he had the account, told him the thing was written by Dr. Addison Alexander, for some magazine or other, under a fictitious signature, and as if from an imaginary town in New Jersey. Nothing could be more in keeping with the habits, or rather the occasional comical fancies, of its reputed author.

The old homestead is changed, and many are dead and gone who once filled it with melodious accents or with honest laughter. The dim picture-gallery, however, still remains, with its evanescent lights and storied walls: and there, in moments of solitary retrospection, memory, with a fond heart but in sober weeds and with light footfall, may walk unobserved and unattended; and, as she sheds those "tears, idle tears," of which the English poet speaks, may renew or forget the sorrows of the present in the sweet vision of the past. At such times, and in such mournfully pleasing occupations,

> "Ante oculos errant domus, * * et forma locorum;
> Succeduntque suis singula facta locis."

There was one who could say of him, "a brother is born for adversity," and that was his own brother James. But he looked to him even more in times of mere perplexity. The sorrowful pastor leaned strongly on the resolute practical wisdom of "Addison," and seldom found it an unsafe dependance. There was no delay and no hesitation in the advice he gave his friends, and he seldom swerved from opinions rendered in this way. One of these was, that it is commonly best for a man to leave home, in order to the attainment of the highest success and usefulness in life. His own case was a peculiar, one but he seemed to think it was a question whether even he might not have achieved more away from the comforts and endearments and restraints of his father's house.

I give below a single but touching evidence of his kindness to his near relatives:

"PRINCETON, Dec. 23d, 1856.

"REVEREND AND DEAR SAM.:

"Please find enclosed my check on Princeton Bank, for fifty dollars, which I hope you will be able to cash without much trouble or expense. Half of the proceeds is to pay for the books I bought of you. Out of the balance, if it were not asking too much of you, I should like to present books to the following individuals:

1. James W. Alexander, Sr.: 2. Elizabeth C. Alexander.: 3. Henry M. Alexander.: 4. Susan M. Alexander.: 5. Henry C. Alexander; and

6. James W. Alexander, Jr., unless (as I suspect) he should prefer a gift in money. If you think so, could you not purchase a gold eagle, put it in a pill box, or wrap it in white paper, as from me? I shall send a picture-book from here to 7. William Alexander; but as it is not very fine, I should like very well to give him something else. I am perfectly aware of the atrocious character of this commission, and astonished at my own audacity in sending it. I would not venture so to do, if I expected to come on during the holidays; but before we meet, I hope you will be over it in one way or another. For my last word is that, if you choose, you may omit the elders, and get something for the juniors, *i.e.*; H. C. A., J. W. A., and W. A.; or for H. and J.; as W. has a book already. I do wish you could find some book for the first, that would be permanently useful and yet ornamental. 'Excuse my liberty,' and accept the compliments of the season, from,

"Yours affectionately,

"J. A. ALEXANDER."

P. S.—Pick up some nice book at your leisure, and accept it for yourself, both as commission and a Christmas-box. If too late for Christmas, you can do something before New Year.

If there was one quality of which he was little suspected, it was affectionate softness. But there are those who can say much in favour of an opinion on this point that is the reverse of the common one. Thus Dr. Hall writes:

"I have often been affected by the *tenderness* of his nature. I think he must have made an effort to repress a strong, underlying, disposition in that direction. It sometimes came out in his preaching, in his sentiments, but particularly his tones. But it was more obvious in private. His sensibilities, I think, were often moved when it was not suspected. In public, in compulsory or official intercourse with men, he may have appeared to assume dignity—perhaps tinged with pride; especially with presuming, forward, conceited people; but I am sure he had a tender heart."

He never did anything by halves. He sends one of his acquaintance a trunk full of books to read, and offers to lend him his whole library. He gets one of his students, who was poor, an admirable place where he could maintain himself and still keep up his studies, and this without solicitation on the part of the needy scholar. He gives up his precious time to another, to sympathize with him and encourage him in a season of mental depression. He offers another to give him the benefit of his own name and emoluments; promises to help him, and begs him to finish a commentary which he himself had projected (and actually begun) on a scale and plan that set at defiance all efforts of imitators or followers. He turns over to his able colleague all the advantage of his own previous researches in Hebrew grammar and oriental philology. These are but illustrations of a characteristic trait of self-abnegation.

But it was the *manner* in which these and a thousand like things were done, that showed the sensitive and noble-hearted Christian gentleman. It was the refined courtesy; the exquisite way in which he avoided the *appearance* of doing a good turn while in reality he did it; the almost prescient sympathy and humanity of feeling by which he knew beforehand what would be most agreeable to the feelings of his friend; it was these things, that proclaimed him to the chosen number who were the recipients of his kind words, or the objects of his still kinder actions, to be not merely the man of generous impulses, but also the man of enlarged New Testament benevolence and the possessor of a warm, constant, tender, though manly and uncringing, human heart.

He had an open hand for all who were in real want. The number of his silent gratuities will never be known. He observed carefully the Bible injunction as to ostentatious giving. We know enough, however, of his kind offices, to enable us to pronounce with confidence on his disposition. He was a true friend to the poor, and to those whose "heart was not haughty." He befriended such both in word and in deed. He reserved his invectives for the wicked, and commonly withheld his rebukes and his sarcasm from those whom he did not consider presumptuous, absurdly or culpably ignorant, foolishly conceited, offensively obtrusive, or arrogantly proud.

"In Israel's courts ne'er sat an Abethdin
With more discerning eyes, or hands more clean;

Unbribed, unsought the wretched to redress,
Swift of despatch, and easy of access."

With regard to his feelings towards those whom he loved to associate with on intimate terms, the testimony of Dr. Hall, of Trenton, will be accepted as that of one who knew him well in all his moods, and who knew him in his lighter moods better, perhaps, than any other man not of his own immediate kin. Dr. Hall writes:

"I can only answer from my own experience, that I always felt the most absolute confidence in his uniform sincerity, and could ask him for any favour with perfect assurance that he would do everything in his power to meet my wishes, If I had not discerned *affection* in his character in this respect, I could not have felt the freedom I did. But without any protestations or professions from him, I felt all the time that he was interested in my welfare; and I have more than once accidentally discovered that he had been contriving to bring about measures that he supposed would gratify me. I remember his offering to lend me his whole library as I might need it, and actually sending me on one occasion a trunk filled with the choicest works for my entertainment: and so he would have continued to do as long as I desired it. He was more disposed to rally his friends than flatter them; and my knowledge of this trait caused me great surprise as well as gratification when I received from him a note of commendation which must have been suggested purely by the impulse of friendship."

He despised the shows and hypocrisies of affected worldly manners. He was not perpetually telling people that he loved them, or signing himself their affectionate or devoted friend. He acted on the maxim of Solomon, that "a man that hath friends must show himself friendly." Sometimes in moments of depressed spirits, or of sudden pique or irritation, he would accost his best friends rather roughly. But who so eager as he to repair his fault, and to "render unto" them "seven-fold into their bosom."

"His mercy e'en the offending crowd will find;
For sure he comes of a forgiving kind."

Nothing could exceed the assiduity of his attentions if any of his friends were sick, or the sincerity of his concern if any of them were "nigh unto death." When any one of them lay upon the bier, he commonly remained silent; but the gravity of his demeanour, and the solemnity of his public instructions, could not fail to impress one with the conviction that his sympathies were in the house of mourning. He would usually under such circumstances absent himself more stringently than ever from all companionship; sometimes locking the door of his room. The reader has not forgotten his stanzas on the little fatherless girl, which are enough to bring the water into eyes of marble; or his heart-searching exercises on occasion of the death of little Harriet Patton; or the wild wail of pathos that came bursting up out of his heart, as he thought of his own preservation and loneliness in a foreign land, and "wept when he remembered" the freshly-sodded grave of poor Rezeau Brown.

It would be an error to suppose that these feelings were not most deeply felt, and most strongly marked, in cases of affliction in his father's or brother's household. Never shall I cease to remember his appearance and manner as he entered my own sick chamber one morning, and presented me with the first copy of his "Mark" that had left his hand. That copy is still on my shelves; and on the fly-leaf are inscribed, in his bold, round handwriting, the letters of my name, the words "from the author," and the date, Sept. 7, 1858. He sat down by me and talked to me in tones of delightful sweetness, almost as if I was a child again. While thus engaged, he was startled by a peculiar catarrhal cough from the bed, and shrank back in visible alarm, and his voice trembled with a species of indescribable sympathy and commiseration. It was evident to me, even then, that he thought my situation far more dangerous than it really was; and it occurred to me that his mind was roving over the seas in search of his absent brother, who might presently be called upon to bear the tidings of another sorrow.

Ah! how much might be added in the way of description

of Dr. Alexander's pleasing relations with his own cherished household, were it not for the natural feelings of those of them who are yet living. It is right, however, for me to say, that the family of which this noble man and sensitive Christian gentleman was a member, feel a solicitude that I should do no injustice to his remarkable domestic character, and a jealousy with regard to this, lest it should be overlooked in the setting forth of his purely intellectual parts and even of his general moral disposition. He was, from the very nature of the case, so little known in this respect, as to give rise to such a fear in the minds of those who knew him best and loved him most heartily. The impression is a common one that he was the same recluse in the bosom of his family that he was to the world. This is a total and most injurious mistake. I have already said enough of his impulsive generosity to his near kindred and to some of his friends; of the delight he took in bestowing upon others, and of how much of this he did secretly and quietly, with so noiseless a movement, indeed, often as to baffle observation. But I have not said much (and it would be hard for anyone to say too much) of the unceasing pleasure he took in the company of those whose presence graced and brightened his hearth at home; of his gentleness and goodness to them, interest in them, and affection for them. I know not in what strong language to tell how tender and sympathetic he was in even the petty household cares of his family. He kept what he called the "Two-Penny Book;" and expressly, if not simply, for the amusement of the children; in which for several years he was in the habit of writing daily, and in which he recorded the name of every visitor who entered the house and every event of the slightest interest connected with the little fortunes of the inmates. One who was at one time, and for years together, a recipient of his personal kindness, lately had an opportunity of looking over this old volume, so full of memories, and was amazed and deeply affected to find the pains he had taken in teaching some of the junior members of the family circle. There it was in black and white: poetry and history, and languages, and what not!

And this, too, in addition to all his other burdens and recreations! His delight in imparting knowledge was truly wonderful; and was only exceeded by his fondness for acquiring it in the first instance.

One who seems to have pierced the "crust of reserve" which lay upon the surface of his manner, and found out the perennial fountain of good feeling and light-hearted humour which was ever bubbling up beneath it, has said that in him he discovered a veritable and striking confirmation of the proverb that, "as ointment and perfume rejoice the heart, so doth a man's friend by hearty counsel." His own affection for his person was quite as great as his awe at his achievements, and in grateful and fitting words he writes:

"My heart always wakes at the remembrance of his genial, instructive conversation, and his loving kindness towards me, so much above any merit or claim, from the beginning of my occasional intercourse with him to the end."

He joyfully adds his humble tribute to the memory of one of the noblest men and Christian philosophers who, by their love of truth and consecration of their powers to the Saviour, have ever adorned the world.

"After leaving the Theological Seminary at Princeton, I saw him seldom, as my professional path lay, most of the time, far away; but always with increasing interest and profit: till, all of a sudden, we heard the affecting news that, after struggling with an insidious and capricious disease longer than any of us had thought, he had laid aside his pen; gathered up his robes; stepped into his chariot; and with a sublime faith in the Captain of his salvation, had gone up to his Home on high." *

* The Rev. Paul E. Stevenson, Paterson, N. J.

CHAPTER XXXII.

The journal for the new year opens with an interesting allusion to that grandest of even Latin obituaries, the concluding words of the Agricola of Tacitus. Many were soon to join in doing similar, though not equal, honours to the memory of the cis-Atlantic admirer of this first of Roman historians.

"Jan. 1. Lectured to the Seniors on the Presbyterian Church of Ireland, abridged from chapters of Reid, which I read yesterday, and my own paraphrase of Kurtz. Finished the Agricola of Tacitus, which I have been reading slowly and with great delight since Dec. 14. The conclusion has an epic grandeur, clothed in the severest prose, and the closing prophecy is made sublime by its complete fulfilment.

"Feb. 28. Lectured on the Apolcaypse (closing the short course begun Jan. 24). Double lectures to the Juniors (Ezra, Nehemiah, Esther, Chronicles), closing the long course begun Sept. 7.

About the beginning of the year, he procured a change of chairs in the Seminary, for reasons which are thus fully and ably presented by the professor who succeeded to his duties in Church History:

"He never," writes Dr. McGill, "seemed to me satisfied with Church History as a department of labour; although its endless variety of methods, in periodology &c., one might have supposed, would suit well the incessant pleasure with which he pursued new plans. Intensely active as he was in changing methods, he preferred to have an immoveable centre, and make all his changes at the circumference; to study one thing, ever the same and ever certain, and range with his diversity from side to side, only to show new beauties, and new brightness of evidence, in what was of record by the inspiration of the Holy Ghost himself.

"Hence, about the beginning of the year 1859, he proposed to me

36*

that Church History should be reunited with Church Government in my department, and that a distinct chair of New Testament Literature be assigned to him, if the Board of Directors and the General Assembly would sanction it. His only hesitancy in urging such an arrangement was the appearance of devolving on me a disproportioned amount of work in the Seminary. Mine, was the apprehension that the students and the Church at large would regret to see any department on which he had entered with his strength, relinquished to any other man. This interchange of views on the subject seemed to terminate the matter at that time. But as the end of the term approached, he spoke of it again; with greater solicitude counselled with all his colleagues and with leading friends of the institution; and at length it was arranged by the Faculty to submit the question to the Board of Directors. The Board approved with entire unanimity, and the General Assembly ordered the change to be made. After the Directors had agreed to this measure, and just before the Assembly met, and while he was yet apprehensive that opposition might be made, he sent me a very long letter,* which I greatly prized, and have kept with carefulness."

He now encloses to Dr. Hall a poem, "written by Sir Knight John K. Hall, of the Boston Encampment, read by Sir Knight Wyzeman Marshall, the tragedian, in a manner which elicited great applause," with the following letter:

'Noble and Gallant Knight, Most Excellent Sir John:

"Allow me to congratulate you on your happy revival of the old alliance between minstrelsy and knighthood. If your prowess is but equal to your lyric inspiration, there is not a windmill that can stand before you for a moment. But although my primary design in writing was to offer you the tribute of my humble but appreciative admiration, I do not deny that I have also an eye to business, and respectfully suggest that if you, or any of your knights or squires, should be so unhappy as to soil your chivalrous costume, it could nowhere be renewed more skilfully or cheaply than by the undersigned, who has recently removed to the great West to carry on this interesting business.

* The letter is one of preëminent ability and friendliness, but turns wholly on imaginary objections to his wishes, and is omitted here on account of its extreme length.

DETROIT STEAM DYEING ESTABLISHMENT.

NO. 16 CONGRESS STREET, EAST.

A. C. ALEXANDER would most respectfully intimate that, more fully to accommodate the wants of the patronizing public, and his large increase of business, he has adopted the improved facility which STEAM gives to the Art of DYEING, having recently fitted up for that purpose. He now *dyes by steam* every description of Silks, Satins, Velvets, Crapes, and Merinos, producing the most brilliant colors and best style of finish that every article will admit of. Shawls of every variety dyed and cleaned.

GENTLEMEN'S CLOTHES CLEANING.

A. C. A. would remind the public that he dyes, cleans, and repairs coats, pants, and vests, restoring the faded lustre so as to improve the appearance of such garments.

"Let me add that the C. in the advertiser's name is cabalistic, like the K. in yours. I would also beg leave to make you acquainted with my friend Smith's "Mammoth Rectifying Establishment," Chicago, where any of your order who have mammoths to be rectified can have it done on the lowest terms, and at the shortest notice. Indeed, I know of no other place where a mammoth can be rectified at all.

"Accept my salutations,

"A. C. ALEXANDER.

"SIR J. K. HALL, KT. May 30, 1859."

The following epistle he wrote to his brother James, who was then in Virginia:

"NEW YORK, June 18th, 1859.

"MY DEAR BROTHER:

"I arrived here on Friday evening on the very day, and almost the very hour, which I had fixed for my return before I started. I have had a very pleasant journey of I don't know how many thousand miles, describing a great circle from New York to New York through Boston, Portland, Quebec, Montreal, Toronto, Buffalo, Detroit, Chicago, Springfield, St. Louis, Vincennes, Cincinnati, Columbus, Pittsburg, Harrisburg, Easton, Somerville, and Elizabethport. I have now daguerreotyped upon my memory a number of new cities, with a good deal of the intervening country. I am as perfectly at home in the streets of Chicago, St. Louis, Cincinnati, and Pittsburg, as in those of Philadelphia or New York. By keeping a look-out for the peculiar features of each new place, I have given each its own physiognomy and countenance. With the great West generally, I was much impressed. The vastness of the distances, and traversed in a short time, and the rapid succession of large cities, have left a singular effect upon my memory and imagination. I am greatly stricken with the freshness, large-soulness and *savoir vivre* of that Western world. Travelling conveniences are in the first style, and the intensity of competition carries everything of that sort to perfection. The physique of the pure Western man is certainly imposing, with a high average of intelligence and spirit, and a curiosity before which Yankeedom must pale its ineffectual fires. Cincinnati is almost a model of a perfect city, although not so picturesque as Pittsburg, which, moreover, is a little London. During my absence, I have read a volume of St. Simon (a most admirable road-book) and Arnoldi on Matthew; the last work which I wish to read before writing, which I think of beginning here next week. I hope to hear of your improved health, and desire to be remembered to Elizabeth and Willy, Dr. and Mrs. and Miss C.

"In haste, yours,

"J. A. A."

Dr. Alexander, if not vacillating or fickle (as was often said to his disparagement), was, as is well known to those who have glanced over these memoirs, amusingly whimsical. As has been well observed by one who understood his character:

> "This love of change and variety in everything but the rock itself on which he rested with childlike and unchanging simplicity, extended to his recreations as well as methods of study and teaching. His vacations of study, during the recess of Seminary exercises, would hardly ever find him resorting to the same place, in summer travelling. He would turn up, sometimes in Canada, sometimes New England, sometimes Virginia, and sometimes, though seldom, in the far West. Nothing but old doctrines and old friends could he adhere to with immutable interest and fondness." *

One of the most remarkable of these journeys was made this year, during the summer recess, when, as we shall presently see more fully, he described 'his great circle,' having New York as his centre, over the wide area which includes the principal cities of the West, and of the British dominions beyond the St. Lawrence. His correspondence with the friends

* Dr. McGill.

at home, and with a Southern newspaper, enables us to tell over some of the incidents of this tour.

I append a fragment of another contribution he made that year to the Staunton Spectator. It was written from Canada, describing graphically a military parade on the Heights of Abraham, and a number of other matters. Following this is a scrap of a letter, going more into particulars, and giving an account of a picturesque interview with a Crimean soldier.

"What makes Quebec particularly interesting is, that it presents to you a glimpse of France and England at the same time, in a proximity and combination which has no existence in the mother-countries; the mass of the people being French Canadians, the under stratum Irish of the lowest class and character, the upper stratum English of the highest quality and cultivation. As a general rule, and one with few exceptions, if you see a genteel person or company, even at a distance, you will hear them on approaching you speak English; if squalid or in tatters, you will hear the Irish brogue; if respectable but odd and antique looking, you will certainly hear French. I tried this rule a hundred times and almost always with the same result. This contrast and confusion of the races is presented in a still more striking manner by two very numerous classes representing them respectively, the soldiery and priesthood. You cannot take a few steps or look out of the window without seeing upon one side the rusty black petticoats of the Catholic clergy, and on the other the bright and spotless uniform of the British army. . . . . . .

"I was fortunate in being at Quebec on Wednesday, the day fixed for the weekly trooping of the column, when I saw a fine review on the noble esplanade. But the next day I had an unexpected and still richer treat, that of following the regiment to the Heights of Abraham and seeing it drilled in sight of the monumental column there inscribed with these words, 'Here Wolfe died victorious, 1759.' This exercise included a lecture by the Colonel on the new system of drill, the whole of which I was enabled to hear, partly by the singularly clear enunciation of the speaker, partly by the zeal of my young French cab-driver, who kept close upon the horses' heels, and once or twice barely saved me from the ignominious defeat experienced by Mr. Pickwick."*

* From the "Staunton Spectator," June 14th, 1859.

Speaking of Quebec, he writes:

"Giving an order for my baggage, I hurried back to the parade ground, and saw the 39th Regiment file into it, to the sound of Bellini's, 'Ah, perché non posso adiarti,' from a splendid band. The inspection and parade were the same as at Montreal, but with surroundings far more interesting. Say what you will, there is a charm in listening to such music, and witnessing such movements, by a part of the finest army and in sight of the strongest citadel and noblest river in America. The parade-ground is an extensive and long green, of the richest, most luxuriant grass I ever saw, with an elevated terrace upon two sides, surmounted by a high stone wall with embrasures, cannon, bombs, and heaps of ball, all ready for use. The weather had been perfect ever since I left Montreal, and the sight of the surrounding country was more like the vale of Zurich than any other scene I could remember. Instead of a wild, barren waste, such as I used to associate with Quebec, you see a beautifully rolling country, sloping up to green hills, and beyond them to blue mountains, dotted all over with villas, cottages, farm-houses, skirts of wood, bounded by the glorious St. Lawrence, which is worthy of its office as the mouth-piece of so many inland seas, and the quaint and picturesque old town, which looks larger than many greater places, because you see so much of it at once.

"After the parade I lingered to converse with the sentry on the rampart near me, who answered all my questions very civilly. When I asked where the regiment was stationed last, he said in the Crimea, and I then observed his silver medal inscribed 'Sebastopol.' He said they had been fourteen months without beds, and gave me some account of the French and Russian armies. The musicians buried the dead. All the musicians are enlisted soldiers under the same discipline. The regiment at Montreal (the 17th) was also in the Crimea.

"It takes six months to make them perfect in the exercise. The sentry told me that at half-past three, I could see a much finer sight in the same place—the drill of the regiment in various manœuvres. Of this I should otherwise have known nothing. Going back to lunch, (on soup and cold meat,) I returned to the esplanade, and saw a sight which I cannot describe, except as the continual breaking up of the body into parts and its sudden reconstruction, the men running at full speed across the ground, dropping on their knees, lying in the grass, then jumping up again, forming into squares, wheeling into column, all by word of command and sound of trumpet, no other music being audible except at their a rival and departure. Meantime, the terrace and the railing on the other sides were crowded with spectators. I stood awhile by two young ladies with the inevitable round hat and two volumes of the Oxonian. Twice, as I leaned upon the fence, it was completely lined upon the other side by red-coats on their knees with their guns pointing through the rails directly at us. After their manœuvres had continued some time, a superior officer, covered with decorations, who had not been present, came to the fence and made a motion with his hand to some one on the ground, whereupon they immediately defiled (or whatever means 'marched off') in single column, five abreast, about eight hundred in all, the officers in the line with the men, except one at the head, and one in the rear, both on horseback, and a single soldier, who shut and locked the big gate, and deposited the key at a house near by, perhaps that of Col. Monroe. This march of the whole body down St. Ann's street to the barracks, was one of the most striking sights I saw, and none the less because so different from what we commonly think martial or military. I have said before that they are trained to march with a firm but light step and without anything like stamping, and to walk without the least approach to swagger—even when off duty. Upon this occasion they carried their guns horizontally with perfect ease, and walked with a sort of swaying motion, indicating freedom from restraint, though perfectly alike in the whole mass, and therefore the result of drilling and long practice. The effect of this poetry of motion was enhanced by the absence of all music, except a gentle tapping on the small drums at the head of the column, which was only audible enough to regulate the movement of the body."

There is a tender allusion to his brother in a letter headed "Buffalo and Detroit," which appeared in a Southern newspaper, July 5th, 1859, and from which I take the subjoined brief extract. His fears were excited by a friendly inquiry from a stranger, who stopped him on his way to dinner. This was at Buffalo. These qualms of affectionate anxiety were however, soon measurably abated, and succeeded by feelings of a very opposite character. The occasion of these new emotions was a sudden and startling demand by an official for his self-identification. Having just referred to something which appeared to him striking proof that he was once more in his native land, he proceeds to say:

"Another indication of the same kind was my being stopped as I went in to my dinner by a gentleman, unknown to me, who under the form of an inquiry, no doubt prompted by the kindest motives, quite destroyed my appetite, that is, so much as had survived the tooth-ache, by suggesting painful apprehensions as to one of my nearest relatives and dearest friends, which were not partially relieved until I had hurried, after swallowing a mouthful, to the post-office, guided and accompanied by a very kind countryman, who had been present at the previous interrogation, and now eagerly continued it, while at the same time he most civilly escorted me as far as his own place of business and then pointed out the rest of the way to the post-office, a fine stone edifice, containing also the United States Courts and custom-house. I here obtained comparative relief from my anxieties, but at the same time entered on a new adventure, more agreeable as past than present, which may serve to entertain some of your readers, few of whom, I reckon, have had occasion to go through the bewildering and mystifying process of *self-identification.*

"Having changed my purpose since I left New York, and now intending to go westward, I had written from Toronto to a member of a well-known New York firm, with which I have intimate relations, requesting him to send by mail to Buffalo a cheque on some bank there for a sufficient sum to carry out my new plan, or a circular letter of credit available in that and other western cities which I thought of visiting. The form in which my correspondent answered my request, was no doubt better than those I had proposed, and not at all the cause or even the occasion of my subsequent experience, as either of the others would have equally required the awful solemnity of *self-identification.*

"The same letter which allayed momentarily the fears already mentioned, brought me a certificate of deposit in a celebrated bank of the great commercial city, with an intimation that it would be cashed by any bank in Buffalo, or any other place *where I could be identified.*

Choosing to undergo this fearful operation with the least delay, and also needing an immediate augmentation of my travelling resources, I crossed the street to the nearest bank, the hour of closing being now at hand, with new sensations partly owing no doubt to a change of weather which had suddenly become oppressive, but in part likewise to the fearful consciousness that I was for the first time to be put upon the proof of my identity, and an accompanying half-delirious doubt of that important fact upon my own part, solaced only by the query, which I urged upon myself as I ascended the bank-steps, 'If I am not myself, who can I be?'

"I wish to be distinctly understood, that the officials of this bank were as polite and kind as possible, and even added thirty minutes to their ordinary business hours for my sole accommodation. But their kindness only aggravated my bewilderment by being evidently mixed with a tremendous doubt of my *identity*, the awful watchword of this conflict with myself about myself, in which I had enlisted. It was in vain that they professed to think it 'all right,' and made faint advances towards the act of paying down the money. My own doubts, as well as theirs must be solved; and though I had the advantage of a previous acquaintance with the subject of inquiry stretching over half a century, I could not as a rational psychologist or honest man, allow them to regard me as myself, when vague suspicions had arisen in my own mind as to that point. My financial correspondent, warily foreseeing this contingency, for which I was mysely exclusively responsible, had named two friends of his own in Buffalo, to whom I could apply for *identification*. As a drowning man is said to grasp at straws, so I, before abandoning the long-cherished dream of my identity, informed my unknown banking friends of this suggestion. To my great joy both names were familiar. Might they look at my letter? Certainly. And at the envelope and postmark. This increased the mystery; but it was now too late to hesitate. Again they said it must be all right, and again I felt that it was all wrong and insisted upon *self-identification*. I would find the gentlemen referred to. They were not far off. The cashier kindly pointed out their office, and proposed to wait an additional half hour for my return.

"I shall never forget the hot and dusty walk that followed, not so much because of these external inconveniences, as on account of the terrific clouds which overhung my hitherto unquestioned, unassailed identity. I reach the building pointed out, a large and stately one of hewn stone, occupied by banks and offices. Directed by a number of bright signs upon the wall, I climb one flight of stairs and then another. An open door displays one of the names to which my letter had referred me. Its owner is not in, and may not be for several hours. The other referee no longer dwells there.

"I retrace my steps. Again it is pronounced 'all right,' but with an evident and natural misgiving, and again I declare my resolution to take nothing till identified. My feeling during that night of suspense and terror, can be likened only to those of the old woman whose real or fictitious sorrows had harrowed but amused my childhood. But, alas! my case was even worse than hers—I could not say as she did, with a groundless but consolatory faith, 'If I be I, as I do hope I be,

I have a little dog at home and he knows me.' 'Whatever little dog' I may have had 'at home' I certainly had none at the American Hotel in Main Street, Buffalo, and as I read a number of 'All the Year Round,' the dark shadows cast by the early chapters of the 'Tale of two Cities,' were surpassed in density by those which now involved my own identity. I slept, but only to dream of some *alter ego*, or to start murmuring *alter et idem!*

"In the morning I must wait till ten o'clock for the opening of the banks, and another hour for the appearance of my referee, a handsome, courteous gentleman, who instantly went with me to another bank down-stairs, where he repeated to the officers the mystic phrase that it was 'all right.' But here the case assumed, at least to my bewildered mind, a new and awful complication. This kind gentleman was perfectly acquainted with my correspondent, but not at all with me. So far as I knew, he had never seen me, nor I him. How then could he prove my identity, as bearer and receiver of the letter, any more than as payer of the certificate? Before me opened an interminable vista of identifications, at the sight of which my brain had well nigh reeled and staggered. I have only a confused recollection of the question being put to my companion, 'Do you know that this is the right man?' and no recollection at all of his reply.

"After this blank in my memory, the money was paid over, and I bore it off with thanks to my endorser, but with a desperate misgiving that the whole process was a failure after all, and that my paper had been cashed, not because I had identified myself, but because my identification had in some mysterious manner been dispensed with. May no Arcadian denizen of Staunton or Waynesboro', Barterbrook or Fishersville ever experience the pangs of an excruciating, yet abortive effort at self-identification!" *

I have said, in another part of this work, that Dr. Alexander loved both the mystery, the protection, and the amusement that are involved in travelling '*incognito.*' In this trait he greatly resembled King Alfred, and that hero of his early fancy "the good Haroun Al Rashid." As might have been expected, this propensity of the whimsical scholar was often the occasion of much secret mirth, and now and then gave rise to a series of diverting adventures.

* From the Staunton Spectator, of July 5th, 1859. That journal was then edited by J. Addison Waddell and Lyttleton Waddell, Jr.

On his return voyage from Europe, in 1853, he thus made the acquaintance of three fair young Canadians, with whom he subsequently kept up a sort of epistolatory correspondence both in prose and verse, and by whom he was recognized as "A——A" and "THE UNKNOWN." But let him tell the story himself.

"When I last returned from Europe, the discomforts of the voyage were much relieved by the company of three Canadian children, little girls returning home from England with their parents. Before we left the Mersey I had been attracted by their gentleness and modesty, the indications of refined and Christian culture. They suffered greatly from sea-sickness, but in the intervals of the disease I renewed my acquaintance with them, and particularly with the second, just eleven years of age. From her I learned without interrogation, that her father was a lawyer of Toronto, and I afterwards discovered that he was a member of the Canadian Parliament. He has since that time held a prominent place in the conservative administration of the province. When I parted with my young friend in Boston harbour, I promised to write to her, and not long after sent her a poetical description of our voyage, which was received so well that I added a second canto and promised a third , but never wrote it, having now exhausted either my material or my inspiration. During this little correspondence I had preserved my incognito, having never told the children who I was or where I lived. After nearly five years' silence, I was prompted by a lady friend, to whom I had related these particulars, to write again, inquiring if Minnie was still living and still willing to receive another canto. Notwithstanding this gratuitous proposal, and the cordial response which it received, I shamefully neglected to perform it; or rather I was too old to resume the sport which had relieved the tedium of a sea voyage half a dozen years before. I was not even roused to action or impelled to composition by the news received about a year ago, that my little correspondent, now almost a woman, had returned to England to complete her education, which she had begun there. Remembering the childish earnestness with which she had declared that she would never cross the sea again, I felt disposed to remind her of this declaration; but inertia or stupidity still conquered, till I visited Toronto for the first time in my course of summer travel, and among other residences in the environs was shown the house of Minnie's father. I think I met her elder sister near it, although six years at that time of life effect great changes, and she certainly would not have known me if she had seen me, which she did not, for she passed me with her eye upon the ground in a profound, but not (I trust) a painful reverie. But even the supposed identity awakened many old associations, under the influence of which I scribbled at the very moment of departure, a few lines intended to remind them of me, and deposited them, with my own hand, on my way to the Niagara steamer, at the office of a morning paper—possibly the wrong one. Whether they were ever published I am still uncertain, as I do not often see Canadian journals; but as authors do not 'willingly let die' the feeblest of their literary offspring, I repeat the verses from memory, and therefore possibly with some diversity of text, which may perplex my editors hereafter:

THRICE TRANSPLANTED.

A SONNET.

From a Volume of Unpublished Poems.

I knew a little fresh Canadian flower,
Transplanted early into English soil,
And fondly nurtured in a fragrant bower,
With sleepless care and unremitting toil,
Then gently moved back to its native bed,
There to take root forever—it was said.
Since that day, long past, I have seen it not,
But lately visited the garden-spot,
Where it had twice upreared its modest head,
Expecting to behold it in full bloom.
But it was gone—not dead, thank God, not dead—
Its early promise withered in the tomb—
But a third time transplanted! May His hand
Spare that sweet blossom yet to blow in its own land.*

TORONTO, May 24, 1859.

A——A.

In the spring or summer of 1860, a letter was received in Princeton addressed by "Minnie" herself to "her unknown friend, A——A." The hand and diction, and the tone of sentiment were all in exquisite good taste; and the letter breathed a spirit of respectful and delicate regard, and of grateful but curious desire. It was perused with high satisfaction, and yet with an interest that was at once keenly ap-

* From the Staunton Spectator of June 28, 1859.

preciative and sorrowfully tender and pensive: for he to whom this beautiful expression of thanks had been sent had now forever laid aside his pen, and ceased his earthly wanderings; having himself gone to "another country."

From Canada Dr. Alexander removed in the early part of July to his brother Samuel's study in New York, and took up again his unfinished work on Matthew.

The great miracle among mere linguists was undoubtedly the Roman Cardinal, Mezzofanti; but his biographer, Dr. Russell, cannot persuade the world that he knew philology. After him, perhaps, comes Jonadab Almanar, the Jew, and then Sir William Jones and others. Few have ever certainly known upwards of twenty languages well, and fewer still have known that many profoundly or even somewhat intimately. It is easy to count, without a basis of fact. Dr. Addison Alexander was once asked by an acquaintance, whose curiosity got the better of his discretion, "how many languages *he* knew." The reply was very much like him: "*I have a smattering of several!*" In order that the reader may know what was the number of tongues, and the degree of excellence, of which the modest scholar spoke so lightly, I append below a catalogue and description which are as exact as I can make them, but are in part conjectural.

The question has been put to me, whether the subject of these biographical sketches was a thorough philologist as well as a mere linguist; and was a lover of comparative etymology and general grammar. The ardent lover of Jones, the friend of Franz Bopp, the pupil of Dr. Pott, the early admirer of Grimm and Humboldt, and the careful student of the more recent efforts of German and English scholarship in this department, as well as of such authors as Freytag, De Sacy, Ewald, Rosenmüller, Thiersch, Buttmann, Winer, Wahl, etc., was not likely to be indifferent to the amazing advances of "the new science." The Repertory is full of articles from his pen implying a keen relish for this species of study and a thorough acquaintance with the labours of the philological experts. Even his magazine articles, newspaper squibs, and letters disclose the same thing. His distaste for metaphysics, and especially German metaphysics, did not extend (as he expressly says, in an article, I think, on Winer) to profound experience and common-sense, to original thought, to refined and cogent logic; even when applied philosophically to the elucidation of the principles of language.

1. Arabic: of which he was a consummate master, from a child, and wrote with some ease, but which he could scarcely be said to speak.

2. Hebrew: ditto.

3. Latin: which he knew profoundly, from a child, and wrote and spoke.

4. Persian: which he knew intimately, from a child, and wrote, but did not speak.

5. Syriac: which he knew intimately, from a child, and perhaps wrote, but did not speak.

6. Chaldee: which he knew as well, or nearly as well, as he did Hebrew, and read with rapidity without a lexicon.

7. Greek: which he knew profoundly, from a child, and wrote, but did not attempt to speak.

8. Italian: which he read with the same facility he did English, and spoke.

9. German: which he knew profoundly, from his youth, and wrote and spoke.

10. Spanish: which he knew thoroughly, and probably wrote and spoke.

11. French: which he read, wrote, and spoke with ease.

12. English: which he knew no less profoundly than familiarly.

13. Ethiopic: which he knew philologically and profoundly, and could read without difficulty.

14. Chinese: of which, in its innumerable details, he had but a smattering, but knew pretty well philologically.

15. Romaic: which he read and wrote with ease.

16. Portuguese: which he read with ease, but perhaps did not attempt to speak.

17. Danish: which he says he soon "read fluently with a dictionary," and probably, in time, without one.

18. Turkish; and 19. Sanscrit: which (soon after he acquired them) he says were "becoming quite familiar," and doubtless became more so.

20. Polish: which he read with ease, though probably with the aid of the lexicon.

21. Malay: which he began in connection with Chinese, and probably read with a dictionary.

22. Coptic: which he knew philologically and, I think, profoundly, and read, though perhaps not with ease.

23. Swedish: which he read with ease; at least with the dictionary.

24. Dutch: which he read, perhaps with ease, and probably without a dictionary, and perhaps learned to speak.

He no doubt had an inkling of the nature, and a glimpse into the structure of many others, which he has not named, and knew part of the vocabulary of others.

Summary: He knew profoundly, not only philologically but linguistically, *i. e.* read, wrote, and spoke well—

1. English.
2. Latin.
3. German.
4. French.
5. (Almost certainly) Italian.
6. (Almost certainly) Spanish.
7. (Probably) Portuguese.

It is quite possible that he knew several others in this way.

He knew profoundly as a philologist, and read without helps, and wrote, but did not speak—*i. e.* not familiarly—

1. Arabic.
2. Hebrew.
3. Persian.
4. Greek (which, however, he may have spoken a little.)
5. Romaic: ditto.
6. Chaldee: which he knew as well, or nearly as well, as he did Hebrew, and read with rapidity without a lexicon.

7. (Probably) Ethiopic, which he certainly read, though perhaps with difficulty.

8. (Probably) Dutch, which he certainly read, though perhaps not with ease.

9. (Possibly) Sanscrit, which he certainly read, though perhaps with some difficulty.

10. (Possibly) Syriac, which he read with perfect ease, but probably did not write.

11. (Possibly) Coptic, which he read, and I think easily, but probably did not write.

12. (Possibly) Danish, which he read without a lexicon, but probably did not write.

13. (Probably) Flemish.

14. (Possibly) Norwegian.

He knew profoundly as a philologist, and read with ease with the help of lexicons—

1. Polish: which it is barely possible he came to read without a dictionary, and even to write.

2. Swedish: ditto.

He knew well, if not profoundly, as a philologist, and could read with the aid of a lexicon, though perhaps not with ease—

1. Malay.

He knew philologically, and pretty well I suppose, but had but a smattering of its details:

1. Chinese: and 2, I think he had some knowledge of Hindostanee.

He also had a masterly acquaintance with the Rabbinical Hebrew, and several dialects of languages which are mentioned in this catalogue.

He no doubt, too, had some slight acquaintance with several other proper languages, as distinguished from mere dialectical variations of one language. He may, indeed, have acquired a few languages of which there is no record.

He was thus a perfect master of probably eight or ten languages; though it is not possible to determine in every instance precisely what ones. Dr. Sears testifies, that when a student in Germany he spoke about as many as Tholuck, which was at least six. He knew profoundly, as a philologist, and wrote, certainly thirteen, probably fourteen or fifteen, possibly nineteen, or even by a chance, over twenty. He knew profoundly as a philologist at least, and read with ease, with the help of the lexicons, almost certainly twenty-one, and probably twenty-two. He knew at least philologically, and well, probably twenty-four. He knew in all, at least slightly, and in one way or other, probably between twenty-five and thirty. He knew, at least well enough for him to claim to know something of them, twenty-five, including English, and excluding mere dialectical variations of any one language.

As has been shown in these memoirs, he did not in later life pursue his linguistic studies with the same absorbing assiduity as in former years; contenting himself, for the most part with refreshing his knowledge of the stock already acquired, or with merely philological investigations, as bearing upon questions of specific or comparative grammar. Had he devoted himself wholly to strange tongues, I think he could have mastered as many as any of the famous linguists, with the solitary exception of Mezzofanti.

He now knows the full meaning of the words, so constantly before his eyes, πολλαὶ μὲν θνητοῖς γλῶτται μία δ' ἀθανάτοισιν.*

* I here subjoin a list of the articles contributed by Dr. Addison Alexander to the Princeton Review, not yet credited to him in these volumes, but on his own authorized list. This includes all the Repertory articles acknowledged by him, from 1843 to 1855 inclusive, when the list was made.

1843.

	PAGES.
Barnes on Episcopacy	386
Smyth on do (?) [The mark of interrogation, is J. A. A.'s]	550

1844.

(Part) Free Church (Hodge)	86
Junkin on Prophecy	262
Bush on Ezekiel	380
Moderatism	403
High low Church	517

1845.

(Part) Sacerdotal Absolution.................................... 43
Pascal.. 252

[Also "Concordances" on Dr. Hall's list, and probably by J. A. A.] (slight)

1846.

Coit's Puritanism.. 122
Kitto's Cyclopædia... 562

1847.

The Eldership.. 42
Historical Theology.. 91
University Education....................................... 336
Jewish History... 378
Apostolical Succession..................................... 539

1848.

Mosaic Legislation... 74
(Part) Spring's Power of the Pulpit........................ 463
Gospels.. 592

1849.

Primitive Presbyters....................................... 116
Davidson's Introduction New Test't......................... 144
Apostleship.. 335
do 542

["Calcutta Review—Khonds," given by Dr. Hall, but not on the author (if "J. A. A.")'s list, and in a totally different style from his. Probably "A. A.'s" *certainly not* "J. A. A.'s."]

1850.

Septuagint... 541

1851.

Test of Ministry... 292
Fairbairn's Typology....................................... 508
Old and New Dispensation................................... 633

1852.

Hengstenberg on Revelation................................. 59
Parrhesia.. 312
Haldanes... 677

1853.

Prophecy and History....................................... 290

1854.

Method of History.. 300
Historical Scriptures...................................... 484 (?)

1855.

Patriarchal History.......... 24
Koeppen's Middle Ages.......... 62
The Coptic Language.......... 388

To this I append the Repertory articles by Dr. Alexander, which appeared after 1855, when he made the authorized list. All the articles on the present supplementary list are on Dr. Hall's list, most of them are on J. W. A.'s, and nearly all are indubitably ascertained, on other evidence, both external and internal, to be by Dr. Addison Alexander. Eli Smith's Arabic Bible (1856) is in his unmistakable style.

1856.

Harmonies of the Gospels.......... 393
Eli Smith's Arabic Bible.......... 732

1857.

Gieseler's Text-Book of Church History.......... 636

1859.

Praying and Preaching.......... 1
Sawyer's New Testament.......... 50

There may chance to be others by his pen, but they have not attracted my notice or that of my informants.

It were needless to describe these articles seriatim. They are, like their forerunners, on a diversity of subjects. It is enough to say of most of them, *ex ungue leonem*.

CHAPTER XXXIII.

The diary of the elder brother for the spring months is a reflex of his feelings during a season of profound nervous and mental depression, connected no doubt with the gradual decay of his physical powers. A journey to the Virginia Springs was determined upon, and he was accordingly taken to the residence of his brother-in-law, near Charlottesville, and afterwards pursued his leisurely way through the ravines and mountain-gorges of the Great Valley, and beyond it. He set out with a part of his family on the 2d day of June, and arrived at Alexandria "amidst a beautiful sunset" on the evening of the 3d.

The next day the party reached the University, and by the 5th, which was the Lord's day, he could write:

> "Clear and cool. Strawberries linger. A truly delightful night's sleep; better, I think, than for six months. I have not coughed since the 3d, in Philadelphia. Let me continue to praise and bless God."

But these appearances of improvement were not the signs of a radical change for the better. His warfare was now almost accomplished; but the declining slopes of the hill were at length irradiated with heavenly sunshine. If his sun went down while it was yet day, it sank in the spotless heavens. The cloud which had so long hung over his propects and happiness was now forever rolled away, and the remaining weeks and days of his life were a serene contemplation of the glory of nature and the more resplendent "glory that was to be revealed in him."

On the 7th, after a better night than common, he took a ride on horseback and bore it well. At five in the afternoon he was driven to the mountain near Judge Rives's. He rode out again the next day, and experienced a little annoyance again from his cough. His third ride was taken on the 9th. He was able to correspond with his friends. The next day he was visited by "the venerable Bishop Meade," whom he describes as "spare, tall, very like his large engraved portrait. Perfect manners. No assumption. Easy conversation. More learned talk than I was prepared for."

On the 12th he was again kept from the sanctuary, and took the opportunity of writing out a most heart-searching prayer for help and comfort. It closes thus:

"And oh! for Jesus's sake make me sweetly submissive to all thy holy will; cheerful in hope; perfect in acquiescence; setting an example of Christian peace and patience. Oh! that my discourse may be always with grace, seasoned with salt, that it may be for the edification of the hearers. And, O my ever glorious God! condescend to lift up thy poor, sunken creature from the earth, and deliver him from those subduing influences which oppress both body and soul. *Jehovah Rophi*, stretch out thy mighty arm for cure. *Jesu Rophi*, vouchsafe to heal, as of old. And oh! graciously pardon for Christ's sake. Amen."

This prayer was perfectly and wonderfully answered. He received what was better than "cure," even entrance into that land where "the inhabitant shall not say, I am sick." As soon as he saw he was not to become a useless burden on the Church and on his friends, the weight was lifted. His spiritual hopes had never been obscured; but now they rose as into a new and more vital atmosphere.

June 15th, he records, "Warm. Thunderstorm last evening, beautiful in the mountains. * * * Waked by a students' charivari." * * *

He refers in another entry to the disappointment of the farmers in regard to their wheat, which was injured by the rains. His brief record one morning contains this abridged sentence, "Vigils and fidgets." Another day the statement is, "Small record, because unwell." He was still able to ride out in the carriage, on the 25th. Two days after, his soul was refreshed by a transient glimpse of one of his brothers. It was their last meeting. They were now among the excitements of the "Public Day," which was as usual "immensely hot." He felt better all day. Monday, the eleventh of July, was set for the mountain journey. Dr. Cabell and his family accompanied the party to the Warm Springs, where everything that is grand and lovely in verdant hillside scenery seemed to meet together for their especial gratification. One day the sunrise, out of creamy mountain mists, was transcendent. It was almost celestial. The patient sufferer read the 104th Psalm, and looking abroad over the enchanting pinnacles cried out, "Oh, how it lifts the soul!"

On the 17th, which was the Lord's Day, he wrote:

"A Sabbath quiet in this lovely spot. Though my health is less encouraging, I thank God that I have so lively a sensibility to the beauties and glories of his creation. The sights, sounds, and odours are all rural, all mountainous. Every bird and flower and tree, and the variety is great, seems placed aright in a beautiful harmony with the whole. Gentle ascents of mountains on several sides, enclosing this happy valley; grassy up to a certain point of their smooth sides, then merging into thick forests, the line of junction being marked with beautiful shades; herds and flocks ever and anon emerging into the light. It is a country of springs, and the sound of water is much in our ears. Oh, that men would praise the Lord for his goodness," &c.

The last entry in his journal was made the next day, and is the following:

"Delightful rains in the night, and this morning. This weak sulphur water has agreed with me admirably. To God do we commit the journey of the morrow!"

While at the warm springs, he had contracted a dysenteric affection which was prevailing in those valleys, but it seemed to yield to the remedies. But on their arrival at the Red Sweet the disease returned, in a modified but uncontrollable form; and on the 31st he fell asleep in Jesus, with his countenance visibly illumined with the hope of a blessed immortality and the sweet consolations of a precious gospel. His dying confession was clear, and uttered with emphatic calmness. "I know whom I have believed, and that he is able to keep that which I have committed unto him against that day."

The body was conveyed from Virginia to Princeton, and was interred by the side of other precious memorials in the old graveyard: Dr. Joseph Addison Alexander stood pale and motionless, as the words of victory were uttered.

The tidings of his brother's death gave him a shock from which he never recovered. The only indication of his feelings at the time he received the dreadful news, which is presented in his journal, is the heavy black line which he drew under the bare record of the fact. But the grief inwardly consumed him. The iron had entered his soul.

He had been sick himself that summer, and had come home looking alarmingly thin and pale and downcast. It was almost as if he had a presentiment of coming evil.

I shall never forget his appearance, or his prayer at family worship, on the evening of the funeral. He was resolute and composed, and his voice did not fail him or even tremble; but it sounded as if he were uttering the prophecy of another startling and irreparable sorrow. Alas, the prediction came too soon, too soon! His tones thrilled through me as he closed the book, and said "let us pray," and with a strange and significant solemnity spoke the words, "O God! Thou art a God of judgment and of mercy, and in mercy and in judgment hast Thou gathered us together here this day."

The tone of the correspondence which he still kept up with his old friend at the State capital now suddenly changes; and it is long before he can resume the air of waggish pleasantry which has seemed to be almost inseparable from this pleasing interchange of good offices and equivocal epithets. His beloved brother was now lying dead in Virginia (though he does not yet know it), and his own heart is almost breaking with grief and anxiety as he writes the hurried sentences which here follow :

"New York, August 1, 1859.

"My dear Sir :

"I left town on Sunday for a day or two, and on returning to resume my work this morning, find that James's sons set off that same day for the South, having heard unfavourable news from their father, and that Sam followed them last night, after preaching in the morning, and receiving a despatch between the services, saying that James was rapidly sinking. He was seized with dysentery on his way from the Warm to the Sweet Springs, where it seems that disease is epidemic. I hear indirectly, through a member of Dr. Cabell's family, that at the beginning of his new attack he suffered nothing, but seemed nearly insensible. We are now in hourly expectation of later news, which will determine my own movements. In the mean time I think it right to let you know what we know, if you have not previously heard it. His wife, in her last letter, earnestly desires the prayers of friends in his behalf, though he may now be far beyond the need of them.

"I cannot yet abandon all hope, though I stand prepared to hear the worst.

"Yours truly,
"J. A. Alexander."

From this time until the first of September he remained in New York, engaged upon his commentary on Matthew. But his work was suddenly arrested on the first of August by the news of the dangerous illness, and on the next day of the death, of his brother James in Virginia. His friends heard but little from him in regard to this great blow. Perhaps the following letter, written a week after the event, contains more of his feelings than he ever uttered in word or by pen :

"New York, August 8, 1859.

"Dearest J.

"I had a delightful sail from Amboy, which is always soothing and refreshing. On the way I read the Adelphi of Terence, a favourite of James's, and containing a passage which I would transcribe if I had it by me; it is so beautiful and simple that I think you would not need a translation. It begins, 'O frater! frater!' I will read it to you some day. I am constantly reminded of our late great loss, in a very singular and unexpected manner. Hundreds of times since I knew that all was over, I have caught myself saying to myself (especially when reading), 'I must tell James that,' or 'what would James say to that?' This makes me sensible that I feel my intellectual and literary loss more poignantly than any other. Yesterday morning I went to the Brick Church; and, being rather late, found Hoge engaged in the second prayer, two thirds of which at least related to James's death, his church, family, &c. Even after he had left the subject he returned to it to pray specially for Henry. He expounded the first Psalm; taking my analysis and interpretation, but amplifying and enforcing with great power and beauty. After going through with a description of the tree, he made a most beautiful and touching application of the passage to our dear departed brother. This was unspeakably affecting, and I cannot now recall it without tears. I may hereafter give you some account of it, but now can only mention one stroke that completely overcame me: After speaking of his rich and varied fruits (as a preacher and a writer), and of his never-fading foliage (as a man and a Christian), he said: 'Even now that he is cut down—no, not cut down—to the root of such trees there is no axe laid—but now that God has gently lifted him, with all his roots and all his fruits above them, to the more congenial soil of Paradise, he is still a tree, a perfect, verdant, fruitful tree, overhanging that river of life the washing of whose waves upon its banks was the music of his soul on earth.' The whole was beautiful and rendered more so by the indications of sincere grief on his own part.

"I spent the intervals between the services at Sam's; where, after reading for an hour or two, I fell asleep and woke up a few minutes before four. This, with the heat and distance, prevented my returning to hear Hoge again; and recollecting that ——— was advertised to preach in Twenty-third Street, I went there, and heard one of the most wonderful performances I ever witnessed. It was a sacramental sermon on the Transfiguration. The whole of it was read, but in the manner of a madman, with the most unnatural, unearthly yells and whispers, sometimes hurrying over half a dozen sentences without regard to stops, and then drawling out what followed with intolerable slowness. There was no appearance of affectation or aiming at effect; for the manner was ridiculous, and just that of a raving maniac. Yet in spite of this, the sermon perfectly enchained me, and I still regard it, on reflection, as one of the most beautiful, original, and powerful discourses I have ever heard. To my surprise he was highly orthodox, not only as to the Trinity and the method of salvation, but even as to Imputation and other sharp points of old Calvinism. It was also intensely Baptist; making the most of burial in baptism, &c.; but this might be expected in a sacramental sermon and among themselves. He gave me some new ideas of the Transfiguration. His idea is that it was typical of the Second Advent, and that Moses and Elijah represented the two classes who will witness it—the dead and those alive upon the earth. His description of Elijah's translation and Moses's burial was transcendent. He suggested 'not as doctrine,' but as his idea, that the body of Moses lay for ages uncorrupted in the valley where God buried him, until he was summoned to the transfiguration. As soon as Peter spake unadvisedly (as Moses did before him), a cloud came over them, and Moses and Elijah disappeared. One reason was, that Peter proposed to make them equal with the Son of God. One of the finest passages was his account of Moses's disappointment; first glorifying him as a legislator, general, prophet, poet, &c., then telling how he turned away from Canaan, and went up into the mount to die alone. The man is a great poetical genius, but with far more appearance of sound doctrine and religious feeling than I ever suspected. I came out before the sacrament; not choosing to be formally excluded from it. At night I heard a Western Methodist in John street (French), an extraordinary preacher of a very different sort from both the others.

"I resumed work this morning, and will continue it a few days. I am actually cheered by the thought that James felt such an interest in my labours and so generously valued them. It is also a consolatory thought that he lived to see the change in my employment, which he had so earnestly desired, and of which he was in fact the author, having never ceased to insist that I should give up Church History and devote myself entirely to Biblical instruction.

"Your brother,

"J. A. A."

From the same, to Dr. Hall:

"PRINCETON, September 1, 1859.

"MY DEAR SIR:

"On returning home this week from my long holiday, I find two letters of yours, not more remote in date than different in tone, and in the recollections which they severally awaken. I have since learned with great regret, that by an unexpected providence, you have been placed in a situation similar to that of James himself eight years ago, when he lost his father and his infant child, the oldest and youngest of our family circle, within a few weeks of each other. I imitate your wise reserve as to the forms and commonplaces of condolence, and shall only say that I sincerely sympathize with you and Mrs. Ingham in this new bereavement. I have no doubt you have often turned in thought to our departed 'son of consolation,' as if he were still living. With a strange, but not unnatural forgetfulness, I find myself looking to him for support, even under the irreparable shock of his own death. I had no conception of my intellectual dependance upon James, until I caught myself continually laying things aside to tell him, as the person who could best appreciate and enjoy them. All this says very loudly, 'Cease ye from man whose breath is in his nostrils,' and shows the grace and wisdom of that constitution which reserves the office of comforter for a divine person. The circumstances which you mention certainly go far to reconcile us to his death at this time; but I feel now and then a disposition to repine at the circumstances themselves. I have no doubt that he shortened his own life by morbid anxieties, connected not merely with his health, but with his pastoral duties. I find it hard to acquiesce without a murmur in the loss of such a man from such a cause, or to reflect without a momentary pang of discontent, that he might have preached for many years with ease and pleasure, but sunk under the weight of other causes. It seems an argument in favour of the old Princeton arrangement which provided both a pastor and a teacher in such cases. But I have already said too much and chide myself.

"My widowed sister is recovering her strength, and was expected to set out for the North about this time with her two sons, who are with her, and Dr. and Mrs. Cabell.

"Truly yours, &c.,

J. A. ALEXANDER."

Not long before he was removed from his labours, his more observing pupils had begun to notice a striking a change in his looks.

"I shall never forget," says one of them,* "how I was startled and saddened by the first conclusive sign to my eye that he was failing. It had been noticed and talked about among us that he was losing flesh and colour, but no serious apprehensions had been excited. Once,

* The Rev. Alfred Yeomans, now of Orange, N. J.

however, in the class-room, as he was lecturing, he sat with his elbow on the arm of the chair, the thumb of his right hand under his chin, and the fore-finger extended and pressed into the cheek. When, after a little while, he withdrew the finger, I happened to look up from my notes, and remarked that the cheek did not spring out again to its round proportions but retained *a deep dent* from the pressure of the finger, as though the flesh were a lump of inelastic clay. The finger print remained for some considerable time, showing how the tissues were losing their elasticity. The sight startled me like an evil omen. Not long after, he was upon his bed from which he rose but briefly, only to return to it and die. I never could rub out that finger-print from my memory. I see it yet, whenever I think of him."

I now lay before the reader certain interesting statements touching the last of Dr. Alexander's various important Seminary changes. The writer of the subjoined extracts is his colleague, Dr. McGill.

"In the autumn of 1858, whilst Dr. Green was yet absent in a journey to Europe, he took charge of the Hebrew department; returning to that elementary instruction in the language which had formerly wearied him and provoked his impatience. The whole term of this employment was one of exhilaration to him; like that of a child recovering possession of a toy which he had been tired of once, and now recognized in all its original attractions. The large class entering that year, eighty-seven in number, were so captivated with his fond and sprightly manner as to form a new estimate of his character and kindness. We little thought this beaming out of his true nature was a playful ray of the setting sun. That class followed him to the grave, in their middle year; mourning not only the loss of a great teacher, but a personal friend also, who had been 'lovely and pleasant in his life.' "

Dr. Green writes, in reference to his last words to his classes:

"After the experiment of a few years in the chair of Church History, he strongly avowed his preference for the work of giving instruction directly based upon the text of Scripture. When the last change was made in the title of his professorship, giving him the New Testament department, he felt that he was precisely suited and that the work before him was more exactly to his mind than it had ever been: that he was just in the position for which the studies of his life prepared him.

"I enclose the last communication made by him to the students and which by his request I read at evening prayers. The last expression in it, you may be interested to know, was suggested by one of your father's letters, who, when absent in Europe, applied to himself that touching Scriptural phrase."

This is the message he sent the students:

"I have hitherto made no communication to the students; partly because I was forbidden to exert myself in any way; partly because I have been living, for the last six weeks, in constant expectation of a speedy return to my accustomed duties. Thus far this expectation has been disappointed, and it still remains entirely uncertain when I shall be able to resume my place as an instructor. I desire to bow submissively under this trying and mysterious dispensation, but at the same time to express my earnest wish and hope, that the classes will not utterly neglect the studies which belong to my department, and in which they made such encouraging proficiency during the first three months of the session.

"I hesitate the less to ask this, because it happens, I may say providentially, that in this more than any former year, these subjects can be prosecuted to a great extent in private, with the aid of the books which we have used or I have recommended. If, however, in addition to these helps, there could be organized a voluntary system of associated labour, or of mutual instruction, whether on a large or a smaller scale, this might cause my absence to be still less felt; and I would gladly make occasional suggestions to the several classes, on the subjects with which they are occupied respectively. But this must depend, of course, upon my actual condition at any given time, and cannot be definitively promised. Even now I must arrest my pen and close by simply but importunately asking the Divine blessing upon all connected with the Seminary, and in turn soliciting their prayers for one who has been, and may still be, so long '*separated from his brethren.*'

"J. A. ALEXANDER.

"Jan. 7th, 1860."

It is but right that I should add to this Dr. Green's own testimony to the worth of his teacher and colleague:

"The reverence with which I have always regarded him is such as to preclude any attempt at an estimate. I do not feel as if it were possible for me to place myself in the attitude of a critic or a judge of himself or of any of his productions. They seem to me as nearly perfect as that which is human can be. The kindness and consideration with which I had ever been treated by him, made me feel when he was taken away that I had lost one of my best friends, as well as of my ablest guides. I did not need the sight of his quivering lip and dropping tears at his father's grave to convince me that he was not, as some imagine him to be, mere intellect; and that beneath his ordinary passionless exterior, there was a deep fount of warm and tender feeling."

It was about this time that he received a visit from one who had been his colleague for a quarter of a century, and his zealous friend and enthusiastic admirer for a much longer period. Of course, I allude to Dr. Charles Hodge. It will be noticed that he prefaces his account with a critical analysis of some of the traits of his remarkable disposition. It will also be noticed that at this time the invalid was trying to persuade himself and others that he was well.

"His mental peculiarities were as remarkable as his intellectual endowments. One of the most marked of these was his inability to do what was distasteful to him. If he did not like any pursuit, or branch of knowledge, or any particular subject, he could not bring himself to attend to it. In the conduct of the Princeton Review, I was often called to suggest his writing on some particular topic. If he expressed any disinclination to it, the matter was at once dropped; for I well knew that however willing he might be to oblige me, or to have the topic discussed, his doing anything with it was out of the question. This peculiarity was probably due, in a good measure, to his mode of education. He was in a great degree self-educated. Being spontaneously devoted to intellectual pursuits, wasting no time, and having no inclination for the unimportant, he was allowed to take his own course. He thus became habituated to studying what was agreeable to him, and unable to bring his mind to bear on what did not interest him.—With this was connected another peculiarity which he had in a remarkable degree. He was voluntarily ignorant of many departments of knowledge with which educated men are generally more or less familiar. This was in a measure true in reference to matters of science, and still more to questions of mental philosophy. His reading was largely in the later German writers, but their philosophical speculations were singularly distasteful to him; and he never gave them a thought.* He would neither read nor talk about them. I have heard him say that when in his historical or other reading he came across any philosophical speculation, he slammed over the pages until he came to something else. It was specially such subjects as anatomy, physiology, hygiene, of which he determined he would know nothing. He had seen how superficial knowledge on this matter had rendered men hypochondriac, and consequently miserable and burdensome. He therefore went to the opposite extreme, and was really so ignorant that he did not know how to take care of himself. That is, he would unconsciously violate the laws of health, especially by exposure, greatly to his own injury. During his last illness, which was preceded by nearly a year of gradual decline, he told me that instead of perspiring freely as was his habit, his skin had been for months without the slightest moisture; and that during all that time his mouth had been so dry he could not wet a postage stamp. When I expressed surprise that those symptoms did not satisfy him that he was seriously unwell, he replied, 'Oh, you know I never put that and that together,' and even within ten days of his death, when remonstrating against his attempting during that session to resume his duties in the seminary, he answered with some impatience, 'I am as well as you are.'

The desolation caused by his brother's decease had told terribly on his constitution. He was then on the downward shelve of the hill; but afterwards began to move under a greatly accelerated momentum. The increase of motion was silent but observable. His flesh, indeed, had decreased rapidly within the last year of his life; and he had begun to look worn and haggard. Students of the early days of his tuition would have hardly recognized him. But these symptoms were aggravated after his brother's death. He, however, complained of nothing except the extreme dryness of his throat, which of late had been almost agonizing.

* His journals show that this remark is only true in the general way in which Dr. Hodge intends it should be taken. He would sometimes, though very rarely indeed, amuse himself with these vagaries.

The first time his nearest relatives at home really thought he was ill, was in the autumn of 1859.

On his return to Princeton, after his great circular tour, he used to take walks among the faded leaves which, though they merely marked the season of the year, almost seemed to foretoken the decay of his own exuberant strength. He probably did this at the urgent request of friends. These little sauntering excursions proved to be too much for him even then. They tired him excessively, and sometimes almost grievously. This was in October. He would complain of weariness even after a short walk, and express a wish to return home.

All through October he was weak and miserable.

It was this unnatural, and in his case unexampled, loss of bodily vigour (together with the previous and startling loss of flesh to which I have elsewhere alluded) that produced the fear in the minds of those who were nearest of kin to him, that there must be something alarming the matter with him.

It was afterwards ascertained that the preceding summer he had had a sudden check of perspiration. He was wearing a linen coat. From this time, so he acknowledged during his sickness, he never perspired again. "His moisture was turned into the drought of summer." From this time his health was never what it had been, and soon after became hopelessly shattered.

About the latter part of October, he began to suffer from a rasping cough. It was the most violent cold he had ever had, and was connected with a slight but distressing difficulty of breathing. He nevertheless attended to all his recitations.

Among the many friends who visited him in the chamber of death, was one * who feels his personal loss to be irreparable, and who testifies in the following terms:

"During his sickness, or decline, I visited him frequently. He was always pleasant, disposed to underrate his own sufferings (scarcely

* The Rev. Dr. Abraham Gosman, of Lawrenceville, one of the translators of Lange.

ever speaking of them, except in reply to some question as to his health), and hopeful of the issue. He could not see what gave his admiring friends so much anxiety and pain. But to us the change was marked and alarming. A little more than a week before his death, I spent a pleasant half hour with him. The conversation was such as to dispel my fears, at least partially. 'The confinement,' he said, 'you know, is pleasant to me. I am among my books, and find no reluctance to work.' He was anxious only about the suspension of his lectures and instruction in the seminary. Losing sight of himself, as his custom was, he entered mainly into the joys and prospects of my own family, saying that as soon as he was able to ride he would make his first visit at my house and see me in my home. I parted from him fondly hoping that I should soon see him again, when, at the close of a Sabbath's labour, the word came that he was gone."

I can discover no material change in his handwriting, so far as it appears in his diaries, until he came to make the very last entry but one; and I am not sure that this is irregular for any other reason than that it is made at the bottom of a page in an immense folio volume. These are the last records he inscribed in his Journal; the very latest being within three days of his death:

"Friday, Jan. 20. Read over my analysis of Matthew xvii—xxviii. Reading as usual. Letter from John Hall, declining to come, except in case of urgent need. Wrote to Moffat, requesting him to preach for me, which he agreed to do.

"Saturday, Jan. 21. Finished the second volume of Stevens's History of Methodism, begun Jan. 3d. Visit from W. H. G. Wrote to Dr. J. H. Jones.

"Lord's Day, Jan. 22." This was his last Sabbath on earth. "Nehemiah in Coverdale; Hodge on 2d Corinthians; Schultz on Deuteronomy; Morning Service and Litany; Episcopal Psalms and Hymns; three of my brother's 'Discourses on Common Topics of Faith and Practice;' ten of Adolphe Monod's Dying Speeches (or *Adieux à ses amis et à l'église*); Anderson's Colonial Church History; The Presbyterian: finished Ecclesiastes in Hebrew, with the Chaldee Paraphrase (begun Dec. 28).

"Monday, Jan. 23.—Finished (in bed) Coverdale's Version of Nehemiah (begun Jan. 11). Visits from Dr. Atwater and Moffat, the latter of whom preached for me in the chapel yesterday. Finished Dickens's Tale of Two Cities, a powerful tragic fiction, unrelieved by any comic element; for Cruncher is a miserable failure. Other reading as usual.

"Tuesday, Jan. 24.—Left the house for the first time since my memorable return on the 28th of November (p. 543). Took a drive with my sister in Dr. Hodge's carriage.

"Wednesday, Jan. 25.—Shaved by Gilbert Scudder. S. D. A. from New York and back. Reading as usual.'

It seems right that the long succession of manuscript entries, which he had kept up so faithfully, should close with these familiar words.

The literary zest was fully as great in him as ever, and his industry as unwearied as it seemed to be unconscious. From November the 28th, the "memorable day" in Philadelphia, to January the 28th, the day of his death, he read more than two books of the Bible (Ecclesiastes and the Song of Solomon) in Hebrew and Chaldee. The version of Canticles he pronounces "most extraordinary." He also read David Trumbull's "Correspondence with a Priest in Valparaiso;" J. J. Gurney's Life; two volumes of Bancroft; much English poetry; the Rev. H. B. Pratt's sermon (in Spanish) on the "Right of the People to the Scriptures"; the weekly religious journals and the missionary papers (both regularly); the Life of Hedley Vicars (which he declares is "a beautiful tale, beautifully told"); the Reminiscences of Rufus Choate; several of the then late numbers of Punch; Johnson's Lives (or most of it); an old article of his own for the Repertory; "Paris and its Environs"; Madame D'Arblay's Journal; the President's Message, and the Reports of the Departments (Dec. 28): and heard read the Life of Daniel Baker and other books and tracts of that sort; "skimmed Evelina;" looked through the Dublin Calendar and examined the Irish Examination Papers. Besides this he read Schultz on Deuteronomy; Hodge on 2 Corinthians; Millhouse's English Grammar (in Italian); nearly or quite all of Rawlinson's Herodotus, and Findlay's "Greece under the Romans"; part of the Thousand and One Nights in

Arabic; the two volumes of Abel Stevens; Helweg's History of the Church of Denmark (in Danish); morsels of Anderson's Colonial History; Aristotle and Plato in Archer Butler's Ancient Philsophy; and a great deal in Coverdale's Bible. His last mark is at the end of the 3d chapter of Esther. He carefully looked through Dr. H. B. Smith's Historical Tables; read several of Irving's stories; perused several articles of Brande's Cyclopædia; examined a new edition of Büchner's Concordanz; pondered the Office for the Visitation of the Sick in the Prussian "Agende"; several of his brother's Discourses; and the Morning Service, Litany, and Hymns of the Book of Common Prayer. Most of the books he handled at this time are copiously marked, and show him to have been in the full possession of all his remarkable powers. The pencil dashes are often critical, often mirthful, sometimes pious, and very often ambiguous. Sometimes he jots down a whole sentence in the margin; sometimes a single word, as (twice, at least) the word "Amen." Almost the last book read, which he mentions in his Journal, is the Tale of Two Cities; which aroused his enthusiasm. I have studiously considered his marks in the two volumes of Abel Stevens, and (though of a much earlier date) in Boston, in Ben Jonson, and in one of the volumes of Irving's Washington, which is cut up like the others; as well as some in Campbell's Lives. The Rev. William Harris, of Towanda, informs me that he has gone over his Rawlinson in the same way, and that (like his Bengel) it is very rich in marginal annotations. The History of Methodism was a devotional as well as literary treat to him.

His mouth and throat now became so dry that he could not moisten a wafer. One cheek would often be burning, and the other cool. He did not seem to know whether it was hot or cold. He would have fires when everybody else was warm; so that this had to be regulated for him. His friends at one time advised a change of climate, and I think one of them consulted Dr. Delafield about it.

In this way it went on, until November, when for several weeks he insisted on taking a trip to Philadelphia every

Saturday, for change of air. On one of these visits, on a Sunday, he was overtaken by a torrent of rain, and drenched to the skin. He had listened in the morning to the Irish pulpit orator, Guinness; and with great though not unmeasured delight. A full account of the matter, and of the whole trip and its consequences, will be found in his later Journals. After his wetting, he got in bed, dried his clothes, then put them on again, and went back to the church and heard Guinness a second time. At the end of the first volume of Dr. Abel Stevens' book on Methodism, which he seems to have had with him as a *vade-mecum* on the rails and in the hotels, occurs the jotting in pencil, "A description worthy of the glorious subject.

"O si sic omnia, et omnes methodistae, i.e. Wesleyani!"

And on the fly-leaf, "Finished in bed at the Girard House, Philadelphia, after a fall and ducking in the street during one of the most violent rains I ever saw or felt, and after twice hearing Henry Grattan Guinness (who, methinks, has made Whitefield his model, and resembles him in some points, but I fear not the most important), Nov. 13, 1859."

He came home very hoarse, yet insisting that his cold was better. It was evident enough to all that it was worse. The hoarseness continued until Monday, Nov. the 28th, when he was taken with a bleeding at the lungs. This was just a week after the memorable Sabbath in Philadelphia.

The hemorrhage, though a most alarming symptom, was regarded as a Providential interference to stop him in a course which was sure to end in a kind of voluntary suicide. For weeks previous, his friends had been in pain to see him going through so much, with a bad cough—growing steadily worse, and yet neglecting all recourse to medical skill. During this whole period he intermitted none of his usual employments. During October and November he increased rather than diminished his labours. He would sometimes go to his lectures with the fever actually on him. It was only the hemorrhage that brought him to his senses, and at last made him fully aware of his imminent danger. He came home perfectly calm, without a single nervous tremor, and yet sufficiently apprized of his state, and as docile as a child to every suggestion of the family, and of the capable physician, an old friend, who was at once called in. Dr. Woodhull found his system thoroughly out of order, and making light of the hemoptysis sought to repair his general constitution. There was not the slightest recurrence of the bleeding after the first ten days; though his cough continued very bad, and he laboured for breath, and had some fever daily. But from this time he steadily improved in every respect but one. He continued to grow weaker.

He was down-stairs, and in his study, all this time; until November the 28th, when he consented to remain on one floor. Until the bleeding from his lungs, there was nothing about him to attract the notice of a stranger, except his dreadful cold. He staid up-stairs a few days, without once going down. With the cessation of hemoptysis, there was manifest improvement in his case in several other respects. The new symptom, startling and even terrifying as it was, procured him a sudden relief, and after a time total exemption, from his cough and the oppressive weight upon his lungs. He soon got into the way of going down to his study again; and would sit there nearly the whole time, until nine at night; as he had done before. This he did to the last. After a few weeks he seemed much better, though the cough held on for a time; his system was in a better state than it was before the alarm was sounded. He was not confined to bed at all except the day he died. Even when at his worst before this, he used to go across the entry into his sister's room, and would often spend the day-light there, reading and talking. He was sitting up most of the time, but sometimes reclined. He was very cheerful and very comfortable, reading a little in the mornings, and enjoying himself greatly. Indeed, he had never seemed to enjoy himself more. He often said it was really "*so luxurious*" to sit up there that his conscience troubled him about it. He was going through a strange experience for him; he had seldom before known what it is to rest! He used to have books and hymns read aloud to him after he had gone to bed for the night. This was so for a month preceding his death. Among the books he thus listened to, was the Life of Daniel Baker. He read himself the Life of Adelaide Newton, and spoke of her departure as "euthanasia." Miss Elliott's "Just as I am," he had repeated to him several times; till he knew it, and often repeated it himself entire. He did not miss one morning reading in Coverdale's Bible, or the Targum of Jonathan; as his pencil marks will show. The last date is Jan. 27, the very day before his death.

The late Dr. Joseph H. Jones, of Philadelphia, shortly before his own decease, wrote the following respecting Dr. Alexander:

"Some time previous to the decline of his health, our correspondence had become less frequent; and I did not see him so often in Philadelphia as heretofore; but that there was no abatement of interest or confidence on his part near the close of his life, I was assured by the following most affecting testimonial. A few days before his death, he wrote from Princeton, requesting me to 'take his place as preacher in the Seminary' on the subsequent Sabbath, and was obliged to decline on the account of the extreme illness of my brother, Judge Jones,* who was then very near his death.

"In my letter, however, I made a conditional promise of preaching for him on some future occasion, if he should desire it. He replied at once, thanking me for the offer, and at the same time, referring to his improving health, expressed the hope that he 'should soon be well.'"

In the first letter he asked Dr. Jones to "take his place in the chapel for one Sabbath and be his guest." The reason for inviting him was his unwillingness to "impose on his colleagues the service which properly belonged to himself." In the second letter he promptly and delicately apologized for "mak-

* Judge Joel Jones, of Philadelphia, a man whose tastes and abilities resembled those of Sir William Jones, of England.

In the funeral oration, Dr. Shields, his pastor, exclaimed: "but yesterday the scholars of the Church were gathered at the grave of its most learned clergyman; there are those present who will deem it no exaggeration to say that to-day we are burying its most learned layman."

ing his request at such a time, not having been apprized of his brother's extreme illness." With regard to Dr. J's proposed assistance, he observed that "he hoped to be so much better as not to need it; but inasmuch as he had been kind enough to offer it, he should be very happy to see, and should expect him."

The next information concerning him received by his friend in Philadelphia, was that of his sudden departure. "From his request," writes Dr. Jones, "that I would be his guest, I inferred that he would take the opportunity to disclose his religious feelings, and probably impart more benefit from the interview than he would receive. There was no expression of them in his letter."

It appears from the daily journal Dr. Alexander was still keeping, that this reply to Dr. Jones's letter was dated January the 21st, just a week before his own death. Dr. Jones winds up an affectionate tribute to his friend, a tribute full of love and admiration, with the familiar words of Horace:

> "Multis ille bonis flebilis occidit;
> Nulli flebilior quam" mihi.

The following letter was among the last from his pen; on the 19th, he wrote to Dr. Hall; on the 20th, a note to Dr. Moffat; and on the 21st, which is actually the last, a note to Dr. Jones.

"PRINCETON, January 18th, 1860.

"REVEREND AND DEAR SAM.:

"The Irvings are repacked; and now that they are gone, I feel as if I should like to spend the money upon something else. It would make no difference to Randolph, and they must be thrown back upon Putnam anyhow. If this view is correct, I wish you would order a large batch of Memorial and Sacramental sermons, to any amount within the price of Irving, and in any proportion that you choose, for Jane and me to give away. The whole sum need not be exhausted in one order. By the bye, I wish you would look in your Washington and see if I have marked how far I read when I was staying with you. I generally scribble such things even in other people's books. * * *

"I beg you not to think of coming out here upon my account.

Though always glad to see you, I should feel much happier to know that you were at your work. Feeling the need of spiritual no less than of bodily medicine, I have invited Dr. Jones, of Philadelphia, to pay me a pastoral visit, and preach for me next Sunday. My cough and oppression have entirely left me, and my present ailment is the non-action of my skin. I have not shed a drop of sweat for many months. It goes off by the kidneys, and the mucous membrane is affected by the skin-disorder. But I like my treatment and believe it will restore me. My situation otherwise is not only comfortable but happy. The students lose nothing, and I am free from all responsiblity and care. I will write the Preface when wanted. I cannot do such things long beforehand. Give my love to the dear children and their parents."

I give below a letter from the late Bishop of Carlisle, which arrived after his friend's decease.

"Basford St. Martin, Mt. Salisbury,
"June 8th, 1860.

"My Dear Sir:

"I am doubly in your debt: first, for your exposition of St. Mark, and now for your sermons. Accept my most sincere thanks for this kind remembrance of me, and remember, I pray you, that if ever you should come to England I shall be too glad to welcome you to my home.

"For the last fifteen years and a half that home has been in this lovely valley in Wiltshire. For the last three years of that period, I have had a three months' annual migration to the neighbouring city of Salisbury, where by the goodness of our God, I had the opportunity of preaching his Gospel, as Canon (not Dean) of the Cathedral.

"You can well understand how my heart is bound up with the spiritual interests of the Church of God in this neighbourhood. You can therefore believe me when I say that I am at the present moment deeply tried. For it has pleased God to call me to a yet higher post in his vineyard, and but a few weeks will have elapsed before I take my place in the far North of England—severing all Southern ties—as overseer of the Diocese of Carlisle. It is a joy to me to succeed such a man as Bishop Villiers has been: but still the pang of parting is bitter.

"Pray for me, my dear sir, that I may be kept faithful, humble, watchful, prayerful. We have had to pass through very deep waters lately. I now see for what they were designed to prepare us.

"Yours for Jesus's sake,
"Saml. Waldegrave."

During the interval between Dec. the 20th, and Jan. the 17th, the hopes of his friends were somewhat revived. The feverish excitement seemed to have left his system. He appeared better than he had been for a year, and said himself he "was better than he had been for *years*." His whole look and expression were much changed, and in the most gratifying way.

One of his relatives, who was with him at the time, wrote to the present biographer soon afterwards: "If you had looked in upon him in his study as he read in his various books, wrote in his journal until the 20th, and in his commentary on Matthew a little each morning till Jan. 18th, ten days before he died, reading with zest the papers and interested in all that was going on, writing letters, etc., you would not have known anything was the matter."

His brother's widow then lived in the adjoining house, and she will never forget his tenderness and generosity to her during these last days.

His sister, Mrs. Alexander, sent him a Christmas dinner, which he relished exceedingly; indeed he was never known to enjoy a dinner more. He appeared most grateful for this and every other similar act of kindness. He spent a really merry day in the good old sense of the word; but from this time he seemed to give up.

On Dec. the 17th, Dr. Hope of the college died suddenly in his chair. Dr. Alexander was much affected by the startling tidings, though he had never been specially intimate with that singularly good and attractive man. Mrs. Green sent him some jelly that day; and he seemed to read the news in the downcast face of the kind friend who brought the refreshment.

I think that up to the last month of his life he judged he might get well; but not so confidently afterwards. His letters and diaries, which had breathed hope, are still full of contentment, but a contentment not wholly produced by earthly expectations. The frequency with which he marked passages relating to the last exercises of good men, and the manner of their dying, is very striking. But still more so, perhaps, is the yet more frequent occurrence of his customary strictures and comments on the style. These marginalia also abound in wit and evince high spirits. The ruling passion never left him in this respect, nor as regards his taste for the most solid, and even forbidding, literature. I draw from this circumstance the animating inference that even when drawing near to the portals of the grave he was himself, and he was calm and even cheerful.

Some of the most remarkable though not the latest of these jottings are to be found in Dr. Stevens's History of Methodism both Wesleyan and Calvinistic. *

One of the last books he read was Adolphe Monod's *Les Adieux;* which I think came in time to be read and sorrowfully pondered by his brother James. The marred pages of his Flavel prove decisively that he was now drawing water out of the wells of salvation. There is a passage about the Resurrection in Dr. Hodge's commentary which he evidently enjoyed, and which it is now a comfort to his friends to read. During the last few weeks it was that he was so greatly revived and exhilarated by committing to memory a number of hymns, and especially Elliott's "Just as I am without one plea," Wesley's two beginning "Come let us anew our journey pursue," † and Watts's "Show pity, Lord, O Lord, forgive."

Nothing could exceed the devotion of his kind and indefatigable physician the late Dr. Woodhull; who had also prolonged the life, and comforted the last hours, of Dr. Archibald Alexander. This feeling was heartily reciprocated by his patient. Dr. Addison Alexander was never forgetful of the wants of his domestics and particularly mindful of the interests

* The most significant places marked in those volumes, are about an old Christian veteran who expected to "die sword in hand," and Whitefield's prediction that he should himself, after his many testimonies when living, "die silent." Both these modes of departure were actually realized in the case of the man who, when himself dying, marked these words with bold pencil strokes.

† The one he most admired, goes on, "With vigour arise." He admired this hymn not only practically, but intellectually—that is, as poetry.

of Marsh, his capable and attentive black man-servant. He has left on record, too, his devout thoughts respecting the spiritual state of old Ben. Sansbury, the eccentric half-breed who having been a useful servant of Dr. Archibald Alexander for twenty years, and after having given the strongest proofs of his fidelity, survived him but a few years.

The dying Christian now seemed to be meekly setting his house in order. He was awaiting the angels—if they should be sent to him; he was perhaps looking for those glorious battlements, of which he had so often and rapturously preached, that "city which hath foundations, whose builder and maker is God."

Yet his love of letters was as strong as ever. The day before he died, I find him not only at his usual tasks, but amusing himself over the pages of Rawlinson's Herodotus. He came down to the last; walking without any effort: rode out on Tuesday; enjoyed it; said he felt better for it; lay down on his settee afterwards, but directed some one to tell Dr. Hodge if he called, that "*he was not lying down because he was weak, for he felt better in every respect.*" During all the days of that week it was seen and deeply felt that he was going down, but it was not dreamed that the end was so near, indeed it was thought that he might linger for years. Though one could not feel that he would ever get well.

Just before the very last, he went about his room repeating to himself, in a plaintive voice, the words of Watts's "Show pity, Lord, O Lord, forgive; Let a repenting rebel live." This he did in a solemn, devotional manner, as if he was expressing his own penitential and prayerful feelings.

On Wednesday he was visited by his brother Samuel, from New York, who thought him much changed, and he told him he was weak; and the next night, Thursday, he told his sister he was getting weaker and must ask the doctor about it. His brother William came the very last day. On Friday he was much exhausted in dressing, but would shave and come down and drive out. This was the last time he ever left the house. He seemed to enjoy the drive,—more, he said, than the first one; but his feebleness was more apparent than ever, when he came to get out of the carriage. There was manifestly an alteration in him; though some of his friends thought he might linger for weeks. But he sat at the table as usual, and ate chicken soup and the leg of a chicken. A connection who saw him that day was greatly shocked at his appearance, and felt that death was written on his face; but never dreamed his end was quite so near. During the afternoon he sat by the fire, reading in the books he usually read in the afternoons. He had a glass of lemonade about four. At six a member of the family took him a bowl of sago, of which he was very fond. He was sitting reading when she went in; spoke as usual; seeming no weaker than he had done all day. When she went back for the bowl, an evident change had come over him—a change in kind rather than degree. It is believed now it was *death*, and had nature been left to itself, he would have survived but a few hours. It was a kind of helpless, sinking look, as the only witness said, "as if he had been trying to get up, and could not."

His mind evidently wandered: he expressed a wish to go to bed: he could not walk across the floor without assistance. A light French mahogany bedstead was brought down to his study. He did not like a wide bed: this was a narrow one. His brother Archibald, who is a physician, and the servant-man were with him all that night. Only once the next day he seemed to know the members of the family. It was when his pillow was arranged to suit him. He said, "that's delightful." He did not speak all day. At about 3½ P.M. he softly fell asleep. He had no suffering: indeed a more painless or quiet death cannot be conceived. An infant's slumber is not more serene and peaceful. "Wonderful! wonderful!" wrote a friend at the time. "And I had always thought it would be so hard for him to die. One lesson taught is 'Take no thought for the morrow.'"

He was in a stupor the whole of the last day and the only day he was in bed. His great resolution; his fixed determination to keep up and stick to his book, probably made his end more sudden than otherwise it would have been. It is likely, too, that it appeared more sudden than it really was. The shock would not have been so considerable, if all had been known. "We know *now*," writes one at the time, "that there was a serious cause for the wasting away of Addison's flesh." Although there were no indications of positive disease visible to the family, yet if he had been at least observant of his own state, or had ever "put this and that together" (as he told Dr. Hodge he never did); in short, if he had been in the least like anybody else as to his bodily condition, and had attended in the most ordinary ways to the care of himself, it is reasonable to think that the collapse might have been averted. Even as his end drew near, he seemed to recognize the languor and prostration only as *a desire to go to bed*, and nothing more; we have all heard of children just before they died saying they were tired, and wanted to go to sleep: and that was all this lofty intellect seemed to know of his own case.

"There is," wrote one of the household, "a sublimity of mercy in all this, to my apprehension, in being allowed to live a life of such enjoyment as a man of intellect and learning, and then give up life like a tired infant going to sleep—free from pain or the slightest anticipation of even physical discomfort. I never heard of such a case. It is a most mysterious thing, and I find myself constantly speculating about it. Sometimes I think, Could it have been consummate skill to keep the end out of our view as long as possible? But no! —a dying man has not strength for any such skill."

He had said that at the first sight of the blood, when on the steamboat with Dr. Hodge, he made up his mind to the worst. He was, however, perfectly free from all nervous fear and apprehensions. But some others, from the beginning, disregarded this symptom except as connected with an obscure and grave disorder which might yet yield to remedies. Among these was his astute friend Dr. Woodhull. His patient often spoke of this with admiration; as being "very little like an empiric" as the doctor had been accused of being. A relative records:

"He so wonderfully concealed the extent of his weakness, that the crash at the last was not really so sudden as it seemed. If it had been anybody else, I might think they were trying to conceal from friends or even from one's self the worst: but I cannot help thinking that in his case it was the unconsciousness of an infant."

Like Whitefield, he *said* nothing. The only words Whitefield uttered in his agony, were, "I am dying." Joseph Addison Alexander uttered none.

And so he died; and "all Israel mourned for him," who had been as the roe * upon the mountain-tops of Judah, the one of all others, "swifter than an eagle," and "stronger than a lion." The ministers of the Presbyterian church in particular wept over him who had given them so liberally of his own regal wardrobe of sanctified scholarship and genius; who had "clothed them with scarlet and other delights; who put on ornaments of gold upon their apparel." And they "lamented with this lamentation: 'How are the mighty fallen, and the weapons of war perished.'"

He was confined to the house just two months. The Seminary students had come to love him with a much more general attachment than in former years, and were overwhelmed with emotion when they heard that the great teacher of whom they were all so proud, was forever silenced.

Dr. McGill remarks, in connection with other observations on this subject:

"Many a student learned the tenderness of his heart, and the overflow of his good-will, in acts of substantial kindness; but only his colleagues knew the extent of his interest in them, and the tender magnanimity with which he watched for their welfare."

The wish of some that a picture should be taken of his appearance after death, was sadly complied with, and the design was executed by Mr. Alfred Yeomans, who thus speaks of his grand ruins:

* See Dean Stanley's comment on the passage in 1 Samuel i : 10, as given in his work on the Jewish Church.

"My last impressions were received as he was lying in his coffin in the Seminary chapel just before the funeral. There had been no recent photograph of his face, and Dr. Hodge was anxious to have some likeness of him as he appeared in his latter days. Learning that I had some little skill with the pencil, the Doctor sent me a request to try an outline of the head and face before the coffin was closed. It lacked but a few minutes of the hour of the funeral. Going hastily into the chapel, I attempted a pencil sketch on the fly-leaf of a music book from the choir gallery, but soon abandoned the effort as a failure. The outline, however, being shown to Dr. Hodge, he was struck with a resemblance due certainly rather to accident than skill, and sent me a request for a copy of it. The last time I was in his study, I saw it hanging there upon the wall. I have this outline before me as I write.

"The cheeks, of course, were much fallen away but the magnificent Websterian dome above the eyebrows seemed larger than ever, by contrast with the shrunken face. Is it not a suggestive fact that death which shrivels up the muscles that more especially pertain to the animal existence, cannot throw down the temple of the mind, or contract its proportions, but leaves it more marble-like and seemingly larger than in life. I had so seldom seen Dr. Addison's full open eye, that in drawing the sketch I could not make anything at all resembling it as in life, and was obliged to leave it closed as in death. Even now a picture of him with the eye cast down and the lid half shut, would be a better likeness to me than one with the eye fully open."

It was the sweet fancy of Dr. William Hoge, who understood him perfectly, that Dr. Addison Alexander was like a man who was allowed for a short time to roam over a great palace; and who would open one door, look in, and then rush to another. If I may be permitted to continue this noble image, he was now not a transient spectator, but a life-long proprietor of a much greater house, where he might forever roam at will.

The Rev. Dr. Wm. H. Green has given me the following account of the Conference in the Oratory, immediately succeeding Dr. Alexander's death:

"The Sabbath afternoon conference on the Sabbath following his death, was the most solemn one I have ever attended. The subject which had been assigned on the previous Sunday, without a thought of the loss which we were to experience in the interval, was, 'The Lord reigneth.' It was the very truth to which our stricken hearts instinctively turned for comfort and repose. Dr. Hodge could not control his voice sufficiently to read the usual chapter. But when the time came for remarks, as he touchingly said, 'We were assembled as a bereaved family, and would spend the time that we were together in talking of him whom we loved and who had been taken from us.' How premature his death appears to human view and how irreparable his loss!"

Dr. Hodge records it as his opinion that,

"His death in the prime of life was like the foundering of a richly laden treasure-ship in mid-ocean. To human view it was a dead loss. So much was expected of him beyond what he had accomplished. Had he lived ten years longer, he would probably have written more in that period than during the preceding thirty years of his literary life. He was gradually overcoming that fastidiousness of taste and judgment which rendered him dissatisfied with his own productions, and which led him to discard or abandon so many projected or partially accomplished works. He has left enough, however, to secure perpetuity to his memory. The public, indeed, can never know him as he was known by his intimate friends. The abiding impression which he made on their minds was, that the power of the man was far beyond his works; that there was in him far more than he had yet revealed; that he was a mine whose treasures had been only partially brought into view or use."

Soon after he was gone, Dr. McGill contributed to the *Presbyterian* the following account of the illness and last hours of Dr. Alexander.

"Owing to the peculiarly retiring habits and remarkable delicacy of the man, and to the extraordinary indifference with which he treated his physical nature and all hygienic science, many of his nearest friends and among these his own colleagues, did not know of his disease till the day of his death. His gigantic mind was in full vigour until Friday last. On the morning of that day he was occupied with his usual course of polyglot reading in the Bible, being accustomed to read the Scriptures in some six different languages as a part of his daily devotions. He seems also to have entertained himself during some part of the day with one of the Greek classics, Herodotus, as a pencil mark on the margin, 'January 27, 1860,' is said to show. In the afternoon of that day he rode out in the open air, for the first time since his attack of hæmorrhage. During that ride, however, which was not continued more than forty-five minutes, a sudden sinking of life came on him, so much so that he was borne almost entirely by the help of others from the carriage to his chamber. This sinking continued all Friday night, and on Saturday he was hardly conscious of anything until he died at half past three o'clock, P. M. His death was perfectly calm, without a struggle, without one heaving breath. He died in his study.

"During the whole confinement from his sickness, about two months, he was cheerful and happy; seeming to regret nothing but his inability for the ordinary duties of his chair in the Seminary. He occasionally expressed a fear that he was not sufficiently chastened in feeling by the affliction upon him. When dissuaded from severer studies, he seemed to find pleasure in committing hymns to memory, and humming them in his study; and these the most simple that could be found, to breathe the childlike trust, with which his heart was leaning on the Saviour. Instead of chanting in Greek the ancient hymn of Clemens Alexandrinus, or any other lyric which a scholar like himself might be supposed to prefer, his favourite hymn was—

"Just as I am, without one plea," &c.

Full of touching kindness towards all his colleagues, he seemed, if possible, to take a deeper place than ever in their love, as he approached his end; and brilliant as his whole career in teaching sacred literature had been, he never, probably, impressed his pupils with more effect and delight than he did this session. He said at the begiuing of it that he had never entered on a Seminary term with so much pleasure and alacrity—speaking of the change made in his title and duties by the last General Assembly.

"The funeral was attended on Tuesday with a very large concourse of friends and distinguished gentlemen, mostly from New Jersey and New York.

"The funeral services were held in the First Presbyterian Church. The sermon was preached by Dr. Hall, of Trenton; and a better discourse for the occasion could not be imagined. It was all the immense congregation of cultivated men, bowed with grief and yearning for comfort, could ask. All were edified with the discriminating and just delineation of the deceased. No one was disappointed; and this is saying much for a sermon over the remains of Joseph Addison Alexander. Dr. Hall was assisted in the solemnities by Drs. Spring, Potts, and Macdonald."

As soon as the melancholy news was known, letters of condolence and sympathy began to pour in from every quarter. The shock was keenly felt, even in Great Britain. Among those who wrote were the late Hon. and Rev. Samuel Waldegrave, afterwards Bishop of Carlisle, and the Rev. Charles Brown, D. D., of Edinburgh, afterwards the able editor and warm eulogist of his sermons.

His friend, Dr. Burrowes, expresses himself as follows:

"In these times, when pride of intellect and philosophy running riot are trying to make havoc of God's truth, and feel it almost a condescension to touch, even for its destruction, our old priceless system of the doctrines of grace, it is refreshing to contemplate the 'simplicity and godly sincerity,' the humility and whole-souled heartiness, with which he took, without the least abatement, these humbling doctrines to his very heart of hearts. The greatest of intellects, the most profound of scholars, he was the humblest of Christians.

'Just as I am, without one plea,
Save that Thy blood was shed for me!'

In this one feeling, all those great powers and attainments centred in life and in death. With all lying around him that talents and reputation could contribute to gratify ambition and intoxicate the heart, he turned away his dying eye to Jesus, and there found rest for his soul. With his home amid as wide and rich an intellectual paradise as is often accessible to the mind of man, he had used these things as not abusing them, and had turned from them to 'live by every word that proceedeth out of the mouth of God.' He was a marvellous instance of the power of God's grace in sobering, and sanctifying, and keeping a man, amid the dangerous and fiery temptations incident to a mind of such powers. Fervent love to Jesus, 'shed abroad in the heart by the Holy Ghost which is given unto us,' was the element in his being which held all his varied knowledge and great attainments in solution, and caused them to enter into combinations that enriched and adorned the living temple of the Redeemer. His crowning glory was, that while he was in fact a self-educated man, he had in reality but one teacher, Christ; and had been taught by Him, 'the truth as it is in Jesus.' Accordingly he held the truth in purity, as the heart receives that truth under the refining and sanctifying power of the Holy Spirit. To him was fulfilled the promise, 'His truth shall be thy shield and buckler.' The buckler borne on the breast of this prince in Israel in his post in front of the hosts embattled around the walls of our Zion, had no mixture of earthy alloy. It was compacted of 'the word of God pure as silver tried in a furnace of earth, purified seven times.' Among the scholars of the age who might be considered his peers, he was like Nestor alone with his entire shield of solid gold among the Grecian princes under the walls of Troy, preëminent above them all by the purity and solidity of this buckler of revealed truth, which threw over all his other intellectual armour a splendour and impenetrable defence.

Αἰὲν ἀριστεύειν, καὶ ὑπείροχον ἔμμεναι ἄλλων·
Μηδὲ γένος πατέρων αἰσχυνέμεν· οἵ μεγ' ἄριστοι·

In the spirit of these grand words of Homer, may we say of him: his character was of the noblest tone and loftiest aim; he distanced all competition; and he shed additional honour on his ancestral fame, though so illustrious."

On the morning after the intelligence of the death of Dr. Alexander reached Danville, the Rev. Dr. E. P. Humphrey, before beginning his daily lecture to the theological students, took notice of that afflictive providence.

Among other things, he said:

. . . .

"Dr. Alexander's whole public life has been given to theological research and instruction. . . . . .

"He had nearly completed his twenty-seventh year as a teacher of theology—dying now in the fifty-first year of his age. The main business of his life, as these statements show, has been with the word of God. It was with great reluctance that he undertook instruction in any other branch of learning; and he embraced the earliest opportunity of release from Church History, and of return to an exclusive attention to the Scriptures. His conception of the science and method of Church History shows that he would have become one of the eminent masters of the subject, if he had given that direction to his vigorous intellect. But he turned from every other form of knowledge to the written Word, in the spirit of the Psalmist: 'My soul breaketh for the longing it hath unto thy judgments at all times.'

"He belonged to a class of men of whom there are but few in

the Church. It did not please the Lord to establish him either in the pastoral charge or in the family state. . . . .

"The fruits of his public labours are to be found, in the first place, in the attainments of the ministers of the Gospel, several hundred in number, who have enjoyed the rare advantages of his instruction; and, still further, in his published writings. The fruits of his proficiency in Divine knowledge were rapidly maturing; and, if we may reverently say so, the loss which the Church has sustained in his premature death is beyond computation. How are all 'his purposes broken off'! A visit to his study, an inspection of his unfinished manuscripts, his incomplete criticisms, his half-developed thoughts and inquiries, and the pencilled margins of his books, would but too painfully teach us the meaning of the parable, 'How is the strong staff broken and the beautiful rod!'

"It is not difficult to determine his characteristics. One of the most obvious of these was breadth and comprehensiveness of mind. He contemplated subjects in their widest as well as their most intimate relations. In his exegetical writings, he is the linguist, closely interrogating the words themselves of Scripture, word by word: he is the philologist also, analyzing the sentence, verse by verse, according to its internal structure and its logical relations to the context: he is more, he is the expounder of the book as a whole, explicating the argument, and tracing the leading idea as it is unfolded from the beginning to the end. . . . .

He does more than that even: He deals with every book not only as a whole in itself, but as a part of the larger and absolute whole, the entire Scriptures, to wit, of both Testaments, the Old and the New. As a logical, in distinction from a verbal, interpreter, he resembled (I am not sure but I ought to say he equalled) John Calvin, who has been hitherto unequalled in that high quality; while as a verbal critic Dr. Alexander excelled that great master of biblical exposition. His eye was both microscopic and telescopic. But his distinction among scholars rests mostly upon the breadth of his general views, by which he not only obtained the mind of the spirit as a whole, but which he used as the true organon for the solution of specific difficulties. His conception of the Scriptures as a history of Redemption, his skill in pointing out the evolution of this history through all the sacred pages and by means of all the Divine dispensations, qualified him, beyond any of his contemporaries, to demonstrate that whole matter to the entire satisfaction of God's people. As a product of this rare gift of discerning the sequences of Scripture, I refer you to his exposition of the Gospel by Mark; which he clearly proves to be not a book of random recollections, as some pretend, nor an abridgment of Matthew's Gospel, as others suggest, nor a collection of unrelated memoirs of Christ, as others still suppose, but a systematic, independent history, composed after a strict method, upon a plan preconceived, rigidly executed, and controlling the selection and arrangement of the materials which were in the possession of the inspired author.

"Another quality in him was his balanced judgment. He was equipoised and ever poised. It would be difficult to discover the instance in which he was blinded by passion or prejudice, or fascinated by novel but insufficient theories, or imposed on by the whims of other men, or the creations of his own quick fancy and brilliant imagination. His eminent judgment was reinforced by his reverence for the Word of God. He sought most diligently the truth intended to be revealed. He allowed himself no liberties with the text which expresses that truth.

"In dealing with places hard to be understood, he states with conscientious accuracy the difficult points involved, suggests the explanations which have been proposed, perhaps offers an original solution, and, with a kind of judicial impartiality, judges both himself and other men, and if the case be so, frankly confesses his inability to solve the problem.

"Not the least of his merit as an interpreter is exhibited in his use of the German critics. He read the language with facility; he had spent some time in study at the universities of Halle and Berlin; and was thoroughly conversant with the critical literature of that country. He fearlessly levied contributions on that whole scholarship, whether of the pantheistic, or the theistic, or the semi-orthodox, or the evangelical school. Yet, with a quick insight into its falsehoods, or half-truths, or sound conclusions, as the case might be, he sifted the wheat from the chaff; he cast the magnet into the sand-heap, and drew therefrom the particles of ore, and then cast the ore itself into the crucible, and purged away the dross that remained, and so extricated the precious from the vile. He went into Egypt, and returned laden with the corn well winnowed, he went again, and tarried long there, but he came forth again, having never once bowed the knee to the idols of the land, prince's idols, but bearing with him the spoils of both; even gold, onyx stones, and embroidery, for the service of the house of the Lord and for the holy garments. This is one of his crowning honours as a Christian scholar, possibly some may think the chief of his great services to the Church of God. No man has done more than he to protect the ministry in this country against the skeptical criticism of Germany; none more, while doing that, to enrich our Biblical literature with the sound results of its truest learning.

"The manner in which his labours are set forth is answerable to their intrinsic value. His pages are adorned with the felicitous expression, the luminous criticism; the argument and conclusion, coherent and compact like a coiled chain or a folded coat of mail; possibly, here and there, a gleam of that trenchant sarcasm, which certain enemies of the truth have the best reason for remembering; but everywhere the fruits of the most patient and exact scholarship, thoroughly divested of the parade of learning. The soundest thinker and the most thorough scholar will best appreciate his merits.

"What has now been said concludes to the judgment that, take him for all in all, in his special province, the interpretation, namely, of the historical, prophetical, and poetical Scriptures (for he attempted nothing in the doctrinal epistles), he was not inferior to any critic of his generation: why should I not add, of any generation? I do not deny that men could be named who have severally surpassed him—one as a linguist, another as a philologist, and another still as an antiquarian, or a logical interpreter, or a dogmatic theologian; but what man has combined more of these qualities, and added to them a faith so sound and orthodox? In whom have these gifts coexisted in a higher average or a juster combination? If it be asked what made him to differ from others, the reply must be, the gracious purpose of God; who bestowed upon him unusual natural endowments, together with rare advantages of parentage, position, culture, erudition, and profession, and then consecrated this gifted man to his own service in the Regeneration.

"In his last published essay,* if I do not mistake the authorship, he discusses the location of the garden of Eden, as determinable by the description of the 'river that went out of Eden to water the garden.' He admits that the problem has not yet been solved, but suggests, with his characteristic breadth of view, that 'in the relation of the antediluvian annals to the later Scriptures, the solution of the question is no doubt to be sought, and will be ultimately found.' The type was hidden from him, but he has beheld that of which it was the type. He has found a guide who has first carried him away in the spirit to a great and high mountain, and shown that great city, the holy Jerusalem, and then has taken him within its gates and shown him a pure river of water of life, clear as crystal, proceeding out of the throne of

* See Princeton Review for January, 1860, p. 90.

God and the Lamb. In the midst of it, and on either side of the river, is there the tree of life, which bears twelve manner of fruits, and yields her fruit every month. What a vision of wisdom and glory has entered the soul of this gifted Biblical scholar! solving the problems which were too intricate for him here; even the most wonderful of them all, the salvation of the sinner by the incarnation and death of the Eternal Son.

"He was buried yesterday in Princeton, near the grave of Jonathan Edwards. From the monument of that great man we may take words expressive of the conflicting emotions which have been again experienced in the dwelling places of the living, and in the everlasting habitations of those who are dead but are alive for evermore.

"'Amissum plorat collegium, plorat et ecclesia;
At, eo recepto, gaudet
Cœlum.'"

INDEX.

Alexander Rev. Archibald, D.D., Father of Joseph Addison Alexander, 1; Removal to Philadelphia, 5; Pastor of old Pine Street (3d Presbyterian) Church, 5; Removal to Fourth Street, 8; One of his Sermons, 10; Removal to Princeton, 12; Method of Teaching his Sons Latin, 21; Opinion of Addison's Mental Capacity in 1817, 23; Letter to Mrs. Graham on Addison's Industry and Tastes, 43; Reminiscences by Dr. Burrowes, 259; His Preaching, 364, 374; Letter to his Son James W. on Addison's proposed Change of Professorship, 665; A Sermon, from Addison's Journal, 426; Received News of Addison's First Sermon, 440; Declining Health, Spring of 1851, 684; His Death, 686; Mrs. Lundy Duncan's Recollections of Him, 489.

Alexander Mrs. Archibald. Her Portrait, by Mooney, 1; Her Character and Attainments, 1; Rev. Dr. Baird on her Excellencies, 2; As an Interpreter of Scripture, 3; Her Decease, 697.

Alexander, Rev. Dr. James W.—Sophomore at Princeton, 24; First Acquaintance with Rev. Dr. Baird, 40; "Cyprian" Papers in the Christian Advocate, 55; German Lessons from Mr. Zadig, 55; Commenced Regular Study of Greek and Latin, 56; Criticism of Edward Irving, 56; Letter to Dr. Hall on American Scenery, 56; Appointed Tutor at Princeton College, 58; His Religious Ardour, 60; Attack of Sickness, 60; Letters to Dr. Hall on Addison's Studies, 155; To Addison, May, 1829, 175; To Addison on Abridgment of Rosenmüller's Alterthumskunde, 192; Connection with the Biblical Repertory, 198; Elected Pastor of Trenton Congregation, 280; Elected to Chair of Belles Lettres, 315; Death of his Little Son Archibald, 346; Essays of "Charles Quill," 410; Imaginative Poetical Sketch of Princeton Homes, 410; Death of his Eldest Child, George, 471; Numerous Calls in 1840 and Afterwards, 481; Elected, but Declined, Presidency of Lafayette, 486; Declined to Resume his Trenton Charge, 491; Lectured before Trenton Mechanic's Institute; Presented with Gold-headed Cane, 492; Installed at Duane Street Church, New York, 595; Colloquies with his Brother Addison, 637; Succeeded Dr. Miller in Princeton Chair of Church History, 665; First Introductory Lecture, 669; Inauguration, 670; Elected to New-York Duane Street Church, 683; Visited England, May, 1851, 684; His Return in October, 685; Death of his Daughter Jessie, 685; Second Installation at Duane Street, 691; "Consolation," his Book Entitled, 698; New York Labors in 1855, 750; Delivered 1855, Princeton Commencement Address, 769; Fifty-Second Anniversary, 1856, of his Baptism, 775; His work on the American Sunday-School, 805; Compelled by Throat Affection to Suspend his Labors, 806; Sent to Europe by his Congregation, 808; Returned to New

York, 815; Letter to Addison on Commentary on Mark, 823; Increasing Weakness; Journey to Virginia Springs, 868; Last Entry in his Diary, 874; His Death, 871.
Alexander H. C. (the author), see Recollections, Appendix C.
Alexander Hon. W. C., Intellectual Contests with his Brother Addison, 30; Article on a Trip to the Levant, 681.
Alexander Stephen. Appointed Adjunct Professor at Princeton, 344.
Alexander. See Also Letters of Dr. Addison Alexander.

Adams, President John Q., His Article on, in the Patriot, 119.
Allgemeine Zeitung, blunder of Would-be Literary Men, 837.
Alumni of Princeton, See Princeton.
American Whig Society, 75, 76.
Arabs, Historical Style of the, 168.
Assembly, See Presbyterian.
Augustine's Confessions, 224.
Baird Rev. Dr. R., Arrival at Princeton as Student, 39; Readings with the Brothers Alexander, 39; Succeeds to Princeton Tutorship, 39; Became one of Addison's Teachers, 41; Principal of Princeton New Academy, 40; His Growing Reputation, 40; Married; resigned for more active Life, 55; Allusion to Addison's Conversion, 220.
Barbour Governor, on Eloquence of Rev. James Waddel, 1.
Beggars, Addison's Kindness to, 436.
Belcher Governor, proposal to name Princeton College after, and his reply, 15.
Bethune Rev. Dr. G. W., Student and Friend of James W. Alexander, 64.
Bible, his love of the, 261.
Biblical History, his lectures on, 806.
Biblical Repertory. First appearance, 195; Changes in Form, in 1830 and 1837, 197; Transferred by Dr. Hodge to an Association, 197; Prosperity in 1841, 523.
Biblical Repertory, See also Princeton Review.
Bishop of Carlisle, Letter to Addison on Appointment to his Diocese, 888.
Blair Rev. D., visits to, 8.
Bolling Mr., a Fellow-Student at Princeton, 127.
Books, his rough treatment of, 678.
Breckinridge Rev. Dr. John, Mr. Bairds predecessor at Princeton, 41; The Death of, 495.
Brown Rezeau, Addison's Bosom Friend at College, 173; Memoir of him, 182; His death, 188; Traits of Character, 189; The only Letter by him discovered, 191.
Brown's Philosophy of the Human Mind, a Criticism of, 168.
Buffalo, the Bank Check and Self-identification, 856.
Burrowes Rev. Dr. George, 36; Reminiscences of Addison, 259, 476.
Calligraphy, Love of, 40.
Campbell Mrs., of Virginia, sketch of him, 31.
Candlish Dr., The preaching of, 707.
Cappadocian Society, 601.
Centennial, See Princeton.
Chalmers Dr. Thomas, Addison compared to, 633; A sketch of, 728.
Chicken College, Addison's when a boy, 29, 90, 91.
Children's Books on the Bible, his Opinion of, 259.
Cicero, a Criticism of, 172.
Classical Knowledge of Great Men, 677.
Cocquerel M., A Sketch of, 722.
Coffee, an Essay on, by Addison and James W., 211.
Colton Calvin, a Criticism of, 526.
Comfort in the Bible, Confessions, &c. 223, 224, 225.
Comfort David, a Fellow-Student, 40.
Commonplace Book at College, 96.
Congregational Union of England, Delegate's Visit to Princeton, 339.
Cooper's Novels, a Criticism of, 150.
Cordolia, Extracts from Byron and Southey, 76.
Coulombe M., French Teacher at Princeton, 132.
Cowper, his Admiration for, 96.
Crimean Soldier and the Military at Quebec, 854.
Cumming Dr., of London, a Sketch of, 713.

Cyprian, a nom de plume of James W. Alexander, in 1824, 55.
Dancing, New Jersey Patriot Discussion on, 102.
Dante, a Criticism of, 169.
Death, Reflections in 1830 on, 238.
Detroit Steam Dyeing Establishment, a Burlesque, 851.
Dunn Rev. Mr., of Germantown, 9.
Duncan Mrs. Lundy, Recollections of Dr. Archibald Alexander, 489.
Edwards Jonathan, Dr. Hall's Allusion to, 14; Inscription on his Monument, 903.
Edwards on the Collections, 224.
English Coldness of Manner, 78.
English Metaphysics, his Notions of, 168.
English Studies, 149 *et seq.*
Episcopacy, a New Theory of, 324.
Exegetical Study, his Method of, 434.
Family Worship at Addison's Home, 787.
Faraday's Character, its Likeness to Addison's, 660.
"Felix Trembled," Anecdote of a Student's Sermon, 570.
Flournoy Thomas, Letters on Addison in 1825, 76; Shake of Addison's Hand in 1845, 78.
Fire Worshippers, His Senior Class Theme, 75.
Forty Years Familiar Letters, 193, 195, 205, 206, 259, 260, 416, 561, 640, 659, 665, 667.
Geographical Research, a Plan for, 354.
Germantown, 8.
German Idealists, Addison's Parodies of, 253.
Graham Mrs., his Aunt, Letter to Dr. Alexander on his Capacity, 23.
Grammars, Foreign, the Construction and Study of, 271.
Greek Exiles at Princeton, 396.
Green Rev. Dr., President of Princeton College, on Princeton in 1793, 16; His Valedictory before Washington, 69.
Griswold, Bishop, A Criticism of, 526.
Guinness, Rev. Henry Grattan, the Irish Pulpit Orator, 884.
Hall Rev. Dr., Addison's Jeu D'esprit on, 837; (see also letters).
Hall, Robert, on Character of Jonathan Edwards, 14.
Halsey Dr. Leroy J., Editor of Dr. Lindsley's Works, 61.
Halyburton Thomas, the Life of, 257.
Hamilton James, Addison's early Latin Teacher, 36; Removal to Nashville University; Return to New Jersey; Death at Nashville, 37.
Hamilton Dr., of London, an account of, 712.
Hare Rev. S. B., His first Latin Teacher.
Hargous M. Louis, His French Lessons from, 161.
Hart J. S., Adjunct Professor at Princeton College, 344; Extract from "The Schoolroom," 608.
Hengstenberg Dr., His Study and Friendship with, 266; Messianic Interpretation, 354.
Hodge Rev. Charles, Editor of the Biblical Repertory, 195; Return from Europe and Address to Class, 197; Resumed sole Editorship, 198.
Hope Dr., of Princeton College, The Sudden Death of, 889.
Hotchkiss Miss, Her care of Addison at School, and his Recollections thereon, 9.
House Mountain, Virginia, 760.
Howell Dr., Princeton Physician, and his son Samuel H. Howell, 394.
Humphrey Rev. Dr. E. P., Address on Addison's Death, 899.
Irving, Edward, Rising into Fame in Scotland, 56; Sketch of, 289.
Jackson, Andrew, His Editorial on, 119.
Janvier Francis D., The Princeton Coach-painter, 70.
Jewish admirers of Addison's learning, 619.
Johnson Dr., and Boswell, an opinion of, 465.
Jones Dr. Joel, of Philadelphia, 886; Reminiscences of Mr. Walsh, 207.
Jones Sir William, Addison's admiration of, 43.
Journal, what its contents were, 504.
Journal, Extracts from, 146 &c., 159, 165, 221, 222, 226-241, 243, 257, 262, 340-344, 351, 352, 354, 355, 356, 359-363, 380, 381, 419, 420,

421, 424, 425, 426, 427, 429-435, 437, 438, 439, 440, 446, 448, 449, 452, 453, 454, 457, 458, 464, 701, 769, 770, 771, 776, 800, 804, 806, 807, 808, 814, 816, 819, 826, 849, 882.

Justice Joseph, of the Trenton Emporium, 126.

King William, a fellow-student of Addison's, 40; Addison's Walks and Companionship with, 127.

Kirk Rev. Dr. E. N., an early Playmate, 21; Was a Pupil of James Hamilton, 37.

Koran, See Languages, Persian.

Lacy Rev. B. T., Account of Dr. Archibald Alexanders' Funeral, 687.

Languages, See Appendix D.

Leighton Archbishop, On the Lord's Prayer, 226.

Lenox James, a visit to; His Collection of Old Bibles, 493.

Letters of Dr. J. A. Alexander, See Appendix to Index—B.

Library, Addison's, in 1828, 158.

Lindsley Rev. Dr. Philip, 37; His Princeton Classical School, 38; His Character and Attainments, 61; Collected Works, Edited by Dr. Halsey, 61; Various tributes to his Worth, 63.

Literary and Philosophical club, a Meeting of, 429.

McCall Hon. Peter, Drawing Lots with Addison for the Valedictory, 88.

McCall Rev. W. S., and the Philadelphia Synod of 1836.

McCarrier Jemmy and Joe, The College Servants, 72; Their Father, 73.

Maclean John, Account of in Centennial Address, 68.

McCleese Mr., Addison's Third Schooling with, 9.

McClung Mrs., Addison's visit to, in 1858, 821.

McDowell Hon. James, Address at Princeton Commencement, 459.

McGill Rev. Dr., Exchange of Princeton Chairs with Addison, 849; Account in the Presbyterian of Addison's Last Illness and Death, 896.

McNeile Dr., of Liverpool, Sketch of his Preaching, 706.

Mansfield, Lord, Early Literary Aspirations, 136.

Martyn Henry, The Oriental Scholar, Criticism of, 173; The Life of, 225.

Melville Dr., of London, A Sketch of, 719.

Messianic Interpretation and Hengstenberg, 354.

Mezzofanti Cardinal, Method of acquiring Languages, 21; Further of Him, 861.

Mickle William Julius, An Imaginary Letter of, 112.

Miller Rev. Dr., Resignation of Church History Chair at Princeton, 663; Last Sickness and Death, 671, 672.

Minnie, One of the Three Young Canadian Ladies, 859.

Missionary Herald, Addison's Fondness for the, 431.

Mohammedan Race, A College Theme, 75.

Mohammedan History, An Essay on, 209.

Mohammedanism, The False Prophet, 267.

Monachism, A College Paper on, 75

Moore Dr., Account of Addison's visit, in 1858, to Mrs. McClung, 821.

Moot Court, the, at Princeton, 45.

Napton Hon. William (Judge), A Student at Princeton and one of Addison's two only Companions in 1823, 40, 45, 52, 53, 65; His Recollections of Princeton Society, and Celebrities, 69, 70.

Nassau Hall, Princeton College, History of, 15.

New-Haven Preachers, A Description of, 700.

New Jersey Bible Society, Executive Committee in 1827, 114.

New Jersey Historical Society, Design of a, 429.

New Jersey Internal Improvement Convention in 1827, 114.

New Jersey Patriot, Description of the, 111.

New Jersey Patriot; for Contributions to, see Addison's Works, &c.

Newman John Henry, A Criticism of, 527.
Newton John, The Writings of, 228.
Onderdonk Bishop, A Criticism of, 526.
Oratorical Warning in Boyhood, Value of, 29.
Oral Discussion, An Opinion upon, 515.
Oriental Languages, See Languages.
Owen on Spiritual Mindedness, 225.
Oxford Tracts, the, and John Henry Newman, 527.
Pains and Pleasures of a College Life —Princeton Valedictory, 88.
Park, Rev. James, Amusing account of Matriculation before Addison, 576.
Parnell's, The Hermit, a quotation from, 283.
Patton, Professor R. B. of Princeton, 97, 98, 100; His School, 212; His edition of Donnegan's Greek Lexicon, 213; Addison's Religious Impressions at his School, 219; Death of Mr. Patton's little daughter Harriet, and its effect on Addison during conversion, 237.
Personal Traits—Early Love of Fiction, 19; Domestic Character, 25; Fondness for Music, 25; Diffidence, 41; Truthfulness, 47; Likeness to Bonaparte, 47; Long Walks, 50; Kindness to Classmates, 53; Memory, 64, 502, 606; Irreproachable Morals, 82; Versatility, 83; Metaphysical Study, 253; Various Personal Traits, 366, 367, 368, 369; Tours about Home, 508; Tastes in Art, 510; Constructive Powers, 622; Not an Innovator, 624; Disdain of Pulpit Arts, 652; His Study and his Library, Habits in, 694.
Philadelphians, Sketches of Old, 8.
Poems, "Ad Joannem," a Young Friend on 15th Birthday, 482; Brown Rezeau, the Death of, 190; "Charity," Extract; Doomed Man, Comments upon, 415; Earliest Efforts, 30; Fall of Ispahan, 140; Flibbertigibbet in liquor, an Imitation of Shelley, 117; Italy, Verses Written in, 304, 312; Juvenile Poems, 32, 33; His own opinion of them, 35; Latin Verses of Mock Condolence with James, 60; Lurid Leper, the, 562; McCarrier Brothers, Facetious Verses on, 72; Motherless Girl, lines to a, 687; Peruvians, the, 96; Princeton, lines on, 54; Tears of Esau, 133; Vision of Greece, 142.
Poems, compared with those of contemporaries, 144.
Pope, Alexander, a criticism on, 194.
Potts, Silas, a young college companion, 9.
Potts, Judge S. G., and the Trenton Emporium, 126.
Pratt, Horace S., Private Tuition from, 39.
Preparation for the Ministry, Addison's Scheme of, 243.
Presbyterian, the, on his Linguistic Attainments, 23.
Presbyterian Emigration from North of Ireland, 4.
Presbyterians, Old and New Schools of, 359.
Presbyterianism, Geneva Letter on, 299, 625.
Presbyterian Philadelphia Synod in 1836, 397.
Presbyterian Assembly of 1837, 408; of 1856, 798.
Presbytery of New Brunswick Centennial Meeting in 1838, 434, 457.
Presidential Contest of Adams and Jackson, 119.
Pressensé M., The Paris Preacher, 722.
Price Mrs., a Friend of Addison's Childhood.
Princeton, Congress Meeting at, in 1783, 16; Slip from Early History, 17; Called the Montpellier of America, 17; Graveyard of and its dead, 18; Society and Celebrities, 40, 67, 156.
Princeton College Alumni, Distinguished, 14; Belcher Hall, Proposed Name, 15; Alumni Association, First Meeting and Officers of, 114; Centennial Extracts, 4, 14, 15, 16, 17, 66, 67, 68, 69; Commencement in Old Times, 66, 67; Chair of History, 663; Commencement, New Jersey Patriot on, 113; Des-

cription of the College, 14; Faculty and Curriculum in 1824, 65; Golden Age, 1844, of, 593; Green, Dr. Ashbel, on appearance in 1783, 16; Moot Court, 45; Nassau Hall, 15; Philologian Society, 100; Round Table and Chronomian Clubs, 63; Suspension Temporary, in 1780, 16.
Princeton Literary Association, 338, 341.
Princeton Magazine of 1850, 681.
Princeton Review, Change of Name, 531.
Princeton Valedictory, Addison's, 88.
Punch, the London, Addison's opinion of Writers of, 665.
Punctuation, an Opinion on, 132.
Quebec, a Description of, 853.
Randolph John, On Candor and Modesty, 47.
Recollections by Relatives, Friends, and Pupils, See Appendix to Index—C.
Reporter A, Instance of Addison's Pulpit-power Over, 648.
Rice Rev. Dr. Benjamin H., 344; His Death, 776.
Rice Rev. Dr. John H., in 1828, 161; Removal to New York, 180.
Riches of the English Language, 51.
Richmond Theatre, Dr. A. Alexander's Sermon on Burning of, 10.
Ridge Recorder, the, Origin and Extracts, 544.
Ritualists and the Chinese, 528.
Rives Hon. W. C., Letter with European Introductions, 284.
Rosenmüller's Alterthumskunde, 192.
Ross James, Addison's Schooling with, 9.
Scott Rev. Dr., of New York, 345.
Scott's Life of Napoleon, a Criticism of, 171.
Scriptural Dramatic Sketches, a Plan for, 399.
Secession, Forebodings of James W. on, 803.
Self-Identification, a Curious Process of, 856.
Sermons, Criticisms of Styles, 178.
Shakespeare, a Criticism of, 166.
Shea, Mr. Sergeant, a Sketch of, 716.
Shelley's Hymn to Intellectual Beauty, 28.
Smith Samuel Stanhope, at Princeton College, 14.
Snowden Dr. Isaac C., Editor Philadelphia Monthly Magazine, 135; Letter to Addison on Contributions to, 137.
Spencer Edmund, a Criticism of, 170.
Steele Revs. Robert and Samuel, 7.
Steele Mr. John, Kindness to Addison, 7.
Stewarts Philosophy of the Human Mind, 255.
Stockton Family, the, 67.
Stories of Old Black, Peter Arun, &c., 163.
Strong Salmon, Head of Dr. Lindsley's School, 38.
Sunday School Journal, a Letter on the, 263.
Swift, Addison, Dickens, and Others, Remarks on, 362.
Thomson Madame, His First School, 7.
Thrice Transplanted, a Sonnet, 860.
Transcendentalism, Amusing Letter on, 521.
Trenton, Emporium of Joseph Justice and Judge Potts, 126.
Turner Mr. W. W., The Abilities of, 635.
Ulster, Account of Early Settlers from, 4.
Vethake Henry, Sketch of, 275.
Waddel Dr. Addison, 6.
Waddel Rev. James, the Blind Preacher, 1.
Waldegrave Hon. and Rev., Letter with Index of Authors, 772.
Walsh Mr. Robert, History and Scholarship of, 204.
Washington George and Pres. Green's Address, 69; Peale's Portrait, 16.
Washington City and Congress, Impressions of, 512.
Westminster Hall and the Law Courts, 715.
Wistar's Magazine, 552 to 564.
Witherspoon Rev. Dr., President of Princeton College, 14.
Wordsworth William, Lines Applied to Francis D. Janvier.
Writings, His Sermons, See Appendix E.

Xenophon, an Estimate of, 176.
Yeomans Dr. Edward, on Addison's Prayers, 378.

APPENDIX A.

PERSONAL HISTORY OF DR. J. A. ALEXANDER.

Birth and Parentage, 1; Ancestry, 4; Removal of Family to Philadelphia, 5; Recollections of Philadelphia during Childhood, 5; Early Study of Latin, 6, 36; Love of the Classics, 7; Last Schooling with Madame Thomson, 7; A Pupil of Mr. Littell, 8; Removal to Fourth St., 8; His First Latin Teacher, Rev. S. B. Hare, 9; His Second Latin Teacher, James Ross, 9; Alexander Magnus, 9; His Manuscript Recollections of Early Life, 10; Removal to Princeton, 12; His Mental Progress, 18; His Early Playmate, E. N. (now Dr.) Kirk, 21; First Lessons in Hebrew, 22; His Mental Capacity in 1817, 23; Teaches himself to Write, 23; First Lessons in Greek, 36; Attends Dr. Lindsley's School at Princeton, 38; Private Teaching by Horace S. Pratt, 39; First Acquaintance with Robert Baird, 39; Moot Court Exercises with W. B. Napton, 40; A Student under Mr. Baird, 40; Edits a Newspaper at the Academy, and aids Formation of a Literary Society, 40, 42; Appearance at Fourteen; likeness to Napoleon Bonaparte, 47; School Feats in English Composition, 50; Attachment to his Brother James, 60; Centennial Address on Princeton of Old Times, 66; Matriculation in 1824, at Fifteen, 73; High Class Standing, 74; American Whig Society, 75; His Paper on Monachism, 75; Growth of Character and Manners, 86; His College Debating Society, 86; Created B.A. 88; Appointed Clerk of Borough of Princeton, 89; First View of the Sea, at Long Branch, 91; His Father's Account of Final Examination and Valedictory, 93; His Princeton Medal for Composition, 93; Declined, in 1827, Tutorship at Princeton College, 97; Picture of, about that Time, 98; Editor of the Patriot, 117; His Library in 1828, 158; Sketch of, at Nineteen, 173; At Twenty, 175; Visit in 1829 to New York, 180; Began Study of Arabic and Persian; Prize Essay, 201; Becomes Teacher of Latin, History, &c., at Prof. Patton's School, 212; Wishes, in 1829, to Settle in the East, 214; Increased Attention to Greek Study, 216; Conversion, His First Deep Religious Impressions, 219, 221; His Journal of the Same, and His Father's Opinion, 221; Resolutions of Religious Training, 235; Twenty-first Birth-day, Solemn Self-devotion to God, 239; Appointed Adjunct Professor of Ancient Languages and Literature, at Princeton, 242; Attack of Scarlet Fever, 242; Resolution to Prepare for the Ministry, 243; Characteristics and Appearance at this Time, 246; Studies During 1831, 252; Religious Experiences, 257, 262; Studies in 1832, 262; Residence with Dr. Vethake, 275.
Sailed for London April 10, 1833, Introductions by W. C. Rives, 284; Farewell Letter to his Mother, 284; Officers of the *Samson*, 285; From Portsmouth to London, 286; Stage Coaches, 286, 292, 293; English People, 287; London, House of Commons, Exeter Hall, &c., 288; Bishops of Winchester and Chester, 288; Chancery, Brougham, Edward Irving, 289; London to Oxford, 292; Edinburgh, House of John Knox, Prof. Lee, 293, 294; Arrived in France, French Politeness, 294; From Dover to Calais, 295; General Lafayette, a Visit to, 295; St. Denis, 297; Munich, the Students' Church, 297; Berne Cathedral Church, 298; Lausanne, a Traveling Companion, 298; Geneva, Church of the Eglise, 299; Visit to D'Aubigne,

302; Franciscan Friar, 308; On to Rome, 310; Via Cassia, 311; Austria, Venice, 314; Halle, Dr. Tholuck, 316; Mr. Sears, and Mr. Haverstick, Tholuck's American Pupils, 316; Daily Life at Halle, 317; Visit to Von Gerlach, 317; Tholuck's Preaching and Lectures, 319; German Life and Customs, 321; Tholuck's Estimate of Addison, 323; Celebrated German Professors, 325; Neander, 327; Return to Princeton, in May, 1834, 332.

Appointed Adjunct Professor of Oriental Literature, at Princeton Theological Seminary, 332; Declines, 361; Biblical and Oriental Labors in, 351; Attends New York Anniversaries, in 1835, 358; Elected but Declines Chair of Oriental and Biblical Literature, in Union Theological Seminary, New York, 380; Companions in 1836, 394; Travels in New Jersey, the Same Year, 395; Attacks of "Jaw Swell," His Old Remedy, 396; Class of 1837, 402; High Pressure Teaching, 405; Severe Illness in 1837, 407; Commenced Notes on Isaiah, 414; Learns Polish, 414; Received, in 1838, as Candidate for License, 435; Licensed, 439; His First Sermon, 440; Journeys to Philadelphia, Washington, &c., 445; Accepted Seminary Professorship Offered in 1835, 445; An Editor of the Biblical Repertory, 450; Residence with his Brother James, 454; Installed in Professorship, Inaugural, 458; Ordination Examination, 469; Tours about Home, 508; Supplied, in 1847, Tenth Church (Dr. Boardman's), in Philadelphia, 639; Residence at House of Dr. Harris, 653; Assists Dr. Cuyler, at Second Presbyterian Church, Philadelphia, 662; Lectured at Close of 1850 at Princeton, 680; Occupying Chair of Ecclesiastical History, 697; Second Journey to Europe, 704.

Sailed, May 18, 1853, for Liverpool, 704; Arrived, 705; Dr. McNeile, 705; Dr. Candlish, 707; Melrose Abbey, 711; Dr. Hamilton, 712; Dr. Cumming, 713; Westminster Hall and the Courts, 715; Sergeant Shea, 716; Judges, 717; Mr. Binney, 718; Dr. Melville, 719; At Paris, 721; M. Cocquerel, M. Pressensé, 722; On the Rhine, 723; The Low Countries, 726; London, 727; Dr. Chalmers, 727; Return Home, 728.

Death of his Aunt, Mrs. Graham, 731; And of his Uncle, Major John Alexander, 737; Autumn 1854 Journal, 737; Visits to Virginia in 1855, 753; Back at Princeton, 769; Preached for his Brother, 775; His Home in 1856, 785; Left New York, 803; Visits, in 1858, to Virginia, and Canada, 819, 820; Declining Health, 831; Manner, in 1858, of Living, 844; Visiting the Sick, 847; Exchanged to Chair of New Testament History, 849; Visit to Quebec, 853; A Crimean Soldier, 853; Acquaintance, in 1853, with Three Young Canadian Ladies, 859; Removed to his Brother Samuel's House, New York, 861; His Brother James' Death, Effect on Addison, 871; His Continued Failure of Health, 875; Assumed Charge of Hebrew Department of Hebrew at Princeton, 876; Last Message and Letter to the Students, 877; His Visible Decline, 879; The Anxiety of his Friends, 880; Seized with Hemorrhage of the Lungs, 884; His Last Letters, 887; The Last Books he Read, 890; Increasing Weakness, 891; His Peaceful End, 892; Conference of the Oratory on the Event, 895; Alfred Yeomans' Impressions of Addison in his Coffin, 895; Dr. McGill's Account of his Illness and Death, 896; His Funeral Sermon, 897; Tribute of Dr. Burrowes, 898: His Grave at Princeton, 18.

APPENDIX B.

LETTERS OF DR. J. A. ALEXANDER.

To His Mother, in 1833, on Sailing for Europe, 284; on July 27, 1846, 615; in 1850, 674.
His Sister Jane, on His Visit to Dr. Moore, 820.
His Brother, Henry M., a Rhyming Letter, 394; from Clifton, in 1855, 757.
His Brother James, probably in 1828, 128, 131; His Early Wish to Settle in the East, 217; From Geneva, 299; Introduction to Isaiah, 602, 603, 610; In 1846, Subject of Unusual Learned Interest, 619; From Geneva, on Presbyterianism, 625; In 1846, Learned Authors, 634; Work on Popular Theology, 660; Literary Subjects, 661; Printing Book of Psalms, 662; In 1852, on Literary Subjects, 692; In 1853, on Ancient Liturgies, Reading English, *et. al.*, 698; Princeton Chair of History, 663; On Interpretation, 701; Anecdote of Pallavicino, 752; Church History, 778; Progress of His Matthew, 828; Money for Presents of Books, 842; In 1859, on Return from Journey, 851; In 1859, on Buffalo and Detroit, 855.
His Brother James' Death, a Letter on, 872.
His Brother Samuel D., New Haven Preachers, 700; In 1854, 738; May, 1855, 753; October, 1856, 803; During His Last Illness, 887.
His wife's Relatives, in 1819, 24.
Canadian Three Ladies, as "The Unknown," 859.
Friend, A. on Projected Work on Isaiah, 474, 475, 476.
Hall, Rev. Dr. John, on Sunday-School Journal, 263; Character of Correspondence with Dr. Hall, 372; With Latin Dictionary, &c., 381; With Word "day" in Several Languages, 398; In 1836, Various Topics, 400; July and August, 1837, 409; On a Parallel Bible, 417; Seminary Instruction, 418; Various Literary Subjects, 428; On Cicero, 465; On Multiplying His Labors, 507; Indiscreet Overwork, 574; On His Doctorate, 591; Sending Student to Preach for Dr. Hall, 597; Ministerial Supplies, 613; Ironical and Playful, 638; Similar to the Retiring Professor, 683; His Extraordinary Desk, 691; On a Cutter, 739; Duties and Engagements, 775; His First Book, 814; With Humorous Poem "by Sir Knight John K. Hall," 850; On Illness of His Brother James, 872; On Death of, 874.
Hodge, Rev. C. W., from New York, in 1856, 800.
John, a Young Friend, with Verses on Fifteenth Birthday, 482.
Little Girl, To a, 859.
Little Pupil, a Letter to, 412.
Old Correspondent, As Transcendentalist, Covenanter, and Ritualist, 521.
Repertory, Questions in Interest of the, 412.
Schaff, Dr., Church History, German Authors, 310; Literary Subjects, 740; Proposed Work by Dr. Schaff, 813.
Scribner, Mr., Proposed Volume of European Travels, 703, 704; On a Popular Church History, 744; Offer of Book on Acts, 751; Reprinting Repertory Essays, and on Book on Acts, 772, 773, 777, 779, 780, 781; Progress of His Book, 805.
Young Pupil, in 1838, 450, 451.

APPENDIX C.

RECOLLECTIONS BY HIS RELATIVES, FRIENDS AND PUPILS.

Alexander H. M. His Youngest Brother, on Addison's Habits while Working on Isaiah, 597.
Alexander H. C. (The Author). Of Addison in 1849, 666; in 1855 to 1858, 785, 826; At Home in 1857, 811; His Innocent Playfulness, 835.
Alexander J. McD. Of him in 1855, 758.

Alexander Dr. Samuel D. On his Labor on Commentaries, 824.
Alexander Dr. Addison. His own MS. Recollections of Early Life, 10.
Adger Dr. J. B. Of him in 1829, 213.
Baird Prof. Henry M. His Preaching, 656.
Baird Dr. His Early Talents and Diffidence, 41; Powers as a Linguist, 45.
Baldwin Hon. J. B. Addison in 1855. 768.
Bolling G. W. A Classmate of College Life, 87.
Breckinridge Judge. Addison in 1828 and 1829, 549.
Burrowes Rev. Dr. Characteristics in 1830, 249, 276; Intellectual Symmetry, 631, 632; Tribute to his Memory, 898.
Cameron Professor. His Memory, 693; Preaching, 817; Day with him in the Cars, 833.
Campbell Charles. College Days, 31. Some years after, 98.
Cattell Dr. W. C. Of, in 1849 and 1850, 733.
Comfort David. His Great Promise, 46; Intellectual Powers, 85.
Cuyler Rev. Dr. Sketch of two Evenings with him, 654.
Dabney Rev. Dr. On Visit to Lexington, 757; Last Visit to him, 798.
Dale Rev. J. W. His Philadelphia Preaching, 644.
Davies Mr. His Preaching, 487.
Ewing James. His Promise as a Preacher, 46.
Favorite Pupil. Recollections, 551.
Field Hon. Richard S. His Power over an Audience, 453.
Friend A. His Method of Study, 588.
Godwin Parke. Recollections, 250.
Gosman Rev. Dr. A close friend. Recollections, 585; At work on Isaiah, 601; His Last Illness, 880.
Graham Mrs. his Aunt. Letter on his mental capacity, 23.
Green Rev. Dr. Addison as a Preacher and Scholar, 365, 569; His Last Words to his Classes, 876; Testimony to his Worth, 877.
Hodge Dr. A. A. Recollections; tribute to Father and Brothers of Addison, 583.
Hall Rev. Dr. John. Life-long Relations with him, 383; Addison before 1841, 496 *et seq.*; Sermon "The City with Foundations," 502; Customary Silence, 516; His Tenderness of Nature, 843; Sincerity and Affection, 845.
Halsey Rev. Dr. L. I. His first and Subsequent Preaching, 442; What he might have Achieved in Literature only, 540.
Hamilton's Opinion of him in 1819, 36.
Harris Rev. Dr. William. His Philadelphia Preaching, 644; Treatment of Books, 679; Abhorrence of Notoriety, 647; Addison at Philadelphia, 653.
Hart Prof. John S., LL.D. Recollections, 99, 349; Princeton Review Articles, 523; Powers of Sarcasm, 531; Preaching at Philadelphia, 641.
Hepburn Prof. Andrew D. Recollections, 420; Lectures and Methods of Teaching, 801; Public Reticence of Opinion, 807, 809.
Hewitt Rev. Dr. His Last Illness, 626.
Hodge Rev. Dr. Charles. Addison in 1834, 333, 334; Early Preaching, 449; Intellectual Ascendency, 506; Aversion to Society, 542; Of Addison for nearly 48 years, 748; Changeableness, 779; Impressions in 1860, 878; Death in the Prime of Life, 896.
Hooper Rev. T. W. The Brothers Alexander, 840.
Humphrey Rev. Dr. E. P. Address on Addison's death, 899.
Jacobus Rev. Dr. Ability as a Commentator, 472; Brooklyn Sermons, 618.
James Henry. Addison at Princeton, 493; Charity of his Nature, 530.
Joline Vandyke. His Character, 82.
Jones Rev. Dr. Beach. His Biblical Scholarship, 784.
Jones Rev. Dr. of Bridgeton. Recollections, 365; Preaching, 650.
Jones Rev. Joseph H. Recollections,

572; Preaching, 645; Last Illness, 886.
King Wm. His Student Days, 48.
Lacy Rev. Dr. B. T. His Preaching, 456; Scholarship, Impartiality, and Candour, 574, 575, 576; His Appearance, 580; Rank as a Divine, 634.
Lady A. Philadelphia Preaching in 1847, 642.
Leftwich Rev. James T. His Preaching, 832.
Lenox James, Esq. Addison in 1841, 493.
Leyburn Rev. Dr. John. Addison in 1830, 247; At Philadelphia, 669.
Leyburn Rev. George. Addison at Princeton, 248.
Little Rev. James. Addison in 1854, 745.
Lord Rev. W. W. Impressions of him, 594.
Lyon Dr. James. Recollections 1832 to 1836, 336.
McCall Mr. Opinion of Addison by the Faculty, 94.
Maclean Rev. Dr. George M. His Early Promise, 46; His Childhood, 86.
McClung Mrs. His youngest Aunt, 763.
McGill Rev. Dr. A. T. Disposition as a Teacher, 335; His Preaching, 651; Goodwill towards Friends, 746; Mobility and Steadfastness, 761; Exchange of Chairs with him, 849; Love of Change, 852; Magnanimity, 894.
Miller Rev. Dr. S. Addison's Return from Europe, 329.
Moore Rev. Dr. T. V. In 1839 and afterwards, 478; Visits to Richmond, 753.
Napton W. B. Moot-court Exercises with, 40; As a Student, 79, 80; His Learning, 83; Habits, 127.
Park Rev. James. Addison at Matriculation, 576.
Philadelphia Lady. His Influence in Society, 643.
Phillips Prof. Charles. His Kindness. 572.
Pupil A. Good Sense and Christian Faith, 620.
Ramsey Rev. Dr. James. Addison in 1836 to 1839, 383 *et seq.*; First and Subsequent Sermons, 440, 441; His Visits to Virginia, 760.
Read Rev. Dr. Charles A. His Pulpit Power, 648; Effect on Newspaper Reporter, 648.
Rice A. A., M.D. His Polygonal Intellect, 548; Rare Humour, 836.
Rice Rev. Dr. John H. Picture in 1828, 161; Hatred of Dulness or Laziness, 368; In his Study, 519; Mental Gifts, 627; In 1853, 730.
Ruffner Rev. Dr. W. H. Preaching, 618; In 1848, 659; Oratorical Specialties, 668; Visits in 1851–3, 697.
Scott Rev. Dr. Recollections, 345; Addison's and Chalmers' Preaching, 633.
Sears Rev. Dr. At Halle, Germany, 320.
Smith Rev. Dr. B. Visits to Addison, 740.
Snowden Rev. Dr. Papers in Philadelphia Magazine, 137.
Sprague Rev. Dr. William B. Addison as a Boy, 408.
Stevenson Rev. Paul Eugene. His Poetical Character, 539; Last Interview, 825; Tribute to him, 848.
Sunday School Times. His Writings and Preaching, 535.
Teese Rev. David. In Class of 1837, 402; While a Licentiate, 468.
Virginia Lady, a Pupil. His Modes of Teaching, 610.
Waddell J. A., Esq. Addison in 1855, 765.
Western Physician. His Preaching, 455.
Wilson Rev. Dr. H. N. Addison in 1834 and 1835, 348; Anecdote, 839.
Wilson Rev. Joseph R. Virginia Visits in 1862, 762, 765.
Yeomans Rev. Dr. E. D. Recollections, 616.
Yeomans Rev. A. Addison's Failing Health, 876; Addison in his Coffin, 895.

APPENDIX D.

LANGUAGES ACQUIRED BY HIM.

Arabic, Facsimile of Translation of Waverley Title Page, 44; Studies of the Koran, 149, &c.; When he Began Study of, 201; Extract on Study of, 271; His great Familiarity with the Language, 274.
Arabic, see also Koran.
Chinese, Study of, 159.
Danish, Study of, 253; His Rapid Acquirement of, 731.
French Studies, Telemaque, &c., 149.
Greek, His First Lessons in, 36.
Hebrew, Studies in, 147, *et seq.*; Inscription in his Hebrew Grammar, 22; Methods of Recitation and Study, 421; Readings of Homer, 128; Study in 1828, 129.
Italian, his Opinion of, 21; Tasso, 132.
Oriental, his Love of, 43; Word "Day" in Several, 398.
Persian, 43, 103, 148, *et seq.*, 201, 590; Koran, 131, 149, 267.
Polish, 414.
Portuguese, 253.
Spanish, Masters Grammar, 132; Don Quixote, &c., 148, &c.
Translation, rigid Method of, 636.
Turkish, began Study of, 253.
Languages he Learned, a list of, 862; Questions on Formation, 132; See also Journal.
Linguists, Comparison of several Celebrated, 861.

APPENDIX E.

HIS WRITINGS—BIBLICAL, LITERARY, AND MISCELLANEOUS.

Acts, Offer to Mr. Scribner, 752; Publication, 782, 882.
Adams, President John Q., Patriot Editorials on, 119.
Assentative People, an Essay on, 764.
Biblical Repertory, Contributions to, 195, 199, 341.
Children's Papers, Wistar's Magazine, &c., 542 to 564.
Church Government, Treatise on, Commenced, 566; at work on and other Labors, 732, 733.
Church History and New Testament Literature, 801.
Coffee, an Essay on, by Addison and James, 211.
"Diagnosis of the I and not I," 253.
Donnegan's Greek Lexicon, Work on New Edition, 213.
Druse, The, an Essay on, 199.
Emporium, The, Contributions to, 85, 126.
Fandango of Osiris, The, 52.
Ham and Eggs, a Plea for Silent Legislation, 515.
High Church Episcopalianism, 528.
Isaiah, Notes on, Commenced, 414, 592; Resumed, 567; With Publisher, 596; Origin of the Work, 604; Early Prophecies published, 604, 611; Second Volume Commenced, 614; Published, 635.
Jewess of Damascus, The, 122.
Johnson Dr., Imitation of, in "Persian Poets."
Justin the Martyr, Extract from Translation, 196.
Koran, Article on the, 267 (See also Languages).
Linn Lane, Story of, 163.
Medley, The, Contributions to, 51 52.
Mohammedan History, 209.
Mohammedanism, Papers on, 75, 209, 267.
Mark, The Introduction to, 820.
Mothers' Magazine, a Brochure in 1820, 675.
Newspapers, Contributions to, 82.
New Jersey Patriot, Contributions to, 101, 112, 116, 119.
"Nothing," a Prize Essay on German Idealists, 254.
Old Black, his Story of, 163.
Oriental Languages, see Languages.
Parallel Bible, a Plan for, 417.
Philadelphia Monthly Magazine, Contributions to, 102, 136.
Presbyterian, The, List of 1832 & 1833 Articles, 281.
Primitive Church Offices, His Work entitled, 567, 683.
Princeton Magazine and Review, Contributions to, 51, 265, 518, 523, 533, 682, 865.
Psalms, His Work on, 666.

Rambler, Spectator, &c., Imitations of, 192.
Rosenmüller's Alterthumskunde, Addison and James' Abridgment of, 192.
"Russia," a College Effort, 75.
Sacred Geography, 192.
Shelly, Flibbertigibbet in Liquor, a Burlesque on, 117.
Souvenir, The, Paper by "Horace Seaford," 102.
Trochylus, Articles under Signature, 112.
True Happiness, an Essay in Boyhood, 412.
Walsh's Quarterly, Oriental Criticisms in, 85.
Wandering Baboon, School Composition, 50.
Wickliffe Johnson, Crowe, and Lane, Story of, 164.
Wistar's Magazine, Origin and Papers in, 552 to 564.
Writings in 1830, 250.

TABLE OF EMENDATIONS.

Always read *humour*, *humorous*, *humourist*, *humorously*.
“ “ *rigour*, *vigour*, *vigorous*, *favour*, *favourite*, *ardour*, *labour*, *honour*, *colour*, *&c.* But *terror*, *horror*, *&c.*
“ “ *without*, or *beyond*, or *not of*, or *except among*, instead of *outside of*.
“ “ *decipher* for *decypher*, &c. And after p. 290, *Dr.* for *Mr.* (J. A. A.)
“ “ *à* for French proposition *a*, and *jusqu'à*, and *Rosenmüller*.
“ “ Latin ablatives *meâ*, *Burgundiâ*, *hâc*, *notâ*, *tuâ*.
“ “ *Tôlômaque*, *Fénelon*, *Molière*, *hôtel*, *méchanicien*, *Beirût*.
“ “ *Pelletière*, *Gerlach*, *Hamill*, *Bascom*, *Talmage*, *Latude*.
“ “ *pôrta*, *doômo*, *pôpolo*.
“ “ *Burnet*, *Biesenthal*, *Mephistopheles*, *Abenmelech*.
“ “ *Conybeare*, *Merle*, *mémoires*, *Realwörterbuch*.
“ “ *wainscoted*, *rhythm*, *Lehrgebäude*, *postilions*, *despatch*.
“ for *διάϱολος* read *διάβολος*; for *Michan*, *Midian*; for *gaizing*, *gazing*.
“ “ *capricios* read *capriccios*; for *mémoirs*, *mémoires*; for *Murkland*, *Mirkhood*.
“ “ *Mascara* read *Mascaron*; for *Neronec*, *Neronc*; for *Maúlria*, *Malaria*.
“ “ *Madame* (Eng.) read *Madam*; for *drank* (partic.), *drunk*; for *Flechia*, *Fléchier*.
“ “ *Poggibousi* read *Poggibonsi*; for *Rorego* (perhaps) *Rovigo*.
“ read *should* for *would* on pp. 735 bis 802, 805, 844.

On page 25, 16th line from top, for *appearances* read *appearance*.
“ “ 26, 13th “ “ “ “ *Arabic* “ *Persian*.
“ “ 59, 17th “ “ “ read thus: ἀπὸ τοῦ θεοῦ.
For επτα επι θηβας, in a letter of “J. A. A.,” read ἑπτὰ ἐπὶ θήβας.
On page 90, 23d line from bottom, for *βουλεις* read *βούλει*.
“ “ “ “ “ “ “ “ *unaccented* Greek words read *accented*.
“ “ 91, 3d “ “ top “ *Gratto* read *gatto*.
“ “ 100 expunge foot-note.
“ “ 112, 2d line from bottom, for *Camolus* read *Camoens*.
“ “ 132, 14th “ “ top, “ *ottara* “ *ottava*.

On page 146, 21st line from bottom, for *Coelio*, read *Caecilium.*

" " 147, 11th " " " " אַרשׁ " אִרשׁ

" " " 9th " " " " אִר " אִרשׁ

" " " 5th " " " " ח " ח

" " 148, 18th " " " " *Novella* " *Novela.*

" " " 23d " " " " *predicadore* " *predicador.*

" " " 2d " " top, " שׁשׁ- " שְׁשׁ-

" " " 12th " " " " *curioso* " *Curioso.*

" " " for Spanish sentence read :

" *No excusarás con el secreto tu dolor ; ántes tendrás que llorar contino si no lagrimás de los ojos, lagrimás de sangre del corazon.*"

On page 175, note, for *Floria d'Italia* read *Storia d'Italia.*

On page 187, 6th line from bottom, for *effort* read *opportunity.*

" " 196, 15th " " top, " σν " σὺ.

" " 204, 1st " " bottom, immediately after foot-note, insert *page* 23.

" " 224, 15th " " " read thus : καταρτίσαι, στηρίξαι, σθενώσαι, θεμελιώσαι.

On page 233, 15th line from bottom, for εξοδος read ἔξοδος.

" " 234, 17th " " top, read thus : ἑνὸς ἐστι χρεία.

" " 255, 11th " " " " *this* read *that.*

" " 270, 4th " " " " *remit* " *emit.*

" " 296, 1st " " " " *entrez* " *entrer.*

" " " " " " " " *l'heur* " *l'heure.*

" " " 4th " " bottom, " *la* " *le.*

" " " 5th " " " " *des* " *de.*

" " 297, 2d " " " " *augst* " *angst.*

" " " " " " " " *witzender* " *schwitzender.*

" " 304, 15th " " top, " ὃ " ὁ.

" " " " " " " " ἄν " ἂν.

" " 311, 4th " " bottom, " *sepolécso* " *sepolcro.*

" " 314, running title, " *Leave* " *Leaves.*

" " " note, " *columne noslrata* read *columna rostrata*

" " 315, 15th line from bottom, " *of date of* read *dated.*

" " 323, 15th " " " " *Hahn* " *Halle.*

" " 329, 18th " erase daggae after *Bonn*, and put after *Paris.*

" " 339, 8th " from top, for *about* read *upon.*

" " 352, 5th " " " " *music* " *mine.*

" " 354, 2d " " " " *gales seem* " *gale seems.*

" " 370, 1st " " " put asterisk after *questions.*

" " 383, 15th " " bottom " *Hall* read *Ramsey.*

" " " 4th " " " " " " "

" " 384, 13th " " top, " *childish* " *childlike.*

" " " 3d " " bottom, " *believe* " *feel.*

On page 419, 12th line from bottom for *reign* read *rain.*
" " 439, 16th " " top, " *rode* " *drove.*
" " 506, 7th " " bottom, after *first* insert *names.*
" " 537, 20th " " top, " *reappear* read *reappears.*
" " 572, 24th " " " " *he* " *I.*
" " 579 put asterisk before foot-note.
" " 583, in page-title, for *Memoirs* read *Memories.*
" " 602, 13th line from bottom, for *use* read *abuse.*
" " 619, 6th " " " " *Luretto* " *Luzzatto.*
" " 620, 1st " " top, " ישאל בכי " בכי ישראל
" " 647, 1st " " bottom, " *on* " *in.*
" " 675, 19th " " " " *New York* " *up-town.*
" " 687, 2d, " " top, put *the only daughter*, &c., in a footnote.
" " 701, 12th " " " " *Stevens's* read *Stephen's.*
" " 709, 14th " " bottom " *was* " *were.*
" " 714, 5th " " " " *Barnabas* " *Barabbas.*
" " 625, 5th " " " " *campana* " (perhaps) *campanae.*
" " " 7th " " " " *omni* " *omnes.*
" " 744, 16th " " top, insert *the* before *pious.*

Sentence from Polybius, on p. 751, evidently wrong; perhaps read ΤΟΙΟΙΣΔΕ ΑΠΙΕΣΤΩΣ, &c.

On page 753, 17th line from bottom, transpose *host* and *pupil.*
" " 854, 4th " " top for *perche* " *perchè.*

CHARLES SCRIBNER. A. C. ARMSTRONG. A. J. PEABODY.

Condensed Catalogue

OF THE PUBLICATIONS OF

CHARLES SCRIBNER & Co.,

654 BROADWAY,

NEW YORK. JANUARY, 1868.

⁂ *The figures in the last column of this Catalogue refer to* CHARLES SCRIBNER & CO.'S *Descriptive Catalogue, copies of which will be sent to any address upon application.*

⁂ *Blanks in the column of prices, except in the case of School Text-Books, the prices of which may be learned from* CHARLES SCRIBNER & CO.'S *Educational Catalogue, indicate that the Works are either out of print or in press.*

⁂ *In this list the names of Books just published are given in* SMALL CAPITALS; *those issued during the year* 1867, *as well as new editions of Works previously produced, are indicated by italics.*

⁂ *The prices here given are for the regular style of binding in cloth. Books furnished in other styles, and their respective prices, may be learned from the Descriptive Catalogue.*

⁂ *Any of these Books will be sent post-paid to any address upon receipt of the price.*

	Volumes.	Size.	Price.	Page
ADAMS, W., D.D.				
THANKSGIVING	1	12mo	$2 00	2
Three Gardens	1	12mo	2 00	1
AGASSIZ, PROF. LOUIS.				
Structure of Animal Life (The)	1	8vo	2 50	2
ALEXANDER, A., D.D.				
Moral Science	1	12mo	1 50	3
ALEXANDER, J. W., D.D.				
Alexander, Archibald, Life of, (Portrait) .	1	12mo	2 00	3
Christian Faith and Practice (Discourses) .	1	12mo	2 00	6
Consolation (Discourses)	1	12mo	2 00	5
Faith (Discourses)	1	12mo	2 00	6
Forty Years' Correspondence with a Friend	2	12mo	4 00	4
Preaching, Thoughts on	1	12mo	2 00	5

	Volumes.	Size.	Price.	Page.
Alexander, J. A., D.D.				
Acts (Commentary)	2	12mo	$4 00	8
Isaiah " (complete)	2	8vo	6 50	7
" " (abridged)	2	12mo	4 00	8
Mark "	1	12mo	2 00	8
Matthew "	1	12mo	2 00	8
Psalms "	3	12mo	6 00	7
New Test. Literature and Ecc. Hist. . .	1	12mo	2 00	9
Sermons (with Portrait)	2	12mo	——	9
Allston, Washington.				
Lectures and Poems	1	12mo	2 50	9
Andrews, Rev. S. J.				
Life of Our Lord	1	post 8vo	3 00	10
Armstrong, G. D., D.D.				
Works of	3	12mo ea.	1 25	11
Bautain, Prof. A.				
Extempore Speaking	1	12mo	1 50	12
Beecher, Rev. H. W.				
Prayers from Plymouth Pulpit . .	1	12mo	1 75	13
Botta, Prof.				
Dante as Poet, Patriot, Philosopher . .	1	crown 8vo	2 50	14
Brace, Charles L.				
Hungary, with Experience of Austrian Police,	1	12mo	——	15
Home Life in Germany	1	12mo	——	14
Norse Folk	1	12mo	2 00	15
Races of Old World	1	post 8vo	2 50	15
Short Sermons for Newsboys	1	16mo	1 50	16
Bushnell, Horace, D.D.				
Character of Jesus	1	18mo	1 00	19
Christ and his Salvation	1	12mo	2 00	19
Christian Nurture	1	12mo	2 00	18
Nature and the Supernatural	1	12mo	2 25	17
New Life, Sermons for	1	12mo	2 00	19
Vicarious Sacrifice, The	1	8vo	3 00	18
Work and Play	1	12mo	2 00	19
Cheever, G. B., D.D.				
Works of	3	12mo	——	20
Clark, Prof. N. G.				
English Language, Elements of	1	12mo	1 25	21
Collier, J. Payne, F.S.A.				
Rarest Books in English Language . . .	4	small 8vo	12 00	21
Conybeare, Rev. W. J., and Howson, Rev. J. S.				
St. Paul, Life and Epistles of (illustrated)	2	8vo	7 50	22

	Volumes.	Size.	Price.	Page.
COOK, PROF. J. P., JR.				
Religion and Chemistry	1	crown 8vo	$2 50	24
CRAIK, GEO. L., LL.D.				
English Literature and Language . .	2	8vo	7 50	23
CROSBY, PROF. HOWARD, D.D.				
New Testament with Notes	1	12mo	1 50	24
CRUMMELL, REV. A.				
Africa, Future of	1	12mo	1 00	—
DANA, A. H.				
Ethical and Physiological Inquiries . .	1	12mo	1 50	25
DANA, R. H.				
Poems and Prose Writings	2	12mo	4 00	25
DAWSON, HENRY B.				
Fœderalist (Univ. Ed.)	1	8vo	3 00	25
" with Notes	1	8vo	3 75	25
DAY, PROF. H. N.				
ENGLISH COMPOSITION	1	12mo	1 50	26
DISCOURSE, (Rhetoric)	1	12mo	1 50	26
Logic	1	12mo	1 50	27
DERBY, EDWARD, EARL OF.				
Homer's Iliad (translated)	2	crown 8vo	5 00	28
DE VERE, M. SCHELE, LL.D.				
Studies in English	1	crown 8vo	2 50	29
DINGMAN, J. H.				
Publisher's Sheet-Book	1	Folio	15 00	29
DRUMMOND, REV. JAS.				
Christian Life, Thoughts for	1	12mo	1 50	30
DUYCKINCK, E. A. and G. L.				
Cyclopædia of Am. Literature (400 Portraits, &c.)	2	royal 8vo	10 00	31
DWIGHT, BENJ. W.				
Philology, Modern	2	8vo	6 00	30
ELLET, MRS. E. F.				
American Revolution, Domestic History of	1	12mo	1 50	32
" " Women of . .	3	12mo	——	33
Pioneer Women of the West	1	12mo	1 50	32
QUEENS OF AM. SOCIETY (13 steel engravings)	1	12mo	2 50	33
ELLIOTT, CHARLES W.				
New England History	2	8vo	6 00	34
EWBANK, THOS.				
Hydraulics	1	8vo	6 00	34
FELTER, S. A.				
Arithmetics, Natural Series of	1	——	——	35-36

	Volumes.	Size.	Price.	Page.
FIELD, HENRY M., D.D.				
Atlantic Telegraph, History of . . .	1	12mo	$1 75	37
FISHER, REV. PROF. GEO. P.				
Supernatural Origin of Christianity . .	1	8vo	2 50	38
Silliman, Benj., LL.D., Life of (Portrait)	2	crown 8vo	5 00	37
FORSYTH, WM.				
Cicero, New Life of (Illustrations) . .	2	crown 8vo	5 00	39
FOWLER W. C., LL.D.				
Sectional Controversy (The)	1	8vo	1 75	39
FROUDE, J. A.				
HISTORY OF ENGLAND	10	crown 8vo	3 00 ea.	40
SHORT STUDIES ON GREAT SUBJECTS . .	1	crown 8vo	3 00	41
GAGE, REV. W. L.				
Carl Ritter, Life of	1	12mo	2 00	42
GASPARIN, COUNT.				
America before Europe	1	12mo	2 00	42
GIBBONS, J. S.				
PUBLIC DEBT OF THE UNITED STATES .	1	crown 8vo	2 00	43
GUIZOT, M.				
Meditations (First and Second Series) .	2	12mo ea.	1 75	43
GUYOT, PROF. ARNOLD.				
Geographies, Wall Maps, Key, etc. . .	–	——	——	44–47
HALL, EDWIN, D.D.				
Puritans and their Principles	1	8vo	2 50	48
HALSEY, REV. LEROY J.				
Bible, Literary Attractions of	1	12mo	1 75	48
HEADLEY, J. T.				
Complete Works of	15			49–53
HEIDELBERG,				
Catechism	1	small 4to	3 50	54
HERBERT, H. W.				
Works of	3	12mo ea.	1 50	54
HOLLAND, DR. J. G. (Timothy Titcomb.)				
Bay-Path. A Novel	1	12mo	2 00	58
Bitter-Sweet. A Poem	1	12mo	1 50	56
Gold Foil	1	12mo	1 75	56
KATHRINA. A Poem	1	12mo	1 50	59
Lessons in Life	1	12mo	1 75	57
Letters to the Joneses	1	12mo	1 75	57
Letters to Young People	1	12mo	1 50	55
Miss Gilbert's Career	1	12mo	2 00	59
Plain Talks on Familiar Subjects . . .	1	12mo	1 75	58

	Volumes.	Size.	Price.	Page.
HOURS AT HOME.				
A FAMILY MAGAZINE	Per annum		$3 00	60
HURST, REV. J. F.				
Rationalism, History of	1	8vo	3 50	61
JAMESON, JUDGE J. A.				
Constitutional Convention	1	8vo	4 50	62
JOHNSON, ANNA C. (MINNIE MYRTLE).				
Cottages of the Alps	1	12mo	——	63
Germany, Peasant Life in	1	12mo	——	63
Myrtle Wreath	1	12mo	1 25	63
JONES, CHARLES COLCOCK, D.D.				
HISTORY OF THE CHURCH OF GOD . . .	2	8vo	ea. 3 50	63
KIRKLAND, MRS. C. M.				
Evening Book	1	12mo	1 25	65
Holidays Abroad.	2	12mo	2 00	65
Patriotic Eloquence	1	12mo	1 75	64
School Garland	1	12mo	——	64
KNOX, REV. J. B.				
St. Thomas, W. I., History of	1	12mo	$1 25	65
LABOULAYE EDOUARD.				
Paris in America	1	12mo	1 25	69
LANGE, PROF. J. P., D.D.				
Commentary on Scriptures, Theolog. and Homiletical: Matthew (1); MARK AND LUKE (1); ACTS (1); JAMES, PETER, JOHN, JUDE (1); CORINTHIANS (1); THESSALONIANS, TIMOTHY, TITUS, PHILEMON, HEBREWS (1); GENESIS, (1)		8vo	ea. 5 00	66–68
LAWRENCE, EUGENE.				
British Historians, Lives of	2	12mo	3 50	69
LIBER LIBRORUM	1	16mo	1 50	70
LORD, JOHN, LL.D.				
OLD ROMAN WORLD	1	crown 8vo	3 00	70
LYNCH, LIEUT. W. F.				
Naval Life	1	12mo	1 50	71
MCLEOD, ALEX., D.D.				
Life of, by Rev. S. B. Wylie.	1	8vo	2 00	114
MACDONALD, J. M., D.D.				
My Father's House	1	12mo	1 50	72
MACLEOD, DONALD,				
Works of	3	12mo	ea. 1 25	71
MAGOON, REV. E. L.				
Living Orators in America	1	12mo	1 75	72
Orators of the American Revolution . .	1	12mo		72

	Volumes.	Size.	Price.	Page
MAINE, HENRY S.				
Ancient Law	1	crown 8vo	$3 00	73
MARSH, HON. GEO. P.				
English Language, Lectures on	1	crown 8vo	3 00	74
" " Origin and History of .	1	crown 8vo	3 00	74
Man and Nature	1	crown 8vo	3 00	75
MARSH, J., D.D.				
Temperance Recollections	1	12mo	2 25	76
MASON, J. M., D.D.				
Complete Works	4	post 8vo	——	76
MEARS, REV. J. W.				
Bible and the Workshop	1	12mo	1 00	76
MITCHELL, DONALD G. (IK MARVEL).				
Dream Life	1	12mo	$1 75	77
Dr. Johns: A Novel	2	12mo	3 50	79
Fresh Gleanings	1	12mo	——	78
Lorgnette, The	1	12mo	——	78
My Farm of Edgewood	1	12mo	1 75	79
Reveries of a Bachelor	1	12mo	1 75	77
RURAL STUDIES	1	12mo	1 75	80
Seven Stories	1	12mo	1 75	78
Wet Days at Edgewood	1	12mo	1 75	80
MITCHEL, PROF. O. M.				
Astronomy of the Bible	1	12mo	1 75	81
Planetary and Stellar Worlds	1	12mo	1 75	81
Popular Astronomy	1	12mo	1 75	81
MORRIS, GEO. P.				
Poetical Works (blue and gold)	1	16mo	1 50	83
MULLER MAX.				
Science of Language, Lectures on . . .	1	crown 8vo	2 50	82
" " " (Second Series)			3 50	82
NEWCOMB, REV. H.				
Missions, Cyclopædia of (32 Maps) . . .	1	8vo	——	83
ORLEANS, DUCHESS OF.				
Memoirs of (Portrait)	1	12mo		86
OWEN, J. J., D.D.				
Commentaries on the New Testament: *Matthew* (1); MARK AND LUKE (1); JOHN (1); ACTS (—), in press; GENESIS (—), in press	1	12mo ea.	1 75	84-85
PAEZ, DON RAMON.				
South America, Wild Scenes in	1	crown 8vo	2 50	86
PAULDING, JAMES K.				
Literary Life of (1); BULLS AND JONATHANS (1); TALES OF THE GOOD WOMAN (1); A BOOK OF VAGARIES (1); DUTCHMAN'S FIRESIDE . . . . each	1	crown 8vo	2 50	87

	Volumes.	Size.	Price.	Page.
PERCE, ELBERT.				
Magnetic Globes			—	88
PERRY, PROF. A. L.				
Political Economy, Elements of	1	crown 8vo	2 50	89
PRENTISS, S. S.				
Life of, by Geo. L. Prentiss, D.D. . . .	2	12mo	3 50	86
PRIME, S. I., D.D.				
Power of Prayer	1	12mo	1 50	90
PUBLIC PRAYER.				
Book of	1	12mo	2 00	13
RANDOLPH, A. D. F.				
Hopefully Waiting, and other Verses . . .	1	16mo	$1 50	90
SCHAFF, P., D.D.				
Apostolic Church, History of	1	8vo	3 75	91
CHRISTIAN " "	3	8vo ea.	3 75	92–93
PERSON OF CHRIST	1	16mo	1 50	94
SEAMAN, E. C.				
Progress of Nations	1	12mo		94
SHEDD, W. G. T., D.D.				
Christian Doctrine, History of	2	8vo	6 50	95
HOMILETICS AND PASTORAL THEOLOGY .	1	8vo	3 50	96
SHELDON, E. A.				
Model Lessons on Objects, etc.				97
SILLIMAN, BEN. M.D.				
Life of, by Professor Geo. P. Fisher . . .	2	crown 8vo	5 00	37
SIMMS, W. G.				
Huguenots in Florida	1	12mo	1 50	—
SMITH, PROF. H. B., D.D.				
Christian Church, History of, in Tabular Form	1	Folio	6 75	98–99
SMITH, J. H.				
Gilead; or, The Vision of All Souls' Hospital	1	12mo	1 50	100
SMITH, MRS. MARY HOWE.				
Lessons on the Globe	1	12mo	0 50	88
SPRING, GARDINER, D.D.				
Personal Reminiscences, etc. (Portrait) .	2	12mo	4 00	100
STANLEY, DEAN A. P.				
Eastern Church	1	8vo	4 00	101
Jewish Church, Lectures on (First Series) .	1	8vo	4 00	101
" " " (Second Series)	1	8vo	5 00	101 / 102
Sermons	1	12mo	1 50	103
STRICKLAND, AGNES.				
QUEENS OF ENGLAND, LIVES OF .	1	12mo	2 00	103

	Volumes.	Size.	Price.	Page.
TAYLOR, GEORGE.				
Indications of the Creator.	1	12mo	1 75	105
TENNEY, S., A.M.				
Natural History	1	crown 8vo	3 00	104
" " Library Edition	1	large 8vo	4 00	104
" " for Schools	1	12mo	2 00	104
TIMOTHY TITCOMB.				
Complete Works of. See HOLLAND.	—	——	——	55-59
TRENCH, RT. REV. R. C.				
Epistles to Seven Churches, Commentary on	1	12mo	1 50	106
Studies in the Gospels	1	8vo	3 00	106
Glossary of English Words	1	12mo	1 50	107
Synonyms of New Testament (1st and 2d Series)	2	12mo ea.	1 25	107
TUCKERMAN, H. T.				
America and her Commentators	1	crown 8vo	2 50	108
TULLIDGE, REV. H.				
Triumphs of the Bible	1	12mo	2 00	108
TUTHILL, MRS. L. C.				
Joy and Care. Book for Young Mothers	1	16mo	1 00	109
VAN SANTVOORD, GEO.				
Lives of Chief Justices of U. S.	1	8vo		109
WHITNEY, PROF. W. D.				
LANGUAGE, AND THE STUDY OF LANGUAGE	1	crown 8vo	2 50	110
WILLIS, N. P.				
Complete Works of				111, 112
WISE, CAPT. H. A.				
Works of	2	12mo ea.	1 75	112
WOOLSEY, PREST. T. D.				
International Law, Introduction to	1	8vo	2 50	113
WYLIE, S. B., D.D.				
McLeod, Alexander, Life of	1	8vo	2 00	114
ZINCKE, F. BARHAM.				
Extemporary Preaching	1	12mo	1 50	114

ILLUSTRATED GIFT-BOOKS.

*** *In this list the prices of the respective works as bound in cloth, full gilt, are given. All of them, however, are furnished in Turkey morocco, and the prices of these editions may be learned by reference to the catalogue.*

	Price.	Page.
ÆSOP'S FABLES	$18 00	117
Bitter-Sweet	9 00	117
Book of Rubies	7 00	119
Christian Armor	15 00	120
Cotter's Saturday Night	5 00	119
FLORAL BELLES	25 00	116
FRED AND MARIA AND ME	$1 50	121
Folk Songs	15 00	115
MY FARM OF EDGEWOOD	10 00	121
Pilgrim's Progress	5 00	120
QUEENS OF AMERICAN SOCIETY	6 00	118

www.ingramcontent.com/pod-product-compliance
Lightning Source LLC
LaVergne TN
LVHW021125110826
845150LV00005B/950

9781425551483